Haunted

ALSO BY LEO BRAUDY

Trying to Be Cool: Growing Up in the 1950s (2013)

The Hollywood Sign: Fantasy and Reality of an American Icon (2011)

On the Waterfront (2005)

From Chivalry to Terrorism: War and the Changing Nature of Masculinity (2003)

Native Informant: Essays on Film, Fiction, and Popular Culture (1992, 2008)

The Frenzy of Renown: Fame and Its History (1986, 1997)

The World in a Frame: What We See in Films (1976, 1984, 2002)

Jean Renoir: The World of His Films (1972, 1989)

The Plot of Time: Narrative Form in Hume, Fielding, and Gibbon (1970, 2003)

Haunted

ON GHOSTS, WITCHES,
VAMPIRES, ZOMBIES, AND OTHER
MONSTERS OF THE NATURAL AND
SUPERNATURAL WORLDS

Leo Braudy

Yale UNIVERSITY PRESS

New Haven and London

Published with assistance from the foundation established in memory of
Philip Hamilton McMillan of the Class of 1894, Yale College.

Yale University Press books may be purchased in quantity for educational,
business, or promotional use. For information, please e-mail sales.press@yale.
edu (U.S. office) or sales@yaleup.co.uk (U.K. office).

Set in Adobe Garamond type by IDS Infotech, Ltd.
Printed in the United States of America.

ISBN 978-0-300-20380-6

Library of Congress Control Number: 2016937700
A catalogue record for this book is available from the British Library.

This paper meets the requirements of ANSI/NISO Z39.48-1992 (Permanence of
Paper).

10 9 8 7 6 5 4 3 2 1

For Dorothy, eternally

Contents

Preface

Who doesn't know the stories? The corpses rising from the grave, the blood-sucking vampires that fly by night, the man-made creature who turns against his creator and murderously stalks the land, the gigantic beast bent on annihilating anything human, the man who has found the magic potion that turns him into a monster. They're as familiar as the story of Moses leading the Israelites out of Egypt, or the Crucifixion, or the Hegira, or the Buddha teaching under the Bodhi tree. But instead of the foundational stories of a religion, they are stories of horror and terror that have generated more and more monsters as they are told and retold over the centuries. They aren't just in books or movies—they are under the bed or they leap out of the closet, they scrape on the window in the dead of night, and they reside patiently in the attic, in the basement, in every patch of darkness and shadow, waiting to pounce.

Why have the monsters born or reborn in past centuries continued to have such a hold on our imaginations? How have they become handy metaphoric ways of describing the dark side of ourselves as well as epithets to hurl at our enemies, as heartless automatons or predatory bloodsuckers or mindless animals, all bent on our destruction? The monsters are before us in both senses: they seem to come from a dark past, but they stand in front of us every day.

Two linked impulses moved me to write *Haunted,* both of which have infused my work since the start. The first is to connect elements in a culture without recourse to a hierarchy of high and low, the "soft" aesthetic values versus the "hard" political and economic ones. The second is to explore how emotions themselves can have a history. *Haunted* is thus very much akin to my earlier books *The Frenzy of Renown* (on the history of fame and the desire to be known) and *From Chivalry to Terrorism* (on the changing relationship between war and ideas of masculinity). It takes a cultural phenomenon that seems to be of the present (here the hordes of zombies, vampires, monsters, and other figures that crowd contemporary culture) and seeks to show not only that it has a history but also how it has evolved. Why it is that these terrifying figures have been so endlessly present since the days of the eighteenth-century political revolutions and the optimism of the Industrial Revolution, when it seemed that politics based on reason and knowledge based on empirical science would have been expected to vanquish such phantasms from human consciousness forever. Instead those fears grew and expanded to furnish a continuing contradiction to and commentary upon the ambitions, assertions, and perhaps pretensions of the modern world itself.

Haunted shares with *Frenzy* and *Chivalry* the conviction that a knowledge of history is crucial for understanding many of those connections that otherwise seem a matter of timeless emotions: the connection to religion and our deepest beliefs—even among the unreligious—about chance, nature, the past, the inner life, and life after death. Through the distorted prism of horror, *Haunted* considers not just the invariable elements of fear, but also how fear is shaped, as well as how those images warp our politics and our understanding of the world. In part my goal is to foster a historical and cultural understanding of the idea of the monstrous as a way of freeing ourselves from the unconscious control of images otherwise rooted in our childhood apprehension of the world of darkness and invisible powers. I don't want to minimize the emotional attraction of these images, or banish them from rational discourse; I want to understand their attraction, as well as the incessant combat between reason and emotion in ourselves and in our public life.

Fear is the pervasive topic of our times. Neuroscientists discuss it in terms of brain function; sociologists and anthropologists investigate it in terms of social attitudes; horror fans luxuriate in its monster shapes and its film and literary history; politicians manipulate it. This book in great part deals with the evolution of a repertoire of monsters and monstrous images that come ready to hand as ways of understanding not only what is abnormal, what is to be hated and despised, but also what is compelling in its supernatural allure. It is commonplace to say that monsters and phantasms have always haunted human dreams. But I am interested here in those historical moments when the scattered fears of the past coalesce into more pervasive terrors, when the old stories meet new circumstances that expand and intensify their meaning.

Many times, in the course of my discussion, I have touched on issues that take up several library shelves, whether in religion, law, literature, science, and elsewhere. Many of these areas of study are controversial, and their authors are often a confusing but heady mixture of the academic, the fan, and the believer. As much as I could within the compass of my argument, I have tried to absorb the insights of scholarship as well as enthusiasm without delving excessively into often fascinating disputes that in themselves are well worth exploring. In its discussion of the relation of horror to religion, for example, *Haunted* is not so much about the intricate historical investigations that have taken place into the nature of belief in demons versus the rarefied realm of demonological theory. Instead, it considers how those long-ago arguments have created a reservoir of imagery that continues to shape popular culture and is drawn upon freely when paranoia and crisis again distort our sense of reality.

Henry James once observed, "Really, universally, relations stop nowhere, and the exquisite problem of the artist is eternally but to draw, by a geometry of his own, the circle in which they shall happily appear to do so." The problem is the same if not more acute for the historian, especially the cultural historian, for what is not connected to innumerable other incidents, events, and trends? Like most historians, I am frustrated about the details I must leave out, the books I have consulted that there is no occasion to mention, and the illustrations I don't have the room to include. But a book must begin and end somewhere, so here I have fashioned a structure that I hope will suggest the many ways literature and art shape a primal emotion like fear into a variety of specific formulas. When I cite some works rather than others, therefore, I'm sure some readers will wonder where their favorites are and be able to add their own nuances. To that end, bibliographical references in the notes supply a preliminary signpost for those readers for whom one region of terror in particular rings a bell and want to delve more deeply. *Haunted* is therefore best seen as an effort to establish a basic taxonomy of fears, the times in which they arose, and their perpetuation down to the present. Like a road map, as you move closer, you discover more and more details, even while you retain what I hope will be a useful sense of its basic patterns.

Thinking about these issues began for me many years ago, in the 1960s, when the questioning of hierarchies of all sorts was in the air. It was helped immeasurably by conversations with some of my colleagues at Columbia

University, including Sacvan Bercovitch, Morris Dickstein, Edward Said, George Stade, and Mike Wood; and continued at Johns Hopkins with Sharon Cameron, Stanley Fish, Jerry McGann, Stephen Orgel, Lee Patterson, and Barry Weller. Some years I spent teaching a class at the University of Southern California called "The Monster and the Detective" helped me work out and refine many of the ideas found here. I would also like to thank Hans-Otto Hügel for printing some of my preliminary thoughts on horror in his *Handbuch Populäre Kultur* (Metzler Verlag, 2003), as well as Amy Wallace, Del Howison, and Scott Bradley for including my comments on horror films in *The Book of Lists: Horror* (HarperCollins, 2008).

My interest in theology was first kindled at Swarthmore College with Linwood Urban, and continued later with the works of Peter Brown, Elaine Pagels, and Karen Armstrong among others. Nowhere in what follows do I specifically cite the work of my old friend Marina Warner, but the spirit of her unique mingling of myth, poetry, and insightful analysis was another inspiration. More recently I have had valuable discussions with Jonathan Kirsch and with Jack Miles, to whom I owe special thanks for his astute and useful comments on a previous draft of the manuscript. Sandra Dijkstra and Elise Capron at the Sandra Dijkstra Literary Agency have smoothed the way with their usual engagement and efficiency. I was pleased to be in contact with Eric Brandt at Yale University Press for the early stages. When he left for northern California and Stanford, I was delighted to have the luck of working with Steve Wasserman, an old friend from Los Angeles now flourishing vigorously in both the East and the West. Eva Skewes, his immensely talented and able editorial assistant, has been a tremendous help in moving the project forward. Finally, to complete the round of happy and fortuitous connections, I want to thank my friends and colleagues at the Los Angeles Institute for the Humanities, which Steve co-founded some years ago, and before whom I presented an early and brief version of *Haunted*. Everyone had interesting comments to make, but I remember especially those of Jon Boorstin, Clifford Johnson, Tom Lutz, John Romano, Mark Swed, and Laurie Winer.

For help in gathering the illustrations, I thank Alan Jutzi and Anita Weaver at the Henry E. Huntington Library; Shannon Supple, Christina Bodnar-Anderson, and Charles James at the University of California, Berkeley Library; Tyson Gaskill at the University of Southern California Library; Iain Calderwood at the British Museum; Karen Lerheim and Ove Kvavik at the Munchmuseet, Oslo, Norway; and David Dees.

Haunted

CHAPTER I

Shaping Fear

We love to be at once, miserable, and unhurt.

—Edward Young, *Conjectures on Original Composition* (1759)

We are all monsters in our subconscious.
That's why we have laws and religion.

—*Forbidden Planet* (1956)

What makes us afraid? What terrifying shapes do we give to the darkness under the bed or the odd noise in the closet, the illegal immigrant or the terrorist? What makes us afraid as individuals, afraid as groups, afraid as nations?

The question of fear is not just a question solely of individual response, the peculiarities of personal strength and weakness. It is also and perhaps even more immediately a question about how a culture responds to events, what names we call what scares us, and how those names help determine how we respond. When I was a child, that name was Hitler. Even though he had been dead for some years, and I was barely ten years old, I had simultaneous fantasies of being attacked by him and then defeating him. For some later ten-year-olds that name might have been Osama bin Laden. For other peoples, in other parts of the world, with other fears, it might be the "Great Satan" of the United States, a Hamas rocket, or an Israeli soldier. Fears may summon up a tentacled, nonhuman monster with ravenous teeth, a rampaging robot, or the boy next door turned into a zombie.

When a mysterious thing happens, we first try to understand it in terms and images we already have learned and internalized for assessing mystery. What's in the closet? What's under the bed? Who is the bogeyman?—they are all shifting questions, inflected by history and culture. For Odysseus and his shipmates, monsters could be man-eaters like the giant Polyphemus or the Sirens, female monsters enticing men to their deaths by their alluring songs.

For English Protestants the monster was the many-headed Hydra of the Catholic Church, for Catholics the diabolic reforms of Martin Luther, John Calvin, and others. There are monsters in the ages before us and monsters right in front of us, and often those new monsters wear the shapes of the old.

So my question about the nature of fear must be expanded to include time: What is the relation between what scares us now and what scared people in the past? Is being afraid something that is hardwired into human nature and never varies over the centuries? Do fears always take the same shapes, or do nations and cultures have distinctive fears that may metamorphose through the centuries? In other words, what is universal about fear, and what is culturally specific in its images and stories? What belongs to a certain era and what transcends time? What is the process by which nameless dreads are named?

Fear indeed might be a reasonable response to potential danger; an emotion to be stimulated and manipulated; an enlivener of action that allows us to take risks; or a stifler of action that encourages a frozen immobility before a threat. Aristotle defined virtue as the midpoint of two vices. Could fear by the same reasoning be the midpoint between paranoia and apathy? Might in some situations fear be a virtue? Does religion need fear to retain its power? Does morality?

Many fears are personal. But when does personal fear become the fear of a whole locality (like the belief that the aristocracy was causing bad harvests in the early French Revolution), and when does it expand to become a national fear (like the paranoia of Cold War America), let alone a worldwide fear? Surely, the expansion of media fuels fear just as it enhances gossip and every other sort of simulated human contact. As the neuroscientist Antonio Damasio has argued, innate behaviors like fear, anger, or disgust require circumstances to give them shape. He uses the phrase "switched on" (which has a more mechanistic air than the rest of his argument implies) to describe the process by which emotional potentials in individual nature become feelings, when they are shaped by the personal and cultural stories in which they make their appearance. My favorite example of this process is how for many years the stereotype of a person with delusions of grandeur has been that he believed he was Napoleon. But who did such a person believe he was before Napoleon existed? As Michiko Iwasaka and Barre Toelken have written about Japanese ghost legends, such stories also "seem to dramatize areas of doubt, ambiguity, anxiety, and concern which are not addressed by 'scientific' means—matters involving human emotions which are strongly connected to cultural values, but for which there are no clear answers."[1]

Humans have been afraid since we first gathered around campfires at night to tell stories of the inhabitants of the darkness that stalked just beyond the edge of light, and some have theorized that fear of the dark, say, is a vestige of the caveman's fear of lurking predators. But that kind of paralyzing fear doesn't seem very conducive to alertness or any other skills the caveman might have needed to survive. Even if fear were a survival mechanism, where does the pleasure in being scared come from, the shivering delight so many take in listening to spooky stories and going to horror films? In the tale of terror, whatever form it takes, we are pulled down the hallway to the door we don't want to open, to see what we have been warned not to see. Curiosity and dread pull us back and forth, until curiosity finally wins. We search out the monstrous in hopes that it won't find us unawares. We peer into the darkened recesses always knowing something horrible may jump out, even from inside ourselves, like the dark side of Dr. Jekyll released in the form of Mr. Hyde, or the gibbering extraterrestrial baby with needle-sharp teeth that bursts from the chest of one of the crewmen in the film *Alien*. What lies behind that door that has to be opened, now finally unlocked? Are we always optimistically running from complacency and toward curiosity? And is the apparition of the monstrous then the punishment for our overweening desire to know?

The traditional Freudian interpretation was that behind that closed door is the primal scene of parental sexuality. Certainly the dark world of horror has an intimate relation to erotic secrecy, but it is obviously limiting to say that of course it's always sex behind the door. The appeal of opening that door is fueled by curiosity, a taste to experience the marvelous, the possibility of unearthing otherwise hidden knowledge that can now finally be revealed and perhaps then understood and controlled. The inner environment of the body and the mind, where feelings are hatched and fears can fester, thus has a close relation with the outside world. All three elements in the complex equation of reality—the individual human brain and body, the tangible world around it, and the larger but less visible world of cultural context—each plays its role.

As civilization developed and knowledge of the physical world expanded, the monster was at first pushed more and more to the periphery of consciousness, like the blank spaces on old maps where the only information is the legend "here there be dragons," or the so-called *babewyns,* grotesque figures that decorate the margins of medieval manuscripts and appear sculpted on churches.[2] Monsters tended to be somewhere else. They were met by Odysseus on his journeys back to home and Penelope; they popped up in travelers' tales of the exotic places of the earth; or they held a mythic, god-like status, like the jackal-headed Anubis of Egypt or the bull-headed Minotaur of Crete. Often they were less real, less likely to be met on an evening's walk in the woods, than they were symbolic. Like the dragon that Saint George defeated, or the Medusa from whom Perseus snatched Andromeda, they were fully formed but also somewhat abstract, strange beasts already primed to be interpreted by priests and scholars as the embodiment of evil, irreligion, and whatever local enemy was at hand. In the age of movies and an expansive popular culture, we have populated the medieval world with monsters of all sorts—flying dragons, comical ogres, wood demons—as well as created pseudo-medieval worlds like those of J. R. R. Tolkien, J. K. Rowling, and Philip Pullman. But in the actual Middle Ages, even when the orthodox suspected there were witches in league with Satan, there were also good witches to whom one could apply to neutralize their evil spells, cure a sickness, or restore the crops (and the humans) to fertility and abundance. In these centuries before electric lights, darkness was more familiar, although often more terrifying, and the invisible world in which witches specialized could be invoked for good as well as evil.

Or so it seemed, until the sixteenth and seventeenth centuries, when Satan's presence in the world began to be felt more palpably, and the number of witch trials and trials for blasphemy and heresy quickly reached epidemic proportions. Especially in the wake of the Reformation and the Counter Reformation of the mid–sixteenth century, the destruction of religious icons in England and the establishment of the Inquisition in Spain, an atmosphere of apprehension, fear, and dread suffused Europe, in which the enemy kingdom of Satan was a handy substitute for the enemy religion, whether Catholic or Protestant. In England particularly, Protestants felt under siege, first from Catholic Spain and later from Catholic France. The conspiracy of Guy Fawkes and his Catholic co-conspirators to blow up the Houses of Parliament in 1605 heightened an already existing paranoia about Catholics that grew throughout the seventeenth century and beyond. In part this widespread anxiety was based on the reasonable belief that Louis XIV, the most powerful monarch in Europe, was masterminding both political and religious pressure on his rivals; and in part it was fueled by the fabrications of some Protestants whose own fears impelled them to exaggerate the threat. Three centuries later a similar mixture of reasonable fears and paranoia is often directed against Islam.

As is the case now, in the seventeenth and eighteenth centuries old certainties and old remedies to cure the impotence of fear seemed useless, old religions were being questioned, and the power of evil seemed more all-consuming than ever before. Just as medieval Christianity had redefined the gods of the old religions of northern Europe—Odin, Thor, Freya—as fiends and demons, many Protestants considered Catholics to be the spawn of Satan, and Catholics often returned the favor. What had been in the more monolithic world of medieval Catholicism a difficult but practicable commerce between the world of material reality and the world of the intangible spirit became instead a polarized opposition, in which Catholics and Protestants competed as experts in the invisible world of faith. Into this unsettled realm walked the monster, the quintessence of all fears. For an Elizabethan royalist like Edmund Spenser, the monster might be called Archimago, the Catholic master of false appearances; for a nonconformist Protestant allegorist like John Bunyan, the monster might be the Giant Despair, who lives in Doubting Castle, lying in wait to catch the wandering Christian as he strays from his faith; while the Independent Protestant John Milton in his epic poem *Paradise Lost* described the mythic monsters and gods of paganism as warped and distorted perceptions of an underlying Christian truth.[3]

These monsters from the past, like Milton's description of Dagon, "Sea Monster, upward Man / And downward Fish," came principally from the fertile imaginations of the writers, engravers, carvers, and painters who attempted to depict the enemies of the Christian world, especially during the Middle Ages.[4] Some of those images in mutated forms persist down to the present as dragons or sea monsters. Others were so dependent upon the culture that gave them birth that they remain only as trivia questions or inspiration for the special effects of the latest horror movie. If, say, we don't live in a culture haunted by the fear of what happens after the heroics of the battlefield, or one in which the fear of vengeful warrior women is not so high, what need is there of the half-woman, half-bird harpy to rend the warrior's flesh, or the half-bird, half-woman Valkyrie to carry him off to Valhalla? Our own anxieties about gender and sexuality, chiefly in the wake of wars that separated the sexes, fashion instead such figures as the vamp of the 1920s and later the femme fatale of film noir, seeming modern figures but with their roots in the ancient past.

It is often easy enough to find ancient origins for contemporary monsters and conclude "they have always been with us." But the more interesting question is why monsters lie quiescent in some ages and in others crowd the imagination. Each age has its own particular fears, and the history of horror is the history of the disquiets of the soul, the inner life, made public, taking on the colorations of the era in which they appear. I will therefore touch on the prehistory of the monstrous and the many worldwide beliefs in gods and demons when they become relevant. But this book is not particularly about the longevity of human fears. It focuses instead on two eras: the first that of the grand rupture in Christianity between Catholicism and Protestantism that revives so many of the fears that created the monsters of the past; and the second, a few centuries before our own, in which the shape of fear, theologically, politically, culturally, literarily, and artistically became an integral part of the books we read, the images we see, the enemies we have, and the beliefs we hold. Of course there are similarities between, say, the ghosts imagined by the Greeks and the Romans, and those who walk the earth in more recent centuries, although more modern monsters like zombies have hardly such long-lived genealogies, while otherwise extremely local monsters like the *vrykolakas,* vampires of eastern Europe and the Balkans, have been transformed by the need for new stories into beings more extravagant than anything in their folktale origins.

It is exactly that evolution and how it came about that most interests me. The modern monster, the most direct ancestor of our own fears and pleasures, does not really make his (and sometimes her) appearance until the later eighteenth century. It was the era of the Enlightenment and the Industrial Revolution, when reason was being invoked to clarify and solve human social problems, and people could look around themselves every day and see the palpable indications that things had changed. Practical discoveries and inventions were coming thick and fast, and international wise men like Voltaire, Rousseau, and Franklin were acknowledged models of the high aspirations of human thought. Yet into this world so bright, so optimistic, and so convinced of its progress toward a grand future came a cataclysmic event, which seemed to mock the limits of human understanding and control of the natural world, while at the same time, particularly for Christian believers, it raised the possibility that perhaps God's plan for the world was not entirely benevolent.

READ MY APOCALYPSE

In the early morning of November 1, 1755, a devastating earthquake and tsunami destroyed much of Lisbon, the capital of Portugal, killing between ten thousand and one hundred thousand people. Since the parting of the Red Sea, few natural events have had such an impact on the way people interpret the world. The effects of the earthquake were in fact felt all over Europe and even in the Caribbean, but because of the extreme destruction and the numerous ways people tried to understand why it happened, it is always referred to as the Lisbon earthquake. And, while the drowning of the Egyptian hosts was considered a mark of God's favor to the Israelites, the Lisbon earthquake proved quite the opposite because it forcefully implied the possibility that perhaps God is not good, or that his power is limited, or that his purposes for the world included death and destruction, even for those who are pious, believing Christians. November 1 was All Saints Day, and most of the population of Lisbon, a city noted for its piety, was in Mass, where churches collapsed on top of them, while all around public buildings, convents, and cathedrals crashed to the ground, although the red-light district suffered only minor damage.

Because of the day on which it occurred, the closeness of the Portuguese government to the Catholic Inquisition, and Portugal's general reputation for being the country most hostile to the new political, scientific, and cultural ideas influencing the rest of Europe, contemporary commentators were immediately stirred to interpret the event in religious terms. Appropriately enough, the Jesuit priests who ran Portugal's schools pointed to the earthquake as evidence that even with its piety, the country was overrun with sinners whom God had set out to punish. For Protestant clergy in the Netherlands as well as Jansenists in France, by contrast, it was God's harsh judgment on Jesuit Catholicism and the Inquisition. For Voltaire, who quickly wrote a poem about the event, the earthquake effectively gave the lie to all religions that were based on the idea of God's benevolence. Coming from their own special interests, the secular mercantile class of Lisbon believed the earthquake was obviously caused by problems in British-Portuguese relations, or by the exploitation of Brazilian natural resources, or perhaps by God's general disapproval of the weak monarchy of José I. For some scientists, the earthquake exemplified the arbitrariness of nature; for others there was no contradiction between natural and supernatural causes because the hand of God worked through earthly processes that themselves had no agenda; and for still others, including the Marquês de Pombal, the prime minister tasked with responding to the catastrophe, all such interpretations were irrelevant to the job of cleaning up the mess.[5]

Whenever some catastrophe, natural or otherwise, occurs, there have always been those who claim the victims deserved God's punishment. The biblical precedent of a flood as a means of cleansing a world suffused with evil found its way into many of the post-Lisbon sermons, just as moralistic interpretations made Hurricane Katrina a judgment on the free and easy lifestyle of New Orleans. Flood myths in particular are a staple of ancient cultures from the Near East to North America to China. Often they feature a culture hero like Gilgamesh or Noah presumably in tune with the long-range purposes of the divine. Water in this way is the original chaos out of which the hero creates a lasting civilized order that, however, is always in danger of slipping back into disorder.

In philosophic terms, this question of why God allows earthquakes and floods to happen in which so many die has been termed *the problem of evil:* What is evil and why should it exist in a world ruled by a benevolent and omnipotent God? Is it part of God's plan? As David Hume phrases the question in his *Dialogues Concerning Natural Religion,* begun in 1750 around the time of an earthquake that shook London, "Is he willing to prevent evil, but not able? Then he is impotent. Is he able, but not willing? Then he is malevolent. Is he both able and willing? Whence then is evil?"

Like the theory of intelligent design in our own time, the issues raised by the Lisbon earthquake occurred in a context of apocalyptic fears. Some of the answers posed by traditional philosophers and theologians sought to quiet those fears by invoking an overall plan that humans may aspire to understand but can never fully grasp. In the past theologians had argued that witchcraft, like other adversities, was a way God used to test the believer's devotion. So too in the time of the earthquake, the Book of Job was cited to support the belief that such disasters were God's way of testing our faith. After all, since God controlled everything, even Satan, all that happened was somehow due to the divine plan. In contrast, writers like Voltaire took the earthquake as definitive proof that any belief in the benevolence, omniscience, and omnipotence of God was wrong. In *Candide,* published four years later, in 1759, he argued against the view of Leibniz and other philosophers that all was for the best for human beings (that is, Europeans) in the "best of all possible worlds." Such a defense was called, in a term coined by Leibniz in 1710, *theodicy.* Like Alexander Pope's long poem *Essay on Man* (1731–35), which sought "to vindicate the ways of God to man," theodicy explained universal evils, pains, and torments as part of a divine plan ultimately incomprehensible to the human mind but to which we must submit. Instead, *Candide* depicted a world filled with accidents and haphazard circumstances, in which the blithely naive hero keeps his cheerfully positive view of life while constantly falling into the worst circumstances, calamities, and unexpected evils, both natural and human. Arriving in Lisbon during the earthquake, Candide and his companion, the optimistic philosopher Pangloss, are arrested by the Inquisition for heresy and set to be executed to appease God's wrath. Pangloss is hanged, Candide flogged, and only the intervention of another earthquake prevents Candide from being executed and allows him to escape.[6]

There had certainly been earthquakes and natural disasters before, includ-
ing the 1750 earthquake in London, which prompted Charles Wesley, John's
brother and a co-founder of Methodism, to write a pamphlet arguing that
God was punishing British moral failures.[7] A few decades later, in 1783, the
Laki volcano erupted in Iceland and spread smoke and ashes across much of
Europe and the rest of the world, significantly enough to be remarked by
Benjamin Franklin and other natural scientists. But none of these events
aroused the psychological, scientific, and religious controversies engendered
by the All Saints Day earthquake in Lisbon. When reports of cataclysmic real-
life events more easily reach a wide audience, they are often interpreted
through the lens of preexisting patterns of thought. Believers were disquieted
everywhere. And not just those who had a philosophic or religious stake in
the matter. The numbers of the dead, their notorious piety, and the destruction of so many obvious innocents stretched to the breaking point the providential interpretation of personal misfortune as God's test of belief. Like 9/11,
the Lisbon earthquake, a material event that happened at a specific time and
place, was just as unequivocally a psychological event whose effect pervaded a
whole culture. In his autobiography, Goethe, who was seven years old at the
time, writes with remembered shivers of the "demon of terror" let loose by the
earthquake. An older observer, Horace Walpole, the author of what is considered the first gothic novel, *The Castle of Utranto* (1765), remarks in his diary
that masquerades at the London pleasure garden Ranelagh had been canceled
because of the earthquake and stayed that way for almost a decade. Perhaps
the authorities didn't want to take a chance without knowing God's view of
such frivolity. In some areas, notes Walpole, bakers who sold bread on Sunday
were also denounced.[8]

The issues raised by the earthquake were stark: Do natural catastrophes
occur because of some moral failing on the part of those destroyed (what
might be called the Sodom and Gomorrah hypothesis), or do they have other,
nonreligious causes susceptible to reason? If it is the first, what did Lisbon do
to deserve this? If the second, how can we understand it, prevent it from happening again, or at least escape its worst consequences? If God controls natural events, but Lisbon was not being punished for its sins, how should the
earthquake be understood in religious terms? Is it that God doesn't care about
human life? Is he arbitrarily vengeful for reasons no human can fathom? Does
a good God in fact rule the world, or did the God who created the world leave
it behind in the care of some more malevolent force? Perhaps the world is
ruled by Satan, with God far away. Or perhaps there is no God at all.[9]

The responses to the Lisbon earthquake therefore take at least two major directions: one is scientific, the other cultural. In accord with the Enlightenment stress on reason, facts started to be gathered and the foundations were laid for what would become the science of seismology. That helped to explain the actions of the physical world, but what about the spiritual, the moral, and the religious implications of the earthquake? One intriguing response that helped bring into being some of the early forms of modern horror was the revival of an otherwise submerged belief from the early centuries of Christianity—Gnosticism. *Gnosticism* is the general term for a group of religions and religious beliefs that emphasize the clash between good and evil. The *gnosis* in Gnosticism referred to secret knowledge or enlightenment that was revealed only to a chosen few. The most successful version, dating from the third century to about the fourteenth century, was Manichaeism. But beyond those religious groups that tried to live by its tenets, *Gnosticism* can also serve as a blanket term for ideas that often persisted as parts of other religions and have as well some clear analogies with present-day popular beliefs in conspiracy theories that assume there is a secret order beneath the surface of reality that only the initiated can perceive.

Gnosticism might be considered one way theologians in the early centuries A.D. tried to answer the question "why do bad things happen to good people?" There were many gnostic groups and many different interpretations of the secret knowledge, but in essence Gnostics, influenced by Zoroastrian theology, believed that the physical world was created by a God or being called the Demiurge (who perhaps shouldn't be capitalized), while the true God was a totally spiritual being whose essence was unknowable and whose dwelling was far away. Gnosticism thus was essentially dualistic, with two principles, the imperfect physical and the perfect spiritual, or, as some defined it, evil versus good, the Old Testament Creator God of vengeance versus the New Testament God of mercy. Just as the material world was a sham reality, so too the human body was a prison for the spirit whose only route to release was a series of steps toward enlightenment, reminiscent of the Platonic ladder of being.[10]

The general lack of a domineering Satan figure in Asian cultures, despite their frequent wealth of lesser demons, and the impact of that absence on their idea of the monstrous can sharpen our sense of its significance in a Judeo-Christian context. In contrast with the frequently dualistic gods of some other religions, the gnostic heritage indicates how good and evil tend typically to be polarized in Christianity. In Hinduism, for example, that dualism is contained within a single god who can be, like Shiva, both destroyer and creator. But there persists in Judeo-Christianity elements of a similarly dualistic view of the divine. In parts of the Old Testament, God's actions, at least from the perspective of human morality, seem to be both good and evil, for example in his treatment of Job or the way he both tempts with the Tree of Knowledge of Good and Evil and simultaneously forbids it. In New Testament Christianity, by contrast, good and evil are clearly opposed to each other. God is defined by his benevolence, while Satan, previously one of God's emissaries, presides over evil. In the Book of Revelation, when the veil is lifted from earthly reality (the literal meaning of "apocalypse") and God's plan is revealed, the answer to the question of evil's existence is shown to be Satan, in the form of a Red Dragon with seven heads.[11]

Satan thus becomes the expression of the originally dualistic nature of Judeo-Christianity, and so gradually metamorphoses from his secondary role in the Book of Job to become first the challenger with Christ for God's favor (in a kind of sibling rivalry), then the ruler of Hell in Dante's *Inferno,* and finally by the sixteenth and seventeenth centuries the direct combatant with God for the control of the human world. Suspicious of such dualistic religions as Gnosticism but aware of their appeal, early Christian theologians like Saint Augustine had insisted that evil was not the opposite of good, a separate active principle on its own, but its distortion; not a turning toward some figure like Satan or the devil, but a turning away from God. As many scholars have argued, however, Christianity, although professedly monotheistic, has never quite been able to purge entirely the dualism of its origins. Alongside the orthodox view of God as the supreme power still flourishes the popular desire to explain the conflict between good and evil in the soul of the individual as a mirror of the more rarefied conflict in heaven. Some theologians phrased this necessary conflict as *sine diabolo nullus deus:* without the devil, there is no God. Or, as the phrase might be turned around, people may claim God is dead, but how can they maintain that if I show them the devil? The pioneering psychologist Carl Jung defined the interconnection somewhat differently, but the point was the same: "Only with Christ did a devil enter the world as the real counterpart of God, and in early Jewish-Christian circles Satan was regarded as Christ's elder brother." Or, as Charlotte Perkins Gilman, a late-nineteenth-century feminist, put it more sardonically: "The devil is a necessary component in male religion because a God without an adversary is inconceivable to the masculine mind."[12]

Without going into the intricate theological details of such dualistic beliefs as Gnosticism, it is easy enough to see how uncertainties about the goodness of God help open the way for a feeling that the world was becoming more and more populated by the followers of Satan. Satan, whose name means "accuser" in Hebrew, begins as a type of Grand Antagonist, sent on his mission against Job (and later Jesus) on behalf of God, somewhat like a mob enforcer who does the dirty work so that the boss can have plausible deniability while he watches from afar. In later developments of Satan's character and theological role, he rises in status to combat with the Deity for every individual human soul. As a result, instead of God being blamed for the evils of the world, the responsibility was transferred to Satan, preserving God's goodness, but in the process enhancing the dualism that had until then remained underground in the Judeo-Christian tradition. Instead of the Gnostic belief in the faraway God of light who rules the universe and the nearby figure of darkness that rules the earth, the earth itself becomes the battleground of a war between God and Satan. It was a combat not unknown to previous eras, and in the next chapter I will look further into its revival in the age of Reformation and Counter Reformation. But the atmosphere of dread it engendered gathered much more strength in the hothouse atmosphere of the eighteenth century, and it was an ambivalence about the nature of good and evil that reemerged full-blown in the gothic and the ensuing tradition of literary and artistic horror.

❧⊙❧

As I hope to show, the more local and traditional forms of horror in the seventeenth century—witches, demons, and the like—often took on an added emotional charge from the international conflicts between Protestants and Catholics. But in the eighteenth century it was the natural world itself that had raised such all-encompassing fears. What the Lisbon earthquake enhanced was an already deeply rooted argument over evil: If the Good God rules everything, why is there pain and death? Could evil be understood in terms of the new categories of scientific and rational understanding, or did it defeat those categories and require a whole other system of understanding? Impelled by a growing interest in empirical science, natural phenomena like the weather had gradually been brought into the realm of understanding and prediction. No longer was weather susceptible to what the philosopher Howard Darmstadter has called "moral climatology," in which every failed crop was the result of bad witchcraft and every fruitful one needed to be supported by good witchcraft. New methods of farming emerged, and success in agriculture became something that human beings could increasingly, although never entirely, ensure. Across Europe in the eighteenth century, diabolic explanations for medical problems were also giving way to more tangible causes, cases against wizards and witches accused of casting spells were dismissed by fact-seeking courts, and, instead of being burnt as accomplices of the devil, offenders against religious orthodoxy were frequently applauded as heroes of Enlightenment thought. Nevertheless larger moral and religious issues remained. Was evil-doing the fault of individuals or of demons? And if it is demons, why does God allow them? The basic question for Christians remained: Is Satan subordinate to God, or are God and Satan equal combatants in the eternal fight between good and evil?

So it happened that, whatever progress there had been made in judicial, political, and medical explanations for what had previously been considered diabolic phenomena, the larger argument over the nature of evil still persisted, as witnessed by the popular phenomena of the artistic world of horror and terror that began to mesmerize Europe in the late eighteenth century. Then, tales of gaping graves and haunted palaces, secret compartments and rotting corpses, vampires and the awakened dead, become the rage for both literary sophisticates and a large novel-reading public, as people opened their minds to imagine what it was like to live in enormous castles, where there were whole wings given over to decay, rooms and furnishings crushed in the jaws of time.

Just as the new sciences based on rationality and empiricism had promised to shake off the cobwebs of supernatural explanations, the imagery and propaganda of the American and French revolutions turned against the traditions of the past and looked toward a more wonderful world to come. The past was the world of monarchical repression and tyranny. Tradition had no claim on respect merely because it was old. Instead of the heavy hand of genealogy and family inheritance, new sources of power, both literally in the shape of mechanized cloth production and metaphorically in the shape of political democracy, were coming into being. As Napoleon would later proclaim, careers would be open to talent, not to money, social position, or family connections.

In this rush toward the future, complained traditionalists like Edmund Burke in *Reflections on the Revolution in France* (1790), the values of the past were being lost. For Burke and other cultural conservatives, political democracy implied a loss of the individual soul along with a loss of traditional sources of power. But even for those whose politics differed from Burke's, the Enlightenment had a dark side. The mysterious and the unexplainable, seemingly banished by the bright light of reason, began to erupt everywhere. Terror was in the air, and, appropriately or paradoxically, Maximilien Robespierre, the impresario of the French Revolution's Festival of Reason, became the central power in the Reign of Terror, where for eleven months denunciations and executions jammed the Parisian days.

At a time of revolutionary uprisings that trumpeted a limitless future, at the moment of an Enlightenment vision of the powers of reason to change the world, the specter of the monstrous harkened back to a gloomy past, where magic and alchemy helped create reality and Satan was a real presence on earth. It was a reaction suitable to uncertain times. In the midst of violence and revolution that contradicted the optimistic view of progress satirized by Voltaire in *Candide,* perhaps the strength to survive could be mustered only by experiencing the forces of terror and the night, at least in the distancing form of art. Emotion had seemed to have been pushed out of the intellectual sphere by scientific reasoning, and a more awestruck spirituality had been repressed in favor of a Clockmaker God who set the universal laws into motion, to be discovered and codified by human geniuses like Newton. But horror supplied an alternate history, and fear promised a new commitment to faith for individuals adrift in a world where personal destiny was more obviously out of their control than ever before. In this new era, emotion comes back in the shape of the monster, a distorted but powerful image of individualism in a world that otherwise seems to have little place for it. Commentators often point to the lack of an Enlightenment in Islamic culture to explain the sway of contemporary fundamentalism, but they ignore Christian Europe's own romance with the irrational, which to some extent the Enlightenment helped bring into being, or at least deeply nurtured as its shadowy twin.

Even before the French Revolution attempted to deify reason as the Supreme Being and rename the months and days to expunge the cult of saints, the literature and art of Europe were beginning to explore areas of the unreasonable and mysterious in what has been called the literature of sensibility. In the midst of a century when writers like the French authors of the *Encyclopédie* attempted to bring together all practical and first-hand knowledge and thereby demonstrate the triumph of empirical reason, there were also writers whose goal was to develop theories of the emotions, specifically in relation to nature and art. As a young man, Edmund Burke had published *A Philosophical Enquiry into the Origin of Our Ideas of the Sublime and Beautiful* (1757) to distinguish the small-scale appreciation of beautiful detail from the awestruck feeling before the majesty of nature. And if there is any connection between his aesthetic ideas, his attack on the French revolutionary cult of reason, and his defense of monarchy, it is an argument about the value of feelings in politics as well as in literature and art, the need to have an emotional connection to the state akin to the emotional connection to a novel or a painting or a landscape.

Not only were there writers about sensibility, there were people who prided themselves on their sensibility, their attunement to feelings, as Jane Austen in *Northanger Abbey* was happy to mock, and in *Sense and Sensibility* to dramatize more complexly. Sensibility could take many forms. In Germany and to a lesser extent in England, the cult of feeling reveled in the medieval and the picturesque; it delved into the folk myths of the countryside, collected old ballads, and aspired to rejuvenate a moribund poetic tradition by tapping ancient sources of imaginative energy; and it sometimes became the basis for a more egalitarian politics and fellow feeling that spurred some of the earliest antislavery movements. In literature it approved those stories that appealed to the heart of the reader along with poetry that exalted the spirit, emphasizing tears as the indication of deep feeling and a feeling of awe before nature as a testament to the renewal of more authentic feeling in the midst of an increasingly "civilized" society. Although frequently falling into the sentimental, the doctrines of sensibility could also include satire that aroused rage against inequities, or pornography that aroused the emotions in other ways. The common element in all these styles and genres, in all these stories and characters, was that they aimed to make their audiences *feel.* Thinking might come later, when the empathy excited, say, for a beaten slave or a lonely castaway could be translated into political action. But instead of feeling and thinking occupying separate contradictory spheres, feeling was the route to thinking, and feeling had the power to go beyond or beneath the rational. Like an underground stream swollen by floods, it could erupt into the overworld and change its shape forever. Even the theological controversy over the Lisbon earthquake might play a role: If God could not be depended upon to fix the inequities of the world anymore, human beings would have to step up.

FEAR ITSELF

With our contemporary sophistication or cynicism we might call the works of feeling that sought to inspire terror "escapism." In the era of the French Revolution, the Marquis de Sade thought that what was happening in art and literature was more harmonized with reality than an escape from it.

He called the terrifying, violent, erotic—and extremely popular—power of Matthew G. Lewis's novel *The Monk*, from 1796, "the inevitable result of the revolutionary shocks which all of Europe had suffered." People had experienced so much misfortune that "to compose works of interest, one had to call upon the aid of hell itself, and to find in the world of make-believe things wherewith one was fully familiar merely by delving into man's daily life in this age of iron." Only fictional terrors could satisfy an audience so used to real ones in their daily lives.[13]

In the more than two centuries since Sade's view of the revolutionary context of the rise of the gothic, of course, there have also been even more explanations—psychological, historical, and cultural—for the genesis of the fears we group under the name of horror. Two of the founders of modern psychology, Sigmund Freud and Carl Jung, made their own attempts to elucidate the power of darkness. Freud considered that repression of the primitive self and its instincts was the price we had to pay for civilization and the creation of a socially acceptable personal identity. Jung, in contrast, thought of the dark self as the shadow, whose power increased the longer it was repressed. His kind of analysis is therefore frequently more attuned to the loss involved by repression in the name of social order and customs, and he frequently draws upon folktales and myths to define that area of the self he called the unconscious. On the cultural level, however, both Freud and Jung suggest that horror might be defined as what every culture, no matter how different, seeks to submerge in the name of social order. Whether fictional terror was an escape from the real world, or a kind of training for its conflicts, was a question taken up by the psychologist Bruno Bettelheim in the twentieth century, when he argued in *The Uses of Enchantment* that stories like the Grimm fairy tales (first published in 1812) helped children master their otherwise overpowering fears of the invisible world. The desire to experience fear, to go to horror movies, to scream on roller coasters, all to a certain extent are explainable through Bettelheim's ideas.[14]

But surrounding the individual effort to master fears by turning them into stories, there is also a historical context for their eruption. In eras when an oversupply of free-floating fear fills the atmosphere, there are more lightning rods raised to experience those fears and to overcome them, including the dusting off of old myths and the invocation of monsters from the past, to deal with the confusions of the present. In this way personal fear is transformed into group fear, whether of a community, a district, or even a nation. It is intriguing to think that the same era that saw the rise of newspapers, newsletters, and other forms of communication also could reasonably be termed the birthplace of widespread and often groundless fears.[15] The establishment of a concept of public opinion and the desire to shape and feed it is inevitably accompanied by the possibility of rumor, false or half-baked information, and bias, to which paranoia is a ready response. Paranoia, after all, can be a form of solace, a distorted effort to regain control in the midst of chaos. Such contemporary best-sellers as *The Da Vinci Code* similarly feed the desire in tumultuous times to believe that there is another, secret history of the world, based on a premeditated and preordained exercise of power. Much like the argument that intelligent design makes against the theory of evolution, such arguments appeal to those who refuse to believe that things have just happened; they had to be planned and controlled by some directing power, whether human, divine, or even diabolical.

Sociologists like Barry Glassner in *The Culture of Fear* have recently documented how a distinct characteristic of the modern world—in which tremendous fears sweep through large segments of the population, fears of terrorism, fears of epidemic diseases, fears of crime, fears of interloping strangers—is abetted by an ever expanding web of communications, manipulated by politicians and newscasters, liberals and conservatives alike.[16] Certainly the speed with which the flimsiest rumor can become viral is something that has changed remarkably since the end of the eighteenth century, as has the daily increasing number of possible sources of information or disinformation. Social scientists have estimated that fear is seven times more likely to spread than any other social attitude. Historically, such bouts of group paranoia can be dated from the seventeenth and eighteenth centuries when the belief that Satan walked the earth (as exemplified in the Salem witch trials) or that armed men supported by foreign invaders or the local aristocracy were on the attack (like the Great Fear of the early French Revolution) aroused fears that reason was helpless to stem. Thus, while fear is always phrased in terms of contemporary issues, it is often animated and shaped by more long-lasting stories and images. Old myths, earlier fears, are repurposed to make sense of the new horrors of the world. Even when other explanations are available, the language of fear gives an emotional weight to the argument. Story floods in to fill the factual gaps in rumor and hearsay. Anti-Semitism and ethnic cleansing become the modern political versions of accusations of heresy and witchcraft. Pandora's box becomes the appropriate image for the prospect of worldwide nuclear destruction. Preschool children make accusations of witchcraft and satanic rituals that come virtually straight out of the works of the Brothers

Grimm. Birther conspiracy theories about Barack Obama's citizenship like-wise draw upon folk tales of the changeling, the demon child.

What is the connection, if any, between the fear of God and the fear of terrorism? One approach will be to try to answer from a psychological and cultural point of view why people gravitate toward the fearful, and therefore why the "reasonable" analysis of sociologists whether fears are justified or not focuses on only part of the question. In *The Culture of Fear,* for example, Glassner maintains with much justification that it is the media world and individual companies—in other words, contemporary capitalism—that invoke fear for their own ends of profit and expansion. In a similar argument, the BBC documentary *The Power of Nightmares* (2004) seeks to demonstrate that neoconservatives and Islamic fundamentalists alike use images of fear to amass power.

However useful that analogy might be, however, it goes only so far to understand the sources, genesis, and imagery of fear. Often the difference between now and then is no more than quantitative. The clash between the language of hope and the language of fear remains the same. In the eighteenth century, industrialization, scientific experimentation, and political revolution promised a new world, just as now the Internet, technological advance, and a globalized economy envision a world coming together economically, politi-cally, and even socially more than it ever has before, highlighting what we can achieve, what power as human beings we have. In the eighteenth century, when the Julian calendar was rejected in favor of the Gregorian in the West, when the French revolutionaries created their own calendar, and when the stock market and betting on the future was becoming the pastime of the rich, time itself would seem to be open to human manipulation. But then as now, the dark underside of progress was visible as well: the consciousness of what had been lost—in the past, in the world of the spirit, in nature—how the world of feeling and the nonrational sources of meaning had been ignored. In some times and places this awareness emerges in the form of fundamentalist religion, in others as a taste for horror films and tales of darkness, and in some uniquely disturbed few the urge to mass murder, suicide bombing, and po-litical assassination. All such responses, though, are at base revolts against and deep anxieties about the future. Even for people who are generally future-oriented, they satisfy the tormenting feeling that what is in danger of vanish-ing must somehow be saved.

✿

Into this world, caught between the overhanging past and the uncertain future, walks the monster, this strange distorted creature, sometimes part human and part animal, sometimes part divine and part diabolical, always a strange amalgamation of contradictory traits, which confuses the categories of rationality and order, creating its own logic and dominating its own space. Whether he is a medieval aristocrat ruling his domain with an iron hand, an actual misshapen being, or a supernatural demon, the monster is a figure of uniqueness—not part of the increasingly orderly system of human relationships and politics that constitutes the modern world. As that world grows ever more complex, the monster continues to exert the fascination of absolute difference. In later works of horror, a man is often the central character, but in the late eighteenth century, at the center of the story is a young woman threatened by mysterious powerful forces. Such a young woman appears preeminently in most of the novels of one great master of the gothic, the best-selling Ann Radcliffe, and she turns up as well in Jane Austen's parody, *Northanger Abbey,* in which she is an avid consumer of such novels as Radcliffe's. Right from the early decades of the gothic novel, then, Austen emphasizes how reading sensational fiction could warp one's view of the world with stereotypes that sink so deeply into one's consciousness that we don't even realize we are using them. The distinction between real-life readers of gothic tales and fictional victims of gothic plots is thus difficult to draw, just as the teenagers in the *Scream* series of satiric horror films can still be murdered, despite their knowledge of horror conventions. But the lure to watch and to read remains. As Sade might approvingly point out, in a world turned upside down by revolutionary violence, personal pleasure is the greatest rebellion of all. Popular art may be escape for some, but it also does crucial cultural work. Like fairy tales for grownups, the popular fiction that starts to become widespread in the later eighteenth century both expresses and then tries to allay the emotional conflicts and contradictions of modern life, where so much of the world appears open and so much is actually closed.

In the course of the nineteenth century, monsters become a more familiar terror than a strange and unprecedented one, for an essential part of the setting in which the literature of feeling emerged was a newly expanded audience for reading itself. Instead of the elite audiences of the seventeenth century and earlier, when the literate were a small portion of the population, the readership of the later eighteenth century was expanding along with the expansion of literacy. In England, circulating libraries began to emerge by midcentury, so people who could not afford to buy many books found them inexpensive to borrow. A large proportion of those books were novels, a new form that appealed so much to this wider audience of impecunious literates that some of their betters complained that servants would get unreasonable expectations when they read tales of foundlings like Tom Jones, who learned by the end of his story that he was actually well-born and soon to be rich. At the same time the supposed revelations of the sexual peccadilloes of public figures (like Marie Antoinette), along with the gothic images of diabolic and pornographic doings behind the facades of cathedrals and castles, increased doubts not only about social hierarchy but also about other political and religious forms of order, authority, and tradition.

Literacy opens up the possibility of experiencing other worlds and other views of reality. Two aspects of the new popular fiction of the later eighteenth century are important here. First is the implicit attack on official "serious" literature and by extension official forms of authority. Governments and churches, all human institutions, in such works are virtually by definition corrupt, or at least guilty until proven innocent. The other aspect is closely connected: the almost unrelenting focus on the life and feelings of individuals, often in opposition to the standards of society. Like the continued existence of folk beliefs under the surface of official church theology, the literature of sentimentality and sensibility implicitly attacked institutions and their repressive ideological systems. The rise of popular fiction in the era of industrial and political revolutions is thus not only due to an increased market of literate readers. It also supplies a temporary imaginative antidote for feelings of personal anonymity that industrialization (and "order," whether revolutionary or traditional) bring with them. Such novels, sometimes realistically but often fancifully, explore issues of power and subjugation, by exaggerating and then by the end of the story resolving conflicts. We have little solid data about the relative numbers of male and female readers at this time, although critics have in the past often stigmatized popular fiction as the recreation of newly leisurely women in particular. But the symbolic role of women in these stories is certain. Defoe's Moll Flanders, toward the beginning of the eighteenth century, surviving by cunning and crime, has an intriguing affinity with Emily St. Aubert, persecuted and imprisoned by the villainous Montoni in Ann Radcliffe's *Mysteries of Udolpho* at the end of the century. Both are responses to an overwhelming world of male authority, and thereby stand in for anyone, male or female, who feels farther down on the social ladder. Who better than women in this society to stand in for the powerless in general? The Marquis de Sade responded to the world of violence he found around himself by creating works of fiction featuring naive women coerced by despotic all-powerful men, in which supererotic violence and lengthy discourses on politics and philosophy have uneasy commerce. Jane Austen, at much the same time, analogously explored in her novels the imbalances of power in a world dominated by male authority and money.

Popular fiction in its most powerful forms evokes extremes of both emotion and repression, and it aims to inspire the physical and psychological effects I mentioned before elation, empathy, crying, fear, hatred, and sexual arousal. So another effect of this wider audience for literature was that many novels began more and more to resemble one another, in the same way that once a film becomes a hit, producers and studios fall over themselves trying to create variations on its success. This is the power of genre—the name for works that tell similar or overlapping stories that fans want to experience again and again. Genres are the categories in the video store or the online rental service that let us go immediately to works that we know will give us pleasure and goose bumps, tears, or joy in the right proportions. It's easy to dismiss the appearance of similar works as a commercial ploy, but the repetition of such stories also serves the needs of their audience. The monster may be unique and unparalleled (in one sense of *original*) but its nature touches such inner fears (in another sense of *original*) that its fans rush to meet it again and again, as Keats said, "half in love with easeful death," if only to show that, once again, they have escaped its clutches.

How have those stories mutated over the centuries, transformed into movie versions, and shaped our sense of reality? One decisive element, not present in either the more realistic setting of *Moll Flanders* or in the human tyranny of *The Mysteries of Udolpho,* that yet plays a crucial part in gothic literature and art, is the supernatural. Can a story of horror and upset be told straightforwardly, or must its telling be, like the essence of the story itself, filled with confusing passages and darkened hallways to nowhere? How then to convey the sense of uncertainty and disheveled perception in a fictional form? Like the architecture of the gothic church or castle, with its catacombs and hidden rooms, secret doors and concealed stairways, the book is often a kind of labyrinth, filled with shifts in time and space. The unsettling story is itself told through confusing and disconcerting movements rather than the seeming one-to-one linearity and transparency of novels that try to convey a picture of an established and rational world.

In Matthew Lewis's *The Monk,* for example, events often occur simultaneously, in a novelistic foretelling of the crosscutting of film. In *The Monk* and even in the more rationalistic novels of Ann Radcliffe, other material is often inserted at odd moments—a farrago of folktales, songs, and poems that break up any causal time scheme that orderly sentences might impose. They convey instead an effort to get beyond the confines of prose into more complex worlds of feeling and understanding. As Lewis's title character, the supposedly holy monk Ambrosio, goes to bed with his lover Matilda, who had been posing as a male acolyte, a lengthy tale of other characters is interposed, complete with mythic figures like the Wandering Jew and the Bleeding Nun, whom the hero of this section takes to be a real person ready for erotic adventures.

Interpolated stories, shifts into poetry or folk ballads, help to undermine the reader's expectations of a plot that will turn out to be totally clear and reasonable with all its loose ends neatly tied up. Of course, all genres rely on repeating and reformulating their basic elements: characters, plots, symbols, and pet phrases. Unlike stories that raise expectations, fears, and apprehensions and then somehow organize and resolve them by the final curtain, there is always an element, and frequently the whole show, in horror that depends precisely upon an inability to resolve them. Does the end leave you satisfied or still on the hook? Just when you feel safe, does a hand rise out of the grave (as in the movie *Carrie*) to grab you by the arm? Or does a shift in perspective, as in the beginning of *The Bride of Frankenstein,* show that the victory over the monster you thought had been won in *Frankenstein* might actually be short-lived? An ending, any ending, seems to imply a final explanation that resolves all uncertainties and allays all doubts. But no matter how much explanation enters the story by the grand finale—and many horror stories of the Radcliffe sort do turn out to be based on misperception and misinterpretation—the fears raised cannot be entirely banished. In the movies more than in literature, this uncertainty can generate sequels. At the end of the film *Halloween,* for example, the hockey-masked killer and escaped lunatic Michael Myers can seemingly be injured by Laurie, the heroine babysitter played by Jamie Lee Curtis, and then shot by his psychiatrist Dr. Loomis (Donald Pleasence). But when they look for his body, it has disappeared, and the question remains, "Can you kill the bogeyman?" It's an unanswered question that in this case manages to generate nine other films, novels based on the films, comic books, Halloween costumes, and more.

Edmund Spenser made a virtually theological point of this clash between the single story and the unending story in the first book of *The Faerie Queene* (1590), back when the first Queen Elizabeth reigned. In the poem, a dragon, allegorically identified as Satan, is terrorizing the kingdom of Eden and threatening the king's daughter Una, who represents the singleness of divine truth. By the end of the book, the Redcrosse Knight, a callow youth at the start, has matured enough that he can defeat the dragon and win Una for his bride. But as the villagers and court come out of their hiding places to celebrate Redcrosse's victory, one "wiser" person warns the others that the seemingly dead and defeated dragon may still be alive, or that inside it there are young dragons waiting to be born. Meanwhile another points out that the dragon's eyes are still open. The point is clear: Evil can never finally be totally and finally defeated; the battle may be won but not the war.

Spenser was in the early throes of writing *The Faerie Queene* while he was a lord deputy in Ireland, engaged in the "reducing of that savage nation to better government and civility," that is, trying to impose English rule in the face of incessant Irish rebellions and even proposing the extreme measure of a forced famine to bring the "barbarous" people to heel. His dragon is in like manner a creature from the barbarous past that must be defeated by the Redcrosse Knight's Christian chivalry. Thus, Spenser draws upon myth to play against as well as interpret the tumult of the present. Here in the last decade of the sixteenth century, we have not yet reached the age of modern horror. But, like Sade's parallel between the terrors of fiction and the terror of a world in revolution, Spenser's poem raises the question of whether real-world fears help generate fictional fears, as they seem to do now in the paranoid atmosphere of terrorism; or whether in some cases they help quench their power, as if horror were a handy way of categorizing and then dismissing real-world monsters. During World War II, for example, the main representatives of the classic monsters appeared primarily in the company of the comedy team of Abbott and Costello in such films as *Abbott and Costello Meet Frankenstein* or *Abbott and Costello Meet Dracula.* But many contemporary horror films would not be complete without some reference to the Nazis, as in *The Exorcist, X-Men,* and *Hell-Boy.*

The issue of whether we can ever ultimately win against the monsters, fictional or real, makes the horror genre especially hospitable to the never ending story. Among the repeated stories drawn upon by literature, theater, and film, there is something particularly exemplary about horror, with its ability to spawn more and more sequels, its virtually endless versions of Frankensteins, Draculas, and Jekyll/Hydes, each a bit different from the other. Along with all the other forms of art and literature meant to arouse the reader's feelings, horror preeminently aims to frighten the reader, to penetrate the room where the book is being read or the painting being viewed or the music being heard, and fill it with intangible spirits whose grotesque shapes are limited only by the imaginations of its audience. At the same time that in the daylight world everything seems geared to the inevitabilities of change and new horizons, such art tosses its audience into the cauldron of inescapable feelings, feelings that have been born in and aroused from an invisible world, set in the present or in the grand and mysterious past. It is a world that readers and viewers can't measure up to, because of their own sense of inner inadequacy and inability to control their lives, as natural or supernatural powers toss them about like a straw in a hurricane.

❧❀❧

> *Glendower.* I can call spirits from the vasty deep.
> *Hotspur.* Why, so can I, or so can any man, But will they come when
> you do call for them?

—Shakespeare, Henry IV, Part 1

Like my previous books on the history of fame and the relationship between war and masculinity, this book is an essay in the cultural shaping of emotions. Just as fame is connected to an enlarged selfhood, and warfare claims to be the prime setting for pride and honor, the experience of fear is a human testing ground as well. All three involve risk, the combined joy and anxiety in crossing boundaries, the desire to leave the tiresomeness of day-to-day "normal" life and step instead into a more awe-inspiring and dreadful world. In what follows I try to explore two prime ways into understanding something of the development of fear from earlier centuries to the present. One is to investigate a human history of attitudes toward death, ghosts, witches, wonders, and portents. The other is to look closely at the period from the late eighteenth century to the present in which that history begins to be shaped into an enormous collection of stories, novels, paintings, and films that aim to excite fear in audiences. I am intrigued by the lure of fear based not on actual tangible experiences, but on the encounter with fictional stories and figures, like the monster, that have pervaded Western culture for the past two centuries and more. Which of the many versions of ghosts and monsters have lasted, and which have been forgotten or ignored? Myths that last are not just timeless stories but also responses to immediate situations, or at least susceptible of being rotated to show those facets most relevant to current fears. Some are stuck in their own times, while others have shown the ability to evolve and respond to new historical situations: Medical advances in cloning and organ transplant give new life to Frankenstein, AIDS rings a turn

on the blood-sucking vampire, and blind consumerism inspires the director
George Romero to think of zombies.

Stirred by such stories, we are drawn to see what we also dread to see. Even
though we know something horrible lies behind that far door, we savor the
suspense of the mystery story and are often disappointed when the payoff
turns out to be deception and manipulation rather than a true compact with
the forces of darkness. Inspired by the world of invisible horrors and terrors
they inhabit, we find in ourselves the urge for the unveiling, the taste for
apocalypse—all cravings that literature and the visual arts may be more able
to describe and even explain than the relentlessly daylight realm of scientific
and sociological analysis. At the same time, in horror's urge to the outrageous,
it may potentially become a subversive critique of mainstream official culture,
a kind of eruption of the repressed. Touching fears well below a culture's consciousness, it may also be mysteriously prophetic. As Stephen King has
pointed out, the otherwise sub-Z movie *Horror of Party Beach* (1964) has a
nuclear waste theme ("Weird Atomic Beasts Who Live Off Human Blood!!!"
says the poster) more than a decade before the very sober *China Syndrome*.[17]

If we don't try to understand the ways our imaginations have been shaped
by these fictional images of horror, our ability to combat authentically dangerous situations is crippled. Demonizing our enemies undermines our ability to win or at least end the conflict by anything less apocalyptic than
Armageddon. Enemies become not just human beings, susceptible to being
contended with through negotiation or normal battle, but nonhuman forces,
part of some universal allegory of good and evil. It goes without saying that
wartime preeminently invites such moral polarization. But the more abso-
lutely the conflict is defined, the less it can be handled in human terms and
the more that wish fulfillment plays a role in the desire to be victorious. Without appreciating how myth and legend can control responses, there is neither
big picture nor nuances, only the either/or of a video game.

I am indebted to the enormous amount of brilliant research and scholarship about what was actually true, for example, about the ways different
countries treated supposed witches, about the evidence for a widespread fear
of vampires unearthed by anthropologists, and about the historical necessity
in certain eras of believing in demons. I am certainly interested in those studies, but they are not my basic concern here. Instead, I want to pursue the
question of how it is that ancient tribal myths, folklore, and superstitions stay
alive and are even nurtured in a world, our own, professedly technological,
scientific, and rational. My focus then is not so much where monsters first

appeared but why they gained such prominence and vitality in the particular historical period of the past two hundred and fifty or so years, when otherwise buried or quiescent local beliefs, images of evil and disruption, became national and international obsessions. There are countless stories about the dead and the undead, the gruesome and the monstrous, just in the West, let alone world culture. Why have some fallen by the wayside and others vigorously survived?

The theologians and lay writers who spent their time in the Middle Ages and later naming and numbering the devils, subdevils, and demons created a vast array of names and functions that has been called "a hideous hodgepodge." Most of these once fearsome creatures have been forgotten or are now only evoked to add an arcane coloring to horror movies and video games. But if fears can be organized into compelling images and stories, they achieve a much longer cultural life. In contrast, then, to the demonologists cataloguing and naming the multitude of terrifying creatures, in what follows I argue that there are four broad provinces of the monstrous and the fearsome. These four provinces also correspond to four prime areas of cultural anxiety in the Western world from the eighteenth century to the present. In other words, these are the monsters of modernity, each commanding a particular area of fear, even while some of its characteristics overlap with the others. They are the monster from nature (like King Kong), the created monster (like Frankenstein), the monster from within (like Mr. Hyde), and the monster from the past (like Dracula). From these, virtually all varieties of the monstrous flow. Instead of being isolated figures, these monsters constitute a system of family resemblances that are modified according to the historical and cultural context in which they appear. Over the past few centuries, each of these sources of fear and sleepless nights has continued to metamorphose beyond its origins without changing its basic nature, and their continuity and recurrence have become a common coin of reference in Western culture.

Three further discussions provide a setting for the discussion of the four fundamental monsters. I begin with a consideration of the relationship between horror and religion, to disentangle one from the other, as well as to show their many similarities. Then, after chapters on the natural monster and the created monster, I turn from the monster to discuss another significant cultural figure, the detective, who as the monster's complement seeks for order and reason as much as the monster creates disorder and fear. Consideration of the detective also helps reestablish the Enlightenment reliance on natural explanations for otherwise baffling events, in contrast with horror's reliance on supernatural interventions from the invisible world. In the final chapter, I consider the coming of modern means of communication, especially the visual media of the movies and television, which have adapted so many of the old stories to their own formats and audience, creating a kind of world folk culture, in which, for example, Indonesian horror movies can modify the motifs and assumptions of American zombie films in light of their own traditions and cultural purposes.

CHAPTER 2

Between Hope and Fear

HORROR AND RELIGION

> People are not liable to be mistaken in their feelings, but they are fre-
> quently wrong in the names they give them, and in their reasonings
> about them.
>
> —Edmund Burke, *A Philosophical Enquiry into the Origin of Our Ideas
> of the Sublime and Beautiful* (1757)

In order to understand what in past religious traditions of fear were co-
alesced by such Europe-wide events as the Lisbon earthquake and such subsequent artistic events as the rise of gothic literature and art, it is necessary to
understand something of the cataclysmic rupture that occurred in the sixteenth century with the Protestant Reformation and the Catholic Counter
Reformation, in which the two great branches of Christianity competed to
convince the wavering faithful which of them had ultimate power over the
divine and diabolic worlds.

In the eighth century, the Eastern Orthodox theologian John Damascene,
summarizing the teachings of the Early Church Fathers, listed six varieties of
fear: shrinking, shame, disgrace, anxiety, consternation, and panic. Of these,
shrinking (fear of something about to happen), shame (fear aroused by an-
ticipation of blame), disgrace (fear arising from a "base act" already committed), and anxiety (fear of failing or misfortune) were fears generated by reality
(not a term he would have used), while consternation and panic were products of the imagination. In the late eighteenth century, John Trusler reflected
some of Damascene's analysis when he distinguished between fear, which acts
upon the mind; terror, which disrupts the senses; and consternation, which
affects the heart, disorders the senses, and "unman[s] us."[1]

So far I have been using words like *horror* and *terror* as if they were interchangeable, and since I am drawing some connections between the monsters

of what is usually called horror fiction or film and the monsters who strike terror in daily life, perhaps that mingled terminology has some point. Like many other earlier eighteenth-century writers, Edmund Burke in his effort to analyze the varieties of feeling that art and nature can evoke uses them almost interchangeably. But by the late eighteenth and early nineteenth centuries, as the vogue for the gothic expanded, some sharper distinctions were being made, especially in the clarification of what was horror and what was terror. Horror, which comes from a Latin word referring to hair standing on end, was often designated as the physical fear, the alarm of immediate jeopardy, the fight-or-flight instinct. When the great eighteenth-century actor-director-playwright David Garrick played *Hamlet*, in the scene when Hamlet first sees his father's ghost, he leaped from his chair with a crash while his specially constructed wig sprang outward to show his fright.

But terror was more abstract and ambiguous. Its root meaning was also to be extremely frightened, a trembling or shuddering reaction of fright and loathing, but it implied as well a sense of the awesome and immeasurable quality of what particularly was so frightening. Horror was what you felt when you saw a monster or a ghost approaching you by night in a ruined castle. Terror with more than a touch of awe was what you felt when you contemplated the grandeur of nature, the immense mountains and crevasses of the Alps, or even the power of God itself. In a strange way, terror was uplifting. Whereas horror made your teeth rattle and your bowels liquefy as you feared for your own safety, terror could either shake the foundations of your belief in a benevolent God or make you feel at one with the universe, a human mote in the sands of time. This sort of meaning may sound far from the way people fear terrorists today. What is uplifting there? But it does mark a connection to deep spiritual feelings that the terrorists themselves claim are their motivation. Creating a generalized, intangible, miasmic fear is clearly a terrorist goal, as it is the goal of many anti-terrorists. Terrorists seek to raise not the more local apprehensions of walking down a dark street and wondering what is going to jump out of a gloomy doorway, but grander fears of a vast and humanly incomprehensible universe.

Ann Radcliffe, the best-selling gothic author of the late eighteenth and early nineteenth centuries, formulates the difference succinctly: "Terror and horror are so far opposite, that the first expands the soul, and awakens the faculties to a high degree of life; the other contracts, freezes, and nearly annihilates them." Horror, in other words, reduces human nature; terror expands it. Both feelings are stirred to some degree by a perception of the external world, but the horror response primarily resides in the physical body, while the combined awe and dread of terror seeps into the soul. Physical fear might enter into terror, as it did in the period of the French Revolution called the Terror, when thousands were sent to the guillotine. But in essence terror was a spiritual reaction. Robespierre, for his part, identified terror with revolutionary clarity: "Terror," he said, was nothing other than "justice, prompt, severe, and inflexible." Ambitious writers (and politicians) therefore aimed to produce terror in their readers, while writers who could produce only a sense of horror in their readers were doing something lower level, akin to a skeleton popping out of closet in a fun house.[2]

Keeping that useful distinction in mind, I will nevertheless generally refer to the artistic shaping of fear by the blanket term we commonly use today: horror. Many of the other words associated with fear have a long history, but the eighteenth century often gives them a crucial twist. Take *gothic* itself. At first, as *goth,* it referred to someone who acted like a barbarian, rude, uncivilized, and ignorant—the Ostrogoths and the Visigoths who attacked and gradually dismembered and destroyed the Roman Empire. Then, in its adjective form the word described the medieval cathedrals that in the seventeenth century were just starting to be looked at with some interest, although they were usually considered, in the gothic way, to be barbaric and crude. Their gloomy interiors and haunted corridors were redolent of the medieval Catholicism that England had broken away from during the Reformation begun by Henry VIII, when many of the buildings were burned and the statues of saints and other holy figures were destroyed as a result of state-sponsored iconoclasm. Protestant Reformers across Europe similarly preached that any images purporting to show the invisible world in general and the divine in particular were to be demolished as objects of idolatry, deployed by the Catholic Church to dazzle the eye and thereby darken the soul.[3]

But an interesting thing happened to these harsh aesthetic and religious judgments as the eighteenth century developed through periods of industrial expansion and political revolution. In England and Germany particularly, myths and folktales that the eighteenth-century rationalist might deride as unworthy of a modern civilized person's attention became the subject of literature and theater, while visual artists delved into the storehouse of horrific images contained in, among other religious sources, the Book of Revelation, while inventing new demons and monsters of their own. Poets wandered in graveyards, communing with the dead and meditating on life, death, and immortality. Folk songs were collected and works by ancient poets exhumed, republished, and imitated in an effort to search for the roots of true poetry and feeling. In 1764, just nine years after the Lisbon earthquake, appeared Horace Walpole's *The Castle of Otranto.*

The more widespread vogue of the gothic did not arrive for some twenty or thirty years after Walpole's novel, but then it continued in literature and also in the other arts well into the nineteenth century. Walpole was a forerunner with no immediate followers. Perhaps the gap in response had something also to do with a lapse of time, both in the sense of chronological age as well as the spirit of the age. Although when Walpole wrote there were revolutionary political stirrings in some countries, a full-scale sense of a tumultuous, apocalyptic age was a few decades in the future, and Walpole's own connection to his work was more narrowly aesthetic than political or cultural. Hardly one to embrace disruption, Walpole was the youngest son of Robert Walpole, the first English politician to be called prime minister (a title originally considered to be an insult). A member of Parliament himself for some thirteen years before *Otranto* was published, Horace Walpole's other significant claim to artistic fame was his construction of Strawberry Hill outside London, an elaborately "gothic" mansion built from the base of a small seventeenth-century cottage. Like the mixture of story with interpolated poems and folk-tales in *The Monk,* Strawberry Hill was a pastiche, mixing turrets and keeps from medieval castles with towers and other interior and exterior details from cathedrals to convey the atmosphere of what Walpole called "gloomth."

Walpole was in his late forties when *Otranto* was published. Some of the later gothic writers, by contrast, were, like many of their contemporaries in the English Romantic movement, comparatively young. Ann Radcliffe was in her twenties when she started publishing her series of gothic tales (1789); William Beckford, who would later build another gothic extravaganza, Fonthill Abbey, in his twenties wrote *Vathek* (1786), the tale of a licentious caliph seeking supernatural power, supposedly translated from the Arabic; and Matthew Lewis was nineteen when he published *The Monk* (1796). As William Wordsworth, himself in his twenties when he and the even younger Samuel Taylor Coleridge published *Lyrical Ballads* (1798), among the first works of English Romantic poetry, later wrote, referring to the era of the French Revolution, "Bliss was it in that dawn to be alive, But *to be young* was very heaven!"[4]

Still another characteristic, beyond that of age, that united many of the gothic writers was a sense of marginality. Although Walpole, Beckford, and Lewis were all members of Parliament and therefore from prominent landed families, all three were also considered sexually suspect and became the targets of gossip and scandal. They help inaugurate a tradition of outsider artists, who gather energy and inspiration from the gothic and horror genres, which stretches down into the twentieth century and beyond. Radcliffe, as a woman, was even more outside eighteenth-century social norms. Although her gender is hardly unique among eighteenth-century novelists, her stories, which almost invariably feature a young woman without family resources threatened by powerful and mysterious male figures, highlight the dilemma of someone outside the protection of a male-dominated social system. Together with others, also often comparatively young, like Lord Byron and Percy Shelley, these authors drew energy from confronting the possibility of transgression, with extravagance and intensity, whether their characters returned safely from the land of taboo or were swallowed up in its sulphurous fumes.

The youth of the late-eighteenth-century gothic writers as well as the Romantics underlined what they considered to be a fresh look at what constituted literary and poetic imagination. But Walpole was one of the first to tap into a stream that was coming closer and closer to the surface. In the midst of turbulent political, social, and technological efforts to move the world into a new future, the past and in particular the Catholic past, which had otherwise been expunged in both England and large parts of Germany by the Protestant Reformation, was becoming more and more alluring. With the closer connection of religion to the state, as in Henry VIII's establishment of the Anglican Church and the *cuius regio, eius religio* (whose land, his religion) argument in Germany, the medieval Catholic characterization of the priest as the intermediary to the supernatural world was lost or at least watered down. Much of the gothic is therefore often situated either in the medieval world (Walpole's *The Castle of Otranto*) or in the more recent past of countries like Spain and Italy that were still strongly Catholic (the novels of Ann Radcliffe, Lewis's *The Monk,* Charles Maturin's *Melmoth the Wanderer*).

༺☙❦❧༻

To appreciate any genre—whether it be horror, detective, science fiction, or romance—requires a belief in its basic formal and storytelling elements. If you don't think people dancing in the street is realistic, forget musicals. If you don't think heroes can be battered unmercifully and then bounce back to win the day, forget action movies. But at the core of horror is a question of belief that goes much deeper, a belief, if only for the moment, in the existence of evil, the possibility for good, and their eternal combat. That so many people in the past (and a goodly number in the present) believed in the ability of witches or other shamans to either summon up demons or thwart them should come as no surprise. If in today's world, cures can be effected through placebos, why couldn't people in the past believe they were infected by a curse? Expectations shape feelings into emotions that can have a physical effect, and the more those expectations are widespread in a culture, the less able the individual is to resist them. To fall victim to a curse therefore might be called a *nocebo*.

Religion and horror are so intimately connected because both are suffused by the distinction between good and evil, and both deal centrally with the uncertain border between life and death. So the question might be asked: Is horror a basically secular form that uses religious trappings, or is it a religious form tricked out in the details of secular reality? One of the basic tenets of all world religions is to say something important (and usually consoling) about the relation between life and death. Many of the rituals of all religions involve not just the way to live a proper life but also the way to face and even defeat death through religious belief. With no guarantee of certainty, they promise a potential control over the uncontrollable. In this way religion asserts its superiority to magic. While spells had to work, prayers could be refused or ignored by God, who never has to give a reason.

In the terms of horror, we must walk down the hall toward that door we know we shouldn't open because as humans we must finally walk into the Valley of Death, and our curiosity about what lies beyond the door is the effort to know what lies beyond the world we know. Death is the end of change. Like the rituals of religion, the repetitions of horror literature and film are a mantra against death, one way of controlling our fears. Like prayers they are formulas connected to basic feelings that have to be validated again and again, repeating and reenacting conflicts and contradictions that can never be finally resolved. Horror in literature, art, films, therefore constitutes a prime way of keeping the spiritual perspective alive in a technological and rational world. Like religion itself, the varieties of horror in art stretch from the trifling and parochial to the embracing and transcendental, from works of power to perfunctory repetitions of mechanical formulas. As the repository of spiritual truths, religion would seem to play the prime role in this effort to connect with and acknowledge the power of the world of mystery and uncertainty. But its social function is frequently ambiguous, for absolute religion can be as tyrannical as absolute reason. In the widely popular gothic novels of Ann Radcliffe, for example, the power of the Catholic Church frequently becomes a tool of villainy, not so that her readers can breathe easily because they live in

Protestant England but so they can savor the chill of being, say, a threatened teenage heroine in Catholic Europe.

What does the connection of religion to horror have to do with the actual practices of religion? To a great extent, there is a fear-faith axis in religion that is replicated in the horror plot. If you believe, you will be afraid, just as "fear of God" is a frequent religious formula. By this logic, it seems that if you don't believe, you will not be afraid. But you hardly have to be Catholic to be terrified reading or watching *The Exorcist,* just as Matthew Lewis's Protestant readers in the late eighteenth century thrilled to the otherwise Catholic setting of satanic rituals and crimes in *The Monk.* Horror thereby detaches fear from a specific religious setting and instills it in whatever definition of darkness and evil its audience supplies. Some practitioners of horror may have specifically religious motives behind their stories, like the Catholic William Peter Blatty, author of *The Exorcist,* or the Mormon Stephenie Meyer, author of the *Twilight* series. But their audiences are much wider than co-religionists, particularly because scriptwriters and directors from a wide variety of faiths and non-faiths translate their works into movies. Then a larger cultural context intervenes, even more so when the world outside is parlous and events seem unexplainable by ordinary ideas of causality and reason.

Horror in many guises thus mirrors aspects of religion like the belief in defeating or at least transcending death. And the worldviews of horror and religion also coincide, meeting in the assumption that there is an invisible spiritual world that parallels, underlies, and infuses the visible physical world. For religion that world of the spirit might contain angels as well as demons. But in horror it tends to be darker—Mr. Hyde more than Dr. Jekyll. Just as religion presents a system of understanding the world, not through scientific details and the interconnection of material circumstance, but through its otherwise hidden system of invisible relationships, so horror turns inside out what usually lurks behind and below the surface of the "normal" world. In a novel like Lewis's *The Monk,* we begin in a superficial social reality and gradually penetrate into the catacombs and dungeons that lie beneath. In the gothic particularly, there is a direct and obvious analogy between the architecture of its gloomy buildings and the recesses of the mind: secret passageways behind the walls; oubliettes, those trapdoors that open abruptly and throw the unwary down into the depths, paintings behind whose seemingly flat surfaces a shadowy world lurks. Stories like these bridge the gap between private fears and public fears, just as fiction itself in whatever form—literature, drama, film—is a seemingly public space that knits together what is daylit and public with what is dark and private. In such tales, what is underneath, what is invisible, becomes the surface, and the reader or viewer is tumbled into whatever darkness he or she feared might be true of the world, while all that we thought we knew for sure, everything solid and stable, vanishes into ghostly vapors.

A PREVALENCE OF GHOSTS AND A
CONSPIRACY OF WITCHES

Turn ye not unto the ghosts, nor unto familiar spirits; seek them not out, to be defiled by them.

—Leviticus, 19:31

It is wonderful that five thousand years have now elapsed since the creation of the world, and still it is undecided whether or not there has ever been an instance of the spirit of any person appearing after death. All argument is against it; but all belief is for it.

—Samuel Johnson

Neither ghosts nor witches are usually considered monsters in even the expanded normal sense of the word. But it is important to look more closely at them before proceeding to monsters proper because ghosts are the observable presence of the world of the dead in the midst of the world of the living, and witches are the prime intermediaries between the visible and the invisible worlds.

Anthropologists have long considered the appearance of funerary practices—commemorating the dead through burial customs and the designation of a special area for their interment—as an essential and early sign of a civilized culture. The active engagement with the dead among the living also extends beyond such care for the burial. Roman families kept *imagines,* wax images of the faces of departed family members, in a special area of the house. Japanese Buddhism has Obon season, a time of year when the dead visit the family, and the family in turn performs rites of ancestor worship. In China, ghost day and ghost month are celebrated as times when all the deceased come to visit the living (versus more usual times when the living pay homage to the dead). Some historians say the practice is related not only to Buddhism, with its ideas of reincarnation, but also to Chinese folk religion, much as Christianity adopted Celtic and other funerary practices.

So long, then, as death and funeral practices have cultural significance, and the living have a sense of obligation to the dead, there is the possibility of ghosts. Since so much of religion is involved with the interplay between life and death, ghosts can also confirm religious beliefs. Whatever their mission may be in appearing to the living—rarely benevolent, often vindictive, or sometimes just by happenstance—the presence of ghosts seems to satisfy the desire to believe that there is some way to cross the line between life and death, between the world of matter and the world of the spirit. As Christianity from its earliest days asserted, Jesus Christ came in the world to defeat death, and the concept of bodily resurrection that unites Christianity and Islam seems to require the idea of the ghost as a demonstration of God's power: Just as the physical being will be restored in the triumph of the world of the spirit, so the spiritual being can enter the physical world at God's pleasure. But even in religions and philosophies without a concept of resurrection the ghost underpins another fundamental belief, the idea of the soul. If the ghost lives after death, what animates it but the human soul, which has outlived the body and, as Socrates argues in the *Phaedo* (which deals with discussions between himself and the students and friends surrounding his deathbed), is immortal. By the same token, a refusal to believe in the existence of ghosts is an attack on the idea of the soul, that intangible substance that makes us human. Some theologians have even considered it an attack on religion itself. So in addition to any mission of revenge, the presence of the ghost also implies the hope of heaven and the reality of the afterlife.

The concept of a soul has two sources: first, it is a central element of many religions, but even before that theological codification, it seems to be an aspect of the human mind and accords with the way people experience themselves. With the increasing and compelling awareness of aging, the question naturally arises: Am I my body or am I something more? What is the *me* that still persists through all those physical changes? As funerary practices imply, in almost all cultures there are beliefs that assume there is a state of being, not defined or limited by the physical body, which dwells inside us until with death it is released from its earthly form. The Egyptians call it *ba;* in Homer it is the *eidolon;* and in Christian terminology it is *anima,* the soul—the other self that lasts when the body is gone, the immortal aspect of identity.

So Dr. Johnson seems right in the lines quoted above: There is something about a belief in the ghost that seems necessary to the human condition, or at least to that aspect of human nature concerned with faith. (I'll pass over his assumption that the world is five thousand years old.) Yet at the same time, as the lines from Leviticus attest, ghosts are not always so kindly viewed, even in a religious context, and their existence has been controversial, especially when religions are in conflict. Perhaps with the warning of Leviticus in mind, very few ghosts appear in the Bible. Along with the frequently invoked injunction from Exodus 22:18, "Thou shalt not suffer a witch to live," the most often cited ghostly scene is the visit of King Saul to the so-called Witch of Endor (1 Samuel 28.3–25). I say "so-called" because the Hebrew text just calls her the "woman," and in terms of what she does—summoning Samuel from the dead—she is more like a medium or a necromancer than what is usually called a witch, either then or now. A necromancer is a person who raises the dead in order to ask questions, usually about the future, that the dead know better than the living, presumably because they, like God, are considered to be outside earthly time and therefore able to access any moment of past, present, and future. It's an ability shared by the ghosts of Charles Dickens's *A Christmas Carol*. There the Ghost of Christmas Yet To Be prophesizes a dismal future for Scrooge that can be changed if he repents his selfishness.[5]

Although in later centuries the biblical story of Samuel would be invoked by some theologians as orthodox support for the reality of ghosts, the original tale, in which Saul seeks advice from the dead prophet Samuel, specifically characterizes this action as deluded and blasphemous, since, in accordance with Jewish law, Saul has himself already banished all magicians and necromancers from the kingdom. Some versions also seem to describe the "witch" as a ventriloquist (literally "someone who speaks from the stomach") and therefore a fraud. The story of the Witch of Endor is therefore as cautionary as the images of the future in *A Christmas Carol* or, say, the noirish version of the village of Bedford Falls in *It's a Wonderful Life*. Its warning is primarily against consulting anyone who claims to traffic with the dead.

In the early centuries of the Christian Church, the reality of ghosts, whether they appeared voluntarily or were invoked, was generally rejected by theologians because their presence implied too crowded and multiplicitous a spirit world for a monotheistic religion to accept. To some extent this point of view reflected the early church's theological roots in prior Jewish theology. But it was also significantly an effort to distinguish itself from paganism, in the same way, for example, that Christianity turned the often benevolent Greek *daimon* into the always malevolent *demon*. In many passages in the gospels, of course, Jesus is described as casting out demons. An early church father like Saint Augustine conclusively considered the belief in demons to be a residue of animism and paganism, the belief that the whole world is inhabited by spirits, and he condemned ghosts as either complete frauds or diabolic creatures summoned by demons. Like the ghosts who appear in

The Golden Ass of Apuleius (second century A.D.), such apparitions came not to promise a heavenly realm, but primarily to torment and delude. In *The City of God* (fourth century A.D.), specifically referring to Apuleius, Augustine argues that the appearances they create are therefore either false or merely tricks of superficial magic. As he remarks in a poignant personal aside, if the dead could return, his mother Monica would never have left him.[6]

Once Christianity triumphed in the West, however, and any competition from paganism had disappeared, ghosts and demons began again to be more or less accepted as an important part of the population of the invisible world. Demonology, the study of their types and abilities, became an accepted sub-discipline of theology with obvious doctrinal justification. Because there can be an alternate self, separate from the body, called the soul, so there can also be an alternate invisible world to the world of the senses. In that invisible world was an alternate ghostly community of the dead, inhabited by beings who knew things otherwise prohibited or unknown to those who still maintain their bodily form. In this way the previously rejected belief that the world is filled with malevolent or benevolent spirits comes back into orthodox Christianity. Both paganism and Catholicism emphasized the infusion of daily life by the spirit world, for good or ill. The ubiquity of saints for every problem large or small, sad or happy occasion, coincides with the pagan sense that the natural world was alive with invisible forces that could confirm the presence of good or evil in daily life. Nevertheless, as befitted a church with an established and growing body of doctrine (unlike the much less codified world of paganism), up through the Middle Ages there was still enough wariness of the magical abilities of Jews and Muslims to make sure that every ghost or demon that came to the attention of the ecclesiastical authorities had to be judged orthodox before being believed.

But the basic question remains whether the belief in the existence of ghosts is dependent on specific religious doctrines or on the general human effort to understand the relationship between life and death. The gap between the learned theology of the hierarchy and the folk beliefs, "superstitions," and emotional understanding of the faithful thus furnished fertile ground for the staying power of less structured and more heartfelt beliefs. Through the Middle Ages, then, two powerful traditions existed, one illiterate, one literate; one with roots in the pre-monotheistic world and individual human feeling, circulated by folktales and folk beliefs; the other with official or semi-official theological sanction, written down and circulated by members of the clergy. In times of settled doctrine, they coexisted. In times of controversy they often clashed. When the oral folktale or local story of an apparition passes through the hands of a literate clerical scribe, it almost inevitably is reinterpreted to express an orthodox point of view, although even then the meaning of the vision may change with changing times. Indeed, the Oxford English Dictionary tells us that the first appearance of *ghost* in the eerie sense (as opposed to the word's meaning as soul, human spirit, or a person's nature in the invisible world) occurs in Geoffrey Chaucer's poem *The Legend of Good Women*, where Dido hears Aeneas tell her that he has to leave their love nest because his father's ghost tells him in a dream that his destiny is to found Rome. Intriguingly, though, Dido does not believe him, suggesting that even by the late fourteenth century, when Chaucer wrote, people were becoming wary of the claims of ghostly visitations in dreams.

Part of the problem was the often contradictory ways the ghost was described, either in theological terms, popular narratives, or visual art, the contrast between just saying there is a spiritual world and then trying to imagine it, make it concrete—as Dante in the *Inferno* vividly depicted the torments, fires, and personnel of Hell. Thus ghosts from the twelfth to the fifteenth centuries were variously described as resembling Lazarus, looking the same as if they were alive, in the form of a naked child, as a phantom in a shroud or white sheet, as a decomposing cadaver or skeleton, and as invisible.

Leaving aside the apparitions of the dead who appear because they are summoned by a medium or necromancer who professes a special connection to the world of the dead, what I might call the voluntary or freelance ghost often has a specific agenda, whatever the religious context in which he or she materializes. (Ghostly gender is another issue that requires speculation, for without a physical body, why have gender, or racial, or any other fleshly distinction?) In a Christian or Shinto or Islamic context, such ghosts often appear for purposes of revenge or to complete unfinished business. Perhaps they have been murdered, perhaps they desire to settle scores with the sinful, either for their own purposes or because they were sent by heaven to redress wrongs. Blood will tell, says the old adage, even if only the killer hears the beats of the telltale heart. But such locally vengeful ghosts also serve, in a religious context, a wider function, and many older ghost stories seem bent on elucidating specific points of religious doctrine, especially about the nature of sin. They represent an admonition, a warning that proper ritual has not been fulfilled. It isn't so much the murder itself as the lack of a proper sermon and gravesite to honor the dead. In this way the ghost serves as a defender of religious orthodoxy, seeking revenge on the living because the proper forms have been ignored. For these reasons, ghosts are often the denizens of a particular place. Now, whole television "reality" shows are based on recording electromagnetic fields, spots of heat and cold, or ultrasonic sound among the archipelago of haunted spots. Invariably, there is some tale of tragedy or crime that explains why this particular place is haunted, although never why another place is not.[7]

To the extent that an afterlife is imagined in classical and Celtic religion, it is almost entirely populated by the warrior dead rather than by children or women, with the prominent exception of the suicide Dido, who refuses to speak to Aeneas when he visits the underworld in the *Aeneid,* just as Ajax refuses to speak to Odysseus in the *Odyssey.* Accordingly, in Celtic and Norse religions the problem of the unseen or forsaken death is avoided by the concept of Valhalla. Warriors slain in battle would be carried there by Valkyries to feast and celebrate; they had no need to return as ghosts who had died without due respect and proper burial. But in the Western tradition generally, as well as in the folklore of Japan and China, when the ghost rises from its unquiet grave, it is often very angry—angry about being dead at all, angry about being dead in the wrong way, angry about not being remembered. Frequently the anger is directed against an individual. But often, as in many Japanese ghost stories, it is a wronged woman who returns as an avenging ghost, *onryou,* in fury against an entire culture in which personal anger, especially in women, is a repressed trait, as in the film *Ju-On: The Grudge.*[8]

At least in English, such anger seems to be an almost etymological necessity, since, although *ghost* corresponds to *spiritus* in Latin, the two words have different implications: *spiritus* comes from words meaning breath (as in *gust*), while *ghost* comes from pre-Germanic words implying rage. The ghost, in other words, is an angry dead person who for whatever reason will not stay dead, and demands that the living somehow make amends. As the common word for ghost in French, *revenant,* implies, ghosts are the ones who come back. The lack of a Valhalla alternative in Christianity may also lie behind the rise of spiritualism in World War I, when the frequent absence of tangible remains of a son, brother, or husband prompted families to hire spiritualist photographers who combined images of the living and the dead to create a picture of those who were lost. The world of the flesh and the world of the spirit came together through the medium of a technology that, in its ability to render the images of those not present, itself resembled a bridge between the visible and the invisible worlds.[9]

The idea that something resembling life exists after death, and that the emotional bonds of love (and hate and revenge) may persist beyond the grave, underlies a large proportion of what the eighteenth century called terror, and what we generally call horror. To a certain extent the resurgence of these forms of fear owe a debt to the history of Christianity, and they are often shaped by the contours of older doctrines. But they also harken back to pre-Christian religion, and even further to the earliest human elaboration of the cult of the dead. All new religions take over some of the beliefs and customs of older religions and tailor them for their own uses. This assimilation can involve the cooptation of physical space, as the cathedral of Chartres was built over the site of the most important Druidic holy spot, and the conquistador church took over the site of the destroyed Aztec Templo Mayor in Mexico City. Edward Gibbon in *The Decline and Fall of the Roman Empire,* like some writers before and many after him, argued that the reason was primarily pragmatic: establishing the new religion in the holy sites of the old showed that past beliefs had been superseded, and that the earlier religion was an imperfect prelude to the new dispensation. Another pervasive tendency of new religions was not to ignore the gods of the old but to redefine them as demons and devils who tempt the righteous away from true belief, as Thor and Odin were considered by Christian Scandinavians in the Middle Ages.

The conflict between old and new religions has some parallels with the distinction between beliefs rooted in time-honored folk custom and those dependent on theological argumentation. A comparatively simple geographic formula seems to account for the difference between conflict and truce: The closer to the center of the religion's temporal power, the more explicitly repressed the old religions are; the farther away, the greater the accommodations to old belief. Just as the creation of the Olympian family of twelve gods in ancient Greece did not end the local practice of ascribing spiritual habitation to virtually every rock, stream, and tree, so too the impress of a systematic Christian theology, in lands far from Rome, often allowed earlier folk beliefs to flourish, if only because they were ignored by the priests of the new religion in the name of conciliating those who still had an emotional relation to the gods of the past. It was a practice particularly prevalent in the areas on the periphery of Europe— Scandinavia, Iceland, Estonia, the Scottish Highlands, and parts of England as well. As Christianity expands into such areas, with their own elaborate preexisting systems of religious beliefs, the effort of the church to subdue mythic beliefs to doctrine and to transform feelings into liturgy could become strained, and the polemical downgrading of the gods of Valhalla somewhat shrill.

Whether it's Christianity in Europe or, say, Buddhism in Japan, organized religion in its early phases often absorbs folk practices and beliefs that seem compatible, only to try to purge them later in the name of theological consistency and priestly authority. The history of Catholicism in Ireland is an intriguing example of both the clash and the syncretizing of such beliefs. Ireland celebrates its saints, and remains deeply devoted to the Catholic Church, but its landscape also includes elves and leprechauns, sacred trees and haunted bogs. A few years ago, I was passing through the town of Killorglin, County Derry. The day happened to be the annual occasion of the Puck Fair, a celebration of the time when a wild goat would be crowned as King Puck because it had warned the town of the coming of an enemy. Some say the goat heralded the advance of Cromwell's army, but since the fair is mentioned at the beginning of the seventeenth century, the ritual seems much more ancient. In any case, it was a surprise to see the statue of the goat itself, which curiously resembles goatlike images of Satan, as depicted in accounts of witches' sabbaths. Whatever its origins, the Puck Fair has some significant relation to the synthesis of paganism and Christianity in Ireland, and perhaps indicates something of its fragility. Shakespeare's metamorphosis of Puck (the word means he-goat in Erse or Irish Gaelic) into a mischievous spirit in *A Midsummer Night's Dream* further illustrates the accommodation between paganism and Christianity in areas of Christendom where churches and cathedrals in the cities and towns rub shoulders with the homes of fairies and other beings in the forests. Shakespeare no doubt derived characters like Puck and Peaseblossom from local Stratford folklore, but, like Queen Mab, "the fairies' midwife" in Mercutio's *Romeo and Juliet* speech, the Celtic traditions that produced the Puck Fair and Maeve, the Queen of Connaught, are there in the background.

This syncretism, as it is termed, of diverse and even contradictory traditions is another example of the ways in which new religions absorb and redefine the stories and the imagery of the religions they replace. It also indicates how believers can often accept a mingled Christian, pre-Christian, and even non-Christian universe with flexible boundaries more casually than do theological systematizers. Perhaps most people are to a certain extent naturally syncretic. We believe contradictory things all the time. More often than not, when emotion enters the equation—fear, love, hatred, disgust—reason often becomes irrelevant. Part of the need for this flexibility in terms of religion is the contradiction between local folk beliefs, related to the land and its people, and the new religion's claim to be an international or universal phenomenon, embracing many different lands and peoples. International Catholicism may have established an authority that swept across borders, but it was also deeply rooted in common perceptions of the round of nature, calling upon the birth and rebirth patterns of the year to validate theological views of the afterlife and bodily resurrection. Even now we still celebrate holidays (Thanksgiving, Christmas, Easter) that have roots in the agricultural calendar and some faint but still distinct connection with the gods and goddesses of planting and harvest. Samhain, the Celtic celebration of the beginning of winter, when the souls of the dead revisited earth, stands behind Halloween; and the midwinter festival of Yule gives way to Christmas. Perhaps most strikingly, the English word for the underworld, unlike many European Latinate terms (*inferno, enfer,* and the like), comes from Hel, the ruler of the realm of the dead in Norse mythology.[10]

An even more conspicuous example of this amalgamation of old and new beliefs is the way English uses *evil,* a word with Old English and Germanic roots that means going over boundaries or beyond limits, while in the Romance languages the more usual word is *mal,* a word of general negation, as in the title of the *Malleus Maleficarum,* the "hammer of witches," written by two Dominican inquisitors in the late fifteenth century to argue the reality of witches and witchcraft. Yet, by an etymological coincidence, in English *evil* is contained in *devil* (a word that otherwise has no linguistic connection), and so the verbal magic of similarity is rung in to cement a relationship that doesn't exist in languages where evil (*mal*) and devil (*diabolus*) have gone their separate ways.

⁕

> For as for Witches, I think not that their witchcraft is any reall power; but yet that they are justly punished, for the false beliefe they have, that they can do such mischiefe, joined with their purpose to do it if they can: their trade being nearer to a new Religion, than to a Craft or Science.

—Thomas Hobbes, *Leviathan* (1651) [11]

Witches who traffic with ghosts and demons are familiar figures in the literature and art of horror. As they often appear in popular culture now, they are primarily individual figures, the witch in her little shack in the woods mixing potions, casting spells, and summoning up the solitary ghost from the dead. But one of the intriguing aspects of witchcraft, astrology, clairvoyance, and other forms of initiating contact with the invisible world is the way each of these types of unofficial knowledge potentially contradicts the imperatives of institutional religion, class structure, and genealogical authority. Even more definitely than when a countryman or peasant consults a local witch to

make sure his crops are plentiful and his children stay healthy, when aristocrats call in a similar figure who is decidedly not a member of the elite court
culture (like a Rasputin), it ruptures the system of social hierarchy and perhaps becomes a tacit admission that whatever inherited authority they have is
fragile at best. So too when movie stars, politicians, and other members of our
contemporary media aristocracy consult with astrologers and other modern
soothsayers, it may be a tribute as well to the fragility of democratic fame and
the need to summon unearthly forces to make sure it endures.

Maleficium, the usual Latin word for witchcraft, was what witches were
accused of, literally "doing evil," which often included copulating with the
devil, kissing his ass, and other combinations of the diabolic and the sexual
that are characteristic of the charge of trafficking with demons.[12] The world
of witches was thus a bizarre inversion of the world of religious orthodoxy,
and demonology itself an officially sanctioned way of publicly discussing and
illustrating otherwise unusual and even blasphemous sexual behavior. But as
religious conflicts followed the Protestant Reformation, and an emerging nationalism, first in England and then elsewhere, began to undermine further
the power of international Catholicism, the formerly local and individual
nature of witches became depicted as a diabolic conspiracy with its own specific rituals—a distorted mirror of mainstream political and religious hierarchy. Particularly during the seventeenth century, established religion, whether
Catholic in continental Europe or Protestant in Germany, England, and
America, tried to characterize the world of witches in particular as a parallel
but evil institution, as bureaucratized as the church itself, with Satan, of
course, at its head and his followers witches who specifically signed a legally
binding pact with the devil.

How were the numerous seemingly isolated local witches, who employed
what Keith Thomas has called "a miscellaneous collection of recipes" and incantations, transformed into an organized force bent on subverting the world?
How in short was superstitious or antisocial behavior transformed into heresy?[13] During the sixteenth and the seventeenth centuries, scattered previous
references to groups of witches called covens and a conclave of witches called
the witches sabbath became much more widespread, with detail upon detail
being added to the description of satanic orgies and conspiracy plans that
supposedly happened there. When it was objected that otherwise poor old
women scattered around the countryside had no way of getting to their infer-
nal meetings, these theorists of witchcraft found it necessary to supply flying
broomsticks as a ready transportation device.[14]

In support of this redefinition of previously homegrown and individual witchy power as in fact premeditated and all-pervasive, James I of England, soon to be the successor of Elizabeth I, linked religious subversion with political subversion, usurpation, and the attack on monarchical divine right authority in his book *Daemonologie* (1597). Writing such a book was hardly inappropriate for James, since the divine right kingship he and other monarchs asserted was equally linked to and justified by the supernatural. Monarchs therefore were well suited to combat diabolical forces. In *News from Scotland,* published by James in 1591 and reprinted as part of *Daemonologie,* he details the confessions of some Danish witches that they tried to assassinate him first by poison and then by summoning up a storm to sink the ship in which he was returning to the British Isles from Denmark with his Danish-born queen, Anne. Later, after succeeding Elizabeth I to the throne, James was a patron of Shakespeare's acting company, and in *Macbeth* the playwright pays due deference to James's views with the tale of an erstwhile political usurper who dabbles in the black arts to gain his way. That the play was probably written in the wake of the Witchcraft Act of 1604, which broadened earlier laws to include the penalty of death, as well as around the time of the thwarted Gunpowder Plot of Guy Fawkes to blow up Parliament (1605), suggests that on this occasion (and for the rest of the century) the diabolic forces are to be identified specifically with the Catholic threat to Protestant England.[15]

The pressures of war, along with the paranoia about one's enemies, created a fertile ground for witch-hunting to flourish. The height of witch trials and executions in Germany lasted from about 1590 to 1630, corresponding in great part with the widespread political and religious conflicts between Catholic and Protestant areas, as each creed attempted to consolidate its power not so much by attacking the other as by undermining any local beliefs and customs that threatened its universal claims to an exclusive relation to God. In England, for example, during the civil war conflicts in the 1640s between the king and Parliament, a young man in his twenties named Matthew Hopkins, calling himself the Witchfinder General, blazed through the east of England in strongly Puritan areas, accusing supposed witches of a pact with the devil even without evidence of maleficium. By the time he died of tuberculosis at the age of twenty-seven in 1647 he was responsible for hanging upward of three hundred women, according to some estimates more than the total of the previous century and a half—around 40 percent of all the witches ever executed in England. In the year of his death, his *Discovery of Witches* was published, a book that became very influential in the New England witch trials that lasted from the late 1640s to the early 1690s. In the aftermath of the Salem witch trials of 1692–93, Hopkins's activities in Norfolk were alluded to with confidence by Cotton Mather in his self-exonerating account, *Wonders of the Invisible World* (1693), where he referred to "the witch-plot" he discovered at Salem and "the witch gang" he thwarted.

There were some accused and actual male witches, but their numbers were small compared with the generally older women who were accused, tried, and executed. In *Discoverie of Witchcraft* (1584), the first major (and generally skeptical) book on witches published in England, Reginald Scot described them as "old, lame, bleare eied, pale, fowle, and full of wrinkles; poore, sullen, superstitious, and papists: or such as know no religion."[16] The usurpation of established priestly power was therefore especially noticeable among women, and connected the persecution of witches to the hostility to women preachers who, during and after the midcentury English Civil Wars, began appearing more and more frequently. Appropriately enough, when Spiritualism made its appearance on the religious scene in the nineteenth century, many of the most successful mediums and clairvoyants were women. In addition to their contacts with the spirit world they also supported antislavery causes and other threats to the established order.[17]

This significant number of women involved in supposedly malevolent or benevolent contact with the spirit world mirrors the tendency of horror to include a distinct strain of social criticism, directed against any handy conventional institution, whether religion, the government, the family, the scientific establishment, paternalism, or any combination thereof. The ritualized religio-legal "testing" of an accused witch was a distinct anomaly in an otherwise sexually more reticent society. In a room crowded with people, often with other women as the prime witnesses, one would be stripped naked in order to inspect her private parts for the devil's marks. The whole process resembles a kind of social pathology, a safety valve to compensate for fears of the unconventional sexuality of older, no longer fertile women who were without any defined social role and so occupied the bottom reaches of the gender hierarchy.[18] Some of this sense of potential social upheaval lies behind the expanded usage of "witch hunt" in the twentieth century to mean the search for any who criticize established authority. The Oxford English Dictionary traces its first literary usage to George Orwell's *Homage to Catalonia* (1938), where he uses it to describe the attitude of Spanish Communists to their Trotskyist rivals. But for Americans the common usage springs from the McCarthy period of anti-Communist fervor and Arthur Miller's play *The Crucible*. Just as Satan and his human followers were at once paradoxically all-powerful yet easy to find and destroy, so J. Edgar Hoover characterized the Communist Party, as at once an apocalyptic threat to the American way of life yet completely containable, so long as Congress kept fully funding the FBI's budget requests.[19]

∽◦✧◦∾

I have alluded several times to the role of the Protestant Reformation and the Catholic Counter Reformation in setting the scene for the Europe-wide eruption of fear of diabolic forces and the accusation that Satan, with the help of his acolytes, was running a church of his own. This effort had two distinct but interwoven causes. First was the necessity among theologians and the priesthood alike to distinguish Protestant from Catholic beliefs; second was the need to police their own borders and assert clerical authority over who controls access to the invisible and supernatural world. With the Reformation it was no longer a time when the Catholic Church was for the most part the only game in town. Now it had to become evangelical and persuasive, just as Protestants of all stripes had already turned out to be. In such an era, both confessions had to look inwardly and locally to stamp out and stigmatize rivals. In that crusade, Protestants and Catholics often had the same general hostility to witches, whether they performed evil or good deeds. In a time of tumult the desire to believe that God is near and deeply concerned with human life meant also that the demonic was equally abroad in the land. In the no man's land between warring versions of Christianity, Satan was a figure of immediate temptation for the individual, no matter how pious. His power would be trumpeted and his defeat would be claimed by all sides.

In the early centuries of Christianity, beliefs that were later attacked as heresies frequently arose from divergent ideas about the nature of Jesus Christ—to what extent he was human and to what extent a god—and his specific relation to God. For those who recognized Jesus as the Christ, he was a figure who somehow combined a physical with a spiritual nature, while for others, hostile to the idea of such a hybrid, he was a false messiah for the same reasons. Many of these controversies were settled for the mainstream church in the fourth century, when church councils addressed the questions of the relationship of the Father to the Son and the role of the Holy Spirit, in effect defining the Trinity, which then became church dogma for the centuries to come. The medieval heresies that stood behind the Reformation focused on different issues, principally having to do with the way the now fully established church had strayed from its early ideals. In essence, they sought to restore moral, doctrinal, and personal purity, and therefore criticized the way an institutional church had become hidebound and corrupt, with a priesthood that separated people from God instead of bringing them closer. Reform meant fundamentally an effort to return to the austere virtues of the early church. Another doctrinal but crucial element in the change was a growing sense of national as opposed to international destiny. God's word in the Bible should be approached directly, not through Latin or Greek, but through vernacular languages like English, French, and German—a process helped along immeasurably by the invention of the printing press in the fifteenth century.

The Protestant Reformation is thus a blanket term for the sixteenth-century break with the Catholic Church made by a variety of groups and movements with somewhat different goals and beliefs. But for our purposes here in understanding the legacy of fear, some general connections might be highlighted. With the rise of Protestantism, the Catholic Church was no longer the only intercessor between God and humans, while Catholicism itself lost its exclusive status and became one church among many. The Protestant attack against the priesthood (even though the Protestant churches would soon enough develop hierarchies of their own) was often extended to the general idea of any intermediaries between the individual and God, ranging from the Virgin Mary to ghosts and saints. Neither priests, nor saints, nor the dead, nor personal good works could help you gain heaven, and the efficacy of holy relics was dismissed as well. Faith alone (*sola fide*) justified you, and only God's grace saved you. While Catholics believed miracles still happened, for Protestants the age of miracles was long gone.[20]

Unfortunately, once Catholic priests, saints, and holy persons with their "counter magic" were removed and a personal relationship with God was asserted, the Protestant individual became more vulnerable to the blandishments of the devil and his diabolic minions, at the same time that potentially benevolent presences like good witches and angels had also been banished. Just as sitting alone with your own copy of the Bible might create a more direct relation to God's word, so too the possible embrace of the devil was equally at hand. Reformers generally had therefore an intense preoccupation with sin and the devil's power, his immediate presence in the world. With the abolition of confession and the priestly ability to absolve sins, demons could have free rein.

In the effort of Protestants of various stripes to consolidate their gains, and the effort of the Catholic Church to fight against the erosion of its power, both focused particularly on folk practices and folk practitioners as their common enemy. For the Protestant Reformers, to reject Catholic rituals and incantations as superstitious remnants of paganism was to condemn the folk beliefs that lay beneath them, which the early church had absorbed to establish its power. Such a broad polemical condemnation, however, had the unforeseen effect of taking away what many of the faithful had considered to be protection against demonic forces. Folk customs contain a wealth of rituals that anthropologists (and theologians) call apotropaic, charms and spells meant to ward off evils usually connected to infertility—poor crops, impotence, barrenness, sickness, bad weather, and so on. In Catholic countries particularly, consultations with witches who claimed to have special knowledge were tolerated so long as they did not infringe upon the rights and privileges of the clergy, some of whom themselves might traffic in herbal cures. Such tolerance corresponded to the distinction in Roman law between the witch who was a healer and a benefit to the community and the witch whose aim was malevolent and destructive. At a time when official medicine was not very advanced and diseases were often thought to be caused by supernatural forces, witches were frequently the prime repository of a long tradition of empirical knowledge kept alive chiefly by women. For rural inhabitants, far from the "advanced" medical knowledge of the day, a reliance on the "wise women" or "white witch" in the countryside for her knowledge of herbs and plants was a reasonable choice. Because of her connection to the natural world, she might also be consulted about issues of fertility and infertility, whether in human beings or crops. Even now, in our supposedly more sophisticated times, when conventional medicine doesn't work, other therapies, often with ancient folk roots, may be tried.

But when both the Protestant Reformation and the Catholic Counter Reformation sought to police more precisely the limits of doctrinal purity, previous local toleration of the use of magic in daily life had to be stamped out as a pagan (and diabolic) practice by officials further up the religious hierarchy. Although the degree of persecution might vary by region and country, depending on the degree of competitiveness between Protestantism and Catholicism in a particular area, in general such "cunning" people, instead of being connected to the earth, the weather, and the seasons, began to be perceived as members of the army of Satan by both sides in the religious war. In fact, there might even be a greater hostility to the "good witch" who helped neighbors in everyday ways, because she made witchcraft an accept-able part of life and helped her neighbors deal with otherwise mysterious events. As Stuart Clark has observed, whether prosecution was conducted by either Protestant or Catholic witch hunters, the result was "an attempt to demonologize the traditional resources favored by ordinary people in need." To the extent that witches helped ameliorate the normal misfortunes of daily life, they undermined political as well as religious authority.[21]

With the Council of Trent, which lasted intermittently from 1547 to 1563, the Catholic Church sought to respond to the attacks of the Reformers by em-phasizing the line between belief and nonbelief, acceptable and unacceptable rituals, and "holy" and "unholy" behavior. In particular the council tried to draw the line between orthodox belief and similar but heterodox "vulgar" and "popular" beliefs that derived from folk religion and "superstition"—ghosts, possession, necromancy, and shape-shifting. In 1585 the papal bull *Coeli et Ter-rae* condemned incantations and necromancy as well as judicial astrology along with other superstitious practices. Exorcism as well was to be limited to only the most carefully vetted clergy, since, with the coming of printing, mystical and religious knowledge (including the text of the Bible), previously confined to a powerful few, had been made widely available for anyone to read and imitate. One practical reason for the resistance of organized religion to the swelling power of the devil was thus the increasing number of lay people doing exor-cisms and practicing witchcraft in accordance with the earlier view that any Christian had the ability to drive out Satan. Even before the convening of the Council of Trent, in the effort to standardize ritual and restrict practices, not only laymen had been restricted but also clerics who were considered to be abusers of divine power, often by imitating local folk practices. As Keith Thomas has pointed out, local magic in the Middle Ages often brought together the rhetoric of Christian prayer with local herbs, incantations, and miracle-producing objects. But with the Counter Reformation, rituals like exorcism were not to be entrusted to lay practitioners or to the untrained, as Father Kar-ras in *The Exorcist* is told by his superiors. As recently as 2014, the Vatican offi-cially confirmed the authority of an international society of exorcists, as part of the church's desire to maintain quality control and keep freelancers out.[22]

After the theological battles of the Reformation and the Counter Refor-mation had somewhat quieted or been swept aside by advances in medicine and jurisprudence, the ghosts and goblins of the past were revived in the liter-ary and artistic gothic of the end of the eighteenth century. It is striking how rooted in local and regional stories these beings are, almost in defiance of the transnational aspirations of both Catholicism and Protestantism. This is the romantic nationalism of the late eighteenth and early nineteenth centuries, when writers and artists in countries aimed to establish their uniqueness by exploring their pasts, especially in Britain and Germany, with, say, the ballad-collecting and novels of Sir Walter Scott, or somewhat later the operas of Richard Wagner. This style of poetic nationalism was the gothic response to both "civilized" Christian belief and the rule of reason. It looks to origins and the past as the source of national identity and authority rather than either to the future or to the atemporal world of reason. In this changing world, ghosts appeared not only in dreams but also walking the earth.[23]

THE WAR AGAINST PURGATORY

Now faith is the substance of things hoped for, the evidence of things unseen.

—Hebrews 2:1

The Romish Doctrine concerning Purgatory, Pardons, Worshipping and Adoration, as well of Images as of Relics, and also Invocation of Saints, is a fond thing, vainly invented, and grounded upon no warranty of Scripture, but rather repugnant to the Word of God.

—*Thirty Nine Articles* (1571)

In the sixteenth century, a bridge opened between death and life that allowed a host of spirits to cross, bringing ghosts into the modern world in quantities far beyond those of the past. The decisive conflict within Christianity that redefined this connection between the visible and the invisible world and allowed this new emigration was the doctrinal split over the concept of purgatory.

The notion that there was an intermediate place between the world of life and the world of death had also been part of pagan religion. Virgil in the *Aeneid* imagines it as a riverbank, where crowds beseech Charon the ferryman to take them across, but he refuses because they are helpless and unburied, and must stay there for a hundred years after death before they can be admitted to the underworld. The important change of realms introduced by Christianity is the concept of heaven. Neither in pagan literature nor in the Old Testament is there a heaven, just underworld lands of the dead inhabited by shades, although there are shreds of an idea resembling purgatory in the Old Testament and the New Testament.[24]

In late medieval Christianity, *limbo,* the Latin word for "edge," became attached to this intermediate zone, for those, like the patriarchs, who lived before the coming of Christ, and infants who died without personal sin (although still with original sin). Presumably this is the place from which Samuel returns in the Witch of Endor story. The impulse to believe in such a place, which was never either accepted or condemned as part of official doctrine by the Catholic Church, seems to reflect a desire to believe that any God worthy of worship would not arbitrarily condemn those whose only mistake was to have lived in the wrong century or to die before achieving adult consciousness. Limbo thus softens an otherwise harsh polarity between good and evil. Helpfully, the idea of a limbo, a purgatory, a reincarnation of souls, or any intermediate zone between life and death also allows a distinction between crime or sin that is irredeemable, and crime or sin that is less drastic and can be extenuated or compensated for. To distinguish degrees of sinning therefore imparts to religion some of the characteristics of a legal system, where issues and circumstances other than the bare sin itself must be considered before judgment is passed. Once you step beyond the Ten Commandments, in other words, a whole host of complications come into play, and the need arises to stigmatize some behaviors and praise others, with various gradations of exoneration in between.

The rise of purgatory as a similar doctrine of intermediacy and intercession owes something to the same desire, although it took a long time to be accepted as church doctrine, and even longer to be thought an actual place. At a basic level the idea of purgatory shares characteristics with the ancient urge to establish funerary practices that include prayer for and honor to the dead. Some theologians have argued that without a concept of purgatory, prayers and any other attention to the dead have no meaning: If the person has gone to heaven or down into hell, why does he or she need to be prayed for? Only if prayers can help them to pass through purgatory to heaven are they of any use. By contrast, an early church father like Saint Augustine was hostile to any belief that punishment in the underworld could be considered a limited and rehabilitative sentence, as well as to the idea that praying somehow offered a release from hell's eternal torment. But at the same time, as Peter Brown has shown, Augustine acknowledged that there were degrees of sinning, the *peccata levia,* the light sins of everyday life, the *non valde mali,* the not-so-bad sins. So, like other religions that developed a concept of possible amelioration (transmigration of souls, reincarnation), Christianity gradually opened up a doctrinal middle ground.[25]

Purgatory thus emerges as a possibility in medieval Christianity about the ninth or tenth century. By then the anti-ghost and anti-demon views of Augustine have been superseded by a variety of emotional and material factors, including the continuing vitality of the folk religion Christianity had ostensibly displaced, the human desire to continue connections with loved ones who have passed, and the need for more church revenues in the midst of endemic medieval warfare. Newly ritualized offerings to the dead and the development of a liturgy of prayers soon followed and were elaborated. Not coincidentally, perhaps, from the early to the late Middle Ages an increasing number of apparitions are recorded of ordinary people who had died, rather than the saints, monarchs, and other high-status individuals who had appeared in dreams and visions before. In addition to these anecdotal stories, the so-called dream vision was a frequent literary device from late antiquity down to the fifteenth century and beyond. As in a later work of faith like John Bunyan's *Pilgrim's Progress,* the dream vision detached the dreamer from his everyday life and allowed access to a new reality, frequently allegorical and symbolic, that offered otherwise inaccessible insights. Cicero's *Somnium Scipionis* (The Dream of Scipio) was a frequent influence. In one of Chaucer's dream visions, a political satire called *The Parliament of Fowls,* he comically falls asleep while reading Cicero's treatise. But in turn, many church authorities began to consider such dream or daylight apparitions potentially heretical, primarily because they happened to individuals without the sanction or intercession of priestly authority. This potential heresy furnished yet another reason to bring ghosts under the protective canopy of doctrine, until late-nineteenth-century psychology, preeminently under the aegis of Sigmund Freud, decisively detached dreams from religion and redefined them as the evidence of unresolved personal problems.[26]

By the late Middle Ages, then, purgatory was becoming an even more attractive concept, both theologically and practically. Dante, of course, used it extensively in what was later called the *Divine Comedy* (set in the spring of 1300 and written between 1308 and 1321), where it takes up the middle third of the poem. But it isn't often appreciated how up-to-date Dante was. Whatever its earlier grassroots existence, purgatory had been made part of official church doctrine only a few decades before he wrote.[27] Some historians have argued that the rising importance of purgatory was due in part to the cult of Mary. Dante's stress on Beatrice, his own intercessor on the way to heaven, may reflect this. In Dante's powerfully persuasive codification of the three prime worlds of the afterlife, both hell and heaven are unchanging places. In hell there is eternal pain, the same punishments over and over again, like Satan in a frozen lake at the core of hell, always chewing the same great sinners. There is no way to get out of the cycle of retribution for sin. Whether it is the good self or the evil self, both are unchanging, without development or expansion.

Purgatory, by contrast, helps answer uncomfortable questions about the relative nature of sinning, which sins were truly unforgivable and which could be purged by repentance and punishment. In such a moral catalogue the gradual development of a nuanced view of purgatory as a specific geographical place—like Dante's mountain that has to be climbed to get to heaven—played a significant role, as did his effort to create the concrete landscape of what was otherwise an invisible world, with all its tormented inhabitants and its final transcendence. In fact, it is the tangibility of both Dante's inferno and his purgatory that is so compelling—the flatterers of the great who swim in shit, the heretics burning in eternal fire. The often brutal physicality of Dante's conception of sin quiets down somewhat when we arrive in purgatory, but it is still strongly felt, for, after all, these sins need purgation. Only in paradise does the physical recede almost entirely, and for that reason it is usually the least read and most abstract part of the poem, even though theologically it is the culmination of Dante's quest.[28]

Purgatory was also validated by the even more ancient Catholic practice of indulgences, by which the sins of the living could be ameliorated by prayer or a sizable monetary contribution. Although the doctrine of purgatory became an important Reformation issue in England and elsewhere, it was in fact indulgences generally that were the main target of Martin Luther's attack on church practices, as it was more than a hundred years earlier by the English reform movement known as the Lollards. (Chaucer's Pardoner, with his knapsack full of "pigges bones"—supposedly relics of the saints—is an emblematic religious con man decried by the earlier reform movement.) The practical and possibly venal side of the growing church interest in purgatory was the amount of money it brought into church coffers, in the shape of those who paid for monks and others to pray periodically for the dead, as well as a variety of ways that the path of the dead through purgatory to heaven could be ensured by prayer and other ceremonies that kept their memory alive. In England, one popular form of such remembrance was the chantry, in which a priest was paid to say continual masses for the dead, often through the donation of lands or other goods or monies to support him. Chantries had existed long before purgatory was an accepted theological concept, but it certainly gave them a push forward; instead of merely being a memorial to the

dead, they would ensure their path to heaven. In some way connected to penance for the murder of Thomas à Becket, for example, Henry II instituted
perpetual chantries for his own soul, and later for the souls of those of his sons
who had died young.

Such lavish memorials, often outfitted with altars, hangings, and other
expensive paraphernalia, were popular among the monarchy, the aristocracy,
and many of the courtiers until the English Reformation of the sixteenth
century, with Henry VIII's attack on the papacy and his separation of the English church from international Catholicism.[29] Stemming from the same issues of churchly corruption that had animated Martin Luther, the early
theologians and publicists of Anglicanism considered purgatory to be just
another example of the ways that the church fattened itself at the expense of
believers. Doctrinally, in what became the general Protestant view, at death
the soul went immediately to heaven or hell depending on its former life;
there was no in-between. To believe that the living could somehow change
the fortunes of the dead was blasphemy, an abrogation of God's power. No
longer would there be a large complement of the dead occupying purgatory
as a way station on the road to heaven from which the living could encourage
their further passage by prayers and other forms of remembrance. The only
other alternative was to wander unsatisfied and discontented on the earth.
Once purgatory was no longer the middle ground between heaven and hell
for those who had passed on to the afterlife, that place was now potentially
taken over by the world of the living. Once again, it had become the more
than temporary abode of a host of supernatural creatures, not only the ghosts
and demons of the past, but also a goodly collection of the monsters from
folklore who later came to populate gothic literature and horror film.

As part of the English Reformation effort to loosen the hold of the Catholic Church, in 1538 the government made the Bible available in English, but
this was only the beginning. Along with the tangible changes in church services came the dissolution of the monasteries, and the iconoclasm that destroyed relics, memorials, and entire churches. Under Edward VI, Henry
VIII's son, there was a wholesale destruction of the religious past. As part of
the attack against purgatory, chantries were abolished, tombs and memorials
destroyed, and even dedicatory brass plaques affixed to church walls and
floors that honored the dead pried off and melted down. Thomas Cromwell,
Henry VIII's chief administrator of the Reformation until his own execution,
was decidedly against the idea of purgatory, while John Rastell, Thomas
More's brother-in-law, first argued in favor of purgatory (1530), and then after

More's execution (1535) somewhat changed his views. In 1549, All Souls Feast Day (November 2), which commemorated the dead, was taken out of the Anglican Church calendar and assimilated to All Saints Day (November 1). An extra effect of the change was to focus more attention on Halloween (October 31), which would increasingly begin to take on the ghostly dimensions it has retained into the present.

For a time the political and theological removal of purgatory from English culture had decisively banished the dead, but gradually they came back. As the sixteenth century wore on, Protestant theologians, despite the Reformation rejection of Catholic doctrines of connections with the dead, began to shape works on the art of dying (*ars moriendi*) on Catholic models. Simply put, human beings want to have a relation to their honored and beloved dead, whatever their religion. The Reformation attack on purgatory opened up a struggle between the doctrinal dictates of religion and its emotional underpinnings, where the attachment to long-held beliefs and the affection for those who have died are in direct conflict with theological orthodoxy. To eradicate the older forms of mourning, in great part because they were historically connected to Catholicism, nevertheless deprived people of satisfying the emotional need to keep some connection with the dear departed. If in the twentieth century the pious mother of the priest and author Andrew Greeley still sprinkled holy water around their house in Oak Park, Illinois, to ward off thunderstorms in tribute to ancient Irish superstitions, it is hardly surprising that sixteenth-century English men and women would want to remember their dead, whatever the theologians said.[30]

In some way, then, the revived presence of ghosts in the world was due to the absence of a theologically defined middle place between heaven and hell. The end of purgatory left the dead who were without an obvious destination below or above to come back and protest that they were no longer being properly remembered. But the theological question remained: Who could be sure whether the ghost was in the service of demons or sent on a mission from God? Even many of the sixteenth-century defenders of purgatory did not say that the supposed existence of ghosts and visions of the dead proved that purgatory existed, because why then had they returned to the world? But whatever you believed about them, ghosts were spellbinding.

That ghosts and witches are important stock figures in stories of horror has to a certain extent veiled their central role in the religious controversies of the past. Except for historians intent on reconstructing that past in its authentic details, most of us have instead an inherited sense of what a ghost or a

witch is from books and movies that themselves are more intent on entertainment than historical or doctrinal accuracy. But this attitude is hardly unprecedented, since the visual staging of horror is itself an old tradition. An
unforeseen result of the theologically promoted iconoclasm of the early generations of Reformers was that the illiterate and lower classes were in effect
deprived of access to any visual expression of Christianity. But with the advent of Elizabethan theater, itself rooted in religious forms like the miracle
and mystery plays that staged biblical and moral stories, the visual representation of kings and saints, heroes and villains, became an art form with a large
audience, literate and not.

It has been estimated that more than fifty ghosts appear on the Elizabethan
stage, most familiarly in Shakespeare's *Hamlet* and *Macbeth,* which has led
some critics to argue that Shakespeare was actually a recusant—that is, a
crypto-Catholic, who even chose to play Old Hamlet's ghost himself. Perhaps,
but he also certainly knew how to amp up his stagecraft with a little sensation-
alism. Did Shakespeare believe in ghosts in any theological sense, or was death
for him, as it is for Hamlet, "The undiscovered country, from whose bourn /
No traveller returns"? As Stephen Greenblatt points out about *Hamlet,* there is a
"bewildering array of hints that the play generates" on both sides of the argument between Catholics and Protestants about the reality of ghosts. Consider
also Puck's description of the coming of dawn in *A Midsummer Night's Dream,*
which wouldn't be out of place in the narration for the Michael Jackson music
video "Thriller," directed by John Landis, in 1982: "yonder shines Aurora's
harbinger; / At whose approach ghosts, wand'ring here and there, / Troop
home to churchyards; damned spirits all, / That in crossways and floods have
burials [that is, as suicides and without the proper rites], / Already to their
wormy beds have gone." Spooky enough, although in the same play Shakespeare is also aware of the role the mind plays in summoning up terrors: "as
imagination bodies forth / The forms of things unknown, the poet's pen / Turns
them to shapes, and gives to airy nothing / A local habitation and a name."
With such a tenuous standard of evidence I wonder whether those same critics
would conclude that Jackson and Landis are recusants as well.[31]

As Shakespeare's employment of ghosts and witches indicates, from the
time of its golden age in the late sixteenth and early seventeenth centuries,
English theater in particular also stressed the enticing theatricality of presenting the otherwise invisible forms of spirits, demonic and others, visibly on
stage. Beyond the human desire to want to continue to have some kind of
emotional relation with departed loved ones, the presence of ghosts brought

the living and the dead closer together. Theology and politics may have been able to banish purgatory for a time, but it was a harder job to expel the dead from the consciousness of the living, and hard as well to dismiss the idea, so validated by emotions, that some state of being, resembling life, exists after death. For the theologians of the English Reformation, however, a belief in ghosts as emissaries from the land of death was "the product of Popish fraud and deception."[32]

An essential part of the Counter Reformation effort to regain its power in the struggle with Protestant Reformers was to emphasize an emotional rather than an intellectual and theological involvement with religious truth, at the same time that both faiths tended to reject any competing popular superstitions. Not surprisingly then, the period of the Counter Reformation constituted a repository of diabolic and satanic imagery, along with vivid depictions of torture and death, that was drawn upon by gothic authors and visual artists two centuries later. Late-eighteenth- and early-nineteenth-century theater also upped the ante on the grisly spectacles of the past with magic lanterns and the newly elaborate special effects, which of course have their descendants in the CGI-enhanced horrors of the present. But the movies surpassed even photography in another important area in the contest of belief and unbelief, especially in ghosts: they seemed to be true. The basic technology and aesthetics of film—the presentation of events that in one sense have already occurred and in another have never occurred—seems predestined to enhance the ambivalent relation of the visible world and the invisible world. With stop motion and visual manipulation, however crudely close to hand, early filmmakers played numerous variations on the "now you see, now you don't" impulse of both magic and ghost hunting.

The iconoclasts had a return engagement with English culture in the mid–seventeenth century after parliamentary forces had defeated and executed King Charles I for treason. By this time as well, visual representation had become associated with the upper classes, particularly the monarchy and the court. At the same time the plethora of demons and other diabolic beings, as well as angels and other divine beings, that had hardly been absent from medieval art was revived and elaborated by the Counter Reformation in Catholic Italy, particularly through extravagant new churches, altarpieces, statues, and paintings that lavishly depicted the torments of hell, the wonders of heaven, and the suffering of the holy. In this style, usually referred to as the baroque, a vast population of otherwise invisible beings was made visible and even dimensional through tricks with perspective and illusion, while in England under the parliamentary rule of Oliver Cromwell, spectacle and theater were stripped away and only music was an officially sanctioned art of performance.

But by the end of the seventeenth and the beginning of the eighteenth century, theater had returned, and it had also become more respectable for Protestants to believe in ghosts. Still, in the face of the increasing expertise of the medical and legal worlds undermining both the power of witches and the existence of demons, when ghosts appeared they were generally subjected to a wide array of empirical inquiries. Daniel Defoe's short pamphlet from 1706, "The Apparition of Mrs. Veal"—or, to give it its full title, "A True Relation of the Apparition of One Mrs. Veal the Next Day after her Death to One Mrs. Bargrave at Canterbury the 8th of September, 1705"—very circumstantially details the apparition in terms of the time of day and the visual circumstance, the ghost's knowledge of details that only she and Mrs. Bargrave knew, and so on. In addition, there are intriguing allusions to a backstory in which Mrs. Veal and Mrs. Bargrave commiserate about the "ill usage" they have suffered from their husbands. Because the pamphlet was published anonymously, some critics have disputed Defoe's authorship, since in a later work that he published under his own name, *A History of the Appearance and Reality of Apparitions* (1727), he proclaims his disbelief in ghosts, although not in the existence of a spirit world. A stronger argument might be that Defoe, one of the first journalists to make a living by his pen, fabricated the story of Mrs. Veal in order to help sell copies of the English translation of Charles Delincourt's *Christian's Defense Against the Fears of Death*, to whose fourth edition his essay was added. In the text, that book is highly recommended by both the ghost of Mrs. Veal and her friend Mrs. Bargrave.[33]

Whatever the merits of the arguments for or against Defoe's authorship, however, there is no reason to think that someone could not have told the story of a ghostly appearance and yet (more than twenty years later) have changed his mind. And it is intriguing to see how even if the story is a total fiction, the author feels it necessary to ground it in a wealth of concrete detail, instead of the frequently vague tales of ghostly visitations in the past. Similarly, many of the later interrogations of the appearance of ghosts were managed by people who wanted to believe in their existence but were objective enough to realize they were being fooled. Samuel Johnson, for example, trusted wholeheartedly in an afterlife and the possibility of ghosts, as his lines prefacing this chapter indicate. But he was also not immune to the view that ghosts might be illusions, demons, misunderstood natural phenomena, or out-and-out frauds, and he was suspicious of the way the Methodist leader

John Wesley had embraced a belief in ghosts as direct evidence of the divine. When Johnson was part of the team of prestigious Londoners investigating the so-called Cock Lane ghost in 1762, he became eager to expose the fraud. So too, in the heyday of late-nineteenth- and early-twentieth-century spiritualism, when England and the United States were filled with mediums who claimed a direct connection to the dead, Harry Houdini, who wanted more than anything to get into contact with his dead mother, ran into constant disappointment and blew the whistle on one fake table-knocker after another. Perhaps ghost hunters are less often unbelievers than they are believers who want incontrovertible proof.

Because the critique of the existence of ghosts may ultimately be a critique of the idea of the soul, the diminution and then resurgence of ghosts in different periods of history is often tied directly to attitudes toward religion in general. For theologians and religious philosophers, the ghost can be a proof of the constant presence of an immaterial, supernatural world, adjacent to or underlying material reality. During and after the English Civil Wars, the breakdown of the relationship of the Anglican Church and the royal government helped foster the growth of numerous new versions of Protestantism, including such familiar groups as the Quakers and Congregationalists, and less familiar ones like the Levellers, Diggers, and Adamites. In response, a group of English theologians and philosophers called the Cambridge Platonists sought to bring together new scientific knowledge with an older religious sense of divine order to argue that ghosts served the theological function of confirming the existence of the afterlife and the immortality of the soul. Joseph Glanvill, for example, could be both a publicist for the experimental method as well as the author of *Sadducismus Triumphatus* (1681), which argued the reality of witches and denounced skeptics about witchcraft as potentially or actually atheistic. The reality of ghosts and demons and witches was thus a vital part of the argument that there was in fact a direct connection between the visible and the invisible worlds. Reason, instead of contradicting faith, could be, in Benjamin Whichcote's phrase (drawn from *Proverbs*), "the candle of the Lord," the way to understanding the spiritual truth behind sensory reality.[34]

But an indispensable lure for the individual believer is that the appearance of ghosts is proof that the afterlife is real, that we are not just bodies but spirits as well. Somewhere, even after I am gone, "I" still exist. To see a ghost could be frightening, but it could also be consoling to know that the one who has died in some sense still exists. Correspondingly, the defenders of ghosts are most articulate in times when the world of public events becomes most

oppressive, whether that is during the endemic sectarian violence of the seventeenth century, or the rise of industrialization in the eighteenth and nineteenth centuries, or the apocalyptic warfare of the twentieth century. In the
face of death and devastation, ghosts may even be soothing, especially if they
appear in the form of lost loved ones.

∾⊙⊚⊙↝

Since the Reformation, then, ghosts and spectral figures are the occasion
for terror, speculation, and investigation, both religious and secular. The
Council of Trent may have tried to draw the line between superstition and
doctrine with a firm hand. But instead of superstition being expunged from
the world, it maintained its hold on human emotions, where kinds of knowledge other than the theological or the scientific were welcome. A high-water
mark of ghostly popularity occurs in the nineteenth and early twentieth centuries, when mediums and clairvoyants professed, like the necromancers of
old, to bring clients into contact with the dead. To the extent that mediums
were connected to any even loosely organized religious group, they were Spiritualists. Predominantly a movement based in the United States and England,
but with groups in Europe and Latin America, Spiritualism first appeared in
the 1840s in the so-called burnt-over district of New York state, which had
earlier, during what was termed the Second Great Awakening, given birth to
Mormonism. It also owed something of its interest in contact with the afterlife to the writings of two eighteenth-century European figures: the radical
theologian Emmanuel Swedenborg, and the pioneer of hypnosis Franz Mesmer.[35] To the extent that a coherent doctrine can be extracted from the variety
of Spiritualist writings and beliefs, it can be characterized culturally as a revolt
against both Victorian rationalism and the polarized heaven and hell of
Christian morality. In Spiritualism there is no heaven and hell but something
analogous to a version of purgatory, where the soul after death can still learn,
ascend through spheres of knowledge, and often pass on that knowledge
through mediums to those who attend their séances. Attacked by the Catholic Church as atheist for its individualist and anti-institutional leanings, Spiritualism appealed particularly to an urban middle-class audience. It gathered
strength as well from aspects of the medium and séance experience like table
knocking ("someone is really there"). New technologies like the telegraph
(which allowed table knocking to be conceived as a kind of Morse code) and
photography, which furnished pictures of ghostly emanations, supplied a
seemingly empirical grounding for Spiritualist activities. Early photography

in fact maintained something of this quasi-mystical potential wherever it appeared. In Japan it encouraged the superstition that a picture of three people should never be taken, because one would die, and even Sigmund Freud refused to be photographed and recorded at the same time for fear it would steal his soul.[36]

As it turned out, many of the investigators of Spiritualist events were themselves magicians who, like Houdini later, were both skeptics and disappointed believers. Whatever the truth of Spiritualist beliefs and experiences, they became a fascination from the mid–nineteenth century onward. In England the Ghost Club was founded in 1862, and the Society for Psychical Research in 1882. Both still exist today. After the death of her young son Willie, Mary Todd Lincoln held séances in the White House to contact him. Robert Browning weighed in with an anti-Spiritualist poem, "Mr. Sludge, the Medium," in 1864. William James, the Harvard psychologist, author of the *Varieties of Religious Experience,* and son of a Swedenborgian minister, offered arguments for the existence of a spirit world, while Madame Helena Blavatsky, the founder of theosophy, a religion with its own ideas about contact with the spirit world, engaged in polemics against the Spiritualists, whose theology she considered not as sophisticated as her own.[37]

On the eve of World War I, a small anthology appeared in the United States with contributions by such literary luminaries as William Dean Howells, Henry James, and Thomas Wentworth Higginson, the mentor of Emily Dickinson. All of the contributors to the book, called *In After Days,* from one point of view or another argued for the existence of an afterlife. The subsequent carnage of World War I, with its obliteration of millions of young men, encouraged the effort to connect the world of the living with the world of the dead. One especially enthusiastic adherent of the movement was Arthur Conan Doyle, who considered himself not a Christian but a Spiritualist, and is of course otherwise best known as the creator of the professedly hyperrational Sherlock Holmes. Conan Doyle, who lost his son in the war, became an enthusiastic publicist for Spiritualism in the 1920s, writing such books as *The Coming of the Fairies* (1921, arguing the truth of photographs of fairies in a Yorkshire garden), *The Case for Spiritual Photography* (1925), and *the History of Spiritualism* (1926).

For anyone trying to reconcile Conan Doyle's Holmes side with his Spiritualist leanings, the way the movies bridge fantasy and reality could be crucial, since early films were rife with "real" ghosts seeking revenge as well as fraudulent ghosts ready to be exposed. Early films even threw themselves into the Spiritualist debate, with skeptical films like *Spiritualism Exposed* (1913) and *Bogus Ghost* (1916), as well as the pro-Spiritualist *The Greatest Question* (1919), although the general tendency of the movies at this point was still to take the side of the debunking magician.

As I discuss in more detail later, beyond such tricks of editing, the movies more substantially reinvigorated the belief in the world of the spirit and its inhabitants by the way they embodied and presented on screen people who were in fact not there. In theater, however impressive the special effects were, it was still theater, happening right in front of you, and remarkable for that immediacy. But the movies inspired a very different, more dreamlike way of perceiving the world, with mysterious entrances and exits, appearances and disappearances. Horror for this reason has become perhaps the most long-lived of all film genres, in great part because its basic assumptions correspond so directly to the nature of the film form itself. In particular, the film screen fosters the impression of an alternate universe, a mirror world that both enhances and distorts our own. As the movies age, we also increasingly watch people singing, dancing, falling in love, involved in every kind of human experience—who are already dead. And if the dead can still show such vitality in the movies, why couldn't they in real life? It may be true of movie stars in particular, but all people who appear in movies exist somewhere between the corporeal world and the spirit world. What's more, instead of being images that might be the object of the iconoclast's urge to destroy, they are instead, in our current language, icons to be venerated for their beauty and fame. And what is life after death if not fame, and isn't the effort to restore their reputations and to be remembered the basic motive of so many of those angry, self-centered ghosts?

RELIGIOUS HORROR: THE MONK *AND* THE EXORCIST

Some thirty years after Walpole's *Castle of Otranto* inaugurated the gothic novel, the nineteen-year-old Matthew G. Lewis wrote and anonymously published *Ambrosio, or the Monk,* a gothic novel filled with scenes of horror and salacious behavior that immediately became immensely popular. Set in early-seventeenth-century Spain, at the time of the Inquisition and in the full throes of the Catholic Counter Reformation, *The Monk* merges an almost comic social satire with scenes of the darkest horror. But unlike the gothic novels of the other best-selling author Ann Radcliffe, in which human tyranny and criminal behavior are discovered to be behind the eerie events, at the end of *The Monk* there is little or no natural explanation for much of what happens, leaving readers inside its supernatural world.

Patriarchal, political, and religious tyranny is hardly a theme unknown before the French and American revolutions. Even at the level of folk myth the ogre, who specifically devours children (sorry, Shrek), is the figure of the threatening adult male, with perhaps some suggestion of Saturn, who ate his children in order to make sure he would not be replaced. (With his mother's help, Jupiter escaped.) Shakespeare's plays are full of despotic fathers, as are later works like Samuel Richardson's novel *Clarissa* (1747). By contrast, in Charles Perrault's Mother Goose stories at the end of the seventeenth century, as well as in those collected by the Brothers Grimm at the beginning of the nineteenth century, the villain is often an evil stepmother (as in Cinderella and Snow White). But almost always the object of the tyranny is a young daughter, very rarely a son, even though the possibility that the son will supplant the father is a more consistent part of the basic myth. The eighteenth-century gothic, with its frequent emphasis on the sins of the fathers, takes this theme over wholesale, with the tyrannical father taking the ogre's place while absorbing some of his mythic characteristics—an image depicted with horrific brilliance in Goya's so-called "black" painting, *Saturn Devouring His Son* (1820–23).[38]

For Ann Radcliffe the sense of unease and apprehension that fill her central female characters coalesces into fear of monstrous despotic male figures that seem to be supernatural but are finally disclosed to be diabolic but still human plotters. Jane Austen in *Northanger Abbey* implies that all the upset and paranoia come from reading too much gothic fiction.[39] But Lewis makes the moral tyranny of church officials and the political and familial tyranny of fathers central to *The Monk*. It was a theme suitable for revival at a time when kings and the patriarchal hierarchy they supported were being overthrown. The belief in sacerdotal monarchy of the old sort, which linked rulers to God, had been eroding for some time. During the English Civil Wars of the seventeenth century, after the execution of Charles I, it had been rejected, then revived for a time under Charles II, rejected again by William and Mary, until Mary's sister Anne became the last English monarch to touch supplicants in a religious healing ceremony. In France, of course, the revolution ended the idea of the sacred monarch even more brutally.[40]

When we enter *The Monk* as readers, we see the main character from afar. He is Ambrosio, "the man of holiness," a popular preacher in Madrid, and he comes into view first through the eyes of an admiring crowd of people, who are not so focused on his sermonizing that they don't have time for flirtation and other not very pious activities. They gossip about Ambrosio's famous godliness, his mysterious birth, and his strict chastity, so much so "that he knows not in what consists the difference of man and woman." A young woman named Antonia feels an affinity with him and wants him to be her confessor. In the next chapter, with a zeroing in that almost foretells movie editing, Ambrosio is ready for his close-up.

It turns out that much of what has been said of him is true, although perhaps he takes too much pride in the way he behaves. His dearest possession is a portrait of the Madonna, whose ideal beauty he worships and contrasts with that of a normal woman whose fleshliness would disgust him. Accordingly, when he receives a letter pleading for mercy from Agnes, a nun who has become pregnant, he immediately turns it over to her prioress for punishment.

The whole plot of *The Monk* is too complex to detail here, but suffice it to say that there are two main movements in it that ultimately converge: first, the downfall of the title character, a story that becomes increasingly supernatural; and second, the story of a pair (or more depending on how you count them) of Radcliffean young women in distress, one a pregnant nun, another being pursued by a lover of whom her family disapproves. Increasing the air of mystery that surrounds Ambrosio is his novice and assistant Rosario, whose face no one has seen. Rosario tells Ambrosio of his sister Matilda, who desperately loved a pure man, then reveals that he in fact is Matilda and she loves Ambrosio. Ambrosio rejects her feelings and tells her she must leave. Matilda is about to commit suicide by stabbing herself when Ambrosio sees her exposed breast and, as "a thousand wild wishes bewildered his imagination," allows her to stay. That night he has a series of dreams in which Matilda and the Madonna mingle. Seeing Rosario-Matilda in the monastery garden, he again tells her to leave and goes to pick a flower for her, is bitten by a snake hidden in a rosebush, and faints into Matilda's arms. His attendants fear the worst, but when they unwrap the bandages the swelling has entirely subsided, and the wound is healed. In a subsequent conversation it turns out that not only has Rosario-Matilda arranged to have the portrait of the Madonna painted to look like her, but she has also sucked the poison out of Ambrosio's hand and will soon die herself, whereupon they give themselves over to consummating their passion—and this is only chapter two of twelve.

So far, nothing very supernatural or even horrific has happened in *The Monk*. Instead we have seen a somewhat psychologically oriented account of how extreme religious purity can turn into sexual obsession, mingled with some obvious biblical symbolism of snakes in gardens, as well as the innuendo of how Matilda cures Ambrosio by sucking out the serpent's poison from his hand. Before the story of Ambrosio continues, while he and Matilda are intertwined in his bed chamber and he forgets "his vows, his sanctity, and his fame," Lewis interposes a long description of Don Raymond's pursuit of Agnes (the pregnant nun who had been so summarily rejected by Ambrosio) and his encounters with the Bleeding Nun and the Wandering Jew, along with an account of his friend Don Lorenzo's love for Antonia.

After this elaborate turn of events, things get more and more complicated: Ambrosio begins to lust for Antonia, who is otherwise under his protection, using a magic mirror to spy on her. Matilda reveals she has witchlike powers and summons up Lucifer in the shape of a beautiful eighteen-year-old boy (perhaps Lewis's image of himself, like Hitchcock's cameos in his movies). Ambrosio attempts to ravish Antonia, but is stopped by her mother Elvira, whom he murders, and who then reappears as a ghost. At the same time, the prioress has told Raymond that Agnes is dead, having been forced to drink poison, "the victim of cruelty and tyrannic superstition." After giving Antonia knockout drops, Ambrosio finally has his way with her, blaming her for luring him on. A crowd of rioters, disgusted with what has happened to Agnes, has meanwhile murdered the prioress, and Lorenzo is searching through the labyrinth of the monastery for Antonia, who screams and tries to break free from Ambrosio. To protect himself, he murders her, but along with Matilda is arrested. Agnes, it turns out, is not dead, but has been put into a coffin with her baby, who dies and putrifies while clinging to her breast. Agnes is then rescued in a slim semblance of a happy ending for her.

But not so much for Ambrosio. The supposed moral power of his asceticism has been mocked, dissipated, and undermined by Lewis's satiric view of piety. Matilda, who has in the novel transformed from a supposed boy into a lusty girl, and then a witch, now turns out to have sold her soul to the devil and is slated to be burned at the stake. Ambrosio summons up the devil to try to escape himself from the flames and signs a contract renouncing "your Creator and his son." Lucifer then tells him that in fact Antonia was his sister, Elvira his mother, and Matilda not a real woman but a spirit sent to tempt him, and expose his pretense to perfection. In fact, when Ambrosio signed the contract, the Inquisition guards were coming to pardon him, not to take him to execution. Digging his nails into Ambrosio's skull, Lucifer carries him off high above the desolate mountains of the Sierra Morena and drops him thousands of feet to the rocky cliffs, where he lingers for six days and dies.

I have recounted some of the high points of the plot of *The Monk* to indicate how Lewis manages to assemble in one volume so many of the basic motifs of the gothic, above all the intimate connection, for a Protestant English audience, between horror and the titillating allure of the older world of Catholicism. At the same time that it looks forward to later psychological accounts of the possession by diabolical forces, *The Monk* also looks back to the orthodox Christian view that Satan, like the demon Pazuzu in *The Exorcist*, is essentially an impersonator and a trickster, adept at finding his victim's weaknesses and exploiting them. In *The Monk* that weakness is Ambrosio's repressed sexual passions, while in *The Exorcist* there are two main sources of weakness: the young Regan's uncertain passage from girlhood to womanhood as well as her need for a trustworthy father figure after her mother Chris's divorce; and the crisis of faith for Father Karras, the priest-psychologist, with his guilt over his mother's lonely death in a New York hospital ward. In both works (William Peter Blatty's novel as well as William Friedkin's film, for which Blatty wrote the script) the realistic level of the story is interwoven with the supernatural. Realist critics might say that *The Exorcist* is "really about" the evils of sexual repression in the Catholic Church or the hysteric susceptibilities of teenage girls, a derivation from the Freudian explanations that underpin Arthur Miller's play *The Crucible,* set during the Salem witch trials of the seventeenth century.

In fact, even in the seventeenth-century heyday of witchcraft, when demonic possession and exorcism were in the forefront of the religious mind, the two most vulnerable groups were considered to be young girls, whose response to internal physical change was confused with external supernatural pressure, and members of female religious orders, most significantly those whose faith was shaky despite their calling.[41] Aldous Huxley's *The Devils of Loudun* (1952) is based on the events leading up to the execution of Urbain Grandier, a French Catholic priest, for witchcraft in 1634, after testimony that he had seduced the nuns of a nearby Ursuline convent and signed a pact with the devil and several demons, which was presented in evidence. The Council of Trent had tried to codify Catholic views on possession and its treatment. But this dictum had for the most part failed to create uniformity of procedures; interpretation as well as punishment were still in the hands of those who could knowingly or unknowingly easily abuse their power. Accordingly, later interpretations of the Grandier case (including Ken Russell's 1971 film *The Devils*) include mass sexual hysteria among the nuns as well as political revenge for his attacks against Cardinal Richelieu.

The potential for teenage girls to believe something is happening to them that they can't control would seem to have a less complicated explanation: the hormonal changes of aging and growth, which appear more unexplainable and momentous to young women than to young men because in a patriarchal society male physical changes are more welcome. But in a time of widespread fear, a religious turn of mind reaches inevitably into the supernatural or at least the preternatural for an explanation. Thus, the atmosphere of horror, with its teasing play between the explainable and the unexplainable, seesaws between the visible and the invisible world. Few readers or viewers leave these stories feeling safe and satisfied that reason has won. In both *The Monk* and *The Exorcist* it is difficult to reduce the events to a single causal account. At various points in *The Monk,* for example, superstition is mocked, but at the same time diabolical events are presented as real.

One important difference between the two stories, despite their similar association between horror and religion, is that *The Exorcist,* even while having Catholic priests as its main characters, seems less involved with specifically Catholic doctrines of good and evil. Crucial to the way *The Exorcist* rereads and re-presents the gothic twins of horror and religion is its focus not in the world of public figures who are shown to have feet (or other parts) of clay but in a somewhat ordinary household (although one where the mother is a movie star); not in a distant Catholic Spain but in an immediately recognizable Washington, D.C. Set in a contemporary secular world where there are many religions and where scientific, physical explanation contrasts sharply with explanations that invoke the invisible world, it attempts instead to inspire a lively sense of the importance of the supernatural, among nonbelievers as well as believers. This is an important change from the possessions of the time of the seventeenth century and earlier, when the victims tended to be the extremely religious rather than the religiously indifferent, giving the opportunity for both Catholic and Protestant exorcists to demonstrate which religion was the true church, with the more powerful magic.[42]

Significantly as well—although in his commentary on the film, Blatty speaks of "the Devil"—the antagonist in *The Exorcist* is not a recognizable Christian version of Satan but a much more ancient demon named Pazuzu, the Sumerian demon of the winds, who hails from northern Iraq and is the bearer of storms and drought. No human agency, witch or otherwise, summons up Pazuzu. Instead, the demon seems bent on a competition between itself and the exorcist Father Merrin, fought out for unnamed reasons over the body of Regan, not the adult male of *The Monk* but a barely prepubescent girl reminiscent of Ann Radcliffe's heroines. Since Merrin is an archaeologist and in the beginning of the film has excavated an amulet image of Pazuzu, is it that the demon is upset at being considered passé and outmoded as a force in the world? In the history of exorcism and possession, the frequency with which such cases arose was often considered an indication of tumultuous, even apocalyptic, times, when God's wrath against human activity allows the devil a freer hand. Is Regan really a possessed demoniac (the technical term), or is she just growing into the kind of child who frightens parents, as the film Regan's mother Chris stars in about 1960s student activism implies? With so much stress from psychological, political, and religious events, it is difficult to come to any final answer about the subtext of *The Exorcist,* let alone why the demon chooses to inhabit this particular girl's body.

Such questions of supernatural or natural explanation are similar to whether in *The Monk* Matilda is actually satanic or just a sexually free woman. Theological explanations collide with psychological explanations, physical explanations, and supernatural explanations, and none of them seem very final. After Merrin has died of a heart attack, at the end of the film (and novel), Father Karras takes the demon into himself and then commits suicide. Although he seems to be triumphant, it is unclear that this is enough to render Pazuzu harmless, let alone "dead." The story may end, but the evil lives on.

Both *The Monk* and *The Exorcist* flirt decisively with a whole host of sexual and religious taboos. Taboo is an important element of both horror and religion, because in each there are things that must be done and things that must not be done, as well as objects that have taken on an aura of the sacred. Interestingly enough, the word *taboo* first appears in English in the 1770s, in the wake of Captain Cook's voyages to Melanesia, just prior to the first great age of gothic literature. Originally meaning sacred, forbidden to people in general and restricted to gods or other authority figures, it quickly expands its meaning to more general usages. Just as the situations of horror invite psychological speculation before there is anything like a discipline of psychology, the fascination with the customs of primitive tribes and the way their practices reflect more civilized behavior is a kind of proto-anthropology, long before anyone thought up phrases like "cultural relativism." Such a difference of perspective on the divine and the diabolic occurs tangentially in *The Exorcist* as well. Max von Sydow, who plays Father Merrin, has commented as a Swede on the lack of a significant devil figure in Scandinavian Christianity, where to the extent he exists is considered to be a comic trickster, along the lines of the Norse god Loki or the Hopi and Zuni Kokopelli.[43]

The Exorcist contains nothing as taboo as Ambrosio's murder of his mother and rape and murder of his sister in *The Monk*. But the concept of the taboo, simultaneously holy and unclean, however more mildly present in *The Exorcist,* is common to them both, and the recognizable closeness to home in the events of *The Exorcist* makes the horror even more palpable to an audience, whether Catholic or not. Like Ambrosio, Father Karras is pulled inexorably toward the taboo, Regan's demonic possession, as a test of his own faltering faith.

Satan in *The Monk* definitely turns out to be the tempter, who tests human submission to God's will, much as he is in the Book of Job, when he is a member of God's court, rather than having any separate power of his own.[44] But in *The Exorcist* the question remains whether the demon's possession of Regan is a red herring. If the basic combat is between the demon and the exorcist Father Merrin, as the prelude in northern Iraq suggests, why should it be fought out on the battleground of a female child, made vulnerable by her growing sexuality, who under the demon's influence becomes monstrous, obscene, and sexualized? Certainly there is a time-honored tradition, especially since the Counter Reformation, that willfulness in children is due to the devil, and that children are closer to and more susceptible to sin. In addition Karras believes he has failed as a good child, and his guilt over his mother's lonely death and his desire to protect Regan (and his underplayed attraction to Chris, Regan's mother) make him vulnerable. Each of the array of doctors, psychiatrists, and priests, not to mention the Jewish detective Kinderman, who look into Regan's case presents a different view of what is happening. Like most of deep horror but particularly religious horror, both *The Monk* and *The Exorcist* keep all those explanatory balls in the air. Explanation remains in the psychoanalytic sense overdetermined; there are just too many possible causes. Some even contradict one another, so you choose what best lets you sleep at night—or not, according to your taste.

THE DEVIL MADE ME DO IT: JAMES HOGG'S CONFESSIONS OF A JUSTIFIED SINNER

As evidence of the Enlightenment emphasis on the empirical study of physical phenomena, one response to the religious dilemma raised by the Lisbon earthquake was to ignore it, blaming neither God nor Satan for the evils that happen in the world. With the advances in medicine, law, and even agriculture, the sphere of the invisible world's influence on the visible was becoming narrower, and the human responsibility to understand widened. Like Descartes's distinction between primary causes (which God has set into motion and are therefore unfathomable to human beings) and secondary causes (which are accessible to human comprehension), a reliance on rational and secular causes did not inevitably leave God or Satan out of the general equation, but put them into a special domain of their own, which intersected less and less with human events. Against those who argued that it is necessary to have religion in order to be moral, and that without a system of supernatural rewards and punishments, people will inevitably embrace anarchy and immorality, the eighteenth century witnessed the gradual growth of will as an element in moral and judicial law. Individuals had to take responsibility for their actions, and across Europe judges and juries were much less eager to accept supernatural explanations for behavior.

The law of previous centuries had often decided guilt or innocence through ordeals, single combats, and torture that purported to show God's intentions by tests of the human body. So too the witch's body was frequently investigated for evidence of a supernumerary breast or spots of flesh ("devil's marks") that could be pricked without pain. By the eighteenth century such practices across Europe gradually gave way to legal procedures involving empirical evidence and direct testimony. Witchcraft and "spectral evidence" were no longer being admitted in law courts, nefarious spells were no longer considered the primary source of ailments, and hexes were generally ruled out as the reason for bad harvests, as more was learned about crop rotation, fertilization techniques, and proper irrigation. To the extent that witchcraft was prosecuted, it was more often for fraud than for blasphemy. When kings, who were supposedly God's representatives on earth, could be overthrown and even executed without the world being destroyed, other time-honored beliefs were in danger of disappearing as well. But still those beliefs retained something of their emotional allure, even as their usefulness in the public world was fading. While the understanding of the natural causes of misfortune continued to expand, the interest in the workings of the supernatural world became more a subject of curiosity and emotional attachment, satisfying some hunger other than that for factual knowledge.

James Hogg, the largely self-educated son of a Scots tenant farmer, worked sporadically as a shepherd into his thirties, while being part of a literary society, composing songs, writing poems and plays. At the age of forty he moved to Edinburgh to concentrate on a literary career. After various ups and downs in the backbiting literary world of Edinburgh, Hogg found himself in his early fifties a character in an ongoing series of drunken conversations in *Blackwood's Magazine* called the "Noctes Ambrosianae," in which he appeared frequently as the "Ettrick Shepherd," a kind of wise but bumptious primitive from the countryside who usually spoke in Scots dialect à la Robert Burns, alternately foolish and insightful.[45] The "Noctes" were a feature of the magazine for more than twelve years, and scholars disagree over what Hogg's attitude was to the caricature, although there is evidence that he himself helped write some of the episodes. He continued to write and publish until the end of his life, but his most surprising and most lasting work, so different from the bulk of his folksy poetry and plays, was the novel *Confessions of a Justified Sinner* (1824), or, to give it its full title, *The Private Memoirs and Confessions of a Justified Sinner: Written by Himself; With a detail of curious traditionary facts and other evidence by the editor.*

In terms of the issues connecting religion to horror, the *Confessions* is part of the gradual transition from a religious view of evil as caused by demonic forces to a secular one that suggests the importance of personal psychology. I will delve further into the psychologizing of the supernatural in the chapter titled "The Monster from Within," which focuses on *Jekyll and Hyde*. For the moment, I am interested instead in the role that religious ideas of the soul and its connection to the spirit world play in laying the groundwork for what later became a more secular explanation of both possession and evil. *Confessions of a Justified Sinner*, set in the Edinburgh area during the early eighteenth century and characterized as coming from a discovered manuscript, falls into two parts, the first narrated by an "editor" and the second by the "sinner" himself in his memoirs. The same incidents are therefore often seen from two different points of view. At the heart of the story is an extreme version of the Calvinist doctrine of predestination, to which Robert Wringhim, the main character, adheres, believing that once someone is predestined to be among the Elect, nothing he does, including the most horrific of crimes, can remove him from God's grace.

Constantly there to convince Robert of his Election whenever he wavers is another character named Gil-Martin, who at various times seems to be the devil and at other times a diabolic side of Robert himself. To complicate things, Robert has a kindly, easygoing brother, George, whom he may have murdered when they meet later in life. (They both have the same mother, who leaves George's father because she disapproves of his casual attitude toward religion and marries a strict clergyman, who, it is suggested although never confirmed, is Robert's father.) With these multiple explanations, including the different points of view of the "editor" and Robert's own writings, Hogg sets his story uneasily between a world suffused with Calvinist doctrines of original sin and total depravity and a world of more psychological explanations, in which the ability to play many roles implies a more metamorphic, willful self than strict ideas of sin would countenance. Yet even here religion had a role to play. Throughout the seventeenth and eighteenth centuries, the ideas of the sixteenth-century Dutch reformer Jacobus Arminius and his emphasis on freedom of the will rather than predestination had become more influential. The doctrine of original sin, first promulgated by Augustine and heavily influential on both Calvinist and Lutheran theology, was qualified, for example, by the ideas of Methodists and others, that the sin of Adam and Eve should not be imputed to all human beings. Grace and repentance were in the hands of the individual rather than foretold from eternity. A new sense of liberty was in the air. Or, as Benjamin Franklin put it more pithily, "God helps those who help themselves."[46]

We would now categorize *Confessions* as a doppelgänger tale in which otherwise separate characters turn out to be aspects of each other. In English this occurs most famously in Edgar Allan Poe's story "William Wilson" and Robert Louis Stevenson's *Dr. Jekyll and Mr. Hyde.* The term *doppelgänger* itself comes out of German romanticism, coined in 1796 by the writer Jean Paul Richter, and the interconnection of selves that the term refers to is a prominent motif in gothic literature. Appropriately enough, according to the Oxford English Dictionary the term first appeared in English in 1824, as "double-goer," in Hogg's main publishing venue, *Blackwood's Magazine,* the same year *Justified Sinner* was published. Earlier examples of the doppelgänger motif in English literature include William Godwin's *Caleb Williams* (1794) and the novels of the American Charles Brockden Brown, especially *Wieland* (1798).[47]

A distinction between the fantastical gothic and the reasonable gothic seems appropriate here, with Matthew Lewis on the fantastical side, Ann Radcliffe on the reasonable, and Hogg somewhere in the middle. In Hogg and other writers who emphasize the psychological aspect of horror, there is little of the preoccupation with the picturesque and scenic description that marks the works of Lewis and Radcliffe. Instead of the roiling outside world conditioning the responses of their characters, it is their inner turmoil and landscape. The American gothic writers, like Brockden Brown and later Hawthorne, without an overhanging past filled with shiver-inducing stories, tend to emphasize the psychological side.

Like Hogg, Brockden Brown is fascinated by the mental world of the religious fanatic, in which everything fits together as a message from either God or Satan. In *Wieland* the title character kills his wife and children after hearing voices that he believes are of divine origin, but actually turn out to be the maneuverings of a mysterious character named Carwin, a "biloquist" (ventriloquist), with designs on Wieland's sister Clara. But, says Carwin, he never told Wieland to commit the murders; that was Wieland's own interpretation of the "voices." After these strange events and the explanations are recounted, Clara, who is the novel's narrator, virtually throws up her hands: "Presently I considered that whether Wieland was a maniac, a faithful servant of his God, the victim of hellish illusions, or the dupe of human imposture, was by no means certain." This pragmatic American viewpoint resembles Ann Radcliffe's attitude toward horror more than Matthew Lewis's. With its multiple perspectives, more rational than irrational, it potentially lets the reader comfortably out of the story rather than, as in *The Monk* or *The Exorcist,* left inside, with its mysteries ultimately unexplained.[48]

CHAPTER 3

Terror, Horror, and the Cult of Nature

The passion caused by the great and sublime in *nature* . . . is Astonishment; and astonishment is that state of the soul, in which all its motions are suspended, with some degree of horror . . . Indeed terror is in all cases whatsoever, either more openly or latently the ruling principle of the sublime.

—Edmund Burke, *A Philosophical Enquiry into the Origin of Our Ideas of the Sublime and Beautiful* (1757)

The genius of Melville [in *Moby-Dick*] is that he saw that this is a country that needs a monster.

—Carlos Fuentes

READING THE MONSTROUS

Whereas words like *terror* and *horror*, along with *dread, fright, scare*, and *fear* itself, generally refer to a physical effect on an observer, there is a whole other class of words in the general realm of the horrific that invoke specific responses to the extraordinary creations of the natural world. Just as *gothic* originates in the realm of architecture to designate the gloomy structures of the distant (usually pre-Reformation) past, a term like *grotesque* also combines an architectural term with its ability to excite a sense of wonder and strangeness. Originally the word came from the Italian for cave, *grotto*. In the late fifteenth century, Raphael Sanzio, more remembered as a great painter, who was then head of antiquities for Rome as well as the chief architect of the Vatican, supervised the partial excavation of Nero's Domus Aurea (Golden House), which had recently been discovered to exist under what was otherwise assumed to be a natural hill near the Colosseum. The site had been discovered in the course of digging a well there, when workmen broke through what was found to be the dome of an enormous room. Lowered down on ropes to explore this vast underground construction, they discovered a series of equally large rooms on whose walls were paintings of mingled human and animal forms fantastically tangled with vegetation, fruits, and flowers that were dubbed *grottesca*—the kind of visual images to be found in grottoes. Down to our own time, this discovery of a marvelous and perhaps terrifying world under the commonplace is mirrored in such places as Freddy's basement lair in *A Nightmare on Elm Street* and the steamy, molten interior of the climactic factory in *The Terminator*.

After the eighteenth century, with the discovery of the buried city of Pompeii, this style was later named *Pompeian* by art historians, but *grotesque* remained as the general term for any abnormal combination of human, animal, and natural elements. Later the term *arabesque,* which described fantastical Moorish designs (although without human and animal forms) was associated with *grotesque* as a similarly astounding and disquieting part of visual art. So it was that when Edgar Allan Poe in 1840 collected previously published short stories (including "William Wilson" and "The Fall of the House of Usher") in a single volume, he called it *Tales of the Grotesque and Arabesque.* For his early-nineteenth-century readers, both terms invoked a combination of startling images that was both titillating and mysterious. Like melodrama on the stage, his stories dared the boundaries of both art and nature by their excesses.

In order to let creative juices flow into works that cross boundaries, there have to be restrictions to be overcome. In the seventeenth century an artist like Inigo Jones could see no contradiction between bringing a formal Palladian style of architecture to England, investigating the building of Stonehenge, and designing strikingly magical stage machinery for the court masques. But by the early eighteenth century the gothic and fantastical were often polemically opposed to neoclassical order and symmetry. As the century wore on and the gothic became more the rage, the taste for the grotesque began to merge with the revival of classical Roman architectural style that began in early-eighteenth-century England and was elaborated by the political rationalists of the French Revolution. Sometimes the gothic revival in architecture produced premeditated wonders, pseudo-medieval buildings like Horace Walpole's Strawberry Hill and William Beckford's Fonthill Abbey. But often, in an odd presaging of the psychological relation between the outer Jekyll and the inner Hyde, a geometric, rectilinear exterior, marked by the rhythm of columns and windows and indebted to Roman precedents, was mated with an interior featuring ornate, sinuous, and undulating lines, sprinkled grotesqueries of fabulous beasts, fruits, flowers, and the occasional detached head, arm, or leg.

All such motifs might be called monstrous by those who disapproved of them. Although the word *monster* is now used for anything outsized, out of the ordinary, or just generally repellent, the original word has fairly specific meanings. In English at least, and to a certain extent in all Romance languages, it tends to have two etymological sources—Latin words meaning "warning" (like *monere*) and Latin words meaning "show" (like *monstrare*). The monster can thus be large, possibly dangerous, strange, but distinctly visible.[1] Whereas demons are spiritual tormentors and thereby connected to religion and morality, monsters are strange permutations of nature, without any discernible individual agendas, except perhaps survival and revenge against their tormentors. Like the inner sin of individuals that supposedly appeared in the outward shape of malformation or unsightliness, the monster could be an observable indication of evil that was otherwise invisible to the naked and untutored eye. Unlike the withered limb or the distorted face, however, where the monster transgressed the standards of the normal was in its frequent amalgamation of the human and the animal, of various animals, of male and female, of the natural and the artificial—in other words, any crossing of the bounds between otherwise distinct contraries. This mixture of traits could convey an aura of either the diabolic or the sacred, for after all the Trinity itself was conglomerate and sometimes depicted as a human being with three heads.[2]

Natural monsters are the most ancient examples of the feared and worshiped. Unlike the vampire, say, they have such variety that it is difficult to compress them into one or even a few prime examples. The recurrent definition of the monster as a mixed form is preserved in human-animal amalgamations that may go back to the animal cults of ancient military cultures: the centaurs and satyrs of Greek mythology, the bird-woman Valkyries and harpies, the werewolf, the northern European selkie (part seal and part human), or the shape-shifting Native American skin-walker. Another early mode of the monster is in the outsized version of a natural or unnatural being (like the giants fought by Hercules, Monstro the Whale in the Disney *Pinocchio,* or the enormous trolls of the Norwegian film *Trollhunter*). Such monsters often emerge from liminal boundary zones, pervaded by night, fog, and mist—the marshes, swamps, and fens where man and nature might be fused together. Grendel and his mother, two of the monsters in *Beowulf,* live in a cave at the bottom of a lake in a swamp. They are creatures of the night and represent something of the dread of darkness and the horrific side of nature more characteristic of earlier peoples than of the worshipers of nature that emerged during the Romantic period of the late eighteenth century, when fear turned into awe.[3]

Teratologists, the scholars of monsters, frequently distinguish three attitudes toward the monstrous: the first, traceable to Aristotle, considers them individual errors in nature, procreative mistakes. Another, typified by the writings of natural philosophers like Pliny the Elder, collected specimens of natural phenomena, tangible or reported, and speculated on the reason they existed. Pliny concluded, for example, that hermaphrodites were generally not omens but aberrations of nature, although he also thought there was a tribe of hermaphrodites in Africa, the usual site of the strange and mysterious for Romans. Finally there was the fascination with the monstrous that came out of a desire to know the future, an urge, like the need to honor the dead, that may be one of the earliest indications of human self-consciousness. In antiquity, there were numerous means to gain this insight and numerous individuals who, usually for a fee but frequently as part of a ceremony, would give their interpretations of abnormal births, comets, the livers of sacrificed animals, by casting lots, oracles, randomly chosen passages from sacred books, and so on.[4]

What kind of attention then is it that the monster from nature or the monstrous in nature demands; what meaning should we tease out from its appearance, and, in particular, what are we being warned against? Whereas ghosts from different cultures often share some of the same characteristics, monsters have much more homegrown specificity, rooted in a particular time and place. One frequent part of the monster's aspect, beyond size and strangeness, is the way he/she/it bridges cultural contradictions fusing the understandable with the incomprehensible. To read the monster in the light of God's purposes helps purge the shock of seeing it and makes the otherwise disrupted universe whole once again. As the poet Marianne Moore has written, "the power of the visible is the invisible."

The monsters of antiquity, like those that populate the *Odyssey*—the Chimera, the Sirens, Scylla and Charybdis—were often natural formations in the landscape turned into monsters. Like the Sphinx of the Oedipus story, with its female face, eagle wings, and lion body, they announced their difference from normality, their potential or actual relation to the world of the gods, by their conglomerate strangeness. When they appear in the labors of Hercules or the adventures of Theseus, these creatures were the more than human enemies that the hero had to defeat. With the Old Testament heroes, the monster enemy became more politicized, whether it was the giant Goliath defeated by David, or the destruction of the temple of the fish god Dagon by Samson. But it is really with Christianity that monsters are fully presented not so much as physical enemies to be defeated as pieces of doctrine that must be heroically interpreted, whether it is the seven-headed dragon of Revelation 12, identified with Satan, the "beast" of Revelation 13, described as part leopard, part bear, and part lion, or the monster Geryon in Dante's *Inferno,* who explicitly symbolizes fraud with his bland human face and scorpion tail. In what may be Christian interpolations in the otherwise pagan epic of *Beowulf,* Grendel and his mother are unambiguously described as descendants of Cain and therefore well situated within a genealogy of those detested by God. Already, therefore, by the early Christian world natural wonders like monsters were portents, evidence of godly or demonic forces active on earth. The pressing need was to redefine the monstrous not as a source of stupefaction or entertainment but as an opportunity for understanding and religious action. That the monster was God's omen also served to give an aura of the divine to the monstrous, because he had seen fit to contravene his laws of creation to bring it into being. As Montaigne writes in his essay "Of a Monstrous Child," "What we call monsters are not so to God."

Once again, as in the later controversy over the Lisbon earthquake, the issue is whether God is primarily benevolent or primarily wrathful: Is he behind the beautiful regularities of nature, the evil disruptions, both, or neither? Does he speak directly or only in riddles that have to be interpreted? When the question is which side God is on, the potential politicization of wonder and portents is thus always a crucial issue. The creators of the Bayeux Tapestry, who are arguing the case for William the Conqueror's rightful takeover of England, not only invoke feudal legal arguments but also include an image of Halley's comet, which flashed across the skies not long after the coronation of Harold Godwinson. For many of William's supporters, it was an indication of God's displeasure with Harold. Harold of course thought otherwise. If you're in power, you don't want to make too much of prodigies and odd events; power depends on regularity. It's the out-of-power person and the usurper who find odd events grist for their point of view. A taste for interpreting prodigies is therefore more the province of potential wizards who want to assert their own brand of power, like the contemporary American evangelicals Jerry Falwell and Pat Robertson, or imams denouncing the Great Satan, who regularly interpret any strange event or natural disaster as a judgment on political policies they dislike.

Like the interpretation of comets and other astronomical marvels, the Middle Ages and the Renaissance also specialized in what the art historian Erwin Panofsky called the *paysage moralisé,* the moralized or interpreted landscape where truth, God's or otherwise, could be found among the rocks, trees, and hills. For medieval Catholicism as much as for a radical Protestant like John Bunyan in the seventeenth century writing *Pilgrim's Progress,* God speaks to us in the metaphors of the world, but our job (Job?) is to find out how to read the truth through the signs of the world without making mistakes. As in the world of animism, where the landscape is populated by hundreds of supernatural beings, and there is transcendental meaning in every leaf and tree, Bunyan's wayfaring Christian needs to realize that the large mud puddle in the road is actually the Slough of Despond, or that the nearby village is actually Vanity Fair. And mistakes are rampant. As Bunyan insists, you can get all the way to the Heavenly City, but make any error of action or interpretation and a fiery chute in front of the Pearly Gates will open and send you directly to hell.

In one sense, then, the monster is another example of the suppressed dualism of Christianity itself. Like the vexed relation between the jealous and vengeful God of the Old Testament and the merciful God of the New Testament, the monster is a hybrid, mirroring malignantly the elements of human and divine in the nature of Jesus, which spawned so many heresies in the early centuries A.D. Even more generally, in whatever culture the monster appears, he/she/it represents an anxiety over contradictions and hybrid forms that challenge otherwise sacrosanct assumptions about difference. At first it seems that the monster is polluted, contaminated by contradictory characteristics that "should not" belong together. Like miscegenation in race relations, the monster is considered impure, "agin' nature." In this narrow and always threatening sense, the monster is a source of fear. But looked at more broadly and sympathetically, the monster also presents the possibility that nature is not what we have assumed it was, and what we have previously considered to be monstrous is actually a normal human potential. In that sense the Frankenstein monster, although all his parts were presumably human in origin, certainly qualifies. Both the Mary Shelley novel and the James Whale film versions (*Frankenstein* and *Bride of Frankenstein*) work hard to counteract the view of monsters as repulsive by presenting a sympathetic character, who desperately wants to be treated like a normal human being.

The modern field of robotics has a term called the "uncanny valley" effect, which hypothesizes that, when robots look more human, up to a point they create empathy with actual human beings; but beyond that point, when they look "too human," revulsion sets in and people are more upset than they would be if the robot looked more like a machine. A certain degree of humanoid resemblance is fine, but too much turns people off. R2-D2 is fine and can even seem cuddly; C-3PO, more humanoid, is still acceptable; Repliee Q2, created at Osaka University in 2003 to look like a young woman, creeps people out. But in contrast with this real-life experience, in horror films the more a humanoid monster seems like a real person, the more likely the audience can have an emotional affinity with it, especially when it turns its face against convention, crosses boundaries, or searches for a sense of personal freedom, like the replicants in *Blade Runner* or the good cyborg of *Terminator 2*. In many such stories, the reaction to the monster by hidebound adults exposes social prejudice, while children can appreciate it as a kindly figure, like Shrek or the characters of *Monsters, Inc.* This potentially benevolent view of the monsters of earth is retained in other ways, such as the images of the giant guardians of London, Gog and Magog (or Gogmagog), displayed annually in the Lord Mayor's Show, and in the United States perhaps most strikingly in the strange costumed mascots who symbolize different sports teams, mocking their foes and celebrating their victories.[5]

A traditional distinction between wonders and miracles declares that while Satan may work wonders through deception, only God can perform miracles. Satan can exaggerate something in the natural world, but only God can create things like monsters that are contrary to natural processes. The only way to tell whether a wonder, a monster, or anything out of the ordinary was a message from God or a delusion engineered by the devil was to be able to interpret them properly, because sometimes they may just be neither—pure natural phenomena. John Milton in *Paradise Lost* describes how Satan disguised as the Serpent lures Eve, "our credulous Mother," to eat of the Tree of Knowledge of Good and Evil and compares Eve's misunderstanding with the way a person lost in a swamp might take the gleam of a will-o'-the-wisp for a helpful light to lead them home, even though, "oft, they say, some evil Spirit attends." As he so often does in the poem, Milton thus combines an empirical description with a more supernatural interpretation ("they say") without resolving the difference. To this day that interpretive dilemma—are wonders the creation of God, of the devil, or of nature?—remains an essential crux for believers. Depending on your point of view, the appearance of the monster might be a warning that signals God's purpose; for others the goals of Satan and his demons. As the *New York Times* in summer of 2012 reported, a knot in a tree trunk in New Jersey that seemed to resemble the Virgin of Guadalupe drew not only believers to marvel, but also skeptics who dismissed the whole thing as superstition, as well as the occasional Jeremiah who warned that this was the work not of God but of Satan.[6]

There's little distance between the vulgar (in the sense of popular) fascination with abnormal human and animal births, comets, and other strange events as wondrous entertainment, and the theological urge to interpret such monsters allegorically as part of a religious message. When the line between the natural and the unnatural is unclear, one response is to look for meaning. But the desire to look at something weird did not always turn into a desire to interpret it. The human taste for the marvelous seems endless, and with the invention of printing, images of the outlandish and the exotic could be disseminated more widely than local gossip could manage. The response was part fascination and part puzzlement. In 1496, for example, Albrecht Dürer published a woodblock print of the so-called Monstrous Sow of Landser, with eight feet, four ears, and two tongues. Dürer himself may have thought the birth of the sow was a portent of coming evil, since he included its image in a series of prints called "Apocalypse," which featured other strange beasts. But even without an appended interpretation it could still be appreciated on its own as a wonder to titillate his audience. Shakespeare later has his vagabond peddler Autolycus in *A Winter's Tale* describe one of his ballads: "Here's one to a very doleful tune, how a usurer's wife was brought to bed of twenty money-bags at a burthen, and how she longed to eat adders' heads and toads carbonadoed." Similarly, when Othello tells how Desdemona was captivated by his adventurer's tales "of the Cannibals that each other eat, / The Anthropophagi, and men whose heads / Do grow beneath their shoulders," he is in the realm of wonder; and Shakespeare draws on stories that go back to Herodotus and beyond about strange races with odd features, like the heads of dogs (the Cynocephali) or enormous feet (the Sciopodes). By the mid–seventeenth century, to accommodate the growing taste for the multiplicity of monsters, erudite terms such as teratology, the discourse of wonders and prodigies, as well as teratoscopy, the practice of understanding the prophetic side of prodigies, were coined.[7]

Accordingly, the wealthy of the Renaissance and after collected evidences of the abnormal and exotic in what was called a *wunderkammer,* a wonder cabinet or collection of curiosities in which the weird, exotic, and monstrous objects of the world (or at least all the collector could afford) were gathered together for the amusement, pleasure, and amazement of whoever was invited to visit. Historians have argued that the fascination with wonders gradually gives way to a more empirical and scientific view of the world, an interest in its regularities and repetitions rather than its unique anomalies. But, although the Protestant Reformation argued that the age of miracles was past, and there would be no more messages from the invisible to the visible world, the urge to believe in miracles, to look for portents, and be amazed by improbabilities and weirdness, particularly in turbulent and confusing times, remained strong. As events speed up and people feel less in control, they often focus on the strange event as an omen of a feared or hoped-for future, or a sign at least that God is interested enough in the world to arrange for strange things to exist.

∽⊙∼

The process by which the unnatural or just peculiar becomes the horrifying requires an interpreter who sees it as a portent of doom, rather than something merely happenstance or pathetic. By the time of the early years of the Reformation, strange images and monstrous births frequently arrived with ready-made interpretations. The individual monster had turned into the generalizable monster. In a time of religious controversy and pitched battles between adherents to one religion or another, they were seized upon as clues to God's purposes, the visible distortion of bodies as pathways to understanding his otherwise invisible intentions. The appearance in 1512 of the so-called monster of Ravenna, a hermaphrodite that was supposedly the result of the mating of a nun and a friar, with wings instead of arms and one large clawed foot, coincided with the battle of Ravenna, in which the papal army was defeated by the French. It was thus interpreted to illustrate God's upset with the Italians for not sufficiently supporting the papacy. A decade later, in a 1523 pamphlet, Martin Luther and Philip Melanchthon turned the polemical tables and argued that the recent appearance of animal monsters—one in Rome in 1495 with the head of an ass, an elephant's foot, and a women's breast and belly, and a calf in Saxony in 1522 that resembled a monk—were symbols of the corruption of the papacy. Dubbed the Papal Ass and the Monk Calf, they may not have been the first but were certainly among the most famous examples of the religious allegorizing of strange events that filled books into the seventeenth century. Together with such anti-Lutheran images as the "Seven-Headed Dr. Martin Luther" and "Luther as a Winesack," they conveyed a polemical message about their inner meaning.[8]

This tradition of associating heretical ideas with bodily distortion, monstrous pregnancy, sexual immorality, infertility, and other visible physical problems served to police behavior, both personal (sexual malfeasance) and theological (blasphemy), by the threat of the monstrous. The idea that a mother's prenatal attitudes and experiences had an influence on the fetus goes back as far as Hippocrates, and the idea of unnatural human-animal mating is preserved in such monsters as the Minotaur, the result of Pasiphaë's love for the Cretan Bull. Like the fused human and animal forms of monsters found in Nero's Golden House, these grotesque images were fantasies of unnatural connection. But in the sixteenth and seventeenth centuries that influence often focused on social, political, and religious issues more than on individual sins or shocking experiences. If a headless baby was said to be born, for example, it was no doubt due to a mother who had breached the natural order of things by not acknowledging her husband or her priest's authority. In an overheated time of religious conflicts, such parallels showed that local events, like personal readings of the Bible, had national, even cosmic significance. Prodigies and their interpretation were thus ways to understand tumultuous times, and to rebuke those who are thought to stray from tradition and "normality." Despite the Protestant idea that the age of miracles had passed, they demonstrated that God had not left the world behind entirely. His eye was still on the sparrow, especially if it was born with an eagle's talons.

Later in the seventeenth century John Dryden drew upon the political tradition of monstrous interpretation in his poem "Absalom and Achitophel." In order to attack the parliamentary enemies of Charles II, he describes the son of Lord Shaftesbury, the head of the anti-court party, as "Got, while his soul did huddled notions try; / And born a shapeless lump, like anarchy." In such a view, the conglomerate form of the monster was most obviously caused by incest, unnatural cohabitation, or some other crime against sexual or political normality. Yet as a sign of God's meaning, no matter how misshapen, the monster's life was his intent. So, even as medical knowledge advanced, abortion was considered blasphemous, no matter what the justification.

One factor at work in the gradual demotion of the strange and monstrous from a privileged position in the hierarchy of belief was the rise of experimental science, as well as the renovation of curiosity as a positive trait rather than a prideful turning away from God and toward the self. In his thirteenth-century *Summa Theologica*, a compendium of the teachings of the Catholic Church, Thomas Aquinas first quotes Augustine's explicit criticism of any close investigation of "the whole mass of material things." Aquinas then lays out the anti-curiosity position for the orthodox Middle Ages, citing four kinds of improper knowledge: literary pleasure, necromancy, knowledge of creatures without knowledge of God, and any search for a truth "too high" for the individual to strive for. The impression he leaves is that contemplation of the visible world, "the eager knowledge of sensible things," for anything other than the praise of God's wondrousness is the gateway to sin. God's world must be accepted, not probed and prized apart.

Historically Christianity has thus always been suspicious of the eye and its tendency to stop at the surface of things. How then to convey in art that unseen world of faith or fear? As the world of experimental science expanded, an inevitable tension arose between the Christian emphasis on the fallibilities of sight (and its potential to lead men astray) and the importance of sight and observation in scientific assumption (Descartes's idea that science should scrutinize things "clear and distinct and close at hand"). The eye could thus simultaneously be entirely denigrated in one kind of language and in another entirely praised. What kind of eye should then be the best to look searchingly at nature?

Nature has always been a complex word that mirrors a complicated reality. For every Lisbon earthquake there are pages of praise of rural life, the bucolic simplicity and innocence of the natural world. Every movement forward in knowledge, politics, and culture generates a nostalgia for a simpler world, a closer relation to the splendor in the grass, the glory in the flower. The speed of the very visible changes wrought by the Industrial Revolution inspired in many people a longing to slow down. Marie Antoinette dressed as a shepherdess; William Wordsworth wandered lonely as a cloud. However, unlike the artificial pastoralism of the French court, with its herd of sheep roving the back lot at Versailles, the Romantic sense of place had a distinct element of the primitive, verging on paganism and a pantheism of the natural world, in which the physical and the spiritual are united. Instead of man being the measure of all things, there was a humbleness before the sublime patterns and grand outcroppings of nature.

The grand theoretical book of this sea change in sensibility was Edmund Burke's *A Philosophical Enquiry into the Origin of Our Ideas of the Sublime and Beautiful*. Like those writers and painters who were to find more inspiration in the emotional excesses of gothic exaggeration than in the orderliness of traditional forms, Burke rejected the idea that true artistic understanding was a compound primarily of good taste and good sense. The sublime, which previously had referred generally to anything heightened and was particularly a characteristic of transcendent writing and poetry, in the hands of Burke was refashioned as both an aesthetic and an emotional category. Reflecting language that was traditionally the province of religious mystics who were trying to put into words their perception of God, Burke described the sense of sublime awe as preeminently a feeling experienced in nature. Like the deists who conceived of a religion without institutions and priestly hierarchies, he sought to account for what had been traditionally considered religious feeling without using traditional religious language. In other terms it might be expressed as the oceanic feeling of being one with the universe, or the sense of human smallness amid an overwhelming natural world, or the feeling that there are other worlds and other realities outside the realm of physical perception—but that the natural world might be a privileged path to them. As Elizabeth Schellenberg has pointed out, the change in attitude can be mapped, among other places, in the successive editions from 1724 to 1778 of Daniel Defoe's *A Tour thro' the Whole Island of Great Britain:* "In the course of those eight editions, the English Lake District is transformed from a region to be dismissed as terrifyingly wild and inhospitable into an object of pleasure."[9]

This burgeoning nostalgia for a direct relation with nature had an effect on other aspects of belief as well. Whereas Protestantism and Catholicism both considered children to be close to the devil and to original sin (hence the need for baptism), the Romantic poets at the cusp of the eighteenth and nineteenth centuries celebrated the child's innocence and deplored the civilization that corrupted it. The Romantic child had arrived on earth, as Wordsworth writes, "trailing clouds of glory," only to be weighed down by chains in the "prison-house" of adulthood. Along with this feeling that nature held secrets that had been lost with the growth of cities and civilization was an assumption that the people who lived closer to nature have a special wisdom and even special powers. In the same era that a belief in witchcraft was being undermined by both the medical and legal communities, the witch and the shaman, with their knowledge of herbs and spells, reentered cultural consciousness through art and literature.

But nature is rarely something in itself. It depends on your past experience and where you're standing in the moment. Walking in Griffith Park in Los Angeles, I saw a young family—parents, children, nieces and nephews—excitedly pointing, raising their cameras. What is it? I asked. A squirrel, they cried. I had the same sense of wonder myself when I took a trip to the savannahs of Africa. From only knowing animals from zoos, I was surprised to see that in nature they all lived together.

The historian of ideas Arthur O. Lovejoy once estimated that there are between thirty and forty major variations in the way eighteenth-century writers used the word *nature,* many of which contradicted others. Nature might be what is outside you or inside you. It might be what is regular and systematic, or what is irregular and random. It could define what is fundamentally human or what is fundamentally animal. It might contradict the conventions of society, politics, culture, and art, or it might be their real meaning. It could be the heart of things or it could be the surface of things. Politically, it could mean freedom (as a return to a lost or repressed human nature) or confinement (as the need to abide by an unchangeable human nature). Artistically, it could mean the need to follow eternal rules or the need to forget all rules. Theologically, it could mean what's permanent or what constantly changes, what is pure (and innocent of thought) or what is impure (and beyond any thought).

Lovejoy's analysis illustrates how arguments based on nature aren't inherently conservative or liberal, but, depending on the circumstances in which they appear, are often radical and oppositional. The invocation of "nature" as a primitive power opposed to everything civilized man has created comes to us particularly from the revolutionary and Romantic era. To a great extent it was a reaction against the revolution in empirical science, when the spiritual view of the natural world as an expression of God had been transformed into a countable, analyzable, and therefore controllable nature that would yield all its secrets to human inquiry and human labor. Unlike the exploitable nature proclaimed by the apostles of industrial and scientific progress, this more emotional view of nature was characterized by the urge to begin again, to get back to roots, and to dispense with all that had burdened the human race in the name of history and so-called civilization.[10]

Two conceptions of nature as a setting for visual and verbal art seem primary: nature as a real place that can be visited and nature as an ideal place like Eden. Often the two clash, especially when human beings intervene to try to control or repurpose nature, for commercial or even idealistic goals. *Jurassic Park* (1993), for example, skillfully combines a seemingly disinterested scientific curiosity with the terror of unleashing an uncontrollable world of natural monsters, while the villain in the *Alien* series is less the space monster than the bland and faceless Company that wants to preserve it for profit.

That nature can be hope and salvation as well as the source of fear may be the inextinguishable residue of our hunter-gatherer and even agricultural past, when cultivation (and culture) created weak boundaries against the mysteries of the forest, the jungle, and the dark. Into that gap came witches, shamans, and other mystical intermediaries who claimed to allay its terrors and expand its blessings through rituals, charms, and incantations. Even now, in a supposedly more technologically sophisticated world (where we have opened up so many of the secrets of nature) and a supposedly more religious world (where we have been promised dominion over the earth), nature remains enigmatic and unexpected, filled with astonishing and overwhelming power. We still retain the same fascination with the roughness and irregularity of nature that fascinated the gothic novelists and painters, just as we are in awe of its excesses, conveyed through news stories and movies about hurricanes, volcanic eruptions, earthquakes, and tsunamis. At least on the evidence of the art, literary and visual, of the past two hundred years, nature continues to show two faces, destroyer and creator. The film director James Cameron, for example, seems to have built his career on the themes of both nature's vengeance against human hubris and the potential benevolence of the acceptance of a natural world in films like *Titanic, The Abyss,* and *Avatar.*

Ever since human beings gathered in villages and cities, therefore, nature had always been ready to hand as a way of criticizing the direction that "civilization" had taken. The Greeks and Romans had their pastorals where shepherds sang, guarded their flocks, and covertly mocked the decadent pleasures of the urban world. It was a less cultivated but still a leisurely world. But in later eras the tension between civilization and nature would become more heated. Montaigne's late-sixteenth-century essay "Of Cannibals" depicts a more violent human nature that is nevertheless uncontaminated by the warping traditions of Europe, and vitally engaged instead in the immediacy of life. In Shakespeare's *The Tempest* Prospero has taken over the island from Caliban, its primitive inhabitant, and pompously tells him how much civilizing benefit that has been and how much he has even been taught to speak. To which Caliban responds bitterly: "You taught me language; and my profit on't / Is, I know how to curse."

By the seventeenth century in England, the appeal to natural wonders was often considered potentially blasphemous, since they suggested a way of understanding the nature of both the real and the spiritual worlds that contradicted religious and political orthodoxy. This occurred with some regularity during the English Civil Wars, when a myriad of breakaway Protestant sects used monstrous portents to counter the teaching of the established church. But even before that, heretics often drew upon the appearance of marvels and wonders to bolster their own heterodox opinions.[11]

Wonder is therefore as much a cultural category as it is proto-scientific. In the *Proceedings* of England's Royal Society, founded in 1660 by the restored king Charles II, whose father Charles I had his own famous wonder cabinet, true scientific advances like Robert Boyle's formulation of the gas laws may rub shoulders with such seemingly tabloid stories as a woman giving birth to cats in Dorset and a fish that can speak in Wales.[12] The Fire and Plague of London a few years later reenergized portent hunting, as seers, necromancers, and ordinary citizens wondered why London had been singled out for what seemed like God's retribution. Not long after, Samuel Pepys, who was fascinated by stories of the anomalous and the monstrous, recorded in his diary his reading of John Spencer's skeptical *A Discourse Concerning Prodigies: Wherein the Vanity of Presages by Them Is Reprehended, and Their True and Proper Ends Asserted and Vindicated* (1665). Spencer had argued that portents do not "necessarily" predict future events, but then hedged his case by presenting the counter argument that they did. There was clearly something more at stake than superstition. A year later the more orthodox believer and natural scientist Boyle published his *Free Inquiry into the Vulgarly Received Notion of Nature*. Nature, said Boyle, turning his ire equally against paganism and Spinoza, was not a separate being that could generate phenomena of its own but subject to God's will. Thus, already in the first century of experimental science, it was possible to validate one's investigation of the natural world by believing either in the inherent cohesiveness of nature or in the plan of God. That this God might be dubbed the Designer or the Watchmaker would not be concertedly argued until the early decades of the eighteenth century, but that new definition of divinity was already in the wings as a way of explaining the mysteries of nature. Still, the question remained: If God's design of nature has a purpose, what is it, and is it possible for human consciousness to understand its meaning?[13]

Whether objects of wonder are isolated miraculous events—or whether they are proto-scientific and thereby connected to an order of the natural world that humans might be able to understand—is the crux of changes from the seventeenth to the eighteenth century. Any conflation of the normal and the abnormal, the pattern and the exception, is what David Hume objected to in his essay "Of Miracles" (1748), in which he argued that God could not simultaneously be credited with the regularities of nature as well as the anomalies, establishing the laws of nature and then contravening them. Like the seventeenth- and eighteenth-century deists, who believed that reason and a close attention to nature were sufficient reason to believe that God is the creator of the world, without any intervention of religious institutions or authority, Hume's God (to the extent Hume was a believer) had established the consistency and plan of nature, not its variances. It was a point of view that echoed Spinoza's idea that natural events were necessary, not arbitrary. (To a certain extent the deist perspective merged Spinoza's view of the unity of God and nature with a refusal to accept unconditionally the authority of institutional religion.) As Alexander Pope had written for Isaac Newton's epitaph: "Nature and Nature's laws lay hid in night: / God said, Let Newton be! and all was light." There was no room in Newton's universe of laws and relationships for any principle of disorder, let alone the demonic—or the miraculous—which would contradict the divine plan. Miracles, Hume maintained, were most often the result of superstition, credulousness, or the desire to promote a particular religion.[14]

So, as the sphere of what can be scientifically investigated expanded, the sphere of the strange and unexplainable (except as evidence of God's will) seemed to contract. Yet the fascination with the strange and unexplainable remained enticing, from the retinues of dwarfs favored by emperors and kings to the ubiquitous raree-shows at street fairs, frequented by members of the Royal Society as well as ordinary Londoners.[15] The wonder cabinets of the aristocracy and middle-class merchants metamorphosed into natural history museums at one end of the spectrum and P. T. Barnum freak shows at the other. The continuing fascination with the conglomerate and contaminated, the questionably human and the resurrected primitive—Yeti, Bigfoot, Sasquatch, even the Loch Ness monster and the Geico caveman—remains a constant in human culture. In the forest there could be strange creatures that combined the human and the animal, perhaps even more so as the wild places are decimated by the onslaught of human progress.[16]

THE POWER OF WORDS AND THE LANGUAGE OF THE INEFFABLE

They say miracles are past, and we have our philosophical persons, to make modern and familiar, things supernatural and causeless. Hence it is that we make trifles of terrors, ensconcing ourselves into seeming knowledge when we should submit ourselves to an unknown fear.

—Shakespeare, *All's Well That Ends Well*

Heard melodies are sweet, but those unheard
Are sweeter; therefore, ye soft pipes, play on;
Not to the sensual ear, but, more endear'd,
Pipe to the spirit ditties of no tone. . . .

—John Keats, "Ode on a Grecian Urn"

In the ages before the expansion of literacy in the eighteenth century, language itself was considered magical. For preliterate societies words and texts, whether spoken or written, often have an aura of power and mystery about them that tends to dissipate as literacy rises, and in those earlier cultures there is frequently no firm distinction between magical language and literacy generally. Literacy was the possession of only a few, and its possession gave them power. Words also were one of the prime gateways between the world of humans and the world of demons. As in many ancient religions, to be able to name demons was to have control over them—and the ability to name was one of the prime gifts of the witch. The authors of the *Malleus Maleficarum* argued that the main human bridge between the visible and the invisible worlds was the witch. Because witches used incantations to work their magic, the faithful therefore needed holy words to combat them. So it is then that, say, priests and other officials of the church were chiefly the ones who wrote as well as prayed. As a result, the plea of "benefit of clergy" allowed clergymen to escape the jurisdiction of secular courts so that they could be tried by more lenient ecclesiastical courts, which often required merely reading a verse in Latin from the Bible for exoneration. As time went on, however, the privilege was in practice extended to laymen who could read, and in this way the Elizabethan poet and dramatist Ben Jonson escaped hanging after killing his fellow actor Gabriel Spencer in a duel.

This connection between learning generally and magical learning in particular is preserved in some English words today. *Grammar,* which may now seem to be only the bane of students and fledgling writers, was once virtually equivalent to the archaic word *gramarye,* the ability to speak the language of the occult. Both words are also linked etymologically with *glamour,* originally meaning an enchantment, and not associated with physical beauty and superficial allure until the twentieth century. Both *glamour* and *gramarye* were revived in their magical meanings during the late eighteenth century, but only *glamour* managed to stick in the common vocabulary. In a more familiar example, in which both the supernatural and the everyday usages are still current, we have *spell* itself: as a noun referring to the verbal formulas of a magician or a witch, and as a verb the knowledge of the accurate order of letters in a word.[17]

But to the extent that explanation is a property of language, and the use of sentences an effort to express the logic of the world, writers who deal in fear and tell tales of terror often suggest that the language they use is inadequate to convey the hyperreality they are describing. In biblical tradition the complexity and ambiguity of words, the difficulty in saying what one means, is a consequence of the Fall. Before then, innocence, plainness, and directness were aspects of words as well as human nature; after then all became much darker. As in the story of the Tower of Babel, the effort to compete with God in knowledge resulted only in confusion and chaos. Deciding which words are true and which are false, which have a touch of the divine and which are the spawn of Satan, becomes an important issue not just for the sciences trying to fashion a language of objectivity but also for the arts trying to convey less verifiable states of being.

The numerous and often contradictory explanations given to any monstrous event in nature correspond in the literature of horror to the variety of contradictory explanations that are part of most works. In brief, there are three major possibilities: the natural, the supernatural, and the hypernatural. The natural explanation assumes a coherent material world that is accessible to human reason and experimentation. The supernatural explanation refers instead to the influence of the invisible world, however that might be defined by religion and belief, including beings and events that have no natural explanation. The hypernatural explanation, often favored by gothic novelists, detective story writers, and horror movie directors, seems at first to be unexplainable by the normal laws of nature (the ghostly figure in the cathedral, the murder in a locked room) but turns out in the end to be explainable (the villain trying to frighten the heiress, the poisonous snake that enters through a vent). They help create as well the "is this real or am I crazy?" plots of such films as *The Cabinet of Dr. Caligari* (1920) and *Shelter Island* (2010), although the need to give an explicit explanation is much more prevalent in literature than in film, a form where the satisfactions of rational closure are not so pressing. Nevertheless, the clash between these different forms of explanation, which are the fruit of the gothic era, are still with us. If only because they generate plots and narrative conflict, they are combatants in a contest that can never be resolved, just as on the moral and theological level the conflict continues between those who argue the intelligibility of evil (Hitler as product of German history and culture) and the unintelligibility of evil (Hitler as demon).[18]

Whether the work is a novel intended to provoke the sense of dread or a painting that attempts to depict dark spirits, neither the verbal nor the visual skills of the artist are sufficient to convey all he intends. An essential part of Edmund Burke's distinction between the sublime and the beautiful was that the intricate detail of the beautiful could be fully expressed while the overwhelming emotion inspired by the sublime was often beyond language. The sublime summoned up the vastness and the magnificence of nature, in darkness, solitude, terror, and vacuity, in the midst of which the ordinary viewer felt small and melancholic. But it was also the realm of the soaring original genius, the unleashed imagination, and an often painful experience that contradicted reason and logic. The beautiful, by contrast, embodied the finite world in its delicacy, smoothness, brightness of color and light. Their difference paralleled the difference between horror and terror: the beautiful was the realm of the physical, the sublime the realm of the metaphysical.[19]

Between these two extremes of art and feeling arose the picturesque, a term coined in the mid–eighteenth century to describe architecture and scenery that evoked strong feeling on the part of the viewer, without being overwhelming (like the awe-inspiring Alps) or trivially beautiful. By now "picturesque" has lost a good deal of its original precision and has come to be used to describe any vaguely pleasant landscape or work of visual art. But in the eighteenth century, when many thirsted for the experience of being in the natural world in order to expand their emotions and enhance their sensibility, the concept of the picturesque provided a way to merge the uplift of the sublime with the detail of the beautiful in a work of art. The earliest cited usages of the word *picturesque* are not about nature per se, but about the enticing picture-like quality of various objects and scenes. William Gilpin is usually given credit for using the word in its now conventional meaning in *Observations on the River Wye and South Wales* (1748). Gilpin was a priest born in Cumberland who was so committed to his ideal of tumbledown beauty that he thought the already roofless cathedral of Tintern Abbey (subject of a later poem by Wordsworth) needed the services of a heavy mallet to make it look more picturesque. In his influential *Essay on Prints* (1768), he called the picturesque the source of the specific beauty in an artistic image and concluded that nature often needed the help of the artist to be truly perfect.[20]

This tweaking or aestheticizing of nature to make it more natural is a characteristic of the manipulated landscape of many eighteenth-century English country houses, where views typically unfold as a spectator walks through the gardens, discovering new perspectives along the way—a plan contrary to that of the typical French garden of the period, which revealed itself all at once as an articulated and often symmetric whole. This contrast between the individual, strolling narrative of English nature and the God's-eye overview of French nature may be one reason why the frequent first-person of gothic fiction was never as popular in France as it was in England and the United States.

The picturesque effect was a goal regularly aspired to by painters in the late eighteenth century and after, so much so that a group of necessary visual motifs developed that turned individual works into a genre virtually independent of the specific artist who created it. The depiction of the irregularity and violence of nature could include twisted trees, a ruined or decaying castle, meandering streams, silhouetted buildings, and craggy hillsides, along with a time of evening that cinematographers today call "magic time," when the last rays of sunlight have not yet left the scene but darkness is coming on. Think, say, of Renfield being met by Dracula's coach at the desolate Borgo Pass, the gloomy laboratory of Henry Frankenstein built high on a steep rocky hill, or, in a later version, the people assembled by the side of the road in *Close Encounters of the Third Kind,* awaiting the appearance of aliens.[21]

As the picturesque reconciles the sublime and the beautiful, so the magic time of gothic painters mediates the world of light and visibility with the world of darkness and invisibility. At these moments, shapes are ambiguous and susceptible to multiple, often contradictory, interpretations. Pools of water echo their surroundings in a mysterious doubling that mirrors the frequent appearances of doppelgängers or other selves in horror tales like Poe's "William Wilson" or Stevenson's *Jekyll and Hyde.* Silhouetted windmills loom like monsters à la *Don Quixote,* and ruined castles regain their ancient power and menace, reflected in the silver sheen of a racing river or the surface of an unfathomable pool. Toward the end of *The Monk,* for example, Ambrosio, saved from the Inquisition by Lucifer, has been transported to a precipice in the Sierra Morena mountains of Spain, to a scene Lewis describes by both sight and sound:

> The disorder of his imagination was increased by the wildness of the surrounding scenery; by the gloomy caverns and steep rocks, rising above each other, and dividing the passing clouds; solitary clusters of trees scattered here and there, among whose thick-twisted branches the wind of night sighed hoarsely and mournfully; the shrill cry of mountain eagles, who had built their nests among these lonely deserts; the stunning roar of torrents, as swelled by late rains they rushed violently down tremendous precipices; and the dark waters of a sluggish stream, which faintly reflected the moon-beams.

Dispensing with the presence of any satanic figure, Edgar Allan Poe, some fifty years later, captured a similar sense of the mystery of the natural world in the first glimpse of the House of Usher:

I looked upon the scene before me—upon the mere house, and the simple landscape features of the domain—upon the bleak walls— upon the vacant eye-like windows—upon a few rank sedges—and upon a few white trunks of decayed trees—with an utter depression of soul which I can compare to no earthly sensation more properly than to the after-dream of the reveler upon opium—the bitter lapse into every-day life—the hideous dropping off of the veil. . . . I reined my horse to the precipitous brink of a black and lurid tarn that lay in un-ruffled luster by the dwelling, and gazed down—but with a shudder even more thrilling than before—upon the remodeled and inverted images of the gray sedge, and the ghastly tree stems, and the vacant and eye-like windows.

In both of these passages, descriptions of nature serve to break through the confines of language into the realm of feeling u general project of the sensibility literature of the later eighteenth century, of which the gothic is a fundamental kind. In works that obviously relied on language—poetry, fic-tion—there was yet a frequent invocation of sights, sounds, and feelings that language was incapable of conveying entirely. With this distrust of language as adequate to convey the most profound thoughts and feelings, it is no won-der that horror literature generally and gothic literature in particular often plays with its own inability to describe fully what its characters see. By the twentieth century, of course, with the growing taste for explicit gory detail, as well as the general ease with which film visually embodies the invisible, the sky darkens, animated vines choke off breath, blood flows more freely, rotting limbs fall off, and fangs grow ever sharper. But in the early years of literary terror, a less explicit description sought to evoke more shapeless fears inside the reader. In *The Monk,* for example, people are always "falling lifeless" to the ground, even though they are still alive, and a common expression of a char-acter when witnessing some fresh horror is "What I felt at that moment lan-guage is unable to describe." This is literature at the edge of disintegration, the horror that can be perceived but never encompassed. Just as cinematic horror is often based on being forced to see what you don't want to see, so in literature it is the unspeakable—as H. P. Lovecraft and Samuel Beckett would have it—the unnamable, the ineffable and awesome grandeur, that leaves you speechless.

The ineffable is what can't be specified or articulated in ordinary language—inchoate ideas, emotions, experiences that evade the effort of language to convey them to others without distortion. The things that move us most are often the most difficult to express. They require instead either silence or some made-up mysterious language that harkens back to the primitive world. Mystics in all religions, when they write about their experiences, stress how vague and approximate is the language in which they can express them; so too the language of horror can often only hint at what it describes.

This literary confrontation with the ineffable corresponds to the urge to go beyond ordinary nature to extraordinary nature, by the way of miraculous births, wonders, or other versions of local miracles. The ineffable also partakes of speechless awe, when contemplating the wonders of nature and feeling. At least two kinds of language are therefore in combat or at least together flourishing by the end of the eighteenth century. The first is a language of growing specificity, a plain language fashioned to express directly the truths of the material world, the insights of science and reason. The other is the more suggestive language of mystery and horror, the insights of religion and art. These two realms correspond to what the psychologist Daniel Kahneman in *Thinking Fast, Thinking Slow* characterizes as two kinds of thinking and perception, the analytic versus the associative. For him thinking fast is implicitly inferior to thinking slow, because its immediate emotional responses yield problematic action, while thinking slow is superior in its ruminative search for causes that can be verified. But it is difficult to maintain this as a hard and fast distinction. Where does it leave the insights gained through emotion and art? Is thinking slow the only way to penetrate mystery? Perhaps the analytic, expository, and strictly causal modes of inquiry need to be sidetracked occasionally in order to discover new insights.

༺ⓞༀ

> Religion is the miracle of direct relationship with the infinite; and dogmas are the reflection of this miracle. Similarly belief in God, and in personal immortality, are not necessarily a part of religion; one can conceive of a religion without God, and it would be pure contemplation of the universe; the desire for personal immortality seems rather to show a lack of religion, since religion assumes a desire to lose oneself in the infinite, rather than to preserve one's own finite self.

—Friedrich Schleiermacher, *Addresses on Religion* (1799)

In different eras, art is called upon to answer the human need to sustain feelings otherwise stunted by official religion. The advent of ghosts to supply a connection with the dead otherwise breached by the Protestant Reformation attack on the idea of purgatory is one example. The changes in attitudes toward religion and the natural world usually called by the general term Romanticism that occurred on the cusp of the eighteenth and nineteenth centuries is another. Just as new artistic forms like the literature of feeling and fear emphasized the inexpressible and the ineffable, so too in religion itself at the end of the eighteenth century the God of reason who underlay and supervised his creation of the natural world was challenged by new beliefs that emphasized the affective rather than the intellectual. In one intriguing example, the so-called "explained supernatural" novels of Ann Radcliffe, in which seemingly uncanny events are shown to have clear human causes, were criticized by readers who would rather have been left in the clutches of the mysterious. Such readers were attracted to her novels in search of a transcendental experience of wonder and mystery, which most of the story supplied, until clarity won out in the end. They were disappointed that a story promising a truth beyond language and logic finally embraced them.[22]

To a certain extent, critics of Radcliffe have explained this kind of ending as the triumph of what they referred to as Protestant reason and logic triumphing over Catholic obfuscation and make-believe. But even within Protestantism itself, the desire for a different kind of relation to God and to religious mystery had already become an important issue. The above quotation from the German theologian Friedrich Schleiermacher is a neatly encapsulated version of some of these ideas that appear also in elements of seventeenth-century Pietism, eighteenth-century Methodism, twentieth-century Christian existentialism, and other religious movements. Instead of the impulse to use the orderliness of nature to prove the existence of God, or the need to demonstrate that despite natural disasters God is good, they emphasized the human awe before the divine. The principal religious relationship in such views is between the individual and God, who is conceived not as a creator of nature or a moral judge, not as a scientist, inventor, or craftsman, or any other human-like authority but as, in the words of Rudolf Otto in *The Idea of the Holy* (1917), a being who is Wholly Other, to which there is no possible analogy. God, in other words, is infinite, man is finite, and the experience of God, akin to that in mysticism, is, in Otto's term, numinous, that is, suffused with a sense of transcendence and the presence of divinity. Instead of being a father or a friend, God is the *mysterium tremendum et fascinans*—a tremendous and fascinating mystery that (like the concept of the sublime in art) is both repellent and alluring to ordinary human perception.

Instead of worrying whether God caused the Lisbon earthquake for unfathomable vengeful reasons of his own, for example, the believer instead concentrates on the godliness of God. The numinous experience is thus, in the formulation of the twentieth-century Jewish theologian Martin Buber, an essentially I–Thou rather than an I–It relation to God, and thus can potentially stand outside any particular earthly institution or mode of understanding.

Both the literature of terror and the cult of nature encompassed a synthesis of emotion and reason in a secular version of religious awe that equally stressed the inexpressible holiness of the experience—what Wordsworth called "the visionary gleam," rather than the strict contrast between the two that preoccupied philosophers like Hume (or Kahneman). The feeling of being overwhelmed, the shiver of experiencing something vastly larger than oneself, the urge to believe in an invisible power, was not only part of the confrontation of the holy, but could also be experienced in the heart of nature as well as in the intensities of the experience of art. At the same time, Methodism and other religions departed from strict Calvinist ideas of predestination to emphasize the need for human will in the drama of grace and repentance.

Despite the invocation of the ineffable, however, the sermon must be preached and the book must be written. And so one of the characteristic forms of the tale of terror is the book without an author, or at least the unauthorized recounting of mysterious events by a supposed witness of them: The discovered manuscript of Walpole's *The Castle of Otranto,* the retold tale of *Frankenstein,* which includes the monster's own narrative; the Chinese box of storytellers in *Wuthering Heights;* the interspersed newspaper clippings, letters, journals, diaries, telegrams, and even a "phonograph diary" that tell the story of *Dracula.*[23] Photography, radio, X-rays, movies—each new technology affords a new chance to delve into the spirit world. The implication is that there is no single presiding author behind the story; it just happened this way, and therefore you must believe it. In our own time, with the latest advanced technology, the so-called "found footage" subgenre of horror reveals itself to be more integral to the history of horror than it might seem at first to be. The more technologically advanced the format, the more seemingly grounded and reasonable the story. Any actual author thus disappears in favor of the supposedly objective authority of videotape or digital recording in such films as *The Blair Witch Project* (1999) and *Paranormal Activity* (2007). One of my personal favorites in this form is *Invasion,* in which virtually the entire film is told from the fixed perspective of a video camera mounted on the dashboard of a police car. In all these examples, from *Otranto* to *Invasion,* the implication is clear:

because no one is in charge, it must be true. Yet at the same time no matter how advanced the technology that helps us see, it cannot protect us from our invisible fears and may even be the instrument of our doom.[24]

By the same token, a straightforward causal narrative method, complete with an obvious or even minimally intrusive author, implies an organized world, not one in which strange events can happen and usually do. Often then, in works of terror, there is a limited first-person narrator or else a dream-like third person. As in the stage or movie musical, when feelings that can't be expressed in ordinary language come out in song and dance, the disruptions and the partial perspectives in the horror tale serve to break up any causal and logical unfolding and to get in touch with a different sense of reality. As the English horror writer Arthur Machen put it, these gaps reveal "the most awful, most secret forces which lie at the heart of things." This kind of nonlinear, noncausal style is as much suited to the horror story as to the avant-garde, as much to the music of Mahler's Fifth Symphony as to the experimental films of Luis Buñuel and Salvador Dalí.[25]

TERROR AND NATURE ON THE PICTURESQUE TOUR

The lure of the picturesque setting and the desire for an emotional work-out compounded of awe and terror intersect in the beginnings of European tourism. Beginning in the late seventeenth century, and usually confined to the wealthy young men of England and northern Europe, the so-called Grand Tour—starting usually in France and proceeding to Spain, Italy, and often Germany, less often Greece—stressed an immersion in the world of classical antiquity and its revival in the Renaissance. In some ways it was a more phys-ical version of the *wunderkammer,* a collection of exotic experiences with the supposed aim of enhancing the young man's education more than any tutor or school could. In their turn, the novels of Ann Radcliffe, with their ex-tended descriptions of Spanish and Italian landscapes, along with such poems as Percy Shelley's paean to the wonders of Mont Blanc were themselves cheaper, pocket-sized Grand Tours for a new audience with enough money for books but not for the extended trips of yore.[26]

The logical next phase was a kind of middle-class adventure tourism, which begins in the early nineteenth century, fueled not only by the desire to see the magical places celebrated in literature and seen in paintings, but also by such practical measures as new forms of transportation and new ways of easing one's journey. On many of these expeditions the search was not so much for the remnants of antiquity or the residue of the great artists of Florence or Rome as some frisson of the evils of the past, but safely encased in a picturesque nostalgia. The first travel guide published by Karl Baedeker dealt with the Rhine, and featured the area near the Lorelei cliffs, in German mythology the home of the Nibelungs and the bane of sailors. This exotic mixture of mythic and actual danger had by this time been domesticated by the dredging and channelizing of the Rhine by river engineers for the delectation of tourists. Whatever piece of landscape had been host to an old tale of ghosts and spirits, magic and mystery, was potentially a goal of Romantic excursion, even more so if it had natural beauty as well. Fingal's Cave on an island off the coast of Scotland, a spot of natural wonder, was popularized by the composer Felix Mendelssohn as another goal for pilgrims of sensibility. Fingal was the subject of a poem by Ossian, a legendary eleventh-century bard, whose writings had been supposedly discovered and translated by James Macpherson to great acclaim and much controversy over forgery in the mid–eighteenth century. Like the Siegfried who would later have his own story, along with the Loreleis, immortalized in Wagner's operas, Ossian was a hero from the distant past who lived when people were closer to nature than they were following the advent of the train, the steamboat, and packaged tourism.[27] Mendelssohn was especially inspired by such settings, and his taste reveals how intermingled the picturesque was with the memory, true or fictional, of titillating adventures and crimes. Here, for example, is his account of another visit in Scotland on the same 1829 tour. The day before he is scheduled to see Sir Walter Scott in Abbotsford, he pops in on Holyrood Chapel in Edinburgh:

> In the evening twilight we went to-day to the palace where Queen Mary lived and loved; a little room is shown there with a winding staircase leading up to the door; up this way they came and found Rizzio in that little room, pulled him out, and three rooms off, there is a dark corner where they murdered him. The chapel close to it is now roofless, grass and ivy grow there, and at that broken altar Mary was crowned Queen of Scotland. Everything round is broken and mouldering and the bright sky shines in. I believe I found to-day in that old chapel the beginning of my Scotch symphony.[28]

Down to today as well, every European town looking to upgrade its tourist image has dug up its murderous and/or diabolic past, refurbished the castle dungeon, and filled the empty building on the town plaza with a torture museum.

While Radcliffe set her novels in the Alps or Italy and Walpole and Lewis in the past and the Continent, the American practitioners of the picturesque gothic, considering themselves already free of religious and political tyranny, saw instead the fearful and awesome potential in a landscape much closer to hand, Charles Brockden Brown's Philadelphia, Nathaniel Hawthorne's New England, or Washington Irving's Hudson Valley, where the Headless Horseman, a figure from Celtic and German folk legend, pursues the hapless schoolmaster Ichabod Crane through the dark night of the Catskills. Just as a natural wonder, without any satanic or criminal past, Niagara Falls became a tourist attraction at around the same time as tourists were carrying their Baedekers along the Rhine, its grandeur evoking the same kind of awe described by Burke and the Romantic poets, the smallness of man in the midst of nature.

So too the paintings by Thomas Cole and Frederic Church of the Hudson River valley, as well as those by Thomas Moran and Albert Bierstadt of Yellowstone and Yosemite, not only drew tourists to those areas but were also instrumental in inspiring federal legislation to preserve nature for awestruck future generations. Winslow Homer's paintings likewise helped popularize the Maine coast as a tourist destination, even as his family, mingling art with commerce, bought property there to develop houses to rent to summer visitors. As William H. McNeil has pointed out, "Romantic regret for a vanishing 'Nature' increased in the nineteenth century as the scale of human intervention [in nature] continued to magnify." Now, of course, we have armchair travels to nature courtesy of the National Geographic and other reality channels.

THE MONSTER FROM NATURE AND THE MOVIES

One of the early Western myths of the powers of nature is the story of Antaeus. Antaeus was the son of Gaea and Poseidon, and therefore part giant and part Olympian god, a transitional figure between the religion of the earth and the religion of the sky. According to the myth, he would challenge passersby to a wrestling match, defeat them, kill them, and collect their skulls to build a temple to his father. Because of his connection to the earth, whenever he was thrown down, he would bound up again with renewed strength. Hercules defeats him by holding him in the air and crushing him to death. But monsters with a special relation to the elements of earth and water particularly continue to prowl the peripheries of human fear, a continuing part of the mythology of nature but more rarely spotted in the literature of horror until the advent of photography and the movies. In a comparatively rare example, Arthur Conan Doyle has a wonderful story in his Professor Challenger series called "When the World Screamed" (1928). Challenger is a proto–Indiana Jones, a globe-trotting adventurer, "a primitive cave-man in a lounge suit." In the story he proves that the earth is actually an organic being, which reacts violently when it is being drilled into, destroying Challenger's equipment and covering everyone present with a noxious fluid.

Despite the many legends of strange races and fabulous creatures that preceded "our" coming, Conan Doyle's story is an unusual instance of a natural monster in literature. It is difficult to characterize the quivering organic earth penetrated by Professor Challenger's drill as resembling anything realistic in our own world. But Conan Doyle's story is, like the almost thirty-year gap between Walpole's *Castle of Otranto* and the flourishing of the gothic, a premonition of things to come. In many latter-day monster stories, human activity has intruded into the realm of the tribal and the ethnic and awakened their rage. Antaeus after all must be defeated, but without a Hercules around, what resources do we have to undo the monstrous damage we ourselves have caused by intruding into the domain of the primitive world with all our modern technology?

Until the rise of movies, the tradition of the artistic contemplation of nature was more generally benign. While Judaism had a more equable relation to the natural world, the Christian ambivalence about nature—due in great part to its polemical need to deny paganism any legitimacy—reinterpreted such ancient stories as Hercules's battle with Antaeus, the son of the earth, as an allegory of pagan defeat. Yet even while God promises humans dominion over the earth, the Old Testament also emphasizes the human debt to nature for its creation (*Adama* = from the earth). The literary critic Leslie Fiedler once wrote that the American equivalent of the European haunted castle was the haunted forest, and that would seem to accord with the sense of America as being without a long civilized past but instead with a closer relation to nature.[29] But in fact the forest and its inhabitants also occupy an important place in the European imagination. The fairies in *A Midsummer's Night's Dream* may seem to play at inconsequential games of love, but Puck associates with ghosts and goblins as well. With the same ambivalence between fun and fear, the image of the hair-covered Wild Man brandishes his club on the shields of some ancient families. So too, the Green Man images that appear on churches and other buildings during the Middle Ages indicate the continuing vitality of pre-Christian traditions about the spirits of nature and the need to placate them even while embracing Christianity.[30] The Robin Hood story also gathers a good deal of its staying power from its roots in the mysteries of the forest. Such figures harken back to kindly but sometimes cruel gods of resurrection and renewal. They are an essential part of the natural calendar, and their continued popularity perhaps another way to pay tribute to the earlier gods Christianity has displaced, by celebrating the connection of the natural world to a magical alternate reality. An argument could be made that an intense focus on physical nature and landscape in literature and art also serves to mingle early modern nationalism with paganism in an homage to local values otherwise in danger of being lost. To invoke the spirits of the land in the time of the rise of nation-states thus becomes a kind of patriotism. Shakespeare in *A Midsummer Night's Dream,* for example, brings together a wealth of local lore about fairies to imagine them as an organized court with a King Oberon and Queen Titania parallel to the monarchs in the human plot, Theseus and Hippolyta, and it is a tradition in the production of the play to have the same actor and actress playing both parts, since the four monarchs never appear in the same scene together.[31]

Burke and the Romantic poets speak eloquently of the awesomeness of nature, but less often of its destructive power, and hardly at all of the monsters it might generate. The chief Romantic image of the conjunction of art and nature is the Aeolian harp, the music played by the wind, without a human creator, nature making art by itself. So far, benevolent enough. Our own image, by contrast, in something like a replay of the explosion of the Lisbon earthquake, is the primitive destructive force of nature unleashed by man in the atomic blast. As technology expands, and we are further from our root, nature seems to become angrier and produce more monsters.

Most natural monsters therefore have to wait for the technologies of visible storytelling before they can have their greatest impact. In part the reason lies in the connection between nature and the ineffable. Unlike the ghost or the demon, the natural monster is entirely tangible. But in literature nature cannot speak for itself and has to be perceived from the outside, by a limited observer or an omniscient narrator, whereas in films the monster can appear dramatically in its terrifying guise, without having to say a word. In the history of both Western and Asian culture, the natural monster, spawned in isolation and discovered by humans only inadvertently, remains a minor player in the horror constellation, until awakened in multitudes by the explosion of the A-bomb at Hiroshima and the fears of the Cold War.

King Kong (1933) is a precursor here. Before making the film, Merian C. Cooper and Ernest B. Schoedsack had collaborated on several films—documentaries, semi-documentaries, and fiction films—that all focused on a setting in the primitive world: a nomadic tribe in Persia (*Grass,* 1925), a poor Thai farmer (*Chang,* 1927), a man who hunts humans for sport *(The Most Dangerous Game,* 1932). With *Kong* they create something like a self-conscious reflection on their own invasive filmmaking, following a film crew sailing to a distant island where there have been reports of a giant gorilla. No need to go through the whole story, which I'm sure is familiar even to many who have never seen the film: the gorilla is captured, brought back to New York to be put on display (shades of Barnum), escapes, and is killed. The final line takes us back to the world of fairy tales: "It was beauty who killed the beast." Like men trapped by a sexually predatory vamp, poor Kong has fallen victim unwittingly to the charms of Fay Wray.

But there are other stories that can be told about Kong's defeat: the need for the civilized world to keep the primitive in a cage for purposes of exhibition only, and the fear when the primitive breaks out. No matter what the specific context, there is always the shadow of a colonialist situation in the stories of natural monsters. We have invaded their territory, disturbing and displacing them from their natural place. We simultaneously see them as threatening but also to be pitied. They are often attracted to "our" women. As far as the men in the film are concerned, the monster pursues the woman for sexual reasons, and they are horrified by the prospect of monster-human miscegenation. But for the spectator the possibility remains that perhaps the natural monster, like the white primitive Tarzan, wants to rescue her from the often clueless "civilized" white men and bring her back to her natural realm. She may scream at first but sometimes later she begins to understand (as in *Kong*) that this is a real friend. Beauty didn't kill the beast; beauty and the beast are instinctive allies against mercenary men, so often out to despoil nature. *King Kong,* like any other film in which the natural monster is humanoid, can therefore support at least two interpretations. In one, it is a racist view of the primitive world, using the gorilla to stand in for black Africans; in another, Kong is the compassionate but doomed hero, the other side of that racism in which the black man is seen as the benevolent alternative to corrupt white civilization. By its connection to a primitive, unspoiled nature and the eagerness of its enemies to contain or destroy it, the story of the natural monster easily transforms into a story of ecological catastrophe.

Unlike more articulate monsters like Dracula or Mr. Hyde, the natural monster in its speechless incoherence is a roomy vessel for the fears that are projected upon it. This potential for social criticism in the film about the natural monster also carries forward into the contemporary preoccupation with zombies, a type of monster that contrasts sharply with the characteristics of that other popular monster, the vampire. The vampire self is often hidden, for instance, while zombies have a very noticeable social dimension.[32] By now, zombies are all shades of the ethnic rainbow, as well as all classes. But, despite the fact that the first American zombie film was called *The White Zombie* and featured Bela Lugosi's efforts to turn a young woman into a zombie for the benefit of her rejected lover, the zombie as part of the voodoo religion of the Caribbean, as well as the zombie in almost all its early film appearances, was black. Earlier versions of the word *zombie* exist from the beginning of the nineteenth century in connection with Caribbean and southern United States folklore about phantoms and ghosts.[33] From 1915 to 1934, Haiti was occupied by American forces, a situation that made exotic elements of voodoo familiar enough to the American public to help foster such Haiti-inflected works as Eugene O'Neill's *The Emperor Jones* (1920; movie, 1933) and Orson Welles's *Voodoo Macbeth* (1936). By 1942, zombie was even the name of a fruit-flavored rum drink. Films like Jacques Tourneur's *I Walked with a Zombie* (1943) underlined the association of zombies with the jungle world of Haiti, the revived dead, and black people. By including the black American comic Mantan Moreland as part of the cast, some distinction between the dull-eyed Caribbean black zombies and the lively American seems intended, although the choice between a threatening zombie stereotype and a familiar African-American stereotype isn't very enticing.[34]

Most monsters, as well as individuals like witches who have a direct connection to the supernatural, have innate abilities of fascination and seductiveness, whereas zombies lack any individual charisma and are perceived primarily as a crowd. In their cannibalistic urges, zombies recall such devouring monsters as the ogre and the fear of being swallowed up. Similarly, while the pallid faces of vampires signal their upper-class white origin even if from a foreign country, zombies are originally people of color, connected to a nature religion, and akin metaphorically to other minority and lower-class groups. Anonymous and almost totally lacking individuality, they embody the threat of a hostile natural world in all its aspects. Like the pod people in the film *Invasion of the Body Snatchers,* they have lost what characterizes them as distinct human beings in order to conform to the mass mind of the group.

At a time when there were widespread fears that Communist indoctrination had brainwashed captured American soldiers in the Korean War, the brain-eating zombie expressed the threat of being absorbed into a soul-crushing collectivity. In Robert A. Heinlein's novel *The Puppet Masters* (1951) a similar monster is the fungus-like alien that takes over individuals and turns them to its purposes. In the post–World War II era, conglomerate monsters also make their appearance, including my comic-book favorite the Heap, a somewhat benevolent monster generated from the body of a World War I German flier who crashed in a Polish swamp. Over the years his body, still with a spark of life force, merged with the vegetation to become a vaguely humanoid mass of foliage, that, when finally animated, moved through the world attacking Nazis and other enemies even more grotesque than itself. But the more prevalent monsters of the period are spawned by the atomic age and take up residence in Japanese films of the 1950s and later, including the archetypal atom-generated monster Godzilla (originally Gojira—part gorilla and part whale) and the roundup film *Destroy All Monsters* (in Japanese, *Charge of the Monsters*), which featured Godzilla and ten other monsters who followed in his wake, including Rodan, the radioactive bird-monster, and King Gedorah, the three-headed monster who strikes lightning from his eyes. No wonder then that the Cold War and its paranoia about the U.S.-Soviet conflict is fertile ground for the monstrous, while the atom bomb presents a persistent example of the unlocking of secrets of nature that might better have been left in mystery. As in *Invasion of the Body Snatchers* or *The Creature from the Black Lagoon,* the new monsters came out of nature or that other mysterious natural realm, outer space.[35]

For this reason it is intriguing how often in the postwar period the existence of the Bomb is connected to ancient myths. In *Kiss Me Deadly* (1956), the detective film that ends with a nuclear blast, for example, the opening of a box that causes a chain reaction is compared to Pandora opening the box that released all the evils in the world. Only the natural monsters of the distant past seem appropriate for these new terrors, as the distraught villain pleads with the femme fatale: "Listen to me, as if I were Cerberus barking with all his heads at the gates of Hell. I will tell you where to take it, but don't . . . don't open the box!"

The great leap forward for the zombie in horror films occurs in the late 1960s with George Romero's *Night of the Living Dead* (1968), in which the zombie (the word is never mentioned), instead of being an exotic black monster birthed in the Caribbean, becomes an all-embracing metaphor for the unthinking attitudes and blind obedience of an entire society. Rather than the serums, potions, and spells of earlier zombie stories, the dead in *Night of the Living Dead* are reanimated by a virus and they sally forth with an immensely lowered IQ and no moral or other consciousness to impede it. Once Romero's film showed how the image of the zombie could apply beyond its origins, the floodgates were open. The zombie in this sense became a more enticing image of the mechanization of modern society than the robot, because the zombie still retained recognizably human traits and was therefore more terrifying. In the Cold War, the zombie could stand in for the group mind Americans attributed to Soviet Communism. Now, our view of terrorists takes on much coloration from the image of the zombie. Whereas to their own audiences they may seem to be heroes sacrificing for the great cause, we tend to see them as faceless suicidal hordes, ideologically and religiously blinkered, out to destroy us. No wonder perhaps that one new characteristic of the zombie introduced in the post 9/11 era has been their speed. Instead of the shambling zombies of old, the new zombies, like terrifying and apocalyptic events themselves, move enormously fast.

These new zombies—like AIDS, swine flu, or the Ebola virus—are arguably the result of an increasingly globalized world in which diseases spread rapidly across continents and populations due to increased commercial contact, ease of transportation, and openness of borders. But, although the natural monster is a crucial player in the array of our fears, it is often the most quiescent of all monsters, which needs to be reawakened by changing cultural circumstances. Even now, when the threats to the earth are more noticeable than ever, there are very few films that try to deal with ecological catastrophe, and when they do exist, like the global-warming disaster film *The Day After Tomorrow* (2004), they tend to be more apocalyptic weather or epidemic disease scenarios, rather than the appearance of individual monsters. The havoc-wreaking monsters in *Cloverfield* (2008) and *Pacific Rim* (2013) may be born from ecological fears, but their genesis is vague enough to make any such connection submerged. An intriguing exception is the Korean film *The Host* (2006), directed by Bong Joon-Ho. There, some years after several bottles of formaldehyde are poured into the polluted Han River in Seoul on the orders of an American military pathologist, a mutated monster resembling a giant fish wreaks havoc in the city. Unlike the multiple zombie monsters, who have been transformed from human beings, usually by the actions of some mysterious disease, the monster in *The Host*, like the monsters released by atomic radiation in the films of the 1950s, is the result of an inadvertent but still culpable distortion of nature by human activity.

The preoccupation with the natural monster therefore has distinct stages in its evolution. The early fascination with the monstrous births of humans and animals as objects of wonder was intricately connected to the desire to interpret them as God's messages to the world. By the eighteenth century this religious and philosophic wonder at the variety of the natural world was being transformed into popular entertainment. Already in *Gulliver's Travels* (1726), Gulliver in Brobdingnag (the land of the giants) is exhibited at the local market day as a natural prodigy and then taken to the big city by the farmer who found him, where "I was shown ten times a-day, to the wonder and satisfaction of all people." By the nineteenth century the exhibition of natural monsters was a principal part of low-level show business for a mass audience, whether in Barnum's American Museum or in the multitude of sideshows, with their bearded ladies, microcephalics, and giants. In the twentieth century Tod Browning's haunting film *Freaks* from 1932 upends the contrast between human and aberrant by making his villains the physically "normal" trapeze artist Cleopatra and her strongman lover Hercules. Their plot to kill the dwarf Hans, whom Cleopatra has married for his money, is thwarted and a revenge is taken by the other members of the sideshow that turns Cleopatra herself into a freak.[36]

Essentially, when advances in medicine and especially in pediatrics lessened the number of such figures, however, the monster from nature became a less significant member of the monster array, and were often, like Joseph Merrick, the Elephant Man of the late nineteenth century, viewed more with sympathy than horror. But with the opening of the Pandora's box of nature that accompanied the discovery and use of the atomic bomb, a whole new generation of natural monsters appeared, some awakened from their long sleep by the Bomb, some changed and distorted by its radiation. Many of the films in which these monsters appeared were themselves, like the monsters of old, hybrids and mutations, crossovers between horror and science fiction: *The Thing, The Creature from the Black Lagoon, Caltiki the Immortal Monster, The Attack of the 50-Foot Woman, The Incredible Shrinking Man, The Beast from 20,000 Fathoms,* and so on. The crucial change in the view of the natural monster is triggered by fears that nature may not be so benevolent after all. The spores that create the pods and the pod people in the first *Invasion of the Body Snatchers* (1956) by the time of the second (1978) have clearly drifted from the last frontier of illegal immigration, outer space, to disguise themselves as beautiful, but deadly, flowers that suck out individual self-consciousness and replace it with bland optimism and agreement. By the

1990s and 2000s the awareness of climate change and the threats to nature by deforestation, mining, and other man-made actions produced another metamorphosis. Instead of the monster being a King Kong, torn from his native habitat to supply the demands of a corrupt show business, or a Godzilla, aroused by war, it was nature itself, distorted by human activity, that wreaked its vengeance by cold, heat, and disease.

CHAPTER 4

Frankenstein, *Robots, and Androids*

HORROR AND THE MANUFACTURED MONSTER

He stood a stranger in this breathing world,
An erring spirit from another hurl'd;
A thing of dark imaginings, that shap'd
By choice the perils he by chance escap'd . . .

—Byron, *Lara* (1814)

Everything must have a beginning. . . . Invention, it must be humbly
admitted, does not consist in creating out of void, but out of chaos.

—Mary Shelley (1831)

Economically, the eighteenth century was the period of that great European leap forward of mechanized progress and population growth called the
Industrial Revolution. Vital to this changing awareness of the material malleability of nature was the way humans now more concertedly than ever were
making nature work for them: turning coal into fire to turn water into steam
to run machines that would create floods of new objects to be bought and
sold. Home to large supplies of coal and iron, the English Midlands in the
mid–eighteenth century became the center of a textile industry that ran on
machines that replaced the hand-woven cloth and handmade clothes of the
past with miles of uniformly made patterns and colors. Instead of individually made weapons, each somewhat different from the other, Eli Whitney in
the American 1790s aspired to create guns made of interchangeable parts, rationally designed and, at least in theory, perfectly replicated versions that were
manufactured in something resembling mass production.

But just as affective forms of religion were trying to win back those who
no longer felt that rational religion was emotionally satisfying, literature, art,
and music began to focus on the cultivation of emotions previously reserved

primarily for religious belief. After centuries of artists who prided themselves primarily on their ability to do better than the past, new, more charismatic roles for the creators of art began to emerge in the atmosphere of the Europe-wide movement of what was then and later called Romanticism, an artistic movement characterized by the fascination with psychologically extreme states and anxieties that were previously almost exclusively the province of religion. That so many in the audience were eager to embrace the literary, visual, and musical works that were part of the new movement strongly suggests that not far below the brave talk of a new power over nature, and a focus on the future rather than the past, was a profound anxiety about the ability of any individual to maintain a sense of balance in the rushing tide of seemingly inexorable forward movement. The collapse or redefinition of old values in the time of revolutions, the march of new inventions and new ways of accomplishing better and more efficiently ancient tasks, nurtured simultaneously an awareness of the new world and a fear about meeting its demands. In such an atmosphere, it is no wonder that writers and artists of all kinds, used to a tradition of standing on the shoulders of the past and paying tribute to its influence, should turn instead to questions of originality.

Surely one of the most wistful lines in eighteenth-century English writing is Edward Young's complaint in his mid-eighteenth-century essay *Conjectures on Original Composition:* "Born *Originals,* how comes it to pass that we die *Copies?*" It might even have a claim on being one of the most haunting lines in all of modern literature, because it encapsulates in a brief phrase all the striving for personal uniqueness amid a pervasive fear of inadequacy that characterizes so many fictional and real people in the two hundred and fifty and more years since it was written. Like a beacon out of a dark forest, it focuses its despair on the innumerable ways the world makes us who we are, obliterating whatever was originally our own by a cascade of preexisting stories, emotions, ideas, and costumes. Alexander the Great ennobled himself by competing with the deeds of Hercules and Achilles; Don Quixote gathered strength for his quest from the tales of heroic medieval knights. But the more modern version of their invocation of bygone greatness to enhance their own is Young's—energy drained, ambition thwarted, by the shadows of the past. When Young wrote, William Wordsworth had not yet arrived to write poems lamenting what happens when the child, who descends from heaven "trailing clouds of glory," turns into the hidebound and limited adult. And it would be a few decades before Jean-Jacques Rousseau politicized Young's sentiment into "Man is born free, but everywhere he is in chains." But their versions only serve to elaborate Young's basic insight into the warping pressure of the modern world upon the inborn sense of who we are.

It's hardly a paradox or even a coincidence that Young should say this at a time when many observers believed the world was getting immeasurably better. All over Europe it seemed, people were waking up from the nightmare of the past. The dead hand of previous thought and prejudice about the world would be thrown off the human mind by thinkers, scientists, and inventors who believed in rationality and progress. The entrepreneurs of early capitalism promoted manufacturing and mechanization, as more and more people were moving away from the almost exclusively rural world of the past to an urban experience that promised more variety, opportunity, and just plain more things to see and buy. With a population approaching a million by the end of the century, London became perhaps the biggest city in the world, its only rival Tokyo.

Edward Young emphasizes this inexorable weight of the past in his lines. The double-edged meaning of originality embodies the paradox: it could mean either going back to the roots, the origin of things, or doing something unprecedented, never before seen on earth. Harold Bloom has called the reaction of poets to this world the dilemma of *belatedness*. They have come too late to the world; everything worth doing has been done; and all they can do is scamper around the ankles of the giants who came before them. In order to free themselves from that triviality, Bloom argues that their only solution is to misread the past in order to create a space within which to define their own achievements. But the more common goal of many was to make the claim of being original, to do extraordinary things for the first time. Victor Frankenstein's desire to create something great and unprecedented, with only a superficial debt to the work of the past, fits neatly within this new world of aspiration.

I therefore would argue that the rise of the literature of horror and terror—and of popular fiction in general—during the time of the Industrial Revolution is not only because of an increased audience of literate readers or (as has been more invidiously argued) leisurely but unsophisticated women. More significantly, the literature of feeling promises a connection for both male and female readers to primitive sources of emotion that could serve as an antidote for the sense of personal anonymity that industrialization and new definitions of order had brought with them. Instead of supplying wisdom, popular fiction then and now stages fantasies of both power and subjugation in a kind of collective therapy that it also seeks to allay or even purge—at least until the next wave of anxiety appears.

The ghost comes from the invisible world to which the witch is often a bridge through her powers. The monster from nature by contrast is a tangible, visible being, sometimes seen as a wonder or a portent. They merge in the modern monster, who has aspects of physical presence as well as the invisible power of inducing terror. Mary Shelley's "creature" in *Frankenstein* (1816), begins a horror tradition of monsters that have adapted over the past two centuries to changing cultural, political, and scientific circumstances. The most important characteristic of these monsters is that they have been created on purpose. Whereas the gothic tales of Walpole, Lewis, and Radcliffe often deal with a supernatural or seemingly supernatural combat with diabolic forces, *Frankenstein* presents the monster as a nonreligious source of fear as well as a child of nature and a sympathetic figure. Like such earlier satiric spokesmen such as Swift's Gulliver, the monster supplies the perspective of an outsider on social norms, exposing their arbitrariness. Peering through his peephole at the De Lacey family, in his own version of a reality show, he tries his best to learn how to behave like a human, not because such behavior is natural but because it is learned.

The Creature in *Frankenstein* is the first in horror literature to be manmade, although there is some precedent in the stories about Roger Bacon, the thirteenth-century philosopher, who is often given credit as an originator of the scientific method. Bacon was reputed to have created a speaking bronze head that could answer any question, a legend that is the basis for *Friar Bacon and Friar Bungay*, a late-sixteenth-century play by Robert Greene.[1] Shelley's character is also the first to be explicitly and continually called a monster, although only by the characters, never by the author herself, when she speaks directly in her various prefaces. He calls himself a monster when he sees his face reflected in a pool of water, a scene that the movies, with their visual emphasis, exploit even further. But just as often he is called "the creature," that is, the created being. The earliest part of the novel that Shelley wrote is in fact the scene of the monster's creation, which begins the present chapter 5. If you come upon it after seeing the Boris Karloff version as well as many later ones, you will be disappointed; the apocalyptic chemistry-lab look exploited by film is more than a century away from the novel, and the moment of creation in the novel passes by almost unnoticed. Mirroring Walpole's account of the inspiration for *The Castle of Otranto,* Shelley describes in her 1831 introduction to the novel how the idea for the story came to her in a dream. This is an intriguing change from the 1817 preface, added one year after the original publication and probably written in great part by Percy Shelley, that stresses the scientific plausibility of the creation of the monster and insists that the novel, unlike the usual stories of ghosts and demons, was not "a mere tale of spectres and enchantments." Experimental science thus offers a way out of the dilemma of natural versus supernatural explanation. The religious may interpret the Lisbon earthquake as God's providence and the empiricists explain it on the basis of their embryonic seismological theories of caverns under the earth. But the creation of the Frankenstein monster draws upon a combination of the ambitions of the mystical medieval science Victor has otherwise put aside and the new science of electricity and galvanism he has been introduced to at Ingolstadt by Professor Waldman. With it, as he says, he will "unfold to the world the deepest mysteries of creation." Just as the coming of Christ promised to believers a victory over death, Victor would rummage among "vaults and charnel houses" for the dead human matter that he will animate and thereby "renew life where death had apparently devoted the body to corruption."[2]

Mary Shelley was not as fascinated with the new science of electricity as was her husband, so there is still a strong touch of the irrational in *Frankenstein,* although it derives not from religious faith so much as from a belief in the power of dreams. In her story of the created monster, the apocalyptic combat between good and evil so familiar to religious horror to a great extent disappears. Neither God, nor Satan, nor ghosts and witches make any substantial appearance in Shelley's novel. In Greene's play, Roger Bacon's abilities are aided by demons, but no such recourse to either the diabolic or the angelic worlds is present in Shelley's *Frankenstein.* When God enters into the language of Victor or the other characters, it is usually in the bland form of an everyday epithet. The rivalry with God as creator is certainly implicit in *Frankenstein,* but unlike the cliché movie invocations of the mad scientist's blasphemous rivalry with the divine, Victor Frankenstein calls directly upon neither God nor Satan as inspiration or competition for his work. Whereas religious horror deals with human characters like Ambrosio in *The Monk* or Faustus who turn from God to Satan, selling their souls for power, pleasure, or some other form of domination, there is also no pact with the devil in *Frankenstein.* It emphasizes instead the goal of making, exploiting the opportunities opened by science to control the processes of nature by defeating death. If anything, the basic competition is not with God but with Nature. While the Creature eavesdrops on the De Lacey family in order to understand human social life, he does compare himself to Satan (from his reading of Milton's *Paradise Lost*), but believes he is worse off, because while Satan in the poem is surrounded by companions, the Creature is "solitary and abhorred." Later in the story, Walton uses a satanic analogy to describe Victor: "What a glorious creature must he have been in the days of his prosperity, when he is thus so noble and godlike in his ruin!" As in the dualistic beliefs of the Manicheans, revived by the Lisbon earthquake, in this world God is distant at best; at worse he may be actively malevolent.

❦

Before looking more closely at the Frankenstein monster, we might pause to consider one of his kissing cousins, the golem.[3] By rights the golem should perhaps have made a figure in the previous chapter on the monster from nature. In the most famous origin story, instead of being created through science, he is made from the earth by Rabbi Loew of Prague. Molding the golem out of mud, the rabbi implants in him a piece of paper inscribed with an animating magical phrase (usually *emaet,* truth). In the 1921 German film of the story, Rabbi Loew also weaves an enchanted circle around the golem and invokes the demon Astaroth as part of the ritual. Unlike Victor Frankenstein in the novel, Rabbi Loew is not aspiring to individual greatness by his creation; he seeks to protect his people, the Jews of Prague, from an emperor who wants to expel or exterminate them. His purposes therefore are much more political than personal, and the golem in its turn is more of a warrior in the conflict than the Shelleyan evidence of an unprecedented ability to create life.

The tale of Rabbi Loew's creation of the golem, along with similar stories, is set in the sixteenth century. It is popularized in literature in the nineteenth century, at a time when Jewish emancipation was a current political issue. By the beginning of the twentieth century, the golem had become a frequent figure in fiction, poetry, and visual representations. The film that codified his image for the future was *The Golem, How He Came into the World* (1921), the third film of a trilogy (the earlier films now lost) that was co-written and co-directed by Paul Wegener. In the film, instead of the animating word being on his forehead or in his mouth, as in the legends, it is hidden under a metal boss in the center of his chest, whose visual descendants can be seen in the costume of the Iron Man series and the central circular power sources of the human-controlled metal giants of Guillermo del Toro's science-fiction film *Pacific Rim* (2013). In all of these, as in Wegener's *Golem* film, this metal core is the source of control as well as vulnerability. Intriguingly, just as Elsa Lanchester plays both Mary Shelley and the Bride of Frankenstein in the 1936 James Whale film, Wegener both helps create the film of the golem and plays the title character—a clue to the way in which creator and created in this variation of the monster story share something of the same aesthetic DNA.[4]

A substantial portion of the look of the Creature in James Whale's *Frankenstein* owes a greater debt to Wegener's golem than to the one Mary Shelley created. But the affinities and differences between the two are instructive in the evolution of this particular branch of terror and horror. Similar to the Creature of the movie, the golem is illiterate and unable to speak. He moves clumsily, and in his dress and demeanor seems to be a caricature of a country bumpkin, 1920s German style. At first, Rabbi Loew uses him as a servant, chopping wood and doing chores. In a comical scene, he marches off to the local grocery with a basket on his arm to present a shopping list to the terror-stricken proprietor. Then Rabbi Loew brings the golem to court at the summons of the emperor, where the golem is captivated by the attentions of the women and entranced by the flowers. There the rabbi presents a phantasmagoric show of Jewish history. Mayhem breaks loose when the show is mocked by members of the court and magical figures from the show cause the roof of the palace to come crashing down. Once the petrified emperor agrees to rescind the edict expelling the Jews, Rabbi Loew instructs the golem to hold up the roof and everyone is saved.

When the rabbi and the golem get back home, however, the golem seems to have developed a mind of his own. He threatens the rabbi, but the rabbi quickly pulls off the metal boss and grabs the animating paper, whereupon the golem falls to the floor, without life. Of course, the creature in *Frankenstein* has no such on-off switch. But some possibility like that will appear in many later versions of the created monster myth, most often in the human-machine amalgams of the android and the cyborg. Toward the end of the film, the golem, who has willfully caused a fire in the ghetto that Rabbi Loew has to use magic to snuff out, escapes from the ghetto and sees a group of children playing. In a moment reminiscent of the scene in *Frankenstein* the movie, in which the Creature unthinkingly tosses little Maria into the lake, the golem picks up a particularly beautiful little blonde girl. But this time, instead of becoming a victim, she innocently detaches his chest boss and he collapses again, no longer a threat.

There are two principal ways to understand the continuing appeal of the golem story once it is reintroduced at the beginning of the twentieth century. The first ties it firmly to the story of the Frankenstein monster: what is the relation of the created being to its creator? The golem is first of all a servant, to Rabbi Loew, strong, inarticulate, and there to be commanded. But every created being also has the potential to be another version of the creator, as well as a potential rebel against him. In the film we first see the rabbi scanning the heavens and reading in the stars the coming threat to the Jews. He creates a being from the earth to protect them, a doppelgänger in physical prowess to body forth his visionary insight. So quickly brought into being, however, the golem, like the Frankenstein monster, has much of the angry but innocent child about him. When this rage and desire to go his own way becomes apparent, the most immediate solution of the creator is to neutralize or destroy him.

The other major implication of both the golem and the Frankenstein story is the possibility of replicating such creatures in the hundreds and the thousands, creating armies of mass-produced monsters that will make human beings unnecessary. When Mary Shelley wrote, industrial production was still in its infancy, and the most familiar kind of machine-created beings that existed were unique ones like chess players, fortune tellers, birds that miraculously sang in their cages, and other clockwork masterpieces. Even so, Victor Frankenstein fears that if he gives the Creature the wife he longs for, they can possibly have children and "spawn a race of devils" that will destroy humans. Automata appear in other contexts during the same period, but once again they are usually the unique wonder machines of the eighteenth century, like Olympia, the "daughter" of Professor Spalanzani, with whom the hero Nathanael falls desperately in love in E. T. A. Hoffman's story "The Sandman" (1816). Olympia is a female automaton perfect in her beauty. After Nathanael discovers she is not real, many young men get "a detectable mistrust of the human form" and insist that "their young ladies should sing and dance in a less than perfect manner, that while being read to they should knit, sew, play with their puppy, and so on, and above all that they should not merely listen but sometimes speak too, and in such a way that what they said gave evidence of some real thinking and feeling behind it." Some hundred and fifty years later, in Ira Levin's *The Stepford Wives* (novel, 1972; film, 1975), suburban husbands have analogously turned their wives into seemingly human robots who are uniformly beautiful and submissive.

∾◌ฺ◌๛

Mary Shelley's father was William Godwin, the political philosopher and author of the novel *Caleb Williams* (1794), often considered the first mystery novel and a pervasive influence on Charles Brockden Brown's *Wieland* as well as the work of Edgar Allan Poe and Robert Louis Stevenson. Her mother,

Mary Wollstonecraft, the pioneering feminist and political radical, had died giving her birth. She met Percy Shelley when she was sixteen and he was twenty-one and married. Expelled from Oxford for his pamphlet *The Necessity of Atheism*, Shelley was an admirer of her father's ideas, and, not incidentally, became a financial supporter of the Godwin family. Mary and Percy duly fell in love. Godwin refused to give his consent to the relationship because of her youth. Escaping his command that they never see each other again, Percy and Mary ran off to the Continent. Mary's first pregnancy ended prematurely, with the baby dying after eleven days. By the spring of 1816, she had another baby, William, and was with Shelley in Paris, along with her stepsister Claire Clairmont (daughter of Godwin's second wife), who was recently the lover of Lord Byron and pregnant with his child. Complicated enough? By the summer of 1816 they had all set off for Lake Geneva to rendezvous with Byron. Byron himself had been married to Annabella Milbanke in January 1815. His daughter Augusta had been born in December, and in April 1816 Byron left England, never to return. He was twenty-eight. Also present during the Lake Geneva summer was Dr. John Polidori, Byron's personal physician, a twenty-one-year-old who had an advance from Byron's publisher to keep a journal of the poet's movements. In the long view of history, Polidori, who died at twenty-six, was also the only other one of the group whose dabbling in the supernatural would bear fruit, through a story titled "The Vampyre," with a main character based on Byron.

The summer of 1816 was one of the wettest and coldest on record since 1783, when the Laki volcano in Iceland erupted and covered Europe with a noxious fog that caused storms and bad weather everywhere. The same year there were also disastrous earthquakes in Calabria and Sicily, in which an estimated thirty thousand people died. But none of these natural disasters excited as much of a clash between religious and scientific reasoning as had the Lisbon earthquake of decades before.[5] In 1816 the culprit in the violent outbreaks of nature was an April 1815 volcanic eruption in Indonesia. Amid the bad weather, the Shelleys had a small cottage and so often spent time at the much grander Villa Diodati, which Byron had rented. One of their visitors was Matthew G. Lewis, the author of *The Monk*. It was there, one literally dark and stormy night, that the group famously set themselves a project to while away the time. After reading to each other German ghost stories, they each undertook to write one of their own. Mary's, of course, was *Frankenstein*. Rarely has an important cultural moment been so documented in the circumstances of its creation, and rarely has it come from such a confluence of significant cultural figures who were at least for a time friends and spent a summer together. From this happenstance moment came the first modern archetype of the monster to break away from the religion-based terrors of the past and create a whole new set of horrors suitable to the modern world. And as an intense moment of creativity among people with their own now-mythic relationships, it inspired three movies of the 1980s, Ken Russell's *Gothic* (1986), Ivan Passer's *Haunted Summer* (1988), and the Italian film *Remando al Viento* (Rowing with the Wind, 1988), with Hugh Grant as Byron.

FIRE FROM HEAVEN

From women's eyes this doctrine I derive:
They sparkle still the right Promethean fire;
They are the books, the arts, the academes,
That show, contain and nourish all the world.

—Shakespeare, *Love's Labor's Lost*

The subtitle of *Frankenstein* is *The New Prometheus.* Prometheus was one of the Titans, the parent gods whose children, Zeus and the Olympian gods, defeated. Like many characters of myth, different stories are told of him, although one common element is that he supported Zeus in the combat with the Titans but later was punished for his actions in support of humans by being chained to a rock in the Caucasus mountains, with an eagle every day eating his liver until, according to another variation of the story, he is released by Hercules. Betrayal by divine authority, even after he has supported it, is therefore one enduring theme of the Prometheus story. The earliest references to Prometheus in English emphasize his creation of humans out of the clay of the earth (like Adam and Eve as well as the monsters of earth) and giving them fire, which he has stolen from Zeus. By the Renaissance the fire had been variously interpreted as the divine spark of life as well as the human capacity for reason and knowledge, an obvious parallel with the punishment of Adam and Eve for eating of the Tree of Knowledge of Good and Evil, with Satan playing the Promethean role.[6]

The emphasis on making that is essential to the mode of the created monster naturally involves a metaphor of parenthood: If I have made you, what is my relation to you? What is my obligation to you? In addition to everything else that was going on in the tumultuous times of the later eighteenth century, the question of the proper education of children was being discussed more extensively than ever before. One prime source in the discussion was

Rousseau's *Émile, or, On Education* (1762), which Mary Shelley read in 1816, the same year she began writing *Frankenstein*.[7] Rousseau's polemical novel concentrates on the role of the parent or teacher in retaining and fostering the innate goodness of the child as he or she matures and enters what is frequently the corrupting influence of society. With the paternalistic authority of both the church and the state being challenged in the revolutionary period, the issue of the relation of generations becomes paramount. Whereas in religious horror the tyrannical parent may appear in a variety of religious and secular guises as an ogre bent on swallowing up children, in the tale of the created monster the creator is frequently a father whose creation desperately seeks recognition and love. In a reversal of the old analogy for justifying political and religious authority by invoking the structure of the family, *Frankenstein* thus begins a compelling theme of likening the horrors visited on the private world of the family to the tyrannies of the public world of political and religious authority. This theme of problematic parenthood, which Freud will later dub the oedipal, appears centrally in Shelley's novel, as evidenced by the customary use of the name Frankenstein for both the monster and the creator.

The figure of Prometheus—as rival with the overbearing and tyrannical gods, as shaper of human nature, as provider of the fire of aspiration and understanding—was also an obvious analogy to the new role for poets and poetry envisioned by the Romantics. And the connection to Satan was not unwelcome in the era's general politicizing of religious imagery. As William Blake had notoriously said, commenting on *Paradise Lost,* "The reason Milton wrote in fetters when he wrote of Angels & God, and at liberty when of Devils & Hell, is because he was a true Poet and of the Devil's party without knowing it!" In other words, by the late eighteenth century Satan's revolt against the overpowering authority of God could be interpreted in terms of the attacks on monarchical authority in the French and American revolutions, as well as the aspiration of poets, in Percy Shelley's words, to be "the unacknowledged legislators of the world."[8] Instead of being the principle of evil, Satan assumes the role of the Great Rebel, challenging the standards of society, revolting against illegitimate authority of all sorts, from fathers to kings to God himself. It was a natural association just waiting to be made, since so many monarchs had argued the divine right of kings, justifying their power as a gift from God like Adam's authority over Eve, and therefore to rebel against them was blasphemy. In addition, even when punished, sinning began to take on a grandeur and a fascination because it dares to step outside the conventions of unquestioning obedience. In this era, the enemy was less the old sinful Satan than the unjustified authority of actual human beings as well as God himself.

So too in the time of revolution, Mozart could revive the seventeenth-century figure of Don Giovanni, and Goethe the sixteenth-century figure of Faust, to explore what it meant to rebel, to assert one's individual nature in the face of despotism, embracing what you had been told is evil. So Mary Shelley in the 1831 introduction recounts one of the German stories translated into French that preoccupied the little group on the shores of Lake Geneva that stormy summer:

> [It was] the tale of the sinful founder of his race whose miserable doom it was to bestow the kiss of death on all the younger sons of his fated house, just when they reached the age of promise. His gigantic, shadowy form, clothed like the ghost in Hamlet, in complete armor, but with the beaver up, was seen at midnight, by the moon's fitful beams, to advance slowly along the gloomy avenue. . . . Eternal sorrow sat upon his face as he bent down and kissed the forehead of the boys, who from that hour withered like flowers snapped upon the stalk.[9]

Goya's painting of Saturn chewing on the body of one of his children is hardly any more graphic a representation of the murderous tyranny of fathers.

Such blasphemous rebellion against God is often a theme in horror. How often have we heard the mad scientist or someone nearby say, "We aren't meant to know these things." There is a shred of this attitude in Shelley's 1831 introduction as she describes the dream that inspired *Frankenstein:* "Frightful must it be, for supremely frightful would be the effect of any human endeavor to mock the stupendous mechanism of the Creator of the world." But surprisingly such a conflict again plays little explicit role in the original story. The universe is not particularly disrupted by the appearance of the created monster, in part because the themes of horror have shifted from the social community of religion to the much more intimate context of the individual and the family.

❧

At the beginning of James Whale's film *The Bride of Frankenstein* (1935), Percy Shelley, Mary Shelley, and Lord Byron are sitting in front of a fire in the villa on the shores of Lake Geneva. Byron is praising what Mary has written for its skin-crawling evocation of terror. Outside thunder and lightning split the sky, and Byron fancies that it is God himself who has brought the turbulent weather down to strike him personally: "I should like to think that an irate Jehovah was pointing those arrows of lightning directly at my head, the unbowed head of George Gordon, Lord Byron, England's greatest sinner." The specific lines are those of the scriptwriter William Hurlbut, but the sentiments accord well with the image that Byron and his audience, fans and detractors, had already created by the time he was with the Shelleys on Lake Geneva. Like the fictional Don Giovanni and Faust, the real-life Byron cultivated a persona of rebellion at the same time that he also presented himself as a wide-eyed naif in the world. A few years after the time on Lake Geneva, Byron began his epic satiric semi-biographical poem *Don Juan,* in which he makes the Don a young innocent, hungry for experience and frequently manipulated by those he meets.

This kind of protagonist, whether a morally ambiguous hero or a morally ambiguous villain, has been called the gothic hero and, in tribute to its real life counterpart, the Byronic hero, whose passionate nature revolts against social inhibitions of all sorts. Such a figure represents the separation of heroic prowess from any specifically moral code. It marks the beginning of the modern tradition of the anti-hero, which could include Heathcliff in Emily Brontë's *Wuthering Heights* (1847), with the romantic allure of his earthy name and his position outside the formal social system, down to tormented contemporary superheroes like Spiderman.[10] Sometimes such characters are imprisoned by circumstances, psychology, and (in the case of Ann Radcliffe's female protagonists) gender that are rendered imagistically by crypts, catacombs, ancient castles, or prisons. In the Byronic or gothic version, the character is usually powerful and charismatic but also agonized and gloomy—and invariably a man, a criminal with a sense of tremendous pride and guilt commingled. The connection of such a character's personal magnetism to criminality and even metaphysical evil may come from the belief that individualism itself is a sin against God, as well as against authority, legitimate or illegitimate. Byron in his poems favored heroes who were wanderers, outcasts, and solitaries, sometimes grand rebels, sometimes small figures in the immenseness of nature. Even if, like Byron, they were aristocrats by inheritance, they would rather be aristocrats of sensibility, at the top of the ladder of being rather than the social ladder. Mary Shelley takes such a figure in Victor Frankenstein and makes him a scientist who wishes to create a new race in his own image.

When Shelley was writing, the word *scientist* had not yet been familiarly used in English, and the predecessor term *sciencist* had itself only recently appeared. But the scientific disciplines Victor studies and then applies to his project of creating an eight-foot artificial human being are among the most advanced of the age. In the early seventeenth century Descartes had formulated his famous maxim, *cogito, ergo sum,* I think therefore I am, to characterize the difference between human nature and animal nature. Animals, he wrote, were *bêtes-machines,* beast-machines, who could not think and only responded mechanistically and instinctually to stimuli. It was acceptable therefore to experiment on them because their screams of pain were only mechanical responses and indicated no self, no *I am,* beneath the skin.[11] With the late seventeenth century, Robert Boyle and Isaac Newton saw no contradiction between what they were doing as "natural philosophers" and pious religious belief. Boyle even published a book late in life called *The Christian Virtuoso* (1690), in which he argued that belief in the regular workings of the universe, the laws of nature, was a mode of divine worship. By the eighteenth century, such a notion of a "clockwork" universe could be invoked as a reason *not* to believe in any need to postulate divine control of nature.

Even earlier, some scientists could already see the possible analogy between machines such as watches and human bodies, or as Boyle referred to them, "living Automata." By the eighteenth century, with an increasing knowledge of human physiology, the possibility that human beings from one point of view were machines was being explored in more detail, perhaps most concertedly in the philosopher-physician Julien Offray de la Mettrie's *L'Homme-Machine* (The Man-Machine, 1748). In that treatise La Mettrie argued the integral relation of mind and body rather than their separation and helped lay the theoretical groundwork for modern medicine. If the human could be mimed by the mechanical, then perhaps human beings themselves had mechanical aspects. That Victor Frankenstein can piece together human body parts to create his monster follows in La Mettrie's wake. When natural philosophers began to be called scientists, the concept of God as the great designer of the natural world was in for some human competition.[12]

MESMERIZERS AND MEDIUMS

I sing the body electric.

—Walt Whitman, *Song of Myself* (1855)

But even if there is a mechanical relation between the parts of the body, how can inert parts be made to work together? La Mettrie defined the relation between body parts as *rapports,* connections, a somewhat vague term. A few

years later, however, Benjamin Franklin made not the first but the most famous experiment to discover the existence of a force that was quickly defined
as the animating connection within individual bodies and in the natural
world generally—electricity. As Patricia Fara has shown in her admirable con-
cise history, electricity swiftly became considered "the greatest scientific invention of the Enlightenment."[13] In the same way that Victor Frankenstein
leaves behind the vague and visionary science of the Middle Ages when he
hears the lectures of Dr. Waldman at Ingolstadt, serious experimenters and
amateur dabblers alike embraced electricity as both scientific wonder and
extravagant entertainment. Percy Shelley was one enthusiast among many,
proposing electrical kites (à la Franklin) "to draw down the lightning from
heaven!"[14] It was a spectacular image that was elaborated visually in the creation scene of *The Bride of Frankenstein* more than a century later. Serious
investigators as well as charlatans flocked in with apparatuses designed to explore electricity further and reap riches from amazed crowds. The line between the gathering of new scientific knowledge and the pleasures of entertainment was ambiguous; wonder had not quite given way to learning, and in
some places, like the high school chemistry lab, with its volcanos of ammo-
nium dichromate and its moons of yellow phosphorous, it still hasn't.

   Experimenters like Franklin and Joseph Priestley were hailed as new versions of Prometheus, not only because they were capturing fire from heaven,
but also because it was a revolutionary period and Prometheus represented
the spirit of liberty, human consciousness revolting against the suffocating
hand of the past, of monarchy, or of paternal power—whatever interpretation
suited you best. Electricity came out of nature, and its harnessing illustrated
how the experimenters themselves were reaching beyond the confines of human society to tap into primal forces unindebted to tradition, family, and
anything else that could limit the human spirit.[15]

   The search to understand the nature of electricity was, like Newton's discovery of gravity, or the almost simultaneous discovery of oxygen by Scheele,
Priestley, and Lavoisier, an effort to establish mathematical formulas or even
invariable laws for forces that were otherwise invisible to ordinary human
perception. In none of these postulations of the invisible connections of
the world was there any need to invoke the presence of God. To the extent
that God made an appearance in such explanations, it was not the high
God of the heavens but the God of nature, not the transcendent order but
immediate material circumstances. Instead of believing, as James I did, that
witches could summon up storms to sink the ships of their enemies, this was

a different view of the connection of the human mind to the nature of things. Unlike Aquinas codifying Christian theology, Newton and Darwin showed the invisible links below the surface of the natural world, and Adam Smith in *The Wealth of Nations* (1776) postulated "the invisible hand" that allowed market economies to work efficiently without the need for an external designer. Unlike earlier theological guidelines for discovering who was a witch or an acolyte of the devil, which often varied depending on circumstances, the new scientific laws were meant to be universally verifiable. Yet in terms of their emotional resonance they satisfied similar purposes—to push human understanding beyond the visible to understand the hidden order of things.

There is no need at this point to go into such scientific leaps forward as Michael Faraday's 1831 demonstration of the relation between magnetism and electricity (in the same year as Mary Shelley's new preface to *Frankenstein*) or James Clerk Maxwell's 1855 paper elaborating and formularizing their connection. These are issues suitable to the history of science, but their significance for this book is how quickly science became seized upon as a metaphor for whatever one believed about the future.

Because a central element of the scientific controversies over electricity was the question of whether human life itself was essentially electrical, the relevance of these newly harnessed forces to the human body was obvious. Magnetism, which had a much longer history in the advance of science, going back to Aristotle and earlier, had often been harnessed for medicinal purposes. Electricity augured to be even more potentially therapeutic, and the discovery of galvanic responses promised not just a cure of ills and enhancement of life for the living but even a reanimation of the dead. The entrepreneurial and pioneering sexologist James Graham learned about Franklin's experiments with electricity on a visit to Philadelphia. Returning to England, he devised various beneficial treatments using electricity that culminated in the "Celestial Bed" at his Temple of Hymen in London's Pall Mall, where he promised eager couples that electricity would replenish "full-toned juvenile virility."[16]

The most popular effort to utilize new scientific knowledge for therapeutic purposes was mesmerism. In 1779 the German physician Franz Anton Mesmer published in French his *Memoir on the Discovery of Animal Magnetism*. For a few years previously Mesmer, who was an early patron of the young Mozart, had attempted and often achieved cures of patients in Germany and Austria, first using actual magnets, and later what he called his own animal magnetism to unlock the barriers in the body to health.[17] His cures were based on the idea that there is an invisible vital fluid that connects every-thing in the world and that magnetism was the way to tap into it. As he states in his first proposition of animal magnetism, "There exists a mutual influence between the celestial bodies, the earth and bodies that are animated" (*les corps animés*). In place of the view in earlier centuries that the world was filled with invisible spirits, usually demons but sometimes angels, mesmerism was an eighteenth-century version of what would now be called a theory of every-thing. It attempted with magnetism, as Newton did with gravity, to under-stand a wide range of phenomena through one simple formula. In a revolutionary age, it was an idea that attracted thinkers and laymen of all sorts. As Immanuel Kant phrased the sentiment in his philosophic effort to separate morality from religion and reformulate it as innate in human nature, "Two things fill the mind with ever new and increasing admiration and awe, the more often and more steadily we reflect on them: the starry sky above me and the moral law within me" (*Critique of Practical Reason,* 1788).

Mesmer's animal magnetism also shared one striking characteristic with Newton's gravity as well as with Lavoisier and Priestley's oxygen: it was invis-ible to the naked eye. Instead of an earlier spiritual world filled with demons, natural philosophers were discovering something of the invisible structure of nature. Newton, Lavoisier, and Priestley, of course, sought to bring their in-visible substances into tangibility through quantifiable experiments.[18] But Mesmer's procedure was more personal and affective than it was either math-ematical on the one hand or theological on the other. Polemically asserting the novelty and superiority of his method, he had clashed with an exorcist-priest whose cures he argued were due less to religious doctrines than to the priest's personal animal magnetism. In trouble with the medical powers that be in Vienna, Mesmer moved to Paris, where he met with instant and wide-spread success that made his doctrine known around France. Despite attacks there by the medical establishment, mesmerism, if not Mesmer himself, at-tracted enough acolytes and believers that it existed as a therapy well into the nineteenth century, when it became indistinguishable from other forms of alternate healing.[19]

Mesmeric doctrine asserted that sickness occurred when the invisible fluid whose free passage created health had somehow been disrupted. Instead of demons or even bodily humors as the cause of the disruption, mesmerism explicitly invoked the powers of the mind, both the patient's and the doctor's, to effect the cure. In a sense it was a forerunner of what we call the placebo effect or, as it was later termed, hypnosis, which is what the term *mesmerism* tends to mean today. Later in the nineteenth century, the pioneering neurologist Jean-Martin Charcot developed techniques of using hypnosis to help treat hysterical paralysis and some other mental diseases, especially in women but also in men, while they were in mesmeric trances. The young Sigmund Freud studied with Charcot in the late 1880s and, although he later developed an account of hysteria that differed from Charcot's, was deeply impressed by Charcot's insight that a hysteric response could be traced to a traumatic incident in the past—a crucial component of psychoanalysis.[20]

Mesmerism was a pervasive fad in Europe in the decades before the French Revolution and continued its attraction well into the nineteenth century, as it spread to England and the United States. In times of general political and social upheaval and disruption, people are often attracted to someone who claims to have a clear (and therapeutic) vision of some simple underlying truth. Mesmer himself was only one of the most successful of an array of supposed healers who gathered eager patients to them. Witches may have been disappearing throughout the eighteenth century as a threat to Christianity, Protestant as well as Catholic. But in their wake came a host of sincere or deceptive practitioners of the invisible arts—pseudoscientists, phrenologists, physiognomists, alchemists, formulators of patent medicines—who served a similar function in a world where science had become a fad in itself. Often they seemed to effect miraculous cures, most dramatically in the area of hysterical paralysis. At a time when much conventional medicine relied on purges and bloodletting, the idea of a gentle cure that claimed to involve the latest scientific discoveries was a comparatively easy sell, for those who had the money to pay for it. In an age of revolution against authority, it was an extra attraction that these cures were not only linked to the new science but also were hotly opposed by more traditional physicians protecting their time-honored rights. Like the concept of liberty, the new science aspired to help create the healthy society as well as the healthy individual.

❧

In the name of science or pseudoscience, many of these new therapies based on electricity and magnetism crossed and recrossed the line between life and death. Luigi Galvani's nephew Giovanni Aldini went perhaps the furthest in this direction by attempting to electrically animate a dead murderer in 1803. *Frankenstein* is thus a characteristic product of its era in the way it emphasizes something of the connection to the invisible world that had been the province of religion, but now with science as the method of understanding rather than theology and belief. "What is life?" was the basic question. What distinguishes it from death, and where is its essence? Instead of focusing on the soul as that vital spirit that survives after death, such studies emphasized the search for the essential spark of life. And those states that seemed ambiguously situated between life and death attracted special attention—suspended animation, the catalepsy that fascinated Edgar Allan Poe in "The Fall of the House of Usher," and somnambulism, about which Dr. Polidori, one of Mary Shelley's companions at Geneva, wrote his doctoral dissertation. While the original meaning of somnambulism referred specifically to sleepwalking, its trance state was also connected to clairvoyance and an ability to see beyond the veils of everyday life, which increasingly began to include a medium's use of a mesmeric or somnambulistic trance to converse with the dead. In a medical context, this shadowland between the living and the dead had somewhat grimmer potential. The physical state of catalepsy so resembled actual death that mistakes could easily be made, as they are (perhaps on purpose) by Roderick Usher. Considering the uncertain state of medical knowledge, many of the more nervous and apprehensive during the nineteenth century hedged their bets against premature burial by installing a wire in their coffins attached to a bell above ground, just in case. As technology improved, the bell was sometimes replaced by a telephone. But it remained an open question whether the increase in medical knowledge dissipated the fear of death or intensified it.[21]

In the course of the nineteenth century the somewhat inchoate movement referred to as Spiritualism redefined the trance state even more specifically as a way to contact the dead and access their wisdom. The "Borderland" was what spiritualists called the realm where the living and the dead could communicate, and often the vehicle of that communication was a woman, sometimes veiled and seated, sometimes dressed fashionably and dancing, but always in a trance. That so many of these performers and mediums were women implies that an ability to make contact with the spirit world was connected to a social marginality in the world of the living. In the era of witch hunting, women were often considered vulnerable to the appeal of Satan and dark forces because of their supposed naïveté, emotionality, and physical weakness. As the image of the female changed in the nineteenth century into the morally purer sex, so the relation to the invisible world changed as well. Intriguingly, in the same year, 1848, that the three Fox sisters in upstate New York started the craze for contacting the dead through table-rapping, the first women's rights convention at Seneca Falls composed the Declaration of

Sentiments and Rights at a table previously used to consult the spirit world. Scientists got into the act as well. Later in the century Thomas Edison even worked on an electrical "valve" that could allow connection to the dead.[22]

At the heart of the spiritual performance was the personal ability of the somnambule to contact God or Jesus or the dead in a manner akin to the desire of more emotionally oriented religious doctrines to circumvent a religious hierarchy and assert a direct relation to the divine. In a sense Spiritualism was a kind of anti-religion, taking over the prerogatives of contact with the spirit world and the dead but without either the organization or the moralizing of traditional religion. After the enormous number of deaths in the American Civil War, the spiritualist belief that contacting the dead was possible became an even more widespread phenomenon, just as it would in England during and after World War I. As the historian Amy Lehman has pointed out, there was an overwhelming element of theatricality in those performances, whether they were the table-rapping séances begun by the Fox sisters, the speaking in tongues by Elizabeth O'Key in England, or the contacts with spirit guides like Anna Cora Mowatt's "Gypsy" and Cora Richmond's Indian woman Ouina. Some performers would bring on a whole cast of different spirit characters, famous and unknown, male and female, old and young, of all ethnicities.[23] In such performances, as in séances, the idea was that the mesmerized performer or the medium was a vessel for the spirits, a physical container for the immaterial soul. All of these efforts, whether scientific or pseudoscientific, recall past attempts to find the physical site of the soul—the intersection of the material and the spiritual worlds. In the Midrash, the Jewish collection of biblical exegesis, is the story of the *luz,* the soul bone in the spine, from which the individual would be reconstituted at Judgment Day. In the same way, Descartes decided that the soul resided in the pineal gland, and various attempts were made during the nineteenth and early twentieth centuries to isolate and weigh the soul. But in the 1870s and later, when mediums claimed to materialize the spirit world separately from themselves as ectoplasm, greater skepticism often resulted.[24]

MAGNETISM AND CHARISMA

Victor Frankenstein specifically tells Walton that "my father had taken the greatest precautions that my mind should be impressed with no supernatural horrors. I do not ever remember to have trembled at a tale of superstition or to have feared the apparition of a spirit." Yet the study required for his own effort to bestow "animation upon lifeless matter" he calls "an almost supernatural enthusiasm." Thinking he is free of the supernatural, he therefore becomes enmeshed in it. Instead of religious horror, the horror he will experience is social, familial, and psychological. No longer required to live in the shadow of the God or a monarch at the top of the human hierarchy, Victor aims to seize his own unique place. Just as the Faustian bargain with the devil in Goethe's rendition had changed from gaining mere magical powers to a search for a transcendent knowledge unparalleled on earth, for Victor the desire for personal immortality has replaced the desire for heaven. The Christian afterlife is thus displaced by a more modern goal—the desire for fame, a trap especially for a scholar and seeker for knowledge like Faust or for Victor Frankenstein, who through his researches wants to bring into being "a new species [that] would bless me as its creator and source." "Where do I fit into the divine plan?" has been replaced by "What should I do to be remembered forever?"

Such ambitions correspond to another popular meaning of animal magnetism—and for which Mesmer was criticized early on—the attractiveness, often with a sexual overtone, that a person can have to others in private life. Released by the new discoveries in electrical and magnetic science, as well as by the revolutionary anti-authoritarian ardor of his era, the supernatural is in Victor himself rather than in the paraphernalia and dramatis personae of gothic horror. Although the name appears nowhere in *Frankenstein,* it is therefore unmistakable how much Victor's singular aspirations to become the creator of a new race also reflect the ambitions of the early nineteenth century's supreme "man of destiny"—Napoleon.

Since the time of the gothic, horror in the West has often been focused on misguided but unlimited ambition, whether it is Ambrosio's urge to be pure and holy in *The Monk* or Victor's to create a new race in *Frankenstein.* What has set the stage for writers and artists to try to explore these diabolic ambitions? In some versions, it is explicitly a combat with God, but it is also in part the feeling in a tumultuous age that God has left the world, or perhaps he was never really in it. Another important influence on these ideas was the French philosopher and historian Comte de Volney, who took his title from a contraction of "Voltaire" and "Ferney," the town in Switzerland where Voltaire spent the last twenty years of his life. Volney's most famous work was *The Ruins of Empire,* in whose English translation Thomas Jefferson played a part and in which Volney argued the political importance of enlightened self-interest. Behind that argument was the assumption that because God has left the world behind, and in effect abandoned us, we must create for ourselves.

Formed naked in body and in mind, man at first found himself thrown, as it were by chance, on a rough and savage land: an orphan, abandoned by the unknown power which had produced him.

Gradually humans then learned to use their environment and expand their abilities until they could proclaim, "It is I who have produced the comforts which surround me; it is I who is the author of my own happiness." But within this self-creation there is always something that undermines the triumph:

> Yes, creative man, receive my homage! Thou hast measured the span of the heavens, calculated the volume of the stars, arrested the lightning in its clouds, subdued seas and storms, subjected all the elements. Ah! How are so many sublime energies allied to so many errors?[25]

Later that summer of 1816, inspired by the highest mountain in Europe, Percy Shelley wrote "Mont Blanc," a poem he described as "a meditation on the nature of power in a Godless universe." The universe may have been without God, but it did have Satan, or at least a satanic figure, an embodiment of distorted human aspiration, to be abhorred but also to invoke sympathy, like the hero-villain of the gothic, or its earthly personification in the charismatic Lord Byron. It was an image of a new kind of public figure that fascinated millions in its mixture of the appalling and the alluring. Recoiling from being like these poets in reality, their audiences desired to be like them in feeling. As Matthew Arnold wrote of Byron after his death,

> What helps it now, that Byron bore,
> With haughty scorn which mock'd the smart,
> Through Europe to the Ætolian shore
> The pageant of his bleeding heart?
> That thousands counted every groan,
> And Europe made his woe her own?

> ("Stanzas from the Grand Chartreuse")

In a world increasingly connected by words and images, it was the beginning of a new age of celebrity, in which fame on earth became a more enticing goal than justification in heaven. Audiences thrilled to the exploits of people they never met, living their own lives in part through these doppelgängers of the self.

Mesmeric healing took place generally in private. In public life, by contrast, animal magnetism was connected to the new political world of popular leaders and adoring admirers through charisma. Originally a religious word signifying anointing, charisma did not itself become secularized until the writing of the sociologist Max Weber in the twentieth century. But in the latter half of the eighteenth century and the beginning of the nineteenth, such figures newly abounded on the international scene: Napoleon, George Washington, Lord Byron. The new brand of charisma possessed by non-royal beings might also be connected to gothic and romantic attitudes, as well as to the emphasis on affective as opposed to rational religion. It was a style of supposedly unconditioned self-creation that would have later political descendants like Nietzsche's idea of the Superman and Ayn Rand's Objectivism.

The name of George du Maurier's character Svengali in his novel *Trilby* (1895) has become the general term for one version of that charismatic animal magnetism. Under the strong metaphoric influence of mesmerism, in the course of the nineteenth century the depiction of the charismatic person (like Byron) who frequently looked away from an audience, gazing into an otherwise invisible future, was transformed into a direct hypnotic appeal. In addition to being an essential aspect of the power enjoyed by Dracula in Bram Stoker's novel (1897), whose mesmeric gaze enthralls his victims, such a look is also characteristic of the matinee idol's and later the movie star's power over an audience. The theatrical connection is hardly coincidental. Bram Stoker was business manager for the Lyceum Theatre in London, which was owned by Sir Henry Irving, a famous actor of the day, on whom Dracula was to a certain extent modeled. Sir Herbert Beerbohm Tree, his main rival as a leading man, played Svengali on stage, and later John Barrymore, the stage and film actor, played Svengali in film (as well as Dr. Jekyll and Mr. Hyde and Sherlock Holmes). This tradition of the monster that lies beneath the guise of the handsome and alluring leading man continues throughout the twentieth century, including such figures as the Draculas of Bela Lugosi, Christopher Lee, and so many more.[26]

FIRST-PERSON SINGULAR

After the devastating seventeenth-century wars of religion, the Enlightenment brought with it the sense that reason, dispensing with the invisible world entirely, may be a way out of conflict. But in response to her husband's vision that poets and men of sensibility were the unacknowledged legislators of the world, Mary Shelley separated horror from religion, connecting it instead to unlimited aspiration, diseased reason, and obsession. No wonder then the dividedness of Victor Frankenstein, who is simultaneously creator and created, and whose creation itself seeks revenge for being born. I have mentioned the virtual obliteration of any religious context from *Frankenstein*. But in the novel Shelley also decisively changes many other associated aspects of the tale of terror.

The satanic here is the search for a powerful kind of knowledge, the hero as maker, originator, and self-originator, unindebted to any past, intent only on the glorious future, who seeks to know and thereby command the basic principles of life. The act of creation is thus linked to the desire for an absolute originality: the pride of being unique, unprecedented, and uncaused by anything that happened before you arrived on the scene. Unlike most of the mad scientists who follow in his footsteps, Victor Frankenstein at least is neither explicitly impotent nor looking to the monster to supply some lack in his psyche. His focus is entirely on the great work he wants to achieve. The urge to such an absolute originality enflames Victor Frankenstein. It is a desire to affirm one's unique identity that is familiar in the young. In an age when monarchs and father figures of many sorts were being overthrown, it became a characteristic of everyone who was trying to make a mark. By now that same urge has become so commonplace that when we read or see *Frankenstein,* it is easier to notice the monster than the monstrous assertions of his creator.

Even more specific to *Frankenstein* is the fact that this is a novel written by a woman about the relations between men, and in particular about the hero's desire to achieve male parthenogenesis—to produce life without the need for a woman or a female principle. Shelley does not create another fearful heroine like those so familiar from the novels of Ann Radcliffe. Instead she focuses on a male protagonist who seeks to create a version of himself. Considering that her own mother died in giving birth to her, the fact that the first scene she writes is that of the creature's creation carries a heavy emotional weight as well, as does the novel's critique of the male urge to self-sufficiency, Victor's "frightful selfishness." *Frankenstein* in this way constitutes a critique of a solipsistic male individualism that uses the methods of science and technology to pave its way to glory. "I will be with you on your wedding night," says the Creature to Victor, for why should Victor need a wedding when he already has a child?

That act of creation is finally more difficult psychologically than Victor is prepared for. By eliminating the feminine from the process of creation, Victor undermines his own chances for any relation to Elizabeth Lavenza, whom the Creature kills as a rival for Victor's affections. The 1931 film interestingly underlines the sexual displacement by renaming Victor as Henry, implying he is no longer a "victor" in his search. At the end of the film, while Henry is recovering from his fall off the burning windmill where the Creature has seemingly died, his father the Baron waits outside the door, having a drink with a cooing covey of maids—even in his age and decrepitude seemingly a more potent figure than Henry inside on the bed. In an intriguing change, heterosexual marriage is thwarted in the novel, but somehow wins out in the film, although very feebly.

The classic 1931 film of *Frankenstein* also illustrates the other ways the movies with their intense visualization have changed the terms of Mary Shelley's novel to convey the image of the created monster to the twentieth century. Many similarities remain. Both the monster of the novel and the monster played by Boris Karloff are lovers of nature. Their reactions to the world are immediate and unpremeditated, like those of a child, and they long, above all, to be accepted, even loved, by their creators. Like Wordsworth's child "trailing clouds of glory," their innocence exposes the corruptions and compromises of normal society and adulthood, where the only compensation for the world they have lost is the embrace of what the Victor calls "maternal nature," which even in the deepest depression fills him with a "sublime ecstasy."

The dissimilarities between novel and film are many, and a good number of them reflect the difference between the time when the novel was written and the era of the film. In the novel we have a monster who reads and appreciates classics of literature, learns to speak, and is articulate enough to have six chapters devoted to his telling of his own story. Science may have brought him into being, but it is literature that nurtures and humanizes him. In the film, by contrast, we find a monster who is inarticulate and speaks primarily in grunts, only able by the time of *The Bride of Frankenstein* to manage a few words, thanks to the tutelage of the blind violinist. In the novel the monster is incredibly agile, running like the wind. In the film the monster stumbles around almost inflexibly, Karloff being outfitted with an iron rod down his back, metal leg braces, and twelve-and-a-half-pound asphalt boots, making up forty-eight pounds of costume in all. In the novel the monster, although his look does repel those he first encounters, can still trail his creator from Europe to England and Scotland without being noticed. In the film the monster is so obviously out of the ordinary that he is immediately recognized and people run away in horror. In the novel the monster has a plan and a clear agenda. For the most part he is in control of his environment and many of the people in it, as he vows revenge on his creator. In the film he may have physical power and be frightening, but he is otherwise manipulated by virtually all he comes into contact with.

To a certain extent many of these differences stem from transferring the story from a verbal to a visual medium that dictates making monstrousness more obvious. In the final chapter I discuss the particularly tight fit of the technology of the movies with such traditional monsters as Shelley's creature, Dracula, and Mr. Hyde. But for the moment the many contrasts between the novel of *Frankenstein* and James Whale's film illustrate the effect of reimagining the story in images as well as words. Whale was an English film and theater director who had been an officer and then a German prisoner of war during World War I, experiences that seem to have influenced the blasted trees and bleak horizons of his *Frankenstein* as well perhaps as enhanced the story's theme of an unleashed technology that creates horror rather than well-being. Other parts of the story are affected by both the medium of film as well as the changing times. Victor in the novel, for example, may think the monster has eyes that look dead, but at least he doesn't have bolts sticking out of his neck. Another factor in 1931 that was not present in 1819 is the Great Depression. *Frankenstein* the novel could be called elegant horror, but the monster of the movie is cheap-suit horror, the contrast with the rest of the cast of characters emphasized still further by promoting Henry's father to the lower ranks of the nobility. The monster therefore could at least subliminally be recognized by the 1931 audience as a representative of the thousands of out-of-work men who haunted the cities and countryside of America, at once a cause of compassion but also extreme fear. Also connected to the period is the monster's inability to master language, which reflects the moment in movie history when silent films were giving way to sound. Like a refugee from a silent movie, he represents a more primitive, less civilized form, but also like a silent movie he may symbolize an earlier stage of growth, again like a child, for which there is some nostalgia and sympathy. In this light another change from the novel to the film, the greater emphasis on the context of Christianity—instead of being entirely about the combat between the scientist and God—also helps characterize the monster (especially in *The Bride of Frankenstein*) as a hapless, even Christ-like victim of mob prejudice.

~∽◎∿~

Do you think I am an automaton?—a machine without feelings? and can bear to have my morsel of bread snatched from my lips, and my drop of living water dashed from my cup? Do you think, because I am poor, obscure, plain, and little, I am soulless and heartless?

—Charlotte Brontë, *Jane Eyre*

What accounts for the longevity of the Frankenstein story? Its essential themes and plot turns have proved to be tremendously adaptable over two centuries, and the fears it arouses continue to have currency. The terrors of *The Monk* seem fairly distant. The tyranny of Catholic monks and nuns or families that force daughters into convents, or ghosts called the Bleeding Nun or the Wandering Jew seem old-fashioned. When such staples of religious fear are revived in films, there is usually an atmosphere of exaggeration verging on campiness. Even the appearance of Satan as an evil principle has a somewhat archaic feel to it. Because these elements have such a specific religious history to them, they seem more fixed and not as susceptible to metamorphosis as the Frankenstein story.

I've mentioned our greater familiarity with organ transplanting and cloning, along with the implication of the increasingly robotic side of medicine that our bodies are basically an assemblage of parts, as well as susceptible to medical mistakes, such as artificial hips and knees put into the wrong limb. Mary Shelley doesn't specify whose body parts Victor used to create the Creature. But later versions of *Frankenstein* or its kindred eagerly supply the criminal brain or a killer's hands. *Donovan's Brain* (novel, 1942; film, 1953), for example, features the disembodied brain of an autocratic millionaire that gradually assumes power over the scientist that has preserved it, while in *The Hands of Orlac,* a short story that spawned several films, the damaged hands of a pianist are replaced by those of a murderer. In Georges Franju's *Les Yeux sans Visage* (Eyes Without a Face), a more compassionate version of similar motifs, a physician father whose daughter has become unbearably disfigured in a car accident tries to graft on the faces of young women he has lured to his laboratory. As the basic idea of detachable human parts put together in new configurations expands from its origins, such baroque variations appear as the transplanting of the head of a rich dying racist (Ray Milland) onto the body (with head) of a black death-row inmate (Rosey Grier) in *The Thing with Two Heads* (1972), or the transplanting of the heart of a lawyer who defended drug dealers (Denzel Washington) into the detective who hated him (Bob Hoskins) in *Heart Condition* (1990). Such gruesome images, like the parts put together to create Frankenstein's monster, stir feelings of horror by the way they violate any conventional notions of bodily integrity. Simultaneously they draw upon the same urge that in the past drew people to public executions and auto-da-fés. In our own time it has created vogues for slasher and torture porn movies that feature gory dismemberment, decapitations, and castration.[27]

Once a single story has spawned a whole genre of stories, its continuing history responds to outside influences as well as internal logic, allowing new possibilities that can expand the story's meaning and its emotional impact. When Victor Frankenstein says that he wants to create a more perfect human race, these are lines that sound differently after what we know about the theory and practice of eugenics, the rise of Hitler, Nazi racial theories, and the Holocaust. By essentially rewriting Genesis, Shelley's story stands behind so many fears and hopes, horrors and achievements, of the modern world.

Mary Shelley's creature is a unique creation. But with the expansion of factories and industrial production, the resemblance between people and machines, as well as the possibility that machines might multiply, becomes a more widespread fear. In Dickens's *Hard Times* (1854), the workers in the mill are referred to as "Hands" by their employers, effectively reducing them to one body part. With the twentieth century, that fear of dehumanization expanded still further, as a more complex industrialization and totalitarianism threatened to turn individuals into pseudo-robots.

In 1921, the same year *The Golem* appeared, Karel Čapek's play *R.U.R.* made its debut, popularizing the word *robot* to describe the mechanical beings who in the play are at first the servants of the humans, but then take over and exterminate the human race. *Robot* is connected to the Czech word for work and in one of its forms was used to describe the labor done by peasants for their overlords. *R.U.R.*, which stands for Rossum's Universal Robots, thus embodies a vision of a mechanical future in which work is done by human-like machines that gradually gain a consciousness of their oppression and then revolt. With the Russian Revolution only a few years in the past, this vision seems as much indebted to current history as to the nascent genre of science fiction. The *Frankenstein* theme of a kind of child who seeks reparation from a detached and indifferent father thus also mirrors intriguingly the revolt against the "little father," Tsar Nicholas II. The twentieth-century world of the revolt of the masses had arrived to merge with the advancing machine civilization to initiate the fearsome possibility of servants rebelling against masters to be free as well as to take revenge for their servitude.

Mass society, whether under communism or capitalism, was bringing with it yet another possible way of understanding the Frankenstein story. This time, instead of the unique eighteenth-century machines of wonder on which La Mettrie modeled his *Man-Machine,* the new machines were the product of interchangeable parts and the assembly-line production methods being pioneered by Henry Ford and others. In Fritz Lang's *Metropolis* (1926), the ruler of the city of the future wants to do away with the human workers and replace them all with robots. To that end he has a robot created to resemble Maria, a female preacher beloved by the workers, which in its turn will incite them to a revolt that can be brutally repressed. The end of *Metropolis* is a little more upbeat than *R. U. R.* The son of the ruler of Metropolis, who has descended to understand the workers' lives and fallen in love with the preacher, brings his father (the Head) together with the leader of the workers (the Hand) through his own role as the Heart, recreating Metropolis as a gigantic Frankenstein-like human body.[28]

As *Metropolis* and so many other films suggest, the crucial issue of the modern age is still the Frankenstein question of to what extent the human and the machine harmonize and to what extent they conflict. These "monsters" are not like the seemingly monstrous villains of the James Bond films, almost every single one of whom wants to rule the world through controlling some technology or another—weapons, communications, and such. Rather, these monsters are technological wonders, tributes to human ingenuity, but with the added burden of self-awareness and the need to develop the less mechanistic aspects of identity. The basic question is less whether such creatures have a soul as whether they can feel. Even in such mega-machine epics as the series of comic books and films of the *Transformer* series, the machines have different degrees of emotional connection. All varieties are possible. There are friendly robots, such as the petlike R2-D2 and the humanoid C-3PO of the *Star Wars* series. By contrast, the computer HAL in *2001* is a robot whose only human characteristic is a voice whose power over the spaceship overrides the commands of the human being to whom he is supposedly subordinate. Transformations are possible as well. The implacable cyborg in *The Terminator* becomes the sympathetic and self-sacrificing cyborg of *Terminator 2.* The replicants of *Blade Runner* turn out to be the most emotionally sensitive characters in the film and, in a frequent twist, we discover that the human hero is actually one of them, another hidden affinity between the hunter and the hunted, like that between Victor and the Creature. In the stories of replicants and cyborgs, where the human side is more apparent, the clash between the human and the nonhuman, the natural and the purposeful creation, is usually a central issue of the plot.[29]

These characterizations are often influenced by the Three Laws of Robotics, which began to be formulated by the science fiction writer Isaac Asimov in his stories of the late 1930s and early 1940s:

1. A robot may not injure a human being or, through inaction, allow a human being to come to harm.
2. A robot must obey the orders given to it by human beings, except where such orders would conflict with the First Law.
3. A robot must protect its own existence as long as such protection does not conflict with the First or Second Law.

Some of the themes of horror shade into science fiction here. It is almost always an apocalyptic and futuristic landscape in which these hybrid monsters appear, because the problematic connection between the near human and the mechanical in them mirrors fears about our own mechanical nature in a technologically enhanced future, a theme, for example, that particularly runs through the films of David Cronenberg. This type of horror thus battens on advances in technology and science: the new knowledge that seems to look toward the future and to free us from the burdens of the past may also be what will destroy us.

In many such stories a central issue is memory—implanted in *Blade Runner*, fragmentary in *Robocop*—for memory as well as the continuous presence through time of one's body are keys to identity: are you human or inhuman? Robots and created monsters generally are born fully formed. If they have a memory of being young, they are on the way to resembling a human, self-conscious and self-aware. In the same spirit Victor Frankenstein tells his story to Walton and the Creature tells his own story so that they will be remembered. With every advance in knowledge, it seems, the fear of losing our originality and turning into copies voiced by Edward Young centuries ago becomes more and more pervasive. We have long known we are made up of genetic parts—my mother's eyes and my father's chin—but not until the science of genetics and the sequencing of the genome could we see so clearly the Frankenstein aspects of ourselves.

The audiences of all the arts look as much for familiar pleasure as they do for the unprecedented. The continuing power of the Frankenstein story is only one example of how a familiar theme mutates. In part because it stood at the beginning of a mingled tradition of hopes for and fears of scientific and technological progress, Mary Shelley's novel in particular engraved itself indelibly into the modern consciousness, igniting the imagination of her readers, and continuing to keep *Frankenstein* alive as a mythic archetype in our own scientific and technological age. The fears that it shapes have varied considerably over the centuries since Shelley wrote. But its lasting usefulness as cultural shorthand for the problems of unbridled individual genius, for the nature of human identity, and for the problems of creation show how much it has conditioned our view of the world.

A story or a character achieves the status of a myth not because it never changes but because its supernatural essence can respond to the change that occurs around it, as the basic story metamorphoses in reaction to new particulars. Paradoxically or appropriately, the story of Victor's Frankenstein's urge to be unique in his creation of the monster has created a persistent genre form that has itself been replicated over and over again. Mary Shelley did not foresee cloning, organ transplant, or the science of robotics, let alone the possibility of recreating through genetic engineering the prehistoric monsters of the past as in *Jurassic Park*. But the story she created has easily mutated to embody them all, including the "Frankenfoods" of genetically modified crops, and any other product brought to the world by advancing science and technology that arouses general anxiety and hostility about the impure and the ersatz and the conglomerate—the monstrous other.

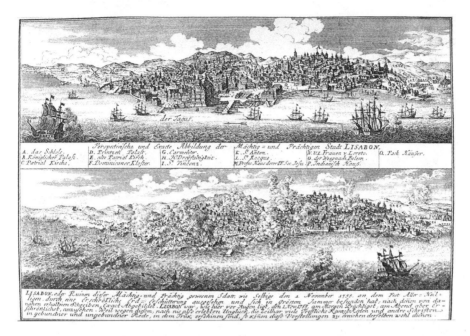

The Lisbon earthquake of 1755 was news all across Europe. This copper engraving made in Zurich just a year later (1756) shows the city before and after, with specific buildings noted. (Kozak Collection, NISEE, University of California, Berkeley)

Francisco de Goya, *Il Sueño de la Razón Produce Monstruos* (1797–99). Depending on how *sueño* is interpreted, the title can be read as "the sleep (or the dream) of reason produces monsters"; either reason is contrary to the monstrous, or they are intimately connected. Stanley Kubrick pays homage to Goya in *The Shining* when Jack Torrance sleeps next to his typewriter. (USC Libraries)

The figure of a winged Monster.

The third caufe is, an abundance of feed & overflowing matter. The fourth, the fame in too little quantity, and deficient. The fift, the force and efficacy of imagination. The fixt, the ftraightneffe of the wombe. The feaventh, the diforderly fite of the party with childe, and the pofition of the parts of the body. The eighth, a fall, ftraine or ftroake, efpecially upon the belly of a woman with child. The ninth, hereditary difeafes, or affects by any other accident. The tenth, the confufion and mingling together of the feed. The eleventh, the craft and wickedneffe of the divell. There are fome others which are accounted for monfters, becaufe they have their originall or effence full of admiration, or doe affume a certaine prodigious forme by the craft of fome begging companions, therefore we will fpeak briefly of them in their place in this our treatife of monfters.

A characteristic monster from the English translation of Ambroise Paré's *Of Monsters and Marvels* (1573), along with some of Paré's comments on the causes of monstrous births. In other monster collections of the period, this creature is frequently referred to as the Monster of Ravenna and its deformities are read allegorically. (Henry E. Huntington Library)

New terror I conceived at the steep plunge.

Canto XVII., line 117.

Gustave Doré, "New terror I conceived at the steep plunge," Canto XVII, line 117 (1861).
Geryon, the monster of Fraud with a conglomerate bestial body and a seemingly honest
human face, carries Dante and Virgil from the seventh to the eighth circle of Hell in the
Inferno. (Henry E. Huntington Library)

Isaac Cruikshank, *Luxury, or the Comforts of a Rumpford* (1801). A young woman reading Matthew Lewis's *The Monk* (1796) pleasures herself. A Rumford stove was a recent domestic innovation that more efficiently directed heat into a room. (British Museum)

William Gillray, *Tales of Wonder!* (1801). Four older women sit around a table for a titillating reading of *The Monk*. The satiric identification of women as particular readers of gothic fiction glosses over the allure of its potentially subversive attack on male social order. (Henry E. Huntington Library)

Frontispiece to Matthew Hopkins, *The Discoverie of Witches* (1647). Hopkins styled himself the Witchfinder General and was a central figure in the executions or deaths in jail of some three hundred women in East Anglia and surrounding areas. The illustration shows witches testifying about the diabolic names of their animal familiars. To know their names bestows power over them. (Henry E. Huntington Library)

Engraving by Robert Thew after a painting by Henry Fuseli, *Hamlet, Horatio, Marcellus, and the Ghost* (from *Hamlet,* Act I, Scene IV), 1796. Fuseli, a Swiss-born artist who spent most of his working life in England, specialized in supernatural subjects, including his notorious painting *The Nightmare* (1781). This image was part of his extensive contribution to John Boydell's Shakespeare Gallery. (Metropolitan Museum of Art, Gertrude and Thomas Jefferson Mumford Collection, Gift of Dorothy Quick Mayer, 1942)

Giovanni Battista Piranesi, "View of a Tomb Outside the Porta del Popolo," from *Le Antichitá Romane* (1756). Piranesi's prints extensively depict the way nature is reclaiming the grandeur of ancient monuments, while the diminished people of the present chat and go about their daily business almost oblivious to the decayed greatness of the past. (Henry E. Huntington Library)

Frontispiece to the 1831 edition of *Frankenstein.* "In the glimmer of the half-extinguished light, I saw the dull, yellow eye of the creature open; it breathed hard, and a convulsive motion agitated its limbs . . . I rushed out of the room." (Henry E. Huntington Library)

Lilliput Camera.

THIS is the handiest, lightest and most easily handled detective camera ever put upon the market. In outward appearance it resembles a small hand bag, being made of fine sole leather and fitted with a sling strap for convenience in carrying. It occupies a space only 4 x 4 x 6 inches, and notwithstanding its small bulk, carries six double holders, which may be filled with glass plates or films and which are emptied and refilled by the operator himself precisely as if in a regular camera.

The lens covers an angle of about 60°, and is adjusted to universal focus, being therefore always in readiness for use. The camera is worked without taking from the case, and all mechanism is entirely concealed from view. The size of picture obtainable is 2½ inches square, and they may be either time or instantaneous exposures at will of the operator, the shutter having an adjustment for either the one or the other. Price, including ruby lamp and plates for 108 exposures, $25.00.

The Concealed Vest Camera.

(Patented.)

THIS MINUTE CAMERA is made to be suspended from the neck of the operator and worn *under* both coat and vest with the lens protruding through the buttonhole of the vest.

It is made of metal, nickel plated, and is provided with circular plate for six exposures without changing.

The camera is 6 inches in diameter, ¾ inch in thickness, and weighs only ½ lb. The lens is of universal focus and concealment almost perfect.

Fine nickel-plated camera, in handsome box, with 6 plates, for 36 pictures, for No. 1, or 24 large pictures for Camera No. 2.

Vest, showing Camera in position.

Nickel or Oxidized Camera, No. 1 (size of picture, 1¾ in.), . each, $10.00
Magic Lantern Size Camera, No. 2 (size of picture, 2½ in.), . each, 15.00

Every camera guaranteed perfect.

From the *Catalogue for Amateurs* (1891), advertisements for a Lilliput camera that can be carried unobtrusively and a concealed vest camera. In the era of the first Sherlock Holmes stories, detective fans were already trying their hands at concealment and crime solving.
(Henry E. Huntington Library)

Spirit photograph from Arthur Conan Doyle, *The Case for Spirit Photography* (1922). Doyle was a strong supporter of the "Crewe Circle," a group headed by the photographer William Hope, and wrote his book in response to skepticism from the Society for Psychical Research. Here Mr. and Mrs. H. East pose with the spirit of their dead son. At the upper right is a photo of their son from life for purposes of comparison. (Henry E. Huntington Library)

Edvard Munch, *The Vampire II* (1893). A woman seems to absorb her lover with her kiss. Originally titled *Love and Pain*, but quickly referred to as "The Vampire," this is one of several visual images Munch made of the subject. (Courtesy of the Munch Museum, Oslo)

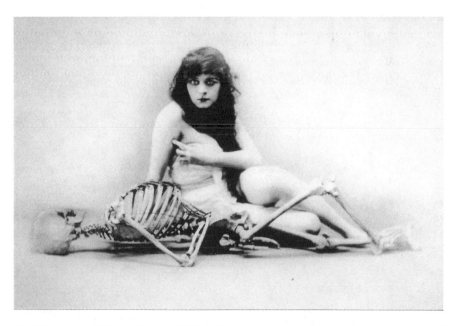

Publicity photo of the movie "vamp" Theda Bara from the 1920s, with a devoured skeleton of one of her amorous victims.

A recent part of the persistent history and flexible relevance of the monster image: vampires as carriers of sexually transmitted disease.

Frankenfoods. (Courtesy of David Dees)

CHAPTER 5

The Detective's Reason

The supernatural is the natural not yet understood.

—Elbert Hubbard (1856–1915)

The monster and the detective are opposite sides of the same coin: the monster is the embodiment of disorder, an eruption into the world of normality, coming from some alien place, from hell, from outer space, from wherever and whatever is not normal. The detective by contrast is the seeker for order. Instead of the unprecedented monster, the detective's quarry is the criminal, the monster reduced to a human scale. Whether it's a locked-room mystery or some other version of the seemingly impossible crime, the detective's discovery of motives and the connection of cause to effect brings the unique and unfathomable into the realm of the familiar and understandable. Instead of the horror story's preoccupation with the ineffable and unspeakable, the detective story would not exist without explanation, archetypally in the scene in which all the suspects are together in the same room and the detective dissipates the mystery, clarifies the otherwise murky sequence of events that led to the crime, and names the guilty.

In the eras before the natural sciences could supply effective explanations for sickness, crop failure, monstrous births, earthquakes, and other misfortunate phenomena, the supernatural was always ready at hand to supply an explanation in its less tangible terms. Yet there is always a detective or mystery story potential when the supernatural horrors let loose in the gothic tale turn out to have a reasonable explanation. At the heart of the detective tale as well might be unexplainable mysteries of human nature, but still the tangible mystery appears to be solved. Each perspective, the explainable and the unexplainable, in some way requires the shadow of the other to play against. Perhaps Goya meant in his image of the sleeping artist that it is not the dream of reason that brings forth monsters but that the monstrous was there in reason itself, when it slept.[1]

In the history of both the tale of horror and the tale of detection, Edgar Allan Poe is the great linchpin or corpus callosum. He writes classic works in both forms, and he, like his detective hero C. Auguste Dupin, has a double consciousness, one side of which faces the inexplicable and the other the comprehensible, while exploring them both. At the same time Poe dispenses with much of the explicit reference in the gothic to religious and political tyranny to depict instead more psychologically resonant images of claustrophobic confinement. Yet the similarities between the two forms remain. Like the monster or the monster-creator, the detective is often a hyper-individual, strange and different. But unlike them he doesn't have to die. He is not defying God, and society tolerates his difference because he serves social interests even though, like Dupin or Holmes, he often seems antisocial himself.

In the 1830s and 1840s, when Poe wrote, the real-life detective was a fairly recent phenomenon, as was the police force itself, with both being directly connected to the growth of cities and the need to organize against crime in those crowded urban spaces. As the loan word *police* implies, the model began in France in 1667, with a decree by Louis XIV establishing a central policing agency for Paris. England lagged behind until the mid-eighteenth-century establishment of the Bow Street Runners in London as a professional force serving the magistrates. But it was not until 1829 that an official Metropolitan Police force was organized by Sir Robert Peel, its officers therefore called the "bobbies." When, according to the Oxford English Dictionary, the word *detective* first appeared, in 1842, it was as an adjective, "the detective police," and it was already noted that unlike the regular police, these men often do not dress in uniform. Earlier, skilled members of the Metropolitan Police, not yet called detectives, solved such crimes as the body-snatching murders of the early 1830s by deducing from articles of clothing found in a well that crimes had been committed. One such officer, Joseph Sadler Thomas, a London police superintendent who helped solve the so-called Italian Boy murder, became a model for the forensic skills of later fictional detectives.

Even before the word, then, detectives were part of a new institutional force in society, professionally committed to solving crimes by a developing sense of what constituted evidence and how to interpret it. At the same time, the literary fascination with crime was growing as well. Thomas De Quincey's satirical essay "On Murder Considered as One of the Fine Arts" (1827) imagines a group of gentlemen who call themselves the Society of Connoisseurs in Murder. "They profess to be curious in homicide; amateurs and dilettanti in the various modes of bloodshed; and, in short, Murder-Fanciers." He envisions this group listening to a lecture speculating about the events and motivations behind the Ratcliff Highway murders of more than a decade earlier. Right at the beginning of crime and detective literature then, the effort of amateurs, real and fictional, to solve an actual crime was already a theme, as it would be a decade or so later in Poe's "Mystery of Marie Rogêt," where, through the fictional guise of Dupin, Poe purports to solve the recent actual murder of Marie Rogers, a cigar-shop hostess in Manhattan.

Poe's more explicit inspiration, however, was not the English mode of crime solving but the French. If Dupin has a real forerunner, it is the Frenchman Eugène Vidocq (1775–1857), who helped found the Sûreté Nationale in 1812 as the investigative arm of the French police and pioneered forensic techniques like ballistics and detailed records of the activities of individual criminals. As a young man, Vidocq had been imprisoned for forgery and sent to the galleys, from which he escaped, then was involved in other criminal activities, was arrested again, became a police spy, and finally was released when his inside information proved valuable. His ability to use his experience outside the law as well as his ability to use disguise to penetrate criminal activities significantly influenced the characterization of the detective as someone whose insight into the criminal mind comes from his own criminal propensities, or at least his ability to empathize with his antagonist. And if Vidocq's time in the galleys and his later tenacious pursuit of criminals rings a bell, it is because both Jean Valjean the escaped convict and Javert the obsessed pursuer in Victor Hugo's *Les Misérables* were modeled on his volatile exploits.[2]

Vidocq had a long and complex career, which influenced the creation and activities of police forces in many countries, and after his time at the Sûreté he founded his own detective agency, the first in the world, which was followed a few years later by the Pinkerton Detective Agency in New York, with its motto "We Never Sleep" and its image of an open eye—the source of the expression "private eye."

Between the publication of Vidocq's best-selling memoirs and the founding of the Pinkertons, and around the time of the founding of the New York Police (1844), Poe wrote his three detective stories featuring Dupin, "The Murders in the Rue Morgue" (1841), "The Mystery of Marie Rogêt"

(1842–43), and "The Purloined Letter" (1844). For Poe, Vidocq represents not the model but a more problematic view of investigation and evidence, against which Dupin defines his own method. Dupin, unlike Vidocq, is not a member of the official police. Instead he is a "young gentleman" from an "illustrious family" who by circumstances has lost most of his inheritance. The word *detective* never appears in the stories. Dupin is instead a gifted amateur with "a peculiar analytic ability," and thereby the progenitor of all the lone-wolf private and consulting detectives to come. He has in his nature something of the divine solipsism of the Romantic artist, on a quest beyond the grasp of most mere mortals. Dupin in "The Murders in the Rue Morgue" specifically criticizes the Parisian police for their lack of a consistent forensic procedure: "The Parisian police, so much extolled for *acumen,* are cunning, but no more. There is no method in their proceedings, beyond the method of the moment." Vidocq, he says, for all his celebrity, is no better: "He impaired his vision by holding the object too close. He might see, perhaps, one or two points with unusual clearness, but in so doing he necessarily lost sight of the matter as a whole."

There have been tales from the beginnings of literature in which a character's search for the answer to a mystery could be likened to the work of the detective. Historians of detective fiction often cite Sophocles' *Oedipus Tyrannos* as a forerunner of the detective plot, for the way in which its unsuspecting hero solves the riddle of the Sphinx only to be sandbagged by his ignorance of his own background. But the original oedipal mystery is the mystery of family relationship, the principal kind of mystery that makes a general appearance in earlier literature, as it does in a revived form in the eighteenth century, with characters like Defoe's Moll Flanders or Fielding's Tom Jones. It is a mystery of family, not a mystery of facts or events, still less a mystery of the universe and who runs it. It is a mystery much more akin to the mysteries that wind their way through gothic tales like Walpole's *Castle of Otranto* than the mysteries that Dupin or Sherlock Holmes or Sam Spade or Philip Marlowe set out to solve. While Oedipus is searching for a personal answer, the modern detective more often has a series of adventures set in a recognizable urban world that he, alone and preeminently, can move freely through, without limitations of neighborhood or class in his search for the crucial facts that will solve the case. The figure of the classic detective thus wears some of the charisma of the tortured gothic hero-villain or the Byronic wanderer. He is usually a solitary with at best a companion to narrate his adventures, never a leader of men or a cog in the apparatus of an institution.

To the extent that they exist, explanations in horror, like those in religion, tend to be centripetal, multiplying and expanding outward. The intellect alone cannot decide on a single answer, "For He can well be loved, but He cannot be thought," as *The Cloud of Unknowing*, a late medieval text of Christian mysticism, would have it. Scientific explanations, logical explanations, detective explanations, tend to be centrifugal, zeroing in on a single, replicable moment of enlightenment: ipso facto, QED, the butler did it. So, like the horror story's conflict between the natural explanation and the supernatural explanation, the areas of experience Poe assigns to the monstrous contrast sharply with what he called ratiocination, "that moral activity which disentangles." Consider these two passages, the first from "The Fall of the House of Usher":

> What was it—I paused to think—what was it that so unnerved me in the contemplation of the House of Usher? It was a mystery all insoluble; nor could I grapple with the shadowy fancies that crowded upon me as I pondered. I was forced to fall back upon the unsatisfactory conclusion that while, beyond doubt, there *are* combinations of very simple natural objects which have the power of thus affecting us, still the analysis of this power lies among considerations beyond our depth

And the second from "Murders in the Rue Morgue," as Dupin explains how he solved the crime:

> My own examination [of the murder room] was somewhat more particular, and was so for the reason I have just given—because here it was, I knew that all apparent impossibilities *must* be proved to be not such in reality. . . . The murderers *did* escape from one of these windows. This being so, they could not have re-fastened the sashes from the inside, as they were found fastened;—the consideration which put a stop, through its obviousness, to the scrutiny of the police in this quarter. Yet the sashes *were* fastened. They *must,* then, have the power of fastening themselves. There was no escape from this conclusion.

Both of these passages, the one filled with an unfathomable mystery that evokes an emotional response of uncertainty and ambiguity, the other engaging with a seemingly impossible mystery to be understood and solved by strict causality and logic, are presented as the observations of a single narrative voice. The mystified first-person narrator of "Usher" cannot fully understand either what he sees in the house or his own feelings about it; the ratiocinative detective follows a chain of logical thought to a necessary, although at first seemingly impossible, conclusion. For the traveler who moves into the world of the supernatural, no understanding of the general laws of nature are relevant to the monstrous reality of the house and what goes on in it; for the detective intent on solving a case, the regularities and causal connections of nature are fundamental.

The nineteenth-century advent of the detective therefore marks the historical moment when literature, in the wake of Enlightenment rationality and Romantic subjectivity, begins to make its own claim on truth telling. The detective appears as a fantasy figure of reason triumphant, even while his personal nature is often that of the charismatic nineteenth-century artist, a Byron of analysis or a Liszt of deductive reasoning. Like sexual desire in the individual, crime is an eruption of the irrational, the barbaric, into the ordered world of civilization and manners. It therefore must be tamed by reason—but also by sympathy and empathy. The detective's truth isn't a transcendental or a spiritual truth. It's a realistic and coherent truth that leads to a social conclusion. The order of reason, like the order of paranoia and the order of story, makes sense of contingency and contradiction. Both horror stories and detective stories thus proceed from an assumption that things are connected, with the difference that horror, like religion, finds that connection in the invisible world, while the detective must believe that the connections, however obscure, are open to discovery. As Holmes says to Watson, "when you have excluded the impossible, whatever remains, however improbable, must be the truth" ("The Beryl Coronet").

The criminal's action tears the social fabric—that is what crime is. The detective is the mythic figure who knits up that ripped fabric with human understanding and insight, sorting out the contradictions between natural crime and supernatural horror through his commitment to both facts and intuition. The essence of detection is the mystery and the solution; and the path to the solution, according to Poe, is logical without being mathematical, inductive without being restricted by prior assumptions or received authority. In short it is a combination of reason with the instinctive insight of the detective himself, which to a certain extent partakes of the irrational. As Poe's narrator remarks of Dupin, "His *method* is a finer thing, a seemingly more supersensual mechanism, than the ordinary processes of rational reckoning. It partakes of the *irrational,* and is therefore the highest kind of ratiocination, since it is not the captive of its own premises."

Through the figure of Dupin, Poe insists that mere factual observation will not suffice. Just as the detective combines an objective mind with a quirky character, facts are inert without the intuition of larger meaning. Like the slow-witted Scotland Yard detective Lestrade in the Sherlock Holmes stories, Monsieur G—, the Prefect in "The Purloined Letter," is prevented from solving the case by his dogged insistence on the precision of his methods, opening every drawer and minutely measuring every square inch of Minister D—'s apartment in hopes of seeing where a hidden recess might be in which the purloined letter will be found. As we discover in the course of the story, the letter is not hidden at all but lies in plain sight and has "escape[d] observation by dint of being excessively obvious." As Holmes will later pronounce, "There is nothing more deceptive than an obvious fact" ("The Boscombe Valley Mystery").

Despite both Dupin's and Holmes's mockery of the merely factual, one significant aspect of the fictional detective's inheritance does concentrate on the amassing of detail and the detective's ability to find the links between otherwise disparate and seemingly lifeless facts. For the detective, it is sight in particular—that fallible sense in many stories of horror and monsters—that, properly used, furnishes the way to the solution. Into the conflict in the tale of horror between whether to call the experience natural or supernatural, the detective introduces the question of evidence and what the detective notices, in contrast with all around him. Is it perhaps too neat a connection that Conan Doyle after receiving his medical degree set up shop as an ophthalmologist, an eye doctor; and when patients failed to show up in any numbers, he then turned to full-time writing?

At the end of the seventeenth century, Cotton Mather in his book on the Salem witch trials *Wonders of the Invisible World* (1693) could include spectral evidence as valid proof for determining the presence of a witch and witchcraft (although not sufficient for conviction). But in the course of the century to follow, the legal systems of many European countries gradually ruled testimony based on "superstition" to be legally inadmissible and accepted only observed and empirical evidence. As in the French and American revolutions, authority of all sorts—political, social, religious—could no longer settle questions. In this way, the nineteenth-century fictional detective also mirrors something of the effort by contemporary theorists to understand and thereby reorganize society on an empirical and anti-authoritarian basis. Whether it is the utilitarianism of Jeremy Bentham, the positivism of Auguste Comte, the communism of Karl Marx and Friedrich Engels, or a host of other social and political theories, each is in some way a rationalist method for curing society's ills.

In a suggestive coincidence, the gap in time between Walpole's pioneering *Castle of Otranto* and the flourishing of the gothic novel is comparable to the one between Poe's short stories and the work of Sir Arthur Conan Doyle. Just as there are some tales of terror, say, between Walpole and *The Monk,* there are also some prominent detectives between Dupin and Sherlock Holmes, including Wilkie Collins's Sergeant Cuff, Dostoyevsky's Porfiry Petrovich in *Crime and Punishment* (1866), and Ebenezer Gryce in the novels of the "mother of the American detective novel," Anna Katharine Green. But such figures, like their real-life counterparts, often came from the lower classes and were hampered when they had to deal with the crimes of people from classes higher than their own. It required first Poe and then the advent of Holmes to move the detective from an intriguing new figure in literature and reality to a cultural icon. Poe's Dupin, like some of his latter fictional colleagues, puts together a multitude of details to create a causal chain that is otherwise invisible to more casual observers. Like Holmes, and unlike Cuff or Petrovich or Gryce, he is a dilettante of criminal investigation, an amateur, a dabbler, and an aesthete. Doyle explicitly said he modeled Sherlock Holmes on Poe's Dupin, but in the passage of some forty years between the two characters' creation, from the 1840s to the 1880s, things have changed. New forms of transportation like trains had become common, along with new tools for communication like the Atlantic cable and new enhancements to familiar institutions, like the greater availability of newsprint. Photography had become widespread, cheap cameras were on the horizon; department stores and new modes of commerce were everywhere. Gas lighting replaced oil lamps on the street, and electric lights were just around the corner.

All of these innovations are important in the change or development of the idea of the detective. But primarily, it is the unofficial side of Holmes that seems to make the most difference. As police departments and agencies of private detectives became more common in the real world, the solitary detective became more important in fiction. Police procedurals and intriguingly eccentric detectives with official connections were still in the future. But it is Holmes's character, as perceived and conveyed to us by Watson, as much as his mysteries, that is so intriguing.

Unlike the frequently ex cathedra tone of such theorists of a new society as Bentham, Comte, or Marx, the idiosyncrasies of the detective always play a significant role in his cases; like the monster, in his most significant nineteenth-century incarnations he is usually observed from the outside. Mary Shelley in *Frankenstein* had brought to the novel of horror a sharp distinction between the third-person perspective of a narrator who sees all that is happening in the story, even able to enter characters' minds, almost like a god, and the first-person narrator whose view of the situation is limited and individually centered. Unlike *The Monk* and the novels of Ann Radcliffe, which maintained a third-person perspective, *Frankenstein* unfolds through a series of letters from William Walton to his sister, Victor Frankenstein's recounting to Walton of the events of his life, and the Creature's own story of what happened to him after he was created. In her use of this multiple perspective, Shelley combines the methods of the epistolary novel of the eighteenth century, which was structured as a series of letters between individual characters (like Samuel Richardson's *Clarissa*), as well as that of such first-person narratives as *Robinson Crusoe*. Both of those methods emphasize the sense of immediacy in the story ("it's happening right now") with a limited degree of reflection on those events. The reader can either take them at face value or be somewhat suspicious about whether the character really understands what he or she is reporting about themselves and their surroundings. Shelley's own turn on this literary inheritance draws upon novels like her father's *Caleb Williams* or Charles Brockden Brown's *Wieland,* in which the narrator is trying to understand a mystery warped by his or her own emotions.

The mingling of third person and first person is a strategy principally suited to the development of horror literature, which draws upon both empathy and distance from its victims of terror. So too the flawed but romantic protagonist in such stories can best be seen at a distance, through the perspective of a conventional character like Walton in *Frankenstein* or through the seemingly objective array of detachment devices (diaries, letters, newspaper clippings) through which we see Dracula. Since we as readers are presumed to be closer to the conventional Walton than we are to Victor Frankenstein, he becomes our bridge to the marvelous and terrifying events of the story. The first person, whether it is that of an observer-sidekick or, later, of the detective himself, is similarly part of the guarantee that these events really happened. So we have the unnamed narrator of Poe's detective stories, who tells us of the adventures of his friend Dupin; the emotional and somewhat unimaginative Mr. Raymond, who introduces us to the meticulous Ebenezer Gryce in Anna Katharine Green's *The Leavenworth Case* (1878); and Dr. John Watson, who famously recounts the cases of Sherlock Holmes beginning with *A Study in Scarlet* (1887). Poe's narrator, Mr. Raymond, and Dr. Watson know all the same facts that the detective does but can't see the solution, beginning a tradition in which the reader is drawn into the story as a fourth character trying to get the answer before the detective does. This technique of viewing the abnormal and subjective through the seemingly normal and objective can also be traced down to the present in such visual forms as the "found footage" in films like *The Blair Witch Project, Paranormal Activity,* and others. In these stories the advanced technology of the video camera supplies the supposed detachment that validates the unusual story, just as in *Dracula* it is also supplied by an up-to-date recording device. But at the same time that these instruments of modern visual technology seem to allow a more objective perspective, they also engender greater fear because their view is essentially confined and claustrophobic. Similar to the effect of the first person in literature, there is no overview, no detached standpoint, by which to view events. As one of the characters in *Paranormal Activity* complains, "You and your stupid camera are the problem."

With the advent of film, then, the possibility also arises that a narrator is fallible and the events are distorted or even a dream. In the pioneering 1920 horror film *The Cabinet of Dr. Caligari,* a visitor to an asylum is talking to one of the patients who tells him that he is there under false pretenses to cover up some dreadful crimes. He proceeds to tell the story of the film, the fiendish Caligari, his somnambulist Cesare, who supposedly can foretell the future while in a trance, how they prey upon small-town fears, how he and a friend discovered their crimes, how the friend was killed, and all the ensuing complications. At the end of the story, the visitor is aghast, but then gradually realizes that all the characters of the story are present in the asylum, including Caligari himself who is the head doctor. So what had seemed to be an objective retelling, reinforced by the power of film itself to mimic reality, turns out to be at least subjective and perhaps a total fantasy.

❧

"The material world," Dupin continued, "abounds with very strict analogies to the immaterial."

In Poe's three stories we find fully formed the bases of the detective novel and story to come—the mystery and the solution, but also the detective who is larger than the specific events he investigates, as the unnamed narrative friend refers to other cases solved by Dupin in a technique that will be exploited even further by Conan Doyle. In addition, Poe sets the pattern for the basic characters of the story—the detective, the sidekick, and the (literally) clueless official police—as well as two of its more lasting puzzles: the impossible crime in a locked room ("Rue Morgue") and the mystery in plain sight ("The Purloined Letter").[3]

We have already seen how the eighteenth century marks the gradual disappearance of religion as the prime mode of understanding the world and the rise of different disciplines, each with its own perspective, from the rational and detached to the irrational and affective. Victor Frankenstein's ambitions embody the belief that science has superseded religion in understanding the mysteries of nature. But as far as *his* creator is concerned, perhaps literature has an even greater claim. The rise of the novel as a major literary form was only one example of the new openness to different narratives that characterizes the period. Just as the various interpretations of the Lisbon earthquake mark the decline of providential thought as the master story of the universe, so the increasing interest in history writing points toward a continuing increase in the varieties of knowledge. The reliance upon religion as the guarantee of epistemological order was giving way to newly competing images of order, not the high God but often the God of nature, the immediate material order in competition with the invisible transcendent order.

W. H. Auden argued that the appeal of detective novels is basically religious because it relieves the reader of guilt, while restoring both innocence and order to the world. G. K. Chesterton with his Father Brown stories tries to bring back something of the religious side of mystery by making his hero-detective an unassuming parish priest. Father Brown's witless competition for solving cases are frequently doctors and/or Presbyterians who, like the Prefect or Lestrade, concentrate too much on the causalities of the material world and not enough on its invisible spiritual connection with the nature of human evil. The word *mystery* itself intriguingly faces in the direction of both the religious and the secular. Even by the end of the nineteenth century it was still a relatively new term to apply to crime and detective stories, not quite having shed its primary meaning of religious mystery. There certainly is a satisfying finality to most detective stories when all the uncertainties are clarified and neatly delivered in the solution. But even if there may be religious elements embedded in it, such stories have a heavily secular overlay. Essential to the detective's effort to solve the mystery is the clue that will unravel it. And "unravel" is the literal truth, since *clue* originally referred to a ball of thread, like the thread Theseus uses to find his way out of the Cretan labyrinth. By the nineteenth century the meaning has extended to refer to a general way of discovering something, although its specifically detective usage did not appear until after midcentury.[4]

UNREAL CITY

Hell is a city much like London.

— Percy Shelley, *Peter Bell the Third* (1819)

In the nineteenth century for the first time in human history more people were beginning to live in cities than in the countryside. Although some detective novels and stories are set in rural areas or small towns, and the way a detective reads clues is reminiscent of a hunter or trapper, it is difficult to think of the modern detective without also situating him in a city. Unlike the monsters from nature who seem indelibly connected to the earthy and preindustrial worlds of agricultural societies, the detective, like the created monster, is an offspring of progress and the growth of complex urban environments that require new skills to navigate and to succeed in.

The philosopher Ronald Dworkin has noted that religions have a scientific and verifiable aspect, in which they make claims about facts, and a values aspect, in which they make claims about the proper way to lead a good life, the existence of God, the nature of the afterlife, and so on. But he argues that there is no "direct bridge" between those two aspects, no decisive way one supports or validates the other. Yet if Poe might be called the linchpin between the horror and the detective ways of looking at the world, his story "The Man of the Crowd" is the tale that seems best to combine them in his own work, and supplies prescient clues about the kind of figure who will embody the spirit of the city. "The Man of the Crowd" is narrated not by a detective, or even an amateur skilled in analysis like Dupin, but at first just a curious someone sitting in his chair in the bow window of a London coffeehouse, watching the ebb and flow of traffic on the street below in the course of a day. At first he sees the people just as a general collection of humanity but gradually he starts to see them as individuals, noticing "the innumerable varieties of figure, dress, air, gait, visage, and expression of countenance." He then notices the similarities between different social groups—the businessmen, the gentlemen of leisure, the senior and junior clerks, as well as the pickpockets, gamblers, and beggars who prey upon them. As the day closes he sees women as well—the young girls returning home from work as well as "the women of the town," from youthful beauty to "the wrinkled, bejeweled and paint-begrimed beldame." When darkness falls and the workaday world ends, the surging crowds become filled with darker possibilities and more sinister faces, and still the observer watches, now pressing his face against the window to see more clearly. Finally his gaze falls upon a single individual, "a decrepit old man, some sixty-five or seventy years of age," who so fascinates him that he gets up out of his seat and leaves his detached point of view to follow that man as he moves rapidly from one end of London to another. Until daybreak the narrator follows the man, wondering where he is going, until they are back in front of the coffeehouse from which he was first observed. Even then the man rushes on and the narrator follows him into the next evening until, "wearied unto death," he gives up. Like the observing detective, the narrator of "The Man of the Crowd" has detachedly watched the world, detailing and cataloguing its many human nuances, until he comes upon a vexing problem and leaves his seat to pursue it. But here there is no specific crime or goal, no aim, no solution. " 'This old man,' I said at length, 'is the type and the genius of deep crime. He refuses to be alone. He is *the man of the crowd.*' "[5]

"Crowd" itself here is well on its way to becoming identified with "mob," masses of people moved by inchoate feelings, manipulated by symbols summoning up images of revolution, revolt, and anarchy that by the end of the century will produce sociological theories of the mass mind in works like Gustave Le Bon's *The Crowd: A Study of the Popular Mind* (1895). But what the narrator of "The Man of the Crowd" sees is possible to be seen primarily in a large city, and in this way he is the inspiration for what Poe's great French fan and translator Charles Baudelaire will call the *flâneur* in his essay "The Painter of Modern Life" (1863), another new kind of person generated by the city, who wanders the streets observing its overflowing variety.[6]

Already in Poe's characterization of Dupin, he is said to be a lover of wandering the city at night and fascinated by strange crimes. Like the kind of contemporary artist celebrated by Baudelaire in his essay, the detective is preeminently a virtuoso knower of the city, who easily moves through it geographically and socially, from the wide, tree-lined streets to the dark alleys, from the luxurious houses of the rich to the hovels of the poor, mastering its physical and social labyrinths, at home with its jargons and its multiple languages. One of the prime functions of the detective is therefore to be an outsider in the urban world of stratified social classes and neighborhoods, yet with entry to all of them. Society to the detective and his reader is a puzzle to be figured out, to be in control of rather than to be controlled by, at least in one's imagination. As Charles Dickens says of his detective Mr. Bucket in *Bleak House* (1852–53), "Otherwise mildly studious in his observation of human nature, on the whole a benignant philosopher not disposed to be severe upon the follies of mankind, Mr. Bucket pervades a vast number of houses and strolls about an infinity of streets, to outward appearance rather languishing for want of an object. ... Time and place cannot bind Mr. Bucket." Or, as Sherlock Holmes says in "The Red-Headed League," "It is a hobby of mine to have an exact knowledge of London." In the labyrinth of the city, one thing leads to another and connections are made by the detective between the most disparate people and events.[7]

The man of the crowd observed by Poe's narrator represents the nervous energy of this newly born and newly perceived city life. Earlier crime literature, from its beginnings in the late seventeenth century onward, was to a great extent made up of romantic but moralistic stories about pirates on the seas and highwaymen on the roads. By the eighteenth century some urban gangsters had entered the picture, in particular Jonathan Wild, whose exploits on both sides of the law as supposed public citizen and actual gang leader were chronicled by both Defoe and Fielding, and who appears in the guise of Macheath in Gay's *The Beggar's Opera*. By the nineteenth century, in contrast, crime is almost exclusively defined as a noxious growth of the city. But urban crime is also simultaneously a window into the surreal side of daily life, a magnet of cohesiveness whereby the scattered complex city, like a haphazard handful of iron filings, turns into pattern and even symmetry. Looking back at the beginning of the twentieth century, G. K. Chesterton called the detective story "the earliest and only form of popular literature in which is expressed some sense of the poetry of modern life."[8] Instead of wonder being excited by exotic objects and people brought from faraway places, the detective and the flâneur emphasize how your own environment can be an object of wonder and perhaps terror. London above all excited such feelings among its writers, painters, and ordinary citizens, although Paris ran it a close second, and St. Petersburg was definitely in the running.

For readers, most of whom were living next to more people than anyone ever had before and knowing so little about them, the detective is an ideal surrogate, whose understanding of the city is solace for its terrors. The flashes of gaslight, the narrow streets, the dark shadows, the coal fires that created the London fog, along with all the people, rushing one way or another—all made London life at night a phantasmagoric spectacle that Poe foreshadows in "The Man of the Crowd." But that scene remains a continual source of images of London throughout the century down into Stevenson's *Jekyll and Hyde*, Stoker's *Dracula*, and beyond (of which more in the chapters to come). Samuel Johnson in the late eighteenth century called London "the great wen" for the way it was spreading into the countryside, swallowing up peripheral small towns. That organic image persists into the nineteenth century, but instead of signifying the kind of variety in which Johnson exulted, it often characterized the city as a kind of monstrous body within which the individual precariously made his way. Because there were more happenstance and accidental relationships between the denizens of the city, the fear of the inability to cope with them could easily arise, along with the sense of dependency on them for one's livelihood. In the dawn of modern populous London at the beginning of the eighteenth century, Daniel Defoe writes *Robinson Crusoe*, whose hero's ability to deal with his perilous situation on the island consoles the reader by implying that, if in similar difficulties, one could figure it all out for oneself, build a boat without the help of a boat builder or make bread without the help of a baker. In a later volume, *Serious Reflections of Robinson Crusoe*, the mariner, now living in London, says that amidst the crowded city he feels more alone than he ever did on the island. Yet Samuel Johnson, some fifty years later, could say that "when one is tired of London, one is tired of life."[9]

In the same era the painter and engraver William Hogarth often portrayed London street scenes as a world of overwhelmingly strange juxtapositions and conglomerations, as much fearful as exciting. Hogarth's vision was admittedly more satiric than nightmarish. Some decades later, the image had shifted. By the mid–nineteenth century, the painter John Martin, who specialized in catastrophic scenes of biblical and historical destruction, only had to depict run-of-the-mill London as itself to get the most extreme effects. As the visiting American Ralph Waldo Emerson wrote to his wife Lidia in 1847, Martin's paintings of the destruction of Babylon are "faithful copies of the West part of London, light, darkness, architecture & all."[10] Similarly, the descriptions of London in the poet James Thomson's 1874 epic "City of Dreadful Night" produce scenes of shadow and gloom that are the ancestors of German expressionism and film noir. In this new city world, the pastoral setting of past literature has become the landscape of a dire apocalypse.

> Although lamps burn along the silent streets,
> Even when moonlight silvers empty squares
> The dark holds countless lanes and close retreats;
> But when the night its sphereless mantle wears
> The open spaces yawn with gloom abysmal,
> The sombre mansions loom immense and dismal,
> The lanes are black as subterranean lairs.

A CASE OF IDENTITY

In Thomson's despairing poem the crowded modern city inspires depression and thoughts of suicide, but for others the city is a place of possibility and discovery, where new identities can be fashioned, and where ambition and the rise to fame is as possible and as alluring as anonymity and disguise. The Holmesian detective preeminently exploits both of those kinds of resources. He is a magnet for those who have mysterious events or crimes they wish to understand as well as a master of masquerade, who can be equally at home in a fashionable party or an opium den. The most obvious aspect of the detective is his ability to command arcane sorts of knowledge, his epistemology. But it is also his ontology, his unique identity, that makes him memorable. Holmes remarks that his art of detection is "an impersonal thing, a thing beyond myself." The detachment rationality requires may also serve as protection against the irrational, rather than something in itself, but there is also something irreducible in the detective's subjectivity. Some time before science and sociology fully understood the observer effect, by which the presence of an engaged spectator changes the phenomenon being observed, the detective story had built it into its basic assumptions.[11]

In order to ascertain the truth of the mysteries Holmes has been handed, he must therefore practice a kind of emotional repression, which brings us to another aspect of the detective that has passed on to its legacy over the decades—his problematic relation to women. To the basic quartet of the detective, the sidekick, the unimaginative official policeman, and the criminal, Doyle adds two further figures—the megalomaniacal master of crime James Moriarty and the elusive female criminal Irene Adler. Moriarty appears in only one story, "The Adventure of the Final Problem" (1893), as well as in the last novel, *The Valley of Fear* (1914), and some critics have argued that his prime function was to help Doyle kill off the Holmes character he was getting tired of writing about (for only a time as it turned out). But the idea of the combat between the master of crime and the master of detection had a resonance and a legacy beyond Doyle's immediate purposes, reaching down into the master criminals who want to rule the world, from Sax Rohmer's Fu Manchu to the antagonists of Ian Fleming's James Bond. Doyle calls Moriarty "the Napoleon of crime," and the combat of charismas between him and Holmes on the cliffs above the Reichenbach Falls resembles the two aspects of the gothic villain, the repellently tyrannic and the melancholic sympathetic, struggling with each other for dominance. Moriarty in this way may also remind us either of Satan or of the Wholly Other God, the *mysterium tremendum et fascinans* postulated by so much of affective religion, now secularized into a kind of mega-gangster.[12]

Criminals with gangs who seek to conquer the world will become more familiar in reality in the twentieth century and beyond. To fight them, the detective or the spy or the innocent bystander must armor himself and sally forth. But the difficulties detectives have with the feminine strike more deeply at their idea of themselves, beneath the armor. Irene Adler and Holmes's wariness of her as well as his admiration look forward to the problems later male detectives will have with women (and perhaps how, even with the advent of feminism, female detectives generally have to highlight their masculine aspects).

As "The Man of the Crowd" implies, a woman alone on the street after dark in nineteenth-century London or Paris is essentially a prostitute. Respectable women rarely go out alone even in daylight, lower-class women who work rush home before darkness falls, and middle-class women rarely leave the home unaccompanied. Because women lack specific social identity beyond the broad categories of young woman, wife, and prostitute, they are difficult to read through the vocational and social clues that Holmes is used to probing. Women are thus variables in a case that are hard to control, and how to control the variables is a prime detective issue. The unique problem of Irene Adler for Holmes is announced at the beginning of the first published Holmes short story (after the novels *A Study in Scarlet* and *The Sign of the Four*), "A Scandal in Bohemia": "To Sherlock Holmes she is always *the* woman." Watson hurries to say that Holmes's feeling for her is nothing like love: "All emotions, and that one particularly, were abhorrent to his cold, precise, but admirably balanced mind. . . . He never spoke of the softer passions, save with a gibe and a sneer." But Irene Adler is somehow different. In a formulation that will echo in detective stories for a century and more, the prince of Bohemia who fears he will be blackmailed by her says, "She has the face of the most beautiful of women, and the mind of the most resolute of men." In order to discover the hiding place of the compromising photograph Adler possesses, Holmes disguises himself first as "a drunken-looking groom" and later as a clergyman. But instead he finds a photograph of Adler herself and a note revealing that she was herself disguised as a "slim youth" who bids Holmes goodnight. Women for the detective are connected to a realm of emotions and sexual feelings that too often divert him from his duty to facts, reason, and the fundamentals of his own profession.

Another early Holmes story highlights the wariness with which the sexes faced each other by the end of the nineteenth century, and especially the masculine need to preserve a sense of threatened autonomy. It is "The Man with the Twisted Lip." When it opens, Watson has been asked to find the husband of a friend of his wife who has become an opium addict. Descending to the darker parts of London, he encounters in an opium den a disguised Holmes, who is pursuing an oddly similar case in which a woman has believed that her missing husband, Neville St. Clair, has been murdered. The St. Clairs live in the countryside in somewhat palatial splendor, from which Mr. St. Clair takes the train every day supposedly to look after his financial interests in the city. On one day, somewhat after Mr. St. Clair has departed, his wife receives a message to pick up a package from a London shipping company and travels into London herself. Walking in an unsavory neighborhood, she believes she sees her husband in an upstairs window of the same opium den. He then vanishes. Unable to enter, she summons the police who find "a crippled wretch of hideous aspect" in the room. After discovering some of St. Clair's possessions and clothing in the room, they conclude that "an abominable crime" has been committed and arrest the man, who is identified as Hugh Boone, a professional beggar well known in the area.

Our cultural memory of Sherlock Holmes is that he immediately discovers what has been going on in the most abstruse and confusing of cases. But in fact he is frequently wrong in his first deductions, and his ability shows as much in his willingness to admit he is wrong as in his miraculous understanding of the meaning of details. Like "A Scandal in Bohemia," "The Man with the Twisted Lip" is another story whose human intricacies seems at first to thwart him. Here Holmes first believes that St. Clair is dead but he is at sea about what relation the beggar Hugh Boone has to his death. Whereupon Mrs. St. Clair shows him a letter posted from her husband after his supposed death assuring her that all will be fine and not to worry. After a night with his pipe and his shag tobacco, however, Holmes has figured it out. "I confess that I have been blind as a mole, but it is better to learn wisdom late, than never learn it at all." Going to Hugh Boone's cell, he sponges off the "repulsive ugliness" to reveal—Neville St. Clair. In fact, St. Clair has made his money and supported his wife in style not by his business interests but by being a beggar, disguised with techniques he learned as an actor when young. Holmes makes him promise that he will never do this again and so the story ends.

"The Man with the Twisted Lip" thus begins with Holmes in disguise and ends with the revelation that disguise is the key to the puzzle of St. Clair's disappearance. Like "A Scandal in Bohemia," there is a kind of combat of disguises, as well as for Doyle the ophthalmologist a foray into the ways the eye can be fooled. The difference between the two stories is that Irene Adler manages to decisively fool Holmes, whereas St. Clair fools him only for a time. More crucially, however, he fools his own wife, who looked on Hugh Boone only with disgust. In this way he joins characters in other Holmes stories who use disguise to fool women who might otherwise be expected to know them well enough not to be fooled, like the stepdaughter who doesn't know her lover is her stepfather in "A Case of Identity." This scenario may mirror Doyle's own sense of the gulf between the sexes, the potentially meta-morphic nature of men and the inability of women (except for Irene Adler) to penetrate their disguises. But it also characterizes the detective's world deeply enough to resonate with his readers. At the end of "The Man with the Twisted Lip," St. Clair must return to the world of respectability, and it is unclear if in fact he will ever tell his wife the source of their prosperity.

The realm of the Anglo-American detective is often split between those writers who are fascinated by the mystery and the unraveling of the secret, on one hand, and those who emphasize the psychology of the detective and the criminal on the other. Both are descendants in their different ways of Dupin and Holmes, and their split into different tributaries appropriately began in the wake of World War I. On one side was an English tradition that empha-sized puzzle solving and was concerned with formulating the basic rules of the genre. Here the detective was often an amateur out to right wrongs and un-ravel crimes when the official police were baffled. T. S. Eliot said that the English detective story was essentially a chess problem, while Raymond Chan-dler more contemptuously termed such writers and their main characters puz-zle solvers. A late-blooming parody and homage to that tradition was the board game Clue, set in an English country house, with a cast of upper-class characters and their servants.[13] The contrasting American tradition featured the hard-boiled detective, and placed its greater emphasis on the detective's character. Instead of the independently wealthy upper-class dilettante, these were professional private eyes who worked between the police and the criminal world, and often had a lively contempt for their frequently rich clients.

The hard-boiled story is not the Holmesian structure of a puzzle that has to be solved with three pipes of tobacco. Instead it is a journey of movement and of character. Holmes does get out on the road, especially in the novels, but he is more often confined to his rooms (where he often figures out a case by logic alone), or to a specific place, like Baskerville Hall. In contrast with the immediate and present tense unfolding of the hard-boiled story, so many of the Holmes stories are retrospective: the crime or the mystery has already happened, and now must be figured out. That retrospective meditation on the problem underlines the English and continental detective's sense of detachment and privilege, his jaundiced separation from the modern world. Instead, the mark of the hard-boiled detective is his immersion in the modern world, with its different ethnic groups, neighborhoods, and sexual orientations, whatever they may be. Instead of the amateur dabbler, he is the common man with an uncommon morality. We may look down on him socially but we are being asked to look up to him morally. Like the knights of old, he begins as a servant, but gradually his skills of violence and his code of honor raise him above those who employ him.

"Hard-boiled" is part of World War I slang, coined to describe the way army drill sergeants treated their men, unsentimental, harsh, cynical, and indifferent to the feelings of others: hard-boiled because any emotional vulnerability was liable to get you killed; unsentimental because sentiment distorted language and language distorted reality. As Ernest Hemingway writes in a well-known passage in *A Farewell to Arms* (1929),

> I was always embarrassed by the words sacred, glorious, and sacrifice and the expression in vain. We had heard them, sometimes standing in the rain almost out of earshot, so that only the shouted words came through, and had read them, on proclamations that were slapped up by billposters over other proclamations, now for a long time, and I had seen nothing sacred, and the things that were glorious had no glory and the sacrifices were like the stockyards at Chicago if nothing was done with the meat except to bury it. There were many words that you could not stand to hear and finally only the names of places had dignity. . . . Abstract words such as glory, honor, courage, or hallow were obscene beside the concrete names of villages, the numbers of roads, the names of rivers, the numbers of regiments and the dates.

Even as the hard-boiled detective may stick to such hard-surfaced facts in solving his case, he still follows in the tradition begun by both Poe's Dupin and Sherlock Holmes of being a special, even peculiar, kind of person. In the first paragraph of "A Scandal in Bohemia," the first Sherlock Holmes short story, Watson refers to Holmes as "the most perfect reasoning and observing machine that the world has seen." Perhaps too many of the imitators of Doyle who sprung up after the first Holmes stories appeared took this description to heart, while disregarding Doyle's emphasis on Holmes's character as well. Instead they invented detectives who applied strict circumstantial logic to all their cases, more like Professor Augustus F. S. X. Van Dusen, whose creator Jacques Futrelle called "the thinking machine." But the more long-lived detectives in the hard-boiled tradition are not just minds putting together facts as they would a jigsaw puzzle.[14]

This new detective's tough exterior emphasized some elements of the character of Dupin and Holmes—an empathy with the criminal world and a willingness to plunge deeply into the life of the city, although his single-minded toughness also resembled something of the image of the solitary American westerner. Now, rather than a gifted amateur and dabbler not part of any official world, he was more often a man alone, in a world of greater violence and more explicit sexual tension, fighting both crime and the police, because detection was not his avocation but his profession. Such figures must have fulfilled some deep cultural need, at least in the United States, since over half of more than four hundred American detective films appear between World War I and World War II. They were hardly ever the prestigious A films, more often the B films that filled the second half of double features, and they included not only white male detectives (twelve Michael Shaynes, fourteen Philo Vances, sixteen Falcons) but also detectives of frequently Asian ethnicity (forty-five Charlie Chans, eight Mr. Motos, six Mr. Wongs), as well as a few female detectives (nine Torchy Blanes, six Hildegarde Withers).[15]

Despite the nod at ethnic and gender variety, however, the hard-boiled style of writing (and selfhood), in authors such as Carol John Daly and Dashiell Hammett, moved the issue of masculinity to the forefront, with the detective preeminently serving to map cultural attitudes toward men, women, and their difference. To the dramatis personae of the detective world a new element was often added, the secretary, sometimes a sidekick but more often the only woman the detective was comfortable with, because she didn't represent either a sexual threat or a sexual opportunity. "You're a good man, sister," says Sam Spade to Effie in *The Maltese Falcon*. Women are the weakness of men, and especially the weakness of the detective. In *The Maltese Falcon,* they include both Iva, the clingy widow of Spade's dead partner, and the femme fatale Brigid O'Shaughnessy. Raymond Chandler formulated the general issue with his usual eloquence:

> Love interest nearly always weakens a mystery story because it creates a
> type of suspense that is antagonistic and not complementary to the

detective's struggles to solve the problem. The kind of love interest that works is the one that complicates the problem by adding to the detective's troubles but which at the same time you instinctively feel will not survive the story. A really good detective never gets married. He would lose his detachment, and this detachment is part of his charm.[16]

Yet that detachment carries with it the fear of attachment. At the end of both the novel and John Huston's film of *The Maltese Falcon,* Spade turns Brigid in for killing Archer: "I won't play the sap for you." And the film ends with Brigid in custody. In the novel, however, there is another scene. Effie, who had continued to believe in Brigid, is upset that he has given her up to the police, even though she knows Brigid was the killer. "So much for your women's intuition," says Spade. Then it is the turn of Archer's widow.

> She said in a small flat voice: "Iva is here."
> Spade, looking down at his desk, nodded almost imperceptibly. "Yes," he said, and shivered. "Well, send her in."

Both horror and detective stories share the premise of mystery. But while horror emphasizes the unconscious and the abnormal, the detective ultimately looks to the pattern beneath the seeming chaos. The way the stories are told also differ. Horror either presents an overarching God's- (sometimes Satan's-) eye view or the intense subjectivity of Poe's claustrophobic narrators, pursued by dark forces. In the detective story our point of view is usually tied to the detective's, even when, as in *The Maltese Falcon,* the presentation is in the third person. We might not understand his motivations, but we carefully follow his trail of deduction and inference. In addition, the dialogue in horror frequently turns on innuendo and high-flown euphemism, while the detective, whether in the English or American tradition, tends to be more straightforward, aiming toward the final revelation of whodunit. While the language of horror verges on the unspeakable, for the detective language must work, explanation is possible. Why a crime has been committed may be lost in the criminal's psyche. But how it was committed is ultimately knowable.

One dark, unmanageable force thus remains in the classic detective story—woman, with the twin temptations of love and sexuality. Critics have often pointed significantly to the frequent presence of male detective partners and sidekicks, and some have argued with varying degrees of persuasiveness that there is a homoerotic undertone that runs through such tales, beginning with Poe's Dupin and the unnamed friend who recounts his adventures. The observation has some truth in it, but it needs qualification. Most important, to what extent is it the result of a positive urge to male bonding, and to what extent is that bonding a reaction against the presence of women and the uncertainty they signify? Watson may have a wife, who appears only tangentially, and Holmes may be preoccupied with Irene Adler, the shape-shifting adventuress. But on their forays into the London underworld and the suburban nests of crime, no woman comes along. There were in fact female sleuths, even in the literature of the 1890s and after, but they didn't achieve the continuing resonance of those whose stories contained only partially veiled allegories of gender uneasiness and conflict. Later, when Dashiell Hammett introduces Nick and Nora Charles, or Erle Stanley Gardner creates Donald Lamm and Bertha Cool, the male and female duo is an innovative response that emphasizes how traditional the male duo had become.

Whether alone or with another, the detective also carries with him his code that protects him against the group mind of both the police and the criminals. If the need to be emotionally cut off is the shortcoming of the new masculinity, the code is its compensation. After the disaster of World War I, it guarantees the individual the possibility of what Hemingway called "a separate peace," turning his face against the abstractions of honor that are just meant to manipulate people. Like a secular version of the medieval knight on a quest for the Holy Grail, the detective's quest is for the answer to the mystery, with words like *quest* and *mystery* themselves announcing the religious tinge of his otherwise worldly arts. When Raymond Chandler's detective Philip Marlowe enters the lavish home of General Sternwood in *The Big Sleep,* he notices a stained-glass panel that shows

> a knight in dark armor rescuing a lady who was tied to a tree and didn't have any clothes on but some long and convenient hair. The knight had pushed the vizor of his helmet back to be sociable, and he was fiddling with the knots on the ropes that tied the lady to the tree and not getting anywhere. I stood there and thought that if I lived in the house, I would sooner or later have to climb up there and help him. (3–4)

Marlowe mocks the medieval conventions in part because he is very much like that knight himself, in a world where knights and ladies and the sense of honor that united them has disappeared, except for the detective's personal code.[17]

The code that buttresses the detective's individualism also keeps him far from any official group. Latter-day fictional detectives who are members of police forces have to negotiate between their own sense of right and the demands of their organizations. But the classic private eye has only himself. This aspect of his ethos also seems connected with what was happening in real crime, outside the pages of fiction and the images of the movies. With the coming of Prohibition in 1919 came the rise of organized crime in America, and with it the café society of the '20s, in which gangsters, members of show business, and the rich mixed. Whatever its moral goals, Prohibition had the effect of making otherwise law-abiding people from all levels of society into at least occasional criminals. Crime and gang violence wasn't just something to be looked upon as a distant sociological phenomenon, a characteristic of immigrants and other members of the underclasses. The big-city sensationalist press treated criminals as celebrities, and filled the front pages with famous murders and gangland killings. In 1931 and 1932 three movies about gangs and the gangster appeared that helped establish the basic pattern—*Little Caesar, The Public Enemy,* and *Scarface.* Like the factual and explanatory side of the detective novel and film, they focused not only on crime but also on a version of sociology in their depiction of Italian and Irish gangsters.

Just as his work defined him in frequent opposition to the police, the detective also was contrasted with the gang. In Hammett's earlier novel *Red Harvest,* his hero, a member of a detective agency who is referred to only as the Continental Op, enters a town with two rival gangs and manipulates them into destroying each other. As an archetypal detective, he is the man between, like his western twin, the lone cowboy hero who comes into town, cleans up the mess of evil and corruption, then leaves.[18] With the stories and novels of Raymond Chandler beginning before World War II, and those of Mickey Spillane starting after World War II, this image of the loner detective becomes more forceful and even strident. In Chandler's often quoted phrase, "down these mean streets a man must come who is not himself mean." His detective Philip Marlowe maintains a vision of himself as the last moral man in a world of corruption, although fully aware of his own complicity in it. As he says in *The Big Sleep,* "I was part of the nastiness now." Yet at the same time he can look down on others he feels are less moral than himself, not only the obvious criminals but also anyone he considers "deviants"—homosexuals, African-Americans, elderly men—anyone outside his conception of the norm. It is an attitude that receives even more blatant expression in Mickey Spillane's novels, where the increased quotient of sex and violence goes along with a casual racist and sexist disgust with any person or group whose way of life he disapproves.

The hard-boiled detective thus carries into later wars the marks of his trench-coated origin in World War I, policing not only crime but also the borders of an embattled masculinity. In the movies his quest is often expressed visually by film noir, which derives from the expressionist photography that characterized German silent horror films. As a cinematic style, film noir is most native to detective and mystery films, but in the late 1940s and 1950s it pervades other genres as well, including romance and even the open spaces of the western. The noir detective, like Mickey Spillane's Mike Hammer, may be a veteran of World War II who has come back to the seeming world of peace only to discover that it's a world of deception and corruption. The detective quest for tangible facts and answers is still there, but in a context of harsh lighting and visual uncertainty, where bodies are broken by shadows and oblique angles, more reminiscent of the creation scene in *Frankenstein* or *The Bride of Frankenstein* than the squared-off and well-lit detective films of the 1930s. The 1930s reliance on the master shot, which gives a full picture of a scene before the camera cuts away to look at individual aspects, disappears, leaving the viewer to piece together the fragments. Film noir as a visual style thus reenergizes the form by emphasizing the psychological aspects of both the detective as well as the mystery, superimposing the dark psychology of the horror world on the world of detective clarity, even as he searches for the clues that will complete the pattern. The viewer is drawn instead into a fatalistic world of darkness, shadows, mists, and rain, where there are few if any solid places to stand, and the search for definitive answers proceeds through a haze of uncertainty. Like the detective, we are invited to read and interpret this confusing place that recedes before us into darkness.[19]

THE DETECTIVE AND THE PSYCHIATRIST

"How does it feel to be a great analyst . . . and a great detective?"

—John Ballantyne to Dr. Constance Petersen in *Spellbound* (1945)

"You may be able to put together the objective jigsaw puzzle while I'm reconstructing the subjective one . . . Objective and subjective, the outer world and the inner, do correspond of course. But sometimes you have to follow the parallel lines almost to infinity before they touch."

—Psychiatrist Dr. Miles Godwin to detective Lew Archer in Ross Macdonald's *The Chill* (1964)

With the need to interpret shadows comes subjectivity, and another characteristic of detective films of this period as well as other genres (especially romance) is the frequently explicit importance of psychology and the presence of psychologists, psychoanalysts, and psychiatrists, legitimate and not. While Huston's version of *The Maltese Falcon* (1941), the third of the films based on Hammett's novel, is sometimes referred to as a film noir, it generally has a realistic texture and even the criminal gang is less menacing than eccentric and even somewhat cozy. A few years later, *Murder, My Sweet* (1944), based on Chandler's *Farewell, My Lovely* (1944), takes place in a virtually paranoid world, a dark, menacing environment that is more expressed visually than it is in the plot. *Falcon* begins with a conventional array of credits, followed by a stock shot of the Golden Gate Bridge and the words "San Francisco" underneath; *Murder, My Sweet*, by contrast, begins with the shot of a white light that we seem to be hovering above. As the credits unfold, we gradually realize that the camera is descending over a table glaringly illuminated with the shadows of people around it. Only by the end does this puzzling image resolve into a police interrogation room, in which Philip Marlowe (Dick Powell), whose eyes are bandaged and blindfolded, begins to tell the story of the movie retrospectively. The whole visual setup of the film forces us at the start to be as disoriented as he is. As in so many film noirs, Marlowe's voiceover is both fallible and subjective, yet it maintains more equanimity than his on-screen physical body, whose actions often verge on the hysterical. There's a definite touch of horror in the way Marlowe in the present tense of the film is so often taken over by emotion. This tension between the cool retrospective self and the hot, somewhat out of control immediate self corresponds in terms of Freudian psychology to the tension between the controlling superego and the instinctual libido. In the hard-boiled detective story, however, it seems that the rational mind needs a healthy dose of unconsciousness before he can solve the case.

Sam Spade is given knockout drops in *The Maltese Falcon* and from his perspective we see Caspar Gutman and the room go out of focus before he loses consciousness. In addition, Spade is even kicked in the head by Wilmer the gunsel.[20] But little is explicitly made of this psychologically: Spade awakens, shakes off whatever vagueness is in his mind, and rifles through the wastepaper basket to find new clues. *Murder, My Sweet,* however, stresses Marlowe's first-person perspective more intensely. Just as his on-screen actions often verge on the frenzied, in a long sequence of the film the Marlowe of *Murder, My Sweet* is rendered unconscious at least three times, most elaborately in a long dream sequence after he has been drugged by the villainous quack-psychiatrist Jules Amthor and locked up in a shady asylum. With its malevolent voices and surreal series of opening doors, it has a family resemblance to the much more elaborate dream sequence created by Salvador Dalí for Alfred Hitchcock's *Spellbound* a year later.[21]

The presence of psychology and psychologists in a detective story immediately raises several issues, most important, the role of the detective's own state of mind in his approach to the crime and to what extent his character and his imperfect perception undermine his grasp of the supposedly objective facts. So many of the classical detectives—Dupin, Holmes, Spade—not to mention their many imitators, are sensitive to the danger of emotion, and stress instead the need to be cool, not just in relation to women but in relation to everything. To solve the case, the detective needs to triumph over his own inner darkness and weaknesses. Personal emotion clouds the mind; attention to material facts and circumstances clears it. But when the detective is drugged or beaten into unconsciousness, the way is open for the unconscious to emerge, everything that logic, causality, clarity, and even civilization itself has covered up.

Freud argued that repression was the price we had paid for civilization, and it's a useful analogy to the basic detective conundrum. He or she is often a loner, outside the social system, living by a personal code. But at the same time he or she also serves to patch up the inadequacies of the system, bringing the knowledge of the outsider to bear in the service of the larger society. To the political question—are detectives liberal or conservative? the only answer is both. Often close in psychological affinity to the criminals they pursue, they are figures equally attractive to left-wing and right-wing writers as critics of a system they ultimately preserve.[22] Sherlock Holmes may mock the police but he basically confirms the social order. He may be separate from that order as an amateur and a quondam aristocrat but he understands the need for rank and manners. In "A Scandal in Bohemia," for example, he derides the king of Bohemia's snobbery, his unwillingness to marry Irene Adler for social reasons, but he still solves the case and preserves the king's reputation. The hard-boiled detective, as he appears in Hammett and later, carries with him instead the desire to avenge the common people against the rich and powerful. "To hell with the rich," says Philip Marlowe in Chandler's *The Big Sleep*. Yet he likes General Sternwood, the decayed man of the past, and is willing to be his servant, or at least his employee, continuing the detective's political ambivalence. But as capitalist culture expands through the nineteenth century and into the twentieth, the detective as an agent of revenge against the social and class pressures that make men feel inadequate becomes stronger. The left could see the detective as a Marxist avenger, the individual against corrupt institutions, with no permanent allies except perhaps for one sympathetic cop or reporter. On the right, the detective considers the system corrupt, but this view stems from an idealism about Americanism and American institutions rather than a distrust of capitalism.[23]

After World War II, for the first time in the history of the genre, an overwhelming mass audience for the detective story was reached by Mickey Spillane's series of novels featuring Mike Hammer, beginning with *I, the Jury* in 1947. By 1965, of the top thirty best-selling books since 1895, Spillane had seven. By 1980, *I, the Jury* alone had sold 225 million books. What explains this explosion of fascination with a cultural figure about a century old? In a postwar world of uncertainty, filled with former soldiers returning home after years in battle to the confusions of peacetime, Hammer is the detective as hero, physically and sexually indomitable, without the need for anyone's help, except perhaps from Velda, his loyal secretary, certainly not from the police, who invariably need *his* help. His quest is for revenge, defined by Old Testament morality (*I, the Jury; Vengeance Is Mine*), and he fights for those who cannot fight for themselves: "After the war I've been almost anxious to get to some of the rats that make up the section of humanity that prey on people." But even though the Spillane detective defines himself as power for the powerless, corruption remains the unkillable monster.

The combat between the detective as the discoverer of facts and the psychiatrist as the detective of the mind takes a dark turn in *I, the Jury* with the standoff between Hammer and the woman he loves, the psychiatrist Charlotte Manning, who turns out to be the murderer. She is the sexual woman, who is also a figure of independent power because she has insight into the minds of men and their actual weakness beneath the exterior bluster. As Hammer says in the final confrontation scene, "How many times have you gone into the frailty of men and seen their weaknesses? It made you afraid. You no longer had the social instincts of a woman—that of being dependent upon a man." In a sense *I, the Jury* is a rewriting of *The Maltese Falcon* for another era. The primary motivation for both quests is to avenge the death of a male associate, partner, or friend; the killer in both is a woman who at first seems to be attractive to the detective. The important difference is that while Sam Spade turns Bridget O'Shaughnessy over to the police, Mike Hammer kills Charlotte Manning. But both demonstrate the real mark of detective virtue, not to be swayed by either female sexuality or the possibility of love in the pursuit of justice.

In their different ways, many of the most memorable detective novels and films from the late 1940s onward ask the same question: Is there still a place for the detective in the postwar world—or is he an archaic figure from the past, a hero no longer relevant? Surrounded and threatened by what he sees as a totally corrupt world of politicians, university intellectuals, Communist agents, feminine men, masculine women, oversexed women, Mike Hammer reasserts the heroic male body, equally at home with extreme violence and aggressive sexuality. In the process he supports the status quo by solving the crime while simultaneously administering his own brand of vigilante justice.

Other writers, contemplating the detective and still convinced of his relevance as a cultural figure, don't quite share Spillane's hostility to the detective of the mind. In a mingling of the detective story with some central gothic themes, Ross Macdonald's detective hero Lew Archer is faced with crimes that can be unraveled only by an understanding of the past, crimes that are often connected to a tangled family history of sin and betrayal, reminiscent of the world of the gothic. Characterized in contrast to Hammer's aggressiveness, Archer is self-effacing, much less physical and more psychologically internal. Instead of grand crimes, he focuses on the problems of seemingly normal people, and his greatest talent for solving the mysteries that face him is his empathy. More interested in people than in facts, he has the usual detective skill of putting facts together, but it is the intricacy of personal and family relationships that draws him. Like Raymond Chandler's, his stories are set in southern California. But whereas Chandler's Los Angeles is a city of insubstantial facades, Macdonald sees it as the place where people come who want to leave their pasts behind and become different persons, clinging precariously to their newfound respectability. As in the tale of horror, the repressed past with all its sin and guilt, as the detective unfolds them, will take its revenge. So many of the characters Lew Archer meets have Jekyll and Hyde personalities, the self from the past wearing the mask of the present in a doubleness that inevitably catches up with them. In a world of people intent on forgetting who they were, Archer is the Rememberer.

With such an investment in the psychology as well as the circumstances of crime, Archer has a close relation in a novel like *The Chill* (1964) to Miles Godwin, the psychologist who is treating some of those involved in the case. As the epigraph to this section illustrates, they are moving in parallel quests,

Archer's objective, Godwin's subjective. With the fading of an un-self-conscious assertion of stoic but aggressive masculinity as an aspect of the detective, the way is open for a greater uncertainty in the detective's quest for a logically discovered conclusion. Instead, even when the circumstances are clear, the mystery of why, the mystery of character, remains. As in so many tales of horror in which the ghosts come to torment the living, neither the sins of the past nor the web of family relations—the myths of self that underlie our behavior—can ever be escaped. As Archer says in *The Chill,* "It's a complex world. The human mind is the most complex thing in it." And the closer we get in the detective stories to the complexities of the human mind, the closer we get to the central issues of horror.[24]

THE FALLIBLE DETECTIVE: KISS ME DEADLY *AND* CHINATOWN

"You don't even know what you're looking for."

—Carl Evello to Mike Hammer in *Kiss Me Deadly*

"You may think you know what you're dealing with. But believe me you don't."

—Noah Cross to J. J. Gittes in *Chinatown*

In the final chapter I will sketch out some of the ways the detective sensibility and skills, through an increased knowledge of science and forensics, manage to survive into the contemporary world, even in the face of the continuingly powerful domination of horror. But before I leave the detective here, I want to take a brief look at two films that severely question both the figure and the genre in which he appears. It's appropriate that while literature tries various ways to bring the detective into the modern world, the movies, with their emphasis on the world of visible circumstances, should be the place where the inadequacy of the detective's reliance on reason and observation are most extensively critiqued. One cause might be the growing awareness of movie artifice itself. The faults of vision and observation are an intriguing theme in literature, but they are central to the movies. Movies know that they are visually made up, and as time goes on, that awareness becomes more often part of their plots and their meaning. But in the detective story there needs to be some objective way of knowing. Otherwise the whole genre has little point. Sight, visual perception, the detective's ability to see better than others, Sherlock Holmes with a magnifying glass, can easily be fallible, with or without recourse to Heisenberg's observer effect, in which the act of observation changes what is being observed. The traditional detective was a master of time and circumstances, almost like a God outside time viewing and understanding the chain of causes. The later detective, no matter how competent, can't avoid being part of the chain of causes and circumstances himself.

I should stress, however, that in both *Kiss Me Deadly* (1955) and *Chinatown* (1974), it is the traditional figure of the private detective that is the center of unsympathetic attention, even though the idea of detection itself, with its assumptions about the rigor of facts, will continue to spawn stories down to the CSIs and NCISs of the present, in which knowledge derived from the law and the lab becomes central to the solution. Compared with Robert Aldrich and A. I. Bezzerides's version of Mike Hammer, and Roman Polanski and Robert Towne's J. J. Gittes, Ross Macdonald has a very positive view of the activities of Lew Archer. But he is still a detective who has changed significantly from the tradition begun by Poe and Doyle. Archer's separateness, his engaged detachment, ensures that the prime emotion in Macdonald's novels is nostalgia, for that same past and its values that so many of his characters reject. So often his villains are people who willfully refuse to remember. The attraction of the detective according to Ross Macdonald seems to have little to do with the social problem of crime, or the pleasure of puzzle solving, but more to the feeling that another America of family and friends and trust between strangers has been lost and the only guardians of its empty treasury are the detectives, the tender, armored professionals of loneliness.

Nostalgia, empathy, or any softer feeling is totally alien to the Mike Hammer of the film *Kiss Me Deadly*. In Spillane, Mike is the straightforward, no-nonsense working-class guy who hates the corruption of the world he finds himself in and is out to cleanse it. In the film of *Kiss Me Deadly*, he's a self-seeking individualist jerk. How does this happen? To question the genre and its major mythic figure is also to question its basic meaning, not only in terms of its view of knowledge but also in terms of its moral assumptions. Usually in the detective story the moral pattern and the pattern of facts are related. When the detective finds the answer, the bad guys are punished. In *Kiss Me Deadly* something different happens.

In essence, *Kiss Me Deadly* plays with our expectations of how a detective like Mike Hammer will behave, and how a detective story will unfold. We begin *in medias res*. A barefoot woman in a trench coat is running down a deserted road. A car appears. She stands blocking it in the middle of the road and its driver grudgingly stops to pick her up. The driver, who turns out to be Mike Hammer, doesn't know what's going on—and neither do we. They talk, elude a police roadblock, another car blocks their way, and they are captured by men whose voices we hear but otherwise see mainly their shoes. Amid odd angles and threatening shadows, she is tortured, and they are both packed into his car, which is sent off the road and explodes. Three days later, Mike wakes up in a hospital bed and begins his detective quest to find the answer. But unlike the majority of detective films, in which our perspective is bound to the detective's vision through voiceover or over-the-shoulder point of view, *Kiss Me Deadly* continually separates us from Hammer's perspective, confining him in dark hallways and narrow staircases. We are encouraged, in other words, not to play along with the detective's point of view, but to seek other angles, even other stories that might be told—which the film supplies in abundance, beginning scenes by focusing on people extraneous to the plot, shooting from impossible angles, overloading the soundtrack and the visual field with classical music, jazz, ballet dancing, opera, abstract art, boxing matches, horse races, not to mention classical and Christian mythology. The beginning of the film just happens; the middle is a wandering trail of unrelated "clues" and "facts" all carefully noted down by Mike; and in the end everything blows up.

Kiss Me Deadly fundamentally tells two stories, one of detective adequacy, the other of detective inadequacy. The first takes seriously the detective's urge to factual certainty and his belief in his ability to find the mysterious object, whatever his motivations. (Hammer in *Kiss Me Deadly* certainly has venal motivations and is altogether a sleazier figure than he is in Spillane.) Still, he is the guy we might expect from *I, the Jury* and other Spillane novels, as well as from the detective tradition. As Pat Chambers, his "friend" on the police force says, "He's got a nose. He can sniff out information like nobody I ever saw." He puts together the facts, tracks down addresses, and writes them all down in his notebook. He knows people in all areas of life, black and white, working class and rich. He is as at home in a garage or a boxing school as he is in a rich gangster's house or talking trash to the police. Women throw themselves at him, while he maintains a cool distance. Men try to attack him and he quickly decks them. He is in virtually every scene.

Hammer in *Kiss Me Deadly* does everything that a detective usually does but it's not enough and it doesn't matter. He represents literal-mindedness in a world of myth and larger-than-life forces. Because the camera shows him to us constantly trapped in shadows and architectural décor, we are being asked to take a critical distance from any assumption of the detective's ability to find the pattern in facts. What is happening is much larger than the narrow world of his attention. Unlike the classic detective story, which tends to go in a straight line toward the goal of solution, here the facts are enigmatic, and the quest more like the path through a labyrinth than an unfolding of truth, a search, as his secretary Velda calls it, for the Great Whatsit. Mike goes around expecting he'll find the answer, but he doesn't really understand what's going on. Clues for him go inward, while the film goes outward to the new great fact in the world, the atom bomb. The final atomic explosion is more mythic than realistic; chain reactions don't happen that way. But it has appropriately exploded, at least for this film, the myth of the detective's dedication to logic and reason, his ability to bring order out of seeming disorder. Instead, in *Kiss Me Deadly* at least, he has succeeded only in creating chaos. In a film crammed with cultural references, at the end all culture and values are gone; only the exploding bomb and the ocean remain, making hash of the detective's vision, his commitment to discovering causes, and his heroic quest and character, along with his myth of himself, as he hobbles along in the surf, supported by his secretary, and the waves smash against them.

The detective story is significantly affected by external events, as knowledge itself becomes a more important issue. In attacking Spillane's heroicized figure of Mike Hammer, *Kiss Me Deadly* may seek to end the detective film as a genre. Almost twenty years later, *Chinatown* tries again, in a world in which the methods of certainty and even the belief that certainty can be achieved have taken even more hits from history. The earlier English detective's preoccupation with exotic details along with an amateur's dabbling in matters of death and violence reflect something in the English character. Likewise, the hard-boiled detective's brashness and belief in his own ability to crack heads and solve cases has something of an American optimism. Hammett (born 1894) and Chandler (born 1888) both served in World War I; Spillane (born 1918) and Macdonald (born 1915) were in World War II. But later detective writers like Sara Paretsky (born 1947) came of age during the Vietnam War and witnessed the coming of such social movements as black power and feminism. By the 1970s, after such national traumas as the assassinations of John and Robert Kennedy and Martin Luther King, Jr., the resignation of Richard Nixon after Watergate, and the cynicism about America's moral position in the world bred by the Vietnam War, that optimism is wearing thin. The American atmosphere instead becomes charged with paranoia about who is really controlling things, along with a mistrust both of government and of the individual's ability to change anything. In such a cultural environment, the detective as an idealized image of the American can-do attitude gives way to a keener appreciation of the paradoxes of his brand of masculine individualism. Traditionally, however limited the detective may be, he (and sometimes she) empowers the audience. But when the detective falters and the quest for the answer, the Great Whatsit, is defeated, we are left adrift.

At the same time that there is a growing cynicism about the effectiveness of the detective's methods and the quality of his character, the decline of the studio system of filmmaking virtually eliminated the old style of serial genre film, in which there could be twenty and thirty versions of the same story with the same hero or heroine.[25] Certainly in film the new detective stories tend to stand alone or encompass only a few films with the same central character. How then to revitalize the form, make it relevant to new audiences? Some popular methods that cut across horror and detective include the intensification of sex and violence in the story, a greater authenticity in relation to the literary sources, and a comic putdown of the genre's assumptions. Others, more native to the detective story, are an aging of characters, as the genre itself has become somewhat exhausted, and an homage to great predecessors, as fictional detectives explicitly invoke the fictional detectives who preceded them.[26]

Unlike the contemporary Los Angeles of *Kiss Me Deadly*, *Chinatown* sets its critique of the detective in the L.A. of the 1930s, somewhere between the time of *The Maltese Falcon* and *The Big Sleep*. But thematically *Chinatown* is an amalgam of *The Chill*'s themes of an overhanging sinful past with the obliviousness of Mike Hammer in *Kiss Me Deadly*. Until the very last shot of *Chinatown,* we learn along with J. J. Gittes, often looking over his shoulder. In this film that so much involves seeing and spying, he is the consummate private eye, using photographs and binoculars, observing with mirrors and through windows, eavesdropping. The look of *Chinatown* is usually referred to as neo-noir, a full-color version of the black-and-white noirs of the past, and a dominant visual style for many of the detective, mystery, and crime films of the 1970s and after. Part of what characterizes neo-noir is the expansion of the dark shadows and night world of noir into daytime as well. There are certainly night scenes in *Chinatown,* especially toward the end, but much of the story occurs during bright sunlight in a world of seeming clarity. Yet it is still overshadowed, this time metaphorically, by the crime that Gittes is trying to unravel. Every time his activities seem to point to the truth, they turn problematic; without the right interpretation the facts he collects are meaningless. Unlike Macdonald's Lew Archer, who understands the ghosts that can come from the past, Gittes, like the film itself, is a creature of immediate time who believes he is its master. But more and more the burden of the past makes itself known in *Chinatown*. As a story of the theft of water, it emphasizes the fluidity of truth rather than its solidity and hardness.

The first crack in his carefully constructed facade comes early in the film when he comes back to his office and insists on telling an off-color and racist joke without realizing there is a woman behind him. As usual, we are in the scene with him, but here we can see something he cannot, and what we see turns out to be crucial, because she is the real Evelyn Mulwray, not the impersonator who hired him to trace her husband's supposed philandering. It seemed that the case was solved and Gittes got front-page praise for his work, but it turns out that he has been fooled. We may learn along with him, but here, not for the last time, we are invited to see beyond him as well. Like Hammer in *Kiss Me Deadly*, Gittes, with his nose to the ground, doesn't understand the big picture. He calls upon his professional skills of snooping and putting together facts, but they are still finally just able to manipulate things and have no insight into people. As he tries to find the pattern of the crimes— the myriad connections between Mulwray and Cross and the water and the DA's office and the corrupt L.A. government—we go along with him because we also want to know the answer, and the search in some sense works. We know the answers at the end. He has been a "good" detective. But the problem is that it does him no good and he is powerless to make anything come out right. In the novel of *The Big Sleep* the detective plot (whodunit) and the moral plot (who is a good person) converge in the last chapter, although Marlowe is left somewhat pining after "Silver Wig"—Mrs. Eddie Mars. In the film's reordering of things, the moral plot, the detective plot, and the romantic plot (Marlowe and Mrs. Rutledge) all come together at the end. But in *Chinatown* that physical solution (whodunit) that Gittes does so well to put together does not issue in a moral solution at all. In fact, the physical solution seems to bring about an immoral solution. All of Gittes's actions inadvertently but decisively make sure that the incest will continue as Katherine is taken off by her father/grandfather, the plot to steal water and incorporate the San Fernando Valley continues unchanged, and the potential romance between Gittes and Evelyn Mulwray dies with her, when he tries to block the gunshot of one detective and makes another aim higher and kill her.

The crimes in both the public and the private spheres will seemingly continue despite everything the detective does. "Forget it, Jake, it's Chinatown," says Gittes's investigator Walsh. Chinatown, like the Great Whatsit of *Kiss Me Deadly*, is a metaphor for our inability to control the world, and it's only the arrogant detective, like Hammer or Gittes, who thinks he can. As the effort in the detective story to dominate crime and chaos through knowledge and facts becomes more difficult, we have moved closer to the themes of horror—the nameless, shapeless monster of atomic power at the end of *Kiss Me Deadly*, the monstrous power of Noah Cross.

But there is another force in both films, the force of aesthetic and visual pattern. Unlike the melancholic end of the detective's search for pattern, the aesthetic pattern is sumptuously fulfilled. The director Roman Polanski appears in *Chinatown* as a gangster who slices Gittes's nose—a reference perhaps specifically to Hammer's famous nose for information in *Kiss Me Deadly* or to the ability of the detective generally to sniff out the buried facts. Thus the classic detective pattern in which the hero connects the material facts is superseded by the director's ability to tell a visually engaging story of detective failure. Throughout the film we have generally been at eye level, seeing everything from Gittes's point of view, learning along with him. At the end of *Chinatown* appears the only overhead shot in the film, as the camera moves upward and Gittes recedes in the distance; the bigger picture has won. Only by rereading, rewatching, as Gittes no longer is able to, can we hope to see what he (and we) have missed, what we have misinterpreted in our uncritical adherence to the detective's perspective.

✌⊙✌

The kind of attack leveled against the detective's basic assumptions about his ability to control the visible world, solve crime, and bring criminals to justice by such films as *Kiss Me Deadly* and *Chinatown* might make us wonder how the series detective is able to maintain his cultural significance. From the 1980s to the present, there are fewer loner detectives, and more police detectives, inspectors, employees of a bureaucracy and a justice system, members of a team. Even though there are still detective novelists with large followings, the private detective is no longer the central cultural figure he was in earlier incarnations. But investigative procedures, the pursuit of witnesses and testimony and facts, still attract wide audiences. Just as the hard-boiled detective's physical and sexual prowess has to a certain extent been coopted by the spy, so his pursuit of clues has been taken over by the lab scientist. Such stories, most often on television, combine the immediate crime with an ongoing workplace drama, in which the personal nature of the detectives involved (always plural) or their subjective responses only occasionally make any impact on the case.

With the exception of the forensically oriented shows like *CSI, Law and Order,* and so on, it turns out that the monster more easily makes repeat appearances than the detective in film, the detective more often than the monster in fiction. The crucial question is why we are at all still willing to trust the first-person, either as a central character or as the narrator of his or her own adventures. One reason might be that the novel can easily hold together the immediate and the retrospective; to do that, the film needs voiceover. There is no voiceover in either *Kiss Me Deadly* or *Chinatown;* the detective is on his own.

Looking at the detectives that have appeared in the novel from the 1960s onward, certain characteristics may justify the reader's trust. When the prime detective is a white male, he often has an intimate relation with some city or locality: John D. McDonald's Travis McGee (first novel, *The Deep Blue Goodbye,* 1964) lives on a houseboat in Florida; Robert B. Parker's Spenser (first novel, *The Godwulf Manuscripts,* 1964) lives in a townhouse in Boston. Over the years it seems that any self-respecting city needs its own fictional detective, or better yet a couple. Like Dupin and Holmes, these latter-day detectives know their own cities intimately, and their adventures are celebrations of city life, not in a chamber of commerce way but through the ability of fiction to make that place magical.

Spenser also presciently (in terms of the evolution of the detective figure) has two prime allies, the black investigator Hawk and the Jewish psychologist Susan Silverman. For these are representatives of groups left out of the traditional definition of the detective—women, gays, blacks, Jews. When they appeared in earlier stories, they were usually marginalized or criminals, but now they can be detectives too.

In the 1950s, Chester Himes's Gravedigger Jones and Coffin Ed Johnson were forerunners. But the real explosion of "new" detectives began in the 1970s and 1980s with Ernest Tidyman's African-American detective John Shaft; Tony Hillerman's Navajo cop, Joe Leaphorn; Joseph Hansen's gay insurance investigator Dave Brandstetter; Hillerman's Hopi cop Jim Chee; as well as Sara Paretsky's V. I. Warshawski and Sue Grafton's Kinsey Millhone, who go beyond female to feminist. So pervasive and continuing a tradition has this been that at the *Los Angeles Times* book prizes in 2014, the prime characters in the mystery and detective nominees were a London detective, a Mississippi attorney, a Dublin cop, a lawyer in Germany, and a Masai detective in Nairobi.

Now, with the appearance of detectives of every race, sexual orientation, and ethnic and national origin, the old ratiocinative side, the solving side of the detective story, has become even less important than the character of the detective, his personal problems, his relations with the members of his team, and whatever other emotional issues the case raises. In other works detection has expanded from a professional calling to a role assumed by an innocent bystander, who might need to solve the crime to exonerate himself, or have other personal motives for getting involved. Everyman can be a detective. One version of the innocent bystander as inadvertent detective was pioneered by Alfred Hitchcock as early as the 1930s. In another interesting example, the Japanese film *Zero Focus* (1961), a recently married woman whose husband has disappeared must travel to a faraway town to figure out what has happened. Walter Mosley's detective hero Easy Rawlins (beginning with *Devil in a Blue Dress,* 1990) can only be an amateur because as an African-American living in 1940s Los Angeles, he can't be an official detective, hard-boiled or not, in the traditional white male sense. But despite the advent of all these detectives who are "different" from the old-style white male detective, the crucial question remains: Does their presence renovate the detective? Does their different nature yield a different perspective? Or are they just the same old detective, looking for the facts, knocking people around—only now with a different face and body but no different attitude?

So many of the old detective themes persist. In *Blade Runner* (1982), featuring a detective of the dystopian future of Los Angeles, the old theme of the nightmare city is pervasive, and there is even a version of the film that features a noir-like voiceover by the main character. At the same time, however, as in *The Chill,* elements of classical horror, like the inability to remember the past and the effort of created beings to become human, abound. Perhaps most common, in both American and foreign versions, is the connection of the detective story to an exploration of the social context, in which the immediate personal case often leads, as in *Chinatown,* into a larger world of public corruption, in which the rich perpetrators, like Noah Cross in *Chinatown,* cannot ultimately be touched.

Such stories and such characters, even when they are members of an official world, perpetuate something basic that characterized even those white male detectives of the past, the outsider looking into the world of established wealth and power with a jaundiced view. As detective reason is taken over by the crime lab and the niceties of the legal system, detective sensibility struggles to maintain its code of honor in whatever world it finds itself.

CHAPTER 6

Jekyll and Hyde

THE MONSTER FROM WITHIN

I have a little shadow that goes in and out with me
And what can be the use of him is more than I can see . . . .
He hasn't got a notion of how children ought to play,
And can only make a fool of me in every sort of way.

—Robert Louis Stevenson, *A Child's Garden of Verses* (1885)

The art of every era generates the symbolic figures it needs to express its hopes and fears. Through the tale of horror, Western culture in general and Anglo-American culture in particular have constructed heroes and monsters to embody those feelings. The detective's character and his way of proceeding is a foil to that story. It illuminates them by its valuing of reason and causality to explain the links between tangible clues rather than the horror story's perplexing of the line between what is visible and what is invisible, what is explainable and what is unexplainable. At the heart of these stories is the unknown and the unseen, and the essential lure is the divided desire to explain or to baffle. As I've mentioned, even the most appreciative readers of Ann Radcliffe's novels were often put off by her endings, in which all the gothic paraphernalia evaporated in the light of a natural explanation of human tyranny and self-interest—as Jane Austen parodied in *Northanger Abbey*. Such an explanation, however, is at the heart of the detective mode: reducing the horrific to the merely criminal and then solving and packaging the mystery. But the temptation of the monstrous always lies beneath.

Why should the monster and the detective have appeared in both the popular and the high arts during the time of one of the greatest changes in history, with the Industrial Revolution, the rise of great cities, the expansion of empires, the transformation of economies, and all the other seemingly impersonal movements we cover with the umbrella term "the modern"? The growing awareness of the complex organization of society, the pressure on individual nature of large-scale institutions, the possibility of increasing political freedom—all engender a greater sensitivity to whatever represses freedom—from both outside and from within. In this light the monster and the detective constitute a Janus-headed response to otherwise meagerly articulated problems in the nineteenth-century idea of both civilized society and personal nature. Horror embodies a hidden culture, often rooted in past belief and "superstition," that has been otherwise repressed by the daylight world of official culture and society, while the detective represents the urge to delve into that darker world and clarify its seemingly intractable mysteries. In the preceding chapter, I chiefly looked at the detective from the point of view of evidence and context, the essentially empirical, material world setting of the detective story and its basis in factuality and causality. But because of the special nature of the detective's character, his weirdness and separateness, the detective story is always also about identity. So too the tales of horror focus not only on questions of epistemology and knowledge but also on questions of personal identity.[1]

The nineteenth-century advent of the detective, as well as the elaboration of the monster beyond its religious and natural roots, reflects and to a certain extent foretells the era of Darwin (*The Origin of Species,* 1859), Marx (*Das Kapital,* 1867), Freud (*The Interpretation of Dreams,* 1900), and other overarching theories of everything. All three of these influential thinkers take the potential for the monstrous out of the world of abnormality and bring it closer to home. To simplify their ideas into broad strokes: Darwin's argument about the process of evolution had the unsettling consequence that human beings are much closer to animals than anyone thought, while implying that no God of good or principle of evil ruled the world; over the course of millions of years, it just happened. Marx's postulation of the class struggle as the engine of history and his metaphor that the capitalist is a bloodsucking vampire on the working class undermined the idea that social hierarchy had any natural justification. Freud's view that civilization was defined by the repression of instincts decisively traced the seeds of insanity to the warping context of the family and society rather than being solely a trait of the aberrant individual. With such powerful ideas in circulation, both horror and detective tales assume cultural roles well beyond escapism and entertainment. Horror most intricately develops its potential to show the essential artifice of social form, social consensus, and social relations, including the demonic side of the family as well as the animal, instinctual, sexual self under the tuxedos and top hats of respectability. With similar materials at its disposal, the detective story tries instead to knit up the torn social fabric and allay or at least explain the bubbling violence that so often exists between individuals by applying logic and the hand of justice.

Like the monster, the detective stands apart from the conventional social order. But whereas the monster's difference is feared, the detective's difference allows a perspective and an insight that normal society either lacks or has forgotten. As the form mutated, it more and more defined itself as an X-ray view of whatever city or environment the detective finds himself or herself in—the social structure, the corruption of institutions and individuals, the labyrinth of streets and neighborhoods. Along with the detective's role in conserving social norms also came a certain amount of racism and sexism as well, even though during the 1920s and 1930s female detectives like Torchy Blane as well as the goodly complement of ethnic detectives—Mr. Wong, Charlie Chan, Mr. Moto—in their own way underlined the detective's basic difference from the settled social world that his work so often supported. As we have seen, especially since the 1970s detectives have come in a rainbow variety of sexual orientations, races, ethnicities, and national backgrounds. Despite these transmutations of the almost exclusively white male detective of the past, the city also remains an integral part of the detective's makeup. Just as any country wanting to assert its presence on the world stage has to have a national airline, any city with claims to importance must have a resident detective. In contrast with the specificity of the detective and his city, the horror story may seem to be transnational and transcultural in its evocation of basic human fears. But the detective's quest for an answer also highlights the darkness that the city and the urban world generally have ignored as they advance into the future.

DOUBLE DETECTIVES AND DOUBLE MONSTERS

With every day, and from both sides of my intelligence, the moral and intellectual, I thus drew steadily nearer to that truth, by whose partial discovery I have been doomed to such a dreadful shipwreck: that man is not truly one, but truly two.

—Stevenson, *The Strange Case of Dr. Jekyll and Mr. Hyde* (1886)

Let me turn our consideration of the detective away from his preoccupation with facts and causes and toward a personal characteristic he shares with one of the prime forms of the monster: his doubleness. Doubleness brings together the otherwise contradictory parts of the self, or the seemingly contradictory preoccupations of a writer or artist. Poe's work, for example, can be separated into his detective stories and his horror stories, but underlying them both is a sense of psychological and physical entrapment that is either surmounted in the detective stories, or succumbed to in the horror stories. Some horror stories treat this physically. In "The Cask of Amontillado," revenge for a slight requires the narrator to wall up his victim in a dank wine cellar. In "The Pit and the Pendulum" the narrator is himself chained and imprisoned as the blade of the pendulum gets closer and closer. In "The Fall of the House of Usher" Roderick Usher's sister is buried alive. Other Poe stories focus on psychological imprisonment. In "The Tell-Tale Heart" the narrator goes mad because he believes he hears the heart of the man he has murdered for no explicit reason still beating beneath the floor. In "William Wilson" the confinement is also psychological, as the "other" William Wilson pursues the narrator through all the episodes of his misbegotten life. And with a twist on the theme of confinement, in "The Masque of the Red Death" Florentine revelers who lock themselves away in a castle to escape the plague in Florence discover that it only brings Death closer. So characters are trapped in tombs, trapped by their family heredity, and trapped by their belief in their own immortality and ability to escape the final page and the end of the story.

The obverse of these tales of often self-created captivity is Dupin's ability to solve impossible mysteries, like the locked-room deaths in "The Murders in the Rue Morgue." But the fact that there are only three of the detective stories and many, many more of the horror stories shows that Poe's fears perhaps outweigh his optimism. Psychologically oriented critics have speculated that the abandonment of Poe's family by his biological father and his tense relation with his adoptive father John Allan lie behind some of these stories and their sense of living in a fearful, suffocating world. He even gives William Wilson his own birthday (although he makes him four years younger), and the character's name implies that he is self-created, the son of himself. But whatever the personal psychological causes, they allowed Poe to turn his special demons into literature that resonated with the fears of millions. Roderick Usher may believe that his family has been specifically cursed for its heredity and therefore his house must fall. But now we know that we all have preexisting conditions.

Poe's Dupin and Doyle's Holmes share this doubleness with the city they both love to wander through. Poe refers to Dupin as "a double Dupin" for the way he brings imagination together with reason and analysis, "the Bi-Part

Soul—the creative and the resolvent."[2] In a sense, Dupin transforms the conflicts and uncertainties of Poe's maddened first-person narrators into the detachment of a third person. Attuned to the minutest detail in his observations, Holmes similarly luxuriates in the contrast of both neighborhoods and human lives in London, the impersonality of his "method" sitting restlessly in tandem with the eccentricity of his personality.

The detective's rootedness in both his empirical view of clues in particular and his emotional affinity with the nature of crime in general bears then an odd resemblance to the mesmerist motto—"God, matter, and motion"—that brings together the material world with the world of the spirit. As Watson describes Holmes at a concert, "In his singular character the dual nature alternately asserted itself and his extreme exactness and astuteness represented, as I have often thought, the reaction against the poetic and contemplative mood which occasionally predominated in him." Doyle's conception of the city is as double as Holmes's nature, with a metaphoric touch that chimes with both Darwin and Freud: "All day the wind had screamed and the rain had beaten against the windows, so that even here in the heart of great hand-made London we were forced to raise our minds for the instant from the routine of life, and to recognize the presence of those great elemental forces which shriek at mankind through the bars of his civilization, like untamed beasts in a cage" ("The Five Orange Pips").[3]

The possibility that the monstrous is not out there and exotic but is somehow inside and "normal," waiting to be released, exists almost from the beginning of the modern tradition of the horror story. Victor Frankenstein, for example, refers to the Creature "nearly in the light of my own vampire, my own spirit let loose from the grave and forced to destroy all that was dear to me." This so-called doppelgänger figure appears often in horror tales of the late eighteenth and well into the nineteenth century, at about the same time that the phenomenon was beginning to be observed scientifically.[4]

In its imaginative manifestation, the doppelgänger, unlike the ghost who comes for revenge or some other reason, resembles a living person, and supposedly foretells doom. If you happened to see your own doppelgänger, it meant that you would soon die. Stories of such presentiments were told of Percy Shelley, Nicolai Gogol, and Abraham Lincoln among many less famous others. The word is of Germanic origin, coined in the late eighteenth century by the writer Jean-Paul Richter. Although it is not used in English until the mid–nineteenth century, the twenty or thirty years following Richter's coinage introduced the type into European literature and drama until it became a common theme easily drawn upon as the demonic counter-part of the socially acceptable self. For writers and artists, it supplied a handy way to express something of the complexity of their own sense of themselves, their dis-ease in social situations, and their self-contradictory moods. Some doppelgängers wander abroad, but often the sense of double-ness is situated within. As Victor Hugo writes in his preface to the unpro-duced play *Cromwell* (1827), a founding document of French romanticism, "Je sens deux hommes en moi" (I feel two men in me). Somewhat earlier Goethe had specified one version of this in a frequently cited passage in *Faust* (1806):

> In me there are two souls, alas, and their
> Division tears my life in two.
> One loves the world, it clutches her, it binds
> Itself to her, clinging with furious lust;
> The other longs to soar beyond the dust
> Into the realm of high ancestral minds.

Goethe's division is between the self that loves the everyday material world and the self that seeks to aspire to greatness. In Hugo's work, Oliver Cromwell is divided over whether or not to aspire to be king. In a late-nineteenth-century sculpture by George Grey Barnard, *The Struggle of the Two Natures in Man*—based on Hugo's lines—which sits in a courtyard of the Metropolitan Museum of Art in New York, the divinity in the human tries to escape its earthly trammels.[5] The doppelgänger in Poe's "William Wilson" is similar—a better self that follows the corrupt narrator from his school days into adult-hood, criticizing and exposing his crimes and extravagances, until in a dark room the frustrated narrator stabs the other William Wilson, only to discover he has murdered himself. Poe's story was his first to be translated into French (1844) and had a great vogue in Europe, possibly also influencing Dos-toyevsky's novel *The Double* (1846; revised, 1866), which also features a double more charming and successful than his original.[6] Such better-self doppelgäng-ers tend to disappear until they are brought back in the American 1930s and 1940s in the guise of what come to be called superheroes with secret identities, and later as the people with abilities that make them different, like the X-Men and the Avengers, as well as Harry Potter. The figure of Batman, whose story has been remade so many times in the past few decades, brings together the detective crime-solver (his first appearance being in *Detective Comics*) with something of the benevolent but tortured monster, replete with masked and doubled villains like the Joker, the Penguin, and Two-Face.

But the nineteenth-century imagination of the double was decidedly darker. Like Goethe, Jekyll also thought that his experiments would release a better self only to discover that it was Mr. Hyde who appeared and gradually took over the original. So too the conflict between selves is more often sharper, between what could roughly be called a "good" self and an "evil" self. The idea of the doppelgänger, which has separated to take on a life of its own, intensifies the division. Instead of a monster like Frankenstein's that is actively created as a separate being who appears metaphorically as a conjoined self, the doppelgänger can be a ghostly double fleetingly glimpsed outside oneself (as in "William Wilson" and the German Expressionist film *The Student of Prague*), or another self that is discovered within, which then comes forth fully bodied, as in *Dr. Jekyll and Mr. Hyde*. Tales of ventriloquist dummies that take over their supposed master, self-animated dolls like Chucky, or the pincushion replicas of movie voodoo similarly follow the basic double theme. In his psychoanalytic terms, Carl Jung argues that this shadow self is more primitive, violent, and even monstrous precisely because it is repressed, but at the same time is often projected outwardly, in the way that the extreme puritan may accuse others of the sins he feels, perhaps unconsciously, most intensely attracted to himself.

Like *The Monk*, with its exploration of the repressed sexuality of Ambrosio that explodes into violence and murder, the doppelgänger represents a proto-psychological effort to plumb the contradictions and complexities of human personality. In its literary genealogy, the doppelgänger reflects a method begun with such first-person novels as Laurence Sterne's *Tristram Shandy*, Goethe's *Sorrows of Young Werther*, and Charlotte Brontë's *Jane Eyre*, in which the author creates a character resembling himself or herself. It also resembles something of the experience of a reader enjoying the possibility of taking on other identities through the form of the novel. As Robert Burns wrote at the same time that the novel was becoming a major literary form (and before the invention of photography), "O wad some Power the giftie gie us / To see oursels as ithers see us!" Like the fan who lives through an idol, the act of reading a novel itself allows such an exploration of otherness, sometimes to exaltation, sometimes to fear and trembling, but always to a degree of empathy.

To a certain extent, the image of the double self, whether doppelgänger or inner Other, echoes cultural changes in the outside world. In the new, more heterogeneous modern urban world, where people of very different types and backgrounds rub shoulders in the chaotic city, the gap between the social self and the inner self becomes more acute. But there is still a contrast to be drawn between the doppelgänger who is another version of yourself, but nevertheless appears to be separate from you, and the doppelgänger from within that surfaces after the scientific experiments of Dr. Jekyll. Whether the other self is evil or good, both Dr. Jekyll and William Wilson are destroyed by the hostility between it and the "normal" self, while the detective manages to control the division and make it work for him. Holmes in particular bodies it forth in his self-stylization as well as his ability to take on disguises as a kind of actor. In this way he foretells the many masked detectives that follow in his wake, like the French serial hero Fantomas, Zorro, Batman, and many more.

Another aspect of the detective's doubling is the sidekick who chronicles his adventures, like Dr. Watson. But the basic question raised by the doppelgänger story is the possibility first that there is no such thing as a single self, and second, despite the better self of "William Wilson," that it is more likely there is actually a monstrous or a criminal self inside the socially acceptable self, and that civilization is a momentary mask for what lies beneath. Another way of asserting this possibility is Holmes's frequently expressed view to Watson that "there is nothing so unnatural as the commonplace." When the pair take a train to investigate a mystery outside London, Watson waxes poetic about the attractiveness of the rural scenery. But Holmes will have none of it: "It is my belief, Watson, founded upon my experience, that the lowest and vilest alleys in London do not present a more dreadful record of sin than does the smiling and beautiful countryside" ("The Copper Beeches"). It does not take much to see "The Man with the Twisted Lip," with its class transformation, disguise, and seeming murder, in this way to be in literary terms a doppelgänger of "Jekyll and Hyde," the natural version of the supernatural exploration of the double self. Both dramatize how the monstrous action, the lower nature, the psychic wound, is closely connected to the gift, what makes you different. At the end of so many of the Jekyll and Hyde movies, when the monstrous features of Hyde return to Jekyll's handsome face, just as when Holmes scrubs the face of the ugly beggar to reveal Neville St. Clair, we know the monster and his crimes are gone, the mystery has been solved, and the world is boring once again.

This close relation between the double detective and the double monster is reflected in the way Stevenson shapes "Jekyll and Hyde" in the form of a criminal investigation. The full title of the novel is *The Strange Case of Dr. Jekyll and Mr. Hyde.* According to the OED, the first published use of *case* occurs in 1838 with the definition of "an incident or set of circumstances requiring investigation by the police or other detective agency." Together with the first appearance of *detective* as an adjective in 1843, as I've mentioned, a vocabulary of official investigation of crime is being established, and the Jekyll/Hyde story, like a series of depositions, is seen from a variety of points of view. Only at the end do we get "Henry Jekyll's Full Statement of the Case." In a sense, then, *Jekyll and Hyde* brings together and even synthesizes the natural and the supernatural explanations, so often at odds in the monster story, without finally giving one priority over the other. The story of horror is presented within a detective-like framework that allows us both to understand it on one level (what happens factually) and not finally understand it on another (what happens imaginatively).

Wandering the city streets with his friend Utterson (yet another duo adrift in the London dark), a young man about town named Enfield begins the narrative by recounting to Utterson the events connected to a mysterious door in the vicinity of a nearby "sinister block of buildings." Some time before, coming home at three in the morning, he had witnessed "a little man" who knocked over and heedlessly trampled a young girl as he raced down the street. With other passersby, Enfield collared the man, whose appearance filled them all with loathing: "I never saw a man I so disliked, and yet I scarce know why. He must be deformed somewhere; he gives a strong feeling of deformity, although I couldn't specify the point." After some argument, the man unlocks the mysterious door, goes inside and emerges with money and a check for the little girl's family. As it turns out, of course, the door is the back way into the house of the highly respectable Dr. Henry Jekyll, specifically into the laboratory where he has completed the experiments and undergone the transformation that turns him into the repellent Mr. Hyde. *Jekyll and Hyde,* like Oscar Wilde's *The Picture of Dorian Gray* (1891), thus explicitly reimagines the problem of the monster not as some being separate and other, but as the dark side of the self. There are suggestions in the story that Dr. Jekyll had a disorderly past that he would rather forget, and the possibility that Hyde is blackmailing him for it is one of the early assumptions of his friends. But like the image of the strange door that mysteriously connects a shadier London neighborhood with a house in a fashionable area, the two selves are connected by the same body. Hyde, in Stevenson's image, is thus the backdoor self through which Jekyll can lose his constricted social identity in the lower parts of the city.

Two years after the publication of *Jekyll and Hyde,* the Jack the Ripper murders occurred in the East End of London. With the exception of semi- or entirely mythic serial killers like the Scottish cannibal leader Sawney Bean and the meat-pie impresario and murderous barber Sweeney Todd, Jack the Ripper was the first real serial killer to catch the public eye and stimulate fascination and shivers. The eighteenth-century "Newgate Calendar," originally a report of the executions for the month, with descriptions of the crimes along with an uplifting account of the criminal's repentance on the steps to the gallows, was the forerunner of both the actual police reports as well as the "penny dreadful" compilations of famous and fictional murders, including the body-snatching essential to early medicine. Along with low-level ripoffs of more celebrated gothic fiction like *The Monk* and new works like *Varney the Vampire,* such stories were part of popular journalism since the early nineteenth century, with a low-cost genre format that competed with the more expensive novel. Aimed especially at working-class males who were part of newly literate classes, their tales of the extremes of human nature both emphasized and supported the reader's normality, even while they allowed him (usually him) to indulge in fantasies of horror and violence.

THE SHADOW KNOWS

If we shadows have offended,
Think but this, and all is mended—
That you have but slumber'd here
While these visions did appear.

—Shakespeare, *A Midsummer's Night's Dream,* V, i, 412–15

The conflation between Stevenson's fiction and the actual events of the Jack the Ripper case was almost immediate, even to the somewhat ludicrous extent that Richard Mansfield, an actor who played Jekyll and Hyde in an early stage version of the story, was suspected of the crimes. Over the years more than five hundred others have been fingered as the Ripper, including Prince Albert Victor, the painter Walter Sickert, and even Lewis Carroll, while a recent book has unequivocally named Aaron Kozminski, a Polish immigrant who was on the suspect list at the time. But the most long-lived popular belief perfectly mirrored Stevenson's own implications that class tension lay behind or beneath these visions of the horror of the double self, and that it was an upper-class man who had descended into the poor neighborhoods of London to murder the lower-class prostitutes who plied their trade there. Jack the Ripper, Mr. Hyde, Dracula—under the cloak of respectability, even aristocracy, is the monster.[7]

Although the young girl trampled by Hyde in the novel is virtually the only woman who makes any appearance, already by the time of the stage adaptation the next year, a love/lust interest was added to the Jekyll and Hyde story in the person of Alice, a vicar's daughter—a plot innovation that becomes more elaborate in the many film versions that followed. Aside from the oblique remarks about Jekyll's past—such as Enfield's theory that he is being blackmailed for a "youthful indiscretion"—the issue of sexuality hardly comes up in the novel. Instead, as Stevenson characterizes it, the release of the Hyde beneath the skin unleashes a whole complex of antisocial traits, rather than any one specifically. Just as Hyde inspires in those who see him a generalized loathing and perception of deformity that seems unrelated to any specific physical trait, the physical body in general is virtually absent from the novel. But, viewed through a Freudian lens, in the *Jekyll and Hyde* films, it turns out that lust and sexual license are almost always designated as the underside of all that respectability. Movies, like theater, with their penchant for the visible, thereby pick out and dramatize the most physical manifestations of the repressed self—sex and violence. Whereas in the novel no one who sees Hyde can manage to articulate more than a vague description—"a little man" arousing "unspeakable terror"—in the many Jekyll and Hyde films all the art of the actor and the makeup man is brought to bear on the distinction between Jekyll's matinee idol features and the shudder-inspiring face of Hyde. So too in the movie versions that begin in the early twentieth century the double man is often supplied with a double woman to match, usually a lower-class woman of easy virtue for Hyde and an almost unattainable upper-class woman for Jekyll.

This is hardly surprising. The natural monster is an anomaly and often precivilized. The created monster as well is defined by his inability to really be human. But just as the Jekyll/Hyde monster displays the doubled face of social respectability and bestial violence, it also reflects the intimate relation between actor and character, performer and role. The natural affinities of the Jekyll/Hyde story for an actor eager to show off his virtuosity were therefore recognized almost immediately, making it the most repeatedly staged and filmed in the annals of monster tales. After several versions in the early years of film, including F. W. Murnau's unauthorized adaptation *The Janus-Head* (1920), the "Great Profile" John Barrymore starred in an American silent version (also 1920) that was popular enough that a pre-Hardy Stan Laurel parodied it in *Dr. Pyckle and Mr. Pryde* (1925). Paramount, which had produced the Barrymore version, came back in the early sound period with a Jekyll and

Hyde starring the equally dashing Fredric March, for which he won an Academy Award for best actor, the first and only to be given to the star of a horror movie until Anthony Hopkins won for *The Silence of the Lambs* (1991), almost sixty years later. I will have more to say about the relation of the coming of sound to the creation of the classic movie monsters in the final chapter, but for now let me just remark how, so usefully for the Jekyll and Hyde story, the consistency of visual image and presence in silent films contrasts with the penchant of sound and image to separate in sound films, and even to contradict each other.

In the early centuries of theater, in both England and on the Continent, a stock character was the hypocrite, often hiding his schemes behind a mask of morality and conventionality. He was a character that the stage was peculiarly able to present, and the derivation of *hypocrite* from the Greek word for actor confirmed the belief that perhaps all acting was hypocrisy. If we therefore trace a genealogy from the hypocrite actor of the seventeenth century to the doppelgänger of the eighteenth and nineteenth centuries to Jekyll and Hyde, we might see the gradual stages by which the belief in a normally cohesive character gradually gives way to the realization that the social self is in general a mask that can caricature or contradict whatever is happening inside. This sense of being two people, of wearing a disguise, of conducting a social masquerade, appears in many American films of the 1930s and 1940s, both negatively for tragic effect and positively for comic effect, but in all cases character is seen as a split, rather than a synthesis.

It's also intriguing to speculate why certain performers seem attracted to such virtuoso turns. In *The Whole Town's Talking* (1935), Edward G. Robinson plays both a timid clerk and a tough gangster. In *The Woman in the Window* (1944), he begins as a meek professor of criminology. Through a series of events he murders the lover of a beautiful woman he has first seen in a painting, is invited to examine the crime scene with his district attorney friend, and is thoroughly enmeshed in a dark world he has before studied only academically—until he wakes up in a comfortable chair in his club and realizes it was all a dream. Some years later, continuing the double theme of his acting career, Robinson in *The Prize* (1963) plays twin brothers, a good American scientist and an evil Soviet scientist. Conrad Veidt (as the good German and his Nazi twin in *Nazi Agent,* 1942), Bette Davis (as sisters in *A Stolen Life,* 1946), and Olivia de Havilland (as sisters in *The Dark Mirror,* 1946) are among other actors who have played such dual roles. Veidt is of special interest since one of his earliest parts was as the somnambulist Cesare in *The Cabinet of*

Dr. Caligari, and so in his own career he expresses how the release of the otherwise sleeping monstrous self in horror metamorphoses into a psychologically more realistic form. But the more supernatural version persists and, like many other horror tropes, is revived in the 1970s with such films as *The Other* (1972, based on a best-selling novel by Tom Tryon), and the twin gynecologists of David Cronenberg's *Dead Ringers* (1988).

World War II generally ushers in more and more intricate "realistic" versions of the Jekyll and Hyde story, featuring willful role-playing, voluntary and involuntary transformation, as well as some more direct versions of the original, including Spencer Tracy's turn in 1941. As it had Barrymore and March, a straightforward version of Jekyll and Hyde attracts an actor's actor like Tracy, who in his film ostentatiously plays the role(s) without the obvious makeup and special effects of the earlier versions. In *The Great Dictator* (1940), Charlie Chaplin makes a more intricate political point of doubling by playing both a Jewish barber and Adenoid Hynkel, his parody of Adolf Hitler. Similarly, Ernst Lubitsch's comic masterpiece *To Be or Not to Be* (1942) features a troupe of Polish actors during the Nazi invasion of Poland who come to play not only the characters in *The Merchant of Venice* but also various Nazis and their victims. In the intricate plot the lead actor of the troupe, played by Jack Benny, must impersonate a high-ranking Nazi spy, with Benny's own egocentric off-screen persona absorbed into his character.

A striking example from this period of what might be called the domestication of the Jekyll and Hyde theme is Alfred Hitchcock's wonderful *Shadow of a Doubt* (1943). Hitchcock's frequent interest in a plot where a seemingly innocent bystander is drawn into crime and complicity with criminals through a virtually subconscious appeal to his own darkness is figured here in the doppelgänger psychic relationship between Uncle Charlie and his niece Charlotte, called Charlie. Uncle Charlie, who has made a career of wooing and then murdering rich widows, comes to hide with his sister's family in her bucolic hometown of Santa Rosa, California, only a few steps ahead of his detective pursuers. His almost telepathic connection with his niece, however, proves to be his undoing, because she gradually puts together the clues to discover his real nature. As his closest bond turns into his worst liability, he finally tries to kill her, but in a twist that reflects the end of Poe's "William Wilson," he succeeds only in being killed himself, sliced in half, we are told, between two trains. This brief account can't do justice to the rich complexities of the film. As a psychological version of a classic nineteenth-century monster, Uncle Charlie is all too human and even at times sympathetic. It is tempting to speculate that these variations on the double theme in the 1940s may have some cultural connections to the war, perhaps to the idea of personality and how it is not a fixed part of the self, but changes according to context, just as wartime itself forces individuals to act in ways that may contradict their earlier ideas of themselves. As the young detective in love with Charlie says at the end of the film, "Every once in a while the world goes crazy—like your Uncle Charlie."[8]

In the postwar period, the double theme received added impetus from the popular fascination with stories of multiple personalities like *The Three Faces of Eve* (book and movie, 1957), for which Joanne Woodward won a Best Actress Oscar, as well as the best-selling *The Search for Bridey Murphy* (book, 1952; movie, 1956), in which an amateur hypnotist claimed to have found that a Colorado housewife could, through what was called hypnotic regression, remember a past life as an Irishwoman born in 1806. *The Three Faces of Eve* mirrored for a contemporary world some of the same issues of dissociative personality disorder that were part of the context in mainstream psychology for *Jekyll and Hyde,* while *Bridey Murphy* harkened back to the various beings released by nineteenth-century mesmerists and mediums. The historical context may have been new, but the fascination with the question of personal identity, the unitary versus the fragmented self, continued.

If we ask what stories in particular, whether presented as real or fictional, capture wide public attention, the flourishing of so many variations on the basic double theme also may indicate an increased consciousness of the flexibility of the concept of the self and its close connection to performance generally.[9] In the years that followed, while the basic motif in the original of opposite selves within the same person could be easily transformed into androgynous versions, like *Dr. Jekyll and Sister Hyde* (1972), or racial versions, like *Dr. Black, Mr. Hyde* (1976), other kinds of contrast were appealing as well. On the dark side there could be the possession by a demonic force, of which *The Exorcist* was only one of many examples. But the most intriguing revamping of the basic double story owed a debt to the counterculture 1960s and the subsequent 1970s questioning of conventional social roles and relationships. A pioneering version was *Freaky Friday* (novel, 1972; movie, 1976), in which a mother and teenage daughter, otherwise at odds, mysteriously exchange bodies and get to understand each other's perspectives. The numerous versions of this plot include children who turn into adults (*Big,* 1988), an exchange between a father and a teenage son (*Vice Versa,* 1988), a bigoted white Los Angeles cop who gets the heart of a black lawyer (*Heart Condition,*

1990), a sexually predatory man who is murdered and reborn as a woman (*Switch*, 1991), as well as many other straightforward or baroquely detailed variations. The one almost invariable element, however, is that the change from one body to another, or the dual occupation of the same body, is the path to understanding social and individual difference, however that difference is defined. Instead of a clash between the two selves, as in the original story, which can end only in death, these more benevolent versions celebrate the flexibility of personal nature and the expansion of self to be gained from empathy with the Other rather than hostility.[10]

MIRROR, MIRROR, ON THE WALL

The primal moment in the traditional story of the doppelgänger is often a scene in which the narrator or main character catches a glimpse of his double, which in folk belief foretells death. The Jewish custom of covering the mirrors in the house while sitting shiva after a funeral seems to reflect something of the same belief. At all costs, the double should not be seen, especially when there is death in the house. A frequent motif in many horror stories is therefore a mysterious portrait or the sense of an eerie presence that turns out to be the fearful person's own reflection in a mirror. The most customary artistic role played by the motif of the mirror is to emphasize vanity, and even more usually female vanity. Narcissus, who fell in love with his own image while gazing into a pool of water, may have been male, but in the stained glass of medieval churches *vanitas* is a woman, and in the secular paintings of the nineteenth century, a few centuries after industrial production had made mirrors available for virtually every budget, women frequently gaze into them, putting on makeup or absorbed by admiring themselves.

But portraits and mirrors are also the evidence of the self seen from the outside, whatever the gender of the perceiver. The evil queen's magic mirror in *Snow White* may seem to come out of an older folktale in which she questions the mirror about her beauty. But the fact that the story was first published by the Brothers Grimm in 1812 suggests that some updating occurred in the process of folk transmission as the mirror became a more familiar household item.

The evil queen (like most in fairy tales a stepmother) may want her opinion of herself validated by the mirror. In *Frankenstein*, when the Creature looks into a forest pool, it is a negative Narcissus moment, because he is repelled by his own face and realizes why he is abhorred by all who see him. But if the mirror or the chance pool of water is a self-reflection in which the viewer can either detest what he sees or luxuriate in it, its reversal of normal visual symmetry makes it a potential doorway to an alternate reality. When Lewis Carroll's Alice, for example, goes through the looking-glass, she enters another world, in which her outside-the-mirror sense of self is severely tested. In *The Student of Prague,* a German film influenced by Poe's "William Wilson" and made twice (1913, 1926), a student sells his soul to the devil and thereby loses his reflection, which leaves the mirror and proceeds to commit crimes in his name.[11]

Thinking of mirrors as a way of externalizing the self naturally leads to thoughts of paintings and portraiture. The rhetorical term for the effort of a literary work to depict a visual work is *ecphrasis,* which literally means to "speak out." It can be used by extension for any attempt in one art to summon up another, but most often it describes the connection between the literary and the visual, like Homer's description of the shield of Achilles in the *Iliad* or Keats's "Ode on a Grecian Urn." In much of literary horror, the monstrous being and the painting are frequently objects of sight that are difficult if not impossible to describe. In "The Fall of the House of Usher," for example, the narrator tells us that it is almost impossible to put into words what Roderick's paintings are like: "If ever mortal painted an idea, that Mortal was Roderick Usher."[12]

But like the mirror, the painting also often has a key role to play in horror. It is most often in the double story that mirrors, paintings, photographs, and visual media generally all have the potential to be used for horrific purposes because they furnish seemingly tangible evidence of the multiple and potentially contradictory aspects of the self. When the unnamed narrator first approaches the house of Usher, he sees a double doubleness, first the house reflected in the mountain lake in front of it, and second "a barely perceptible fissure, which, extending from the roof of the building in front, made its way down the wall in a zigzag direction, until it became lost in the sullen waters of the tarn." Yet another doubling will of course appear, in the relation of Roderick Usher and his sister Madeline.

The change from a verbal to an almost entirely visual format in the era of silent film obviously has a considerable impact on the way such stories are told and retold. In how many films does a character walking through a gloomy house, holding only a candle or a flashlight, become horrified to see a figure at the end of the dark hallway, only to discover that it is himself reflected in a mirror? I will consider the impact of turning horror stories into horror theater, horror movies, and horror television at more length in the final chapter, but for now I turn to a few remarks on how, in the era before motion pictures, the mysterious portrait and the mirror played special roles.

The mirror reflects whatever lies in front of it and thereby seems to imply a kind of self-recognition, for better or worse. The painting, by contrast, is at least at first glance an idealized version of the real person. But often, as in Hawthorne's *House of the Seven Gables,* it conceals a secret chamber or a secret passage that leads into the murkier and more threatening corners of the house and the self. Like the descent into the dank catacombs beneath the gaudy cathedral, to go behind the painting can be a way into the repressed past and its otherwise unspeakable horrors. Portraits thus both allure and falsify. Whether through the painter's eye or the camera's eye, the self is seen from the outside, and no matter how positive the image, we see Another. The eye reveals, and the eye deceives. Ambrosio in *The Monk* has a cherished portrait of the Madonna that he worships. But he later discovers that his trusted male servant Rosario is actually the woman Matilda, who is in love with him and has arranged to have herself painted as the Madonna—a revelation that quickly reveals the carnality beneath Ambrosio's spiritual adoration. As in much of Christian theology, temptation enters primarily through the eye, whether it is in the form of lust or avarice or other of the deadly sins. Poe once again helped to elaborate some of these basic motifs. In addition to the mirror that at the end of the story reveals the symbiotic relationship between the two William Wilsons, in another of his tales, "The Oval Portrait," a man obsessed with painting his wife works endlessly on her portrait without realizing that he is absorbing her life force into it. When the portrait is finished, he discovers that she is dead. This turn on the doubled relation of a painting to the person painted emphasizes the artist's role in stealing something of the person's essence by his depiction, in a kind of vampirism, just as some primitive tribesmen refused the request of early explorers to photograph them, out of fear that taking their image would mean the imprisonment or theft of their souls.[13]

The lure of the art object that mesmerizes the viewer by its spiritual power, as Ambrosio is mesmerized by the portrait of the Madonna, is another way in which English gothic fiction pays a debt to the Catholic imagery otherwise rejected by the Reformation. The drained visual world of Protestantism may doctrinally set its face against the divine as well as the diabolical iconicity and theatricality of Catholicism, but by the same token it lays itself open to be fascinated and even dominated by that same imagery. In a sense, it is a habit of mind still with us. To fall in love with the image without knowing the reality, to see in either the beloved or the repulsive Other a narcissistic reflection of oneself, neatly encapsulates the fan's attitude toward the star and perhaps the whole psychological underpinning of modern fame.

The final decade or so of the nineteenth century that embraced the first appearances of Jekyll and Hyde, Jack the Ripper, Sherlock Holmes, Dracula, and the early writings of Sigmund Freud also saw the publication of another intriguing work about doubleness, Oscar Wilde's *The Picture of Dorian Gray.* It first appeared in May 1890 in *Lippincott's Magazine,* where Conan Doyle's second Holmes novel *The Sign of the Four* had appeared in the February issue. Six more chapters were added to *Dorian Gray* before its publication as a book in 1891. Six silent-film versions of the story have been recorded and one great sound film version in 1945, directed by Albert Lewin, who, appropriately enough, was one of Hollywood's greatest art collectors.

In the style of Wilde's notorious epigrams ("The only way to get rid of a temptation is to yield to it"), here he reverses some of the basic motifs of the double story in *Dorian,* turning the painting, whose charming surface hides the darkness that lies behind it, into the true picture of Dorian's soul. He is first seen by Lord Henry Wotton as a painting being finished by the artist Basil Hallward. Lord Henry then meets the real Dorian, who expresses a desire to remain forever like the painting. Launched on a life of corruption as he descends from his luxurious home into the back streets of London in search of prey, Dorian stays youthful and beautiful while the painting becomes more and more grotesque. In Wilde's witty inversion of the role of the painting in gothic fiction and film, Dorian retains a perfect social and personal facade while the painting reveals what lies beneath.

Wilde wrote in a letter in 1894 that "Basil Hallward is what I think I am: Lord Henry is what the world thinks me: Dorian is what I would like to be—in other ages, perhaps." This tripling of Wilde's own identification with his characters may top the doubling theme within the novel. But its nested personas only emphasize how Dorian's sense of himself remains so concertedly superficial. Enchanted by Lord Henry's way with an aphoristic paradox ("I love acting. It is so much more real than life"), Dorian organizes his own life in terms of the desire to maintain his surface charm and beauty, while the Hallward painting registers the aging voluptuary he has become. As Wilde puts it, "Through some strange quickening of inner life the leprosies of sin were slowly eating the thing away." While Lord Henry mockingly compares theater and reality, Dorian accepts that the theatrical show of surfaces *is* reality. Basil sees through Lord Henry's verbal play—"You never say a moral

thing, and you never do a wrong thing"—but Dorian, blinded by his desire
to remain the youthful charmer he was, does not. Even as Lord Henry, like
the Wilde his audience celebrates, uses paradoxical wit to puncture and lam-
poon conventional thinking ("It is only shallow people who do not judge by
appearances"), Dorian takes his words as a guide to life. While Lord Henry
sees words as play, Dorian considers them to be reality. So it is appropriate
that his image in the painting turns into his reality, while his physical self remains as unchanged as a piece of sculpture. Finally, disgusted with the painting after he has murdered Basil, who painted it, Dorian stabs the portrait and
dies. It has become his real self. No one who discovers the body at first even
realizes that the "withered, wrinkled, and loathsome of visage" corpse is
Dorian. He is finally recognized only by his rings. Appropriately in terms of
its Jekyll and Hyde forebears, in the 1946 film of *The Picture of Dorian Gray,*
the last shots shows the portrait returning to "normal" while the real face of
Dorian becomes monstrous.[14]

HORROR ON THE COUCH

[Satan is speaking:] The mind is its own place, and in itself
Can make a Heaven of Hell, a Hell of Heaven.

—John Milton, *Paradise Lost* (1667)

I sent my Soul through the Invisible
Some letter of that After-Life to spell:
And by and by my Soul returned to me,
And answer'd 'I myself am Heav'n and Hell.'

—*The Rubaiyat of Omar Khayyam,* translated
by Edward Fitzgerald (1859)

Like the pattern in *Jekyll and Hyde* of a supernatural core inside a realistic
"case," the only supernatural element at the heart of *Dorian Gray* is the portrait itself. As befits an age becoming more and more attuned to the dark
labyrinths of personal psychology, this supernatural element in the novel has
been interpreted to be "about" something more specific. Dorian seeks to
dominate his emotions while all around him people fall victim to vague or
unspeakable sins, dying, committing suicide, or otherwise destroyed by his
actions, while he lives on with no one believing anything bad about him because he is still so young and beautiful. What is the moral to Wilde's tale of
the doubled self? Biographically, is it a kind of self-critique of the urge to be

a public figure with a fixed persona? Or, in the context of the "decadent" 1890s, is it a revolt against Victorian repression in the name of another way of being in public that emphasized self-stylization and mannered performance? Moralistically, does it indict or just satirize the belief that the ravages of age are worse than the ravages of sin?

Or is the book perhaps "about" homosexuality itself—the secret that dare not speak its name? All these and many other interpretations have been made of *Dorian Gray* and *Jekyll and Hyde* and so many previous and subsequent doppelgänger stories. The result is usually a reduction of the power of the stories, at the same time that it condescends to the authors, who are assumed to be unaware of the implications of their own stories. But *Dorian Gray,* like *Jekyll and Hyde,* shares with Poe the sense of secrets that cannot be revealed even on one's deathbed—whatever those secrets are. After Dorian kills Basil Hallward, for example, he blackmails a former friend, Alan Campbell, into destroying the body by saying he will reveal to Campbell's wife some secret sin—homosexuality, philandering, drug taking—which is never specified. Such stories use the trope of the mysterious and ineffable not primarily because of some social reticence or veiled purpose, but because it embraces a whole range of dark possibilities. To reduce such an all-encompassing secret to a personal pathology, predilection, or passion limits the allure of the story, psychoanalyzing the author through the story. To read, say, *Dorian Gray* through the lens of Wilde's biography and his later trial and imprisonment for sodomy reduces the power of a story that invites the reader to imagine what he or she might sacrifice to remain forever youthful and unchanged. Whatever the individual psychic drama that fueled his work, art allowed him to touch a universal chord. *Dorian Gray* in this way is a dark prelude to more comic variations on the double story of age-swapping like *Freaky Friday, Vice Versa,* and *Big.*

The doppelgänger story almost ostentatiously invites a psychological reading. But earlier works like *The Monk* and *Frankenstein,* as well as stories like E. T. A. Hoffmann's "The Sandman," also illustrate how close gothic horror comes to psychological intuition. In their writings, Lewis, Shelley, Hoffmann and others, during the Romantic period, could convey acute insights into human fears without the benefit of an actual discipline of psychology and its specialized language. Critics have long praised Shakespeare for his insight into human behavior and philosophers like John Locke for their early efforts to understand the complexities of personality and character. But it was in this era at the end of the eighteenth and the beginning of the nineteenth century that many traumas and phobias were first being concertedly explored in the context of the supernatural, which only many decades later would be treated more systematically by modern psychology and psychoanalysis. Just as growing scientific and medical knowledge narrowed the sphere of religious explanation, the literature of horror suggested that such fears might be part of the self rather than an aspect of the world outside, and that they may have to do as much if not more with upbringing and nurturing than with the effect of diabolical forces. So many horror stories from this period can retrospectively be interpreted as inner landscapes shaped by personal problems with which we have become more familiar. They retain their power, however, even when they are critically reduced to an assortment of symptoms, since their implications are often political and social as well as psychological, for example, in their preoccupation with the tyranny of fathers and other religious and political authorities.

In the nature of such works, *The Monk* allows multiple explanations: Ambrosio may make a pact with the devil, but he was also brought up to be morally pure, to not know the difference between a man and a woman, and thus to be prey to his own repressed emotions of lust and power. In like manner, at various points in the story, Matilda appears as a disguised young man, a virtuous woman in love with Ambrosio, a sexually abandoned young woman, a witch, and a demon. What in fact is she? Is her sexual avidity satanic or just her own lust? Unlike Radcliffe's final revelations of what is in fact going on behind the supernatural facade, Lewis never makes it clear. But it was apparent to Lewis and others how much sin was the product of the mind rather than Satan. The real danger posed by Satan was thus not the theatrical power to cause earthquakes or stunt crops, but the ability to elicit potential desires that already existed within the self. He was the Tempter, not compelling people to do evil against their will so much as releasing their own inner longings to violate conventional morality.[15] Especially when the fear of an Other is supported by general cultural beliefs in invisible, external forces out to get you, it is often difficult or impossible to tell the difference between something happening inside you and something outside. Psychological explanation, in other words, puts the source of guilt and fear back into the self without any need for an external tempter. The double speaks your own dark thoughts.

A crucial factor in the transformation of the double story into a story of twins or personal psychology during the course of the twentieth century is of course the pervasive awareness and popularization of the Freudian scrutiny of the hidden aspects of the self. The virtually simultaneous rise in the 1890s of a psychoanalytically oriented psychology widens the impact of the stories of fictional horror into an exploration of the darknesses we all have. The human image at the end of the nineteenth century was changing in decisive ways. Virginia Woolf famously and provocatively said, "On or about December 1910, human character changed." But if that gnomic statement has any truth in it, the groundwork was being laid in the last decade or so of the previous century, and the change was not from one conception of character to another, equally solid, but from a unified sense of self to a more fragmented— or more complex and layered—sense. It is a central era in cultural history that brings together stories such as *Jekyll and Hyde* and *Dorian Gray* with the embryonic discipline of psychoanalysis (a word coined by Freud in 1896). When John Locke in the late seventeenth century considered the riddle of contradictory aspects of personality, he compared a man drunk to a man sober, but in the Freudian perspective, so shadowed by the gothic view of the self, the nexus was who you were when conscious and who you were when you were unconscious. Psychoanalysis thus supplied a seemingly more systematic language to connect the various tales of the shadow and the double with individual mental problems. That language and that connection then served to send the idea of the double forward in a more self-conscious way.

The awareness and investigation of multiple personalities existing within the same person was a special fascination of early psychology, and in the decade or so prior to Stevenson's publication of *Jekyll and Hyde* there are many mentions in the medical literature of the question of multiple personalities. The mesmeric therapy of releasing other internal identities as a source of health and, not incidentally, entertainment emphasized what was called "double consciousness" (referred to by John Elliotson, a prominent London physician and teacher, in the 1830s), which became a frequent term of art in early psychiatry as well, which is used to imply a conflict or doubling of the self in Freud and Breuer's *Studies in Hysteria* (1895).[16]

Here then were some of the ideas about the hidden aspects of the self that were in the air during a time, the Victorian age, that is popularly associated with personal repression of all sorts, especially sexual. The rise of psychoanalysis heralded a revival of the themes of gothic and Romantic horror, now viewed through the lens of both personal pathology and anthropologically influenced cross-cultural mythography. To Freud's perspective, Carl Jung added the idea that there is also a collective unconscious, which is the repository of all human history and experienced almost exclusively through myths and symbols. But it is hardly necessary to go all the way back into the

primitive past with Jung to appreciate how from the time of the gothic onward Anglo-European culture was developing its own set of stories, motifs,
and characters to body forth fears and terrors. In 1914, Otto Rank, a prominent Viennese psychoanalyst, published a study of the doppelgänger that
explored examples from both literature (including *Dorian Gray*) and film
(*The Student of Prague*). Although a close associate of Freud's, Rank delved
into areas of anthropology and folklore that bring his work close to that
of Jung as well. He cites Freud's view that the original double was the soul.
But finally he concludes that in the modern world it is "the defective
capacity for love" that creates the double, and follows Freud in situating the
apparition of the double in a paradoxical narcissism: "So it happens that the
double, who personifies narcissistic self-love, becomes an unequivocal rival in
sexual love." But whatever the explanations of these various theorists of human psychology and however helpful they might have been to individual
patients, explaining hardly diminished the power of the double story and its
ability to frighten.[17]

Psychology as a developing discipline in the nineteenth century thus gradually replaces the conflict between the natural and the supernatural with one
between the conscious and the subconscious or unconscious mind, a division
that exists in everyone but is most acute in those with mental disease or dis-
turbances. A phrase like "alter ego," which from the sixteenth century onward
had referred to a close friend who was like another self, began to mean instead
a submerged part of oneself, a substitute personality, and the term *double
consciousness* came into vogue. There's a close resemblance between the double
consciousness described by nineteenth-century psychologists and writers and
what in religious had been called and treated as possession.[18] For psychology
it was a dissociative personality disorder generally known as *dementia praecox*.
Locke in the late seventeenth century defined consciousness as the ability to
perceive what is happening in our minds, an elaboration of the Descartes
dictum "I think therefore I am." When a thought or feeling is below the level
of perception or repressed by consciousness, it is first called subconscious, an
adjective that does not appear until a little less than a century and a half later,
during the heyday of mesmerism and later hypnosis in England, when aspects
of the self that seemed to contradict daylight respectability were being unleashed for the purposes of both therapy and entertainment. But *subconscious*
as both adjective and noun generally loses out as either a popular term or,
later, a technical term in psychoanalysis to *unconscious*. Somewhat earlier,
Samuel Taylor Coleridge, whose own poems show a distinct gothic influence,

focused on how the interplay between the conscious and the unconscious was crucial to the creation of great art:

> In every work of art there is a reconcilement of the external with the internal; the conscious is so impressed on the unconscious as to appear in it. . . . He who combines the two is the man of genius; and for that reason he must partake of both. Hence there is in genius itself an unconscious activity; nay, that is the genius in the man of genius.[19]

For most people, the world of dreams is the clearest example of the potentiality for other selves and other visions in a place where the conscious and the unconscious meet. As I've mentioned, the Roman and medieval literary form of the dream vision defined the world of dreams as the path to an alternate view of reality, frequently employed to satirize traditional politics and religion. Dreams had been considered potentially heretical by the church because they might be interpreted without priestly mediation, and therefore became subversive to theological orthodoxy and authority. But an essential characteristic of the gothic was how it implicitly raised through dreams the question of the psychology of deep feelings, decades before the codification of a discipline called psychology, and more than a hundred years before Freud's *Interpretation of Dreams* initiated an alternate system of interpretation, with the psychoanalyst as its minister.

A prime example of the gothic reliance on dreams as an expression of repressed desire is the way Ambrosio in *The Monk* cannot sort out the relation between his religious and his carnal desires. As we have seen, after the young novice Rosario confesses to him that he is in fact a woman, Matilda, who loves him, "a thousand opposing sentiments combatted in Ambrosio's bosom." When he rejects her plea for understanding and tells her she must leave, she threatens to stab herself in the chest, revealing to Ambrosio "the beauteous orb" of her breast. Undone, he says she can stay. When she leaves him, he prays to the picture of the Madonna to help him repress his emotions, unaware that it is actually the likeness of Matilda. Then he sleeps, and dreams of her, while "his unsatisfied desires placed before him the most lustful and provoking images, and he rioted in joys till then unknown to him." Another self, otherwise repressed by his upbringing, has been awakened.

Mesmerism, and later hypnosis, used a trance state to evoke other selves for professedly therapeutic purposes, while in the world of horror fiction walked more malevolent somnambulists like Cesare of *The Cabinet of Dr. Caligari*. Freddy Krueger, the child-molesting janitor in the *Nightmare on*

Elm Street series of films, who is murdered by outraged parents and then returns to prey on the children in their sleep, brings that particular monstrous
tradition into the late twentieth century. The alien pods that take over human
beings in their sleep in *Invasion of the Body Snatchers* similarly update the
theme of vulnerable sleep with a science-fiction twist.

In a more prosaic way, consciousness dictated who you were in the
daylight and unconsciousness who you were at night, asleep. The frequent
preoccupation in the gothic period with the terrors that visit the sleeper thus
began to take on the coloration of personal psychology as well as horror-story
tradition. Incubi (male creatures who prey on women at night) and succubi
(female creatures who prey on men at night), like Goya's illustration of the
sleep of Reason producing monsters, emphasize the defenselessness of the
sleeping brain to its own dark imaginings. Henry Fuseli's frequently repro-
duced painting *The Nightmare* (1781) explicitly portrays the connection
between the horrific and the erotic with its image of a gnome-like incubus
sitting on the sprawled body of a young woman, while a mad horse peers
from behind a curtain. Fuseli was fascinated by dreams and frequently
depicted such figures as the ghost in *Hamlet* and the witches in *Macbeth*. The
horse is his visual-verbal joke, since the "mare" in nightmare doesn't refer to
that animal but comes from *mara*, a female demon that lies on your chest at
night and causes suffocation.[20]

Appropriately enough for the dense connection between psychoanalysis
and horror, Ernest Jones, like Rank a close associate of Freud's, published
On the Nightmare, a study of "the inherent connection between intrapsychic
dread and repressed sexual impulses," graced with a reproduction of Fuseli's
painting as its frontispiece. However acute the analysis in Freudian categories
that came later, the basic connection between the fearful and the erotic was
not lost on the readers of the Romantic period. However useful was the urge
toward analysis and systematization brought on by modern psychology, there
was still more than a touch of the gothic view of the self at its heart. The unconscious, that necessary place where the demons that plagued more superstitious ages now resided, that other self that hinders us from our conscious
goals, was, after all, invisible. No one could point to where it physically could
be seen and examined.[21]

CHAPTER 7

Dracula and the Haunted Present

The tradition of all the dead generations weighs like a nightmare on the brain of the living.

—Karl Marx, *The Eighteenth Brumaire of Louis Bonaparte* (1852)

Whoever struggles with monsters may see to it that he does not thereby become a monster. And when you look long into an abyss, the abyss also looks into you.

—Nietzsche, *Beyond Good and Evil* (1886)

THE DISCOVERY OF THE PAST

Although the common view of the European Renaissance stresses its vision of a new future, that future was often culturally and politically an explicit revival of the cultural and political past, a rebirth that looked back to the Roman republic of the early centuries B.C. The great artists and thinkers of the Renaissance turned against the recent past—especially the Middle Ages—to both imitate and then exceed a more ancient world. This double vision of a revived past that would energize the present and create a new future gave rise in the seventeenth century to an ongoing intellectual argument that lasted about a hundred years. It was called the conflict between the Ancients and the Moderns. In essence the argument went: Was the present better than the past, or a mere footnote to its lost greatness? To a large extent the answers broke down on disciplinary lines: Writers and artists pointed to the greater humane wisdom of the past, while scientists and medical men proclaimed the superiority of their understanding of the physical world. After all, in addition to its witch hunts and religious wars, the seventeenth was also the century of new findings in astronomy, chemistry (gas laws), physics (gravity), biology (the circulation of the blood), and mathematics (analytic geometry and calculus), to name only a few. But even the new generation of scientists wasn't entirely hostile to the ancients. As Newton remarked, his discoveries came by standing on the shoulders of giants, and he spent a good deal of his intellectual time trying to establish a parallel chronology linking the most significant events of the classical and the biblical worlds.

Whether you were an Ancient or a Modern, you occupied common ground in your opposition to the Middle Ages, or the dark ages, as they were beginning to be called by the end of the seventeenth century, a world of barbarism rather than the "civilization" cherished by the partisans of both Ancients and Moderns. The eighteenth-century Enlightenment continued the attack. As the past was being swept aside, by industrialization, by economic growth, and by revolution, the northern European tribes—Gauls, Goths, Celts—were defined as brutes and savages. Instead of clarity and scientific reason, the medieval period was characterized by magic and mystery. As we have seen, *gothick* had been the word in English used to insult the period, the adjective form of *goth,* meaning a barbarian, with that final *k* thrown in to further mock their archaic world. Even though some political philosophers were beginning to understand the actual political and economic intricacies of the medieval feudal system, and even though the late medieval poet Geoffrey Chaucer was already being considered one of the greatest English writers, the world on the other side of Henry VIII's separation of England from international Catholicism was generally viewed with distaste and intellectual condescension. In fact, argued their partisans, writers like Chaucer, as well as Dante, Petrarch, and Boccaccio in Italy, and Rabelais and Montaigne in France, were themselves heralding a future nationalistic and linguistic rebirth, their literary models and influences as much Roman as they were part of the national literatures they helped create.

The most obvious reminders of the difference between past and present in many European countries were ruins, the enigmatic but awesome fragments of the Roman past, the Celtic past, and beyond. By the fifteenth and sixteenth centuries some contemporary Romans had begun to dig up and venerate their past, even while many others used classical ruins as handy brickyards and marble quarries, incorporating fragments into their own buildings, until the practice was outlawed in the eighteenth century. Still, the reverence for the past persisted among scholars and ordinary citizens alike. The discovery of Nero's Domus Aurea buried beneath the Esquiline Hill was only one of several symbolic Renaissance recoveries of past vitality and grandeur. The Apollo Belvedere was discovered in the sixteenth century, and the equestrian statue of Marcus Aurelius, previously thought to represent the first Christian emperor Constantine, was moved to a new place of honor on the Capitoline Hill during its redesign by Michelangelo, who had begun his sculpting career in Florence by making fake Roman pieces for wealthy collectors.

What this past meant and questions like who built these often colossal but ruined monuments varied from country to country. In England, in contrast with Rome, it is only toward the end of Elizabeth I's reign in the late sixteenth century that learned scholars and historians tried to understand their own monumental broken arches and fallen walls. A great part of the difference was that in Italy, of course, the ruins were primarily Roman, while in England there were three basic kinds: the pre-Roman ruins generally known as gothic or Celtic; the Roman; and the more recent remnants of medieval cathedrals, churches, and abbeys roofless, gutted, and often torn down by the agents of Edward VI's militant anti-Catholic iconoclasm. William Camden's *Britannia* (1586) attempted for the first time a historical and geographic survey of all England and Ireland, noting ruins from a variety of periods about which he was often informed by a network of local antiquaries. In seventeenth-century England, for instance, speculation about the origins of Stonehenge ran high. Royalist writers argued that it was the seat of Danish kings, while those with more parliamentary sympathies considered it a relic of the British past exclusively—the creation of indigenous Druids (although in fact it had been in existence for thousands of years before them). Rarely was the argument about the bygone world uncontaminated by politics. When the question of the past was raised in the late eighteenth century, for example, those embracing a left politics, like the French revolutionaries, preferred the togas of the Roman republic and a world before Christianity, while conservatives like Edmund Burke buttressed their support of monarchy by celebrating the continuity (and the divine sanction) that stretched back into more shadowy eras.[1]

But such a political polarization hardly does justice to the wide variety of ways the past was used to enlighten, instruct, and occasionally terrify the present. Even though the ignorance of history is ritually grieved over at times, we take for granted that there is a past and that there is a sequence of events we call history, if only in history books themselves or in timelines or chronologies. We speak of generations and baby boomers and the differences between the X, Y, and Z generations because we have in front of us a constant media scrutiny of changes in attitudes, even while we watch movies and television set in a variety of pasts, realistic and fictional, often vaunting their research and authenticity, at least in the length of dresses and the cut of trousers, if not in faces and emotions. But for a great part of human history there was in effect no sense of history as we know it. There were myths and stories about the past, but little precise understanding of how the past differed from the present, except in the broadest and most extreme ways. In the ninth-century Old English poem *Beowulf*, considered one of the earliest works of English literature, there is mention of the *enta geweorc*, the works of giants, still visible in the countryside. Shakespeare in his Roman plays, for instance, like *Julius Caesar* or *Antony and Cleopatra*, knows that Romans did not have a moral prohibition against suicide, so heroic characters like Brutus or Cleopatra can commit the act with impunity and even with a certain honor, whereas suicide in the Christian world remains a moral problem, as Hamlet mulls over in his "to be or not to be" speech. Suicide as the marker of difference between the classical and the Christian worlds stands in for a whole array of unexplored cultural differences. But when Hamlet lies dying and Horatio tells him he will join him by drinking poison himself—"I am more an antique Roman than a Dane"—Hamlet replies that Horatio must remain alive to tell his story.

Perhaps the question of the past and its relevance to the present emerges periodically in human culture when a society gets conscious enough of its own nature to wonder how much it has exceeded or fallen from those standards. While the people of Shakespeare's day could not readily explore the special nature of the past, they were eager to differentiate themselves from those in the present, whether they were other Europeans or the primitive tribes of Africa and the Americas, whose customs were not their own. In any period of rapid modernization, whether it is the Industrial Revolution of the eighteenth century or the nineteenth-century end of the Tokugawa shogunate in Japan, the need arises to eradicate or at least diminish the importance of the past and its old ways. Such a time of uncertainty can easily give rise to stories that generally fit the description of horror, because horror can serve as a form of cultural compensation that dramatizes the difficulty a modern world of whatever form has in dealing with threats that draw their power from the past. Greek myths of the defeat of a race of giants and monsters that allowed the coming of a more "advanced" civilization abound. Even in the *Iliad* the aged and cranky Nestor frequently mocks the Achaean heroes in comparison with the great men who used to be around. Colossal ruins stimulated a sense of inferiority before the greatness of antiquity. Through their unavoidable examples, the optimistic sense of ascendancy, progress, and the coming of a new dawn was undermined by an awareness of the seemingly inevitable fall of the empires of the past. Seventeenth-century painters working in Italy, such as Claude Lorrain, Nicolas Poussin, and Salvator Rosa, had often produced paintings in which natural landscapes were mingled with ruined castles, Roman temples, and tumbled aqueducts that conveyed a cautionary appreciation for how decisively the mighty had fallen, as nature reclaimed the buildings that embodied human aspiration.

Later in the eighteenth century the etchings of Giovanni Battista Piranesi even more elaborately contrasted the crumbling opulence of the past with the smallness of the present, depicting the half-destroyed monuments of Rome, their cracks and crevices festooned with grass, weeds, and the occasional tree, while tiny people marvel at their decayed grandeur. From one perspective, nature had swallowed up the grandiose creations of humans; from another, the still living classical heritage had so outlasted its origins that it seemed part of nature itself. The French painter Hubert Robert enlarged this theme with his portrayals of the contrast between the common events of daily life and the overpowering past, Roman women doing their laundry amid fallen columns and arched vaults. It was a motif that attracted painters in many countries and continued into the later nineteenth century, as artists from the United States arrived to spend their obligatory time in Italy. Otherwise best known for his landscape paintings of the Hudson River, Thomas Cole, after a time in Italy, painted a five-part series titled "The Course of Empire" (1834–36) from savagery to pastoral ease, to the height of civilization, to apocalyptic destruction, and finally to desolation clearly based on Rome and drawing upon Edward Gibbon's *Decline and Fall of the Roman Empire* as well as the Comte de Volney's *Ruins of Empire,* the work that also influenced Mary Shelley in the writing of *Frankenstein.*[2]

The historian Jean Starobinski has argued that by the eighteenth century ruins had lost some of their emotional weight due to a more empirical awareness of their actual origins: at that time, "emotional feeling for ruins had to compete against the awakening of modern historical thinking, which gradually depoeticized the ruins as its investigations became more methodical." The ability to date ruins, to give them a precise place in history, he continues, "destroys the sense of the *immemorial.*"[3] But, as we have seen in other instances, the rise of a scientific and technological investigation of phenomena hardly erases entirely the mysterious aura of things and the emotions, the awe mingled of fear and admiration, they inspire. The awareness of the collapse of the great empires of the past into ruins could induce melancholy or at least a jaundiced attitude toward the empire building of the present. At the same time, it could inspire desires to return at least metaphorically to a less industrialized and more visionary world. The rich owners of country estates would often commission their architects to include premeditated ruins, usually Roman in style, with a political edge, praising the lost virtue of the past and denigrating the corrupt present.

Napoleon set the standard for the new empire builders by gathering to himself the lost greatness of the past. When he launched his Mediterranean campaign in Egypt and Syria (1798–1801), his effort to associate himself with the pharaohs was aided by a large group of archaeologists, artists, and writers he, like Alexander the Great entering Persia, brought along to document their stay and produce an enormous volume celebrating their discoveries. A decade or more later, perhaps with Napoleon's defeat at Waterloo in mind and stimulated as well by the British Museum's acquisition of an enormous chunk of a statue of Ramesses II, Percy Shelley wrote the sonnet "Ozymandias" (1818), which simultaneously laments both the lost grandeur of the past as well as the emptiness and transience of supposed greatness. It includes the ironic line "Look upon my works, ye mighty, and despair," when in fact nothing of Ozymandias's kingdom remains but fragments half covered by desert sand. The past here, instead of being the source of an ideal vision of new greatness that it might have been for Napoleon, brandishes instead the clutching skeletal hand of inevitable doom.

The eighteenth century in England pushed these contradictory tendencies forward, just at a time when all around the emblems of progress and the future like factories and bridges and paved roads were becoming more and more apparent. The nature of light changed as oil lamps replaced candles, making the experience of darkness, especially in growing cities, less normal and thus potentially more fraught with danger and uncertainty. This intensified urban setting, most marked in London's rise to become one of the biggest cities in the world, was accompanied, as we have seen, with an increased preoccupation with the natural world. The French revolutionaries even devised an entirely new calendar with the months named for natural phenomena like snow or harvest rather than gods or rulers. Everywhere there was a sense at the end of the eighteenth century that a new world was being born.

But in a world that promises openness and unlimited opportunity for self-creation, the failure to take advantage of those opportunities becomes a tremendous burden. How can any individual strive toward the promise of the future while evading the pressure of the past? Politically as well, the new world of revolutionary hopes in the United States and France brought a great anxiety not just in those countries but throughout Europe—the fear of leaving the past, along with its grandeur and power, behind. With so many signs all around that history was moving forward, what had been lost? What if the past, with all its ghosts, came back to haunt the giddy, sunlit present? Thus in the late eighteenth century fears began to arise whose forms have persisted into our own day in the shape of monsters that often help define whatever new threats appear on the horizon.

∾⦿∾

To the extent that popular culture is, as it is so often called, escapism, we can reasonably ask what we are supposed to be escaping from. The answer might lie in its ability to simultaneously arouse fears, allay them, but never quite extinguish them. Perpetual battles characterize the modern world: the questioning of the ability of traditional authority to meet new challenges versus the embrace of traditional authority as the only guide to the present and the future; the unseating of the old powers versus the desire to take on the mantle of their legitimacy; the belief in individual will versus the belief in God's foreknowledge. One solution, derived from both nature and the past, was a periodic re-anointing in the primitive. In England this took the form of a Celtic revival, in which the previously scorned barbarians were celebrated for their sense of honor, military prowess, and closeness to nature.

Historically the Celts were an Indo-European tribe originating in the area of southwestern Germany and eastern France that spread across Europe in the second millennium B.C. as far west as Ireland and east as the Ukraine. They never called themselves Celts; that was their Greek name, and it appears for the first time in English and French in the seventeenth century and was often used interchangeably with "Gauls," a linguistic connection still preserved in Wales, "Le Pays de Galles," as well as in such far-flung areas as Galicia in Spain and Galicia in Poland. The early indigenous inhabitants of Britain and Ireland were a branch of the Celts, and Julius Caesar ran into them as part of an essentially failed expedition to Britain in 55 and 54 B.C. As Caesar among other writers testifies, both the Greeks and the Romans considered the Celts (let's stay with that name) both great warriors and barbarians, admiring them for their stoic honor and strength. Depending on your point of view, you might also consider them a breath of fresh air in the midst of Roman vice and corruption, as Tacitus seems to imply in some parts of *Germania,* his book about the German tribes.

A hundred years or so after Caesar, the emperor Claudius was more militarily successful, but Ireland still remained less colonized by the Romans than was England, so the Celtic influence there continued to be strong. Some centuries later, a Romano-Briton with a Celtic name fought against the Saxon invaders and gained an everlasting fame. His name was Arthur, which means "bear" in Celtic.⁴ The Romans had brought Christianity to England, but with the fall of Rome, there was a reversion to paganism and then a re-Christianization a few centuries later. This seesaw between paganism and Christianity was characteristic of Scandinavia as well. In fact, the connection between Scandinavia and the British Isles was strong. Perhaps oddly, but appropriately, for a poem considered to stand at the beginning of English literature, *Beowulf* is set in Scandinavia and features a heroic pagan warrior along with a cast of monsters and duels to the death. Whatever lines in it have even the appearance of a Christian perspective are few, and may have been added later. By the same token, the ways in which Christianity entrenched itself in Ireland are intriguing as well. In the snakes that Saint Patrick (also a Romano-Briton) supposedly drove out of the island we see a significant Druidic symbol, while the Christian Trinity meshed well with the Celtic emphasis on symbolic groups of three. In the sixth century Pope Gregory the Great explicitly enjoined Augustine, the first archbishop of Canterbury, to bring together the "good" myths of the Celtic and Norse past with the Christian dispensation, while stigmatizing the evil. Before Christianity decisively takes hold, however, those who wanted to hedge their bets might pay obeisance to both traditions, as tombstones in northern Europe decorated at once with the cross and Thor's hammer seem to imply.⁵

Perhaps more than any other European version, Celtic Christianity seemed to be able to weave together old practices and folklore with the new religion, simultaneously hospitable to beliefs in elves and leprechauns as well as in the calendar of saints. As the historian R. F. Foster puts it, "the rich and varied rural lore of fairies, charms, banshees, superstitions, 'special days,' rituals, sympathetic magic and amulets could and did live alongside the Irish Christianity of the countryside, and could even be assimilated into it."⁶ Paganism and Christianity had already merged in the images of Christ as the good shepherd as well as the youthful athlete and warrior. It was an accommodation that could merge the ideals of the priesthood with those of a court-controlled military society under a ruler like Charlemagne, and it influenced the later creation of such fictional heroes as Sir Galahad, the pure knight.

If any group in the British Isles might be considered "gothick" in the eighteenth-century sense, then, it was the Irish and perhaps the Highland Scots, both groups in which the Celtic inheritance was strong. The Irish had been a thorn in the side of the English government from the Reformation onward, refusing generally to give up their Catholic faith and frequently mounting rebellions against the English presence in Northern Ireland, until the armies of Oliver Cromwell in the mid–seventeenth century succeeded in establishing military rule over the island. From the time of the Reformation, the English generally viewed the Irish as basically uncivilized, conflating their Catholicism with paganism. Edmund Spenser, who created the villainous Catholic manipulator of images Archimago, wrote a good portion of *The Faerie Queene* in his Irish estate in County Cork. He later argued in *A View of the Present State of Ireland* (unpublished during his lifetime) that the Irish would never be subjugated by the English unless their culture and language were totally obliterated. Yet Ireland was not the only part of Britain that pre-served something of the pre-Christian past. The English language itself re-tains a good deal, even though we often don't realize it. *God,* for example, is the Old English and Old Norse word, rather than the Greek *theos* or Latin *deus. Heaven* comes from the Old English for edge or sharp stone, perhaps related to the idea that if lightning came from the sky, it was like the spark from striking a stone. *Easter* comes from Eostre, the Anglo-Saxon goddess of the dawn and the spring, whereas in French (Pâques) and Italian (Pasqua) it derives from the Hebrew Pesach (Passover). And of course there are the days of the week: Sun-day, Moon-day, Tiw's day, Woden's day, Thor's day, Frige's day, and Saturn's day—the only one with a Latin origin.[7]

In the decades around and after the appearance of *The Castle of Otranto* and before the vogue for the English gothic gathered maximum strength, there was an increasing appreciation for the long-slighted folk culture of En-gland, Scotland, and Ireland, which frequently linked it to a sense of death, the past, and the all-embracing landscape. The seventeenth-century imperial-ist effort to abolish and eradicate local customs and traditions, reflected in Spenser's *Present State of Ireland,* turned into an eighteenth-century fascina-tion with them. Instead of ignoring the past or actively rejecting it in the name of reason or revolution, such studies gave the past an aura that turned the despised gothick into the admired gothic. Poets like William Collins and Thomas Gray praised the inspired bardic poets of the past, with Collins writ-ing an "Ode on the Popular Superstitions of the Highlands." Similarly in search of the ancient roots of pure poetic inspiration, James Macpherson had claimed to have translated the work of the tenth-century bard Ossian, re-nowned for his defiance of the invading English king Edward I, while anti-quarians like Bishop Thomas Percy traveled the British Isles in search of folk songs and ballads, which he called "Reliques of Ancient English Poetry."

Such books found ready audiences not only in England but also in Germany as well, where members of the *Sturm und Drang* movement like Johann Gottfried Herder wrote approvingly of Ossian and "the Songs of Ancient Peoples." Herder, like Bishop Percy and Herder's countryman Gottfried August Bürger, was also a collector and publisher of folk songs. In their turn such works inspired literary-minded young men, like the young Walter Scott, to try his hand at translating such German folk ballads as "The Erl King," and a few years later to publish his own book of collected ballads, *The Minstrelsy of the Scottish Border* (1803). It was a fruitful period for recapturing olden stories in poetry and prose, with the Brothers Grimms' influential volume *Children's and Household Tales* first appearing in 1812. Taken together, the Ossian poems of Macpherson, the ballad collections of Bishop Percy, and Scott's minstrelsy represent a delving into the past as a way of criticizing the present by reinvigorating the otherwise lost emotional world of times gone by—not incidentally, the world of the rural poor.

The gothic period thus embodied a double sense of the past: in gothic horror, it was the monstrous place from which we must escape, as well as the benevolent site of a unified experience of nature and spirituality that has been lost through the rush toward the modern future. This past is preeminently connected to the English land, in which a pre-Christian religion rooted in nature grew and thrived. Such a past was always present to take its revenges, most often when it had been forgotten or ignored in favor of the movement toward a technological and rational utopia. Its lasting presence in the English imagination continued to produce a host of stories, novels, and films in which sweetly bucolic rural villages of the Olde Englande sort turn out to be filled with witches, devil worshipers, or adherents of various pre-Christian religions of nature.

The Renaissance to some extent had revived the Roman past in an international movement to shake off the intellectual and artistic restrictions of the Middle Ages. But its eighteenth-century inheritors often had more nationalist motives in mind. Like the renovation of gothic as the mysterious and enticing rather than the barbaric and dismissible, the Celtic/Norse past in the nineteenth century was also revived as an antidote for the ills of British civilization—the cult of the Celtic. What the Celtic connection could contribute to more urbanized British civilization was a closer connection both to nature and to a sense of individual character. In visual art the Roman copy of the third century B.C. statue of "The Dying Gaul" was widely admired, inspiring a poetic tribute by Byron in *Childe Harold's Pilgrimage.* It was brought to the Louvre by Napoleon's armies, and became a necessary stop on the Grand Tour for young upper-class Englishmen when it was later returned to Rome. England, of course, had often cherished a political lineage that went back to King Arthur and beyond. In the twelfth century, during the reign of Henry II, the discovery of the bones of Arthur and Guinevere was announced by the Norman court in an effort to legitimize its connection to the Anglo-Saxon past. By the nineteenth century, works such as Tennyson's *Idylls of the King* (1859–85) and Matthew Arnold's 1867 lectures "The Study of Celtic Literature" added more artistic and intellectual cachet to the romanticizing of the Celtic past. Arnold tries to be measured in his assessment of Celtic virtues and faults. At his most positive he says:

> In a certain measure the children of Taliesin and Ossian have now an opportunity for renewing the famous feat of the Greeks, and conquering their conquerors. No service England can render the Celts by giving you a share in her many good qualities, can surpass that which the Celts can at this moment render England, by communicating to us some of theirs.

Arnold wrote in an era when both Irish culture and Welsh culture were being attacked as barbaric, and only a few decades earlier one opponent of political reform was popularly considered to have called the Irish "alien in blood, in language, and in religion." But in his lectures Arnold argues for recognizing "the poetical Celtic nature in us . . . [i]ts chord of penetrating passion and melancholy," the inner Celt as well as the conquering Saxon:

> . . . and where do we get it from? The Celts, with their vehement reaction against the despotism of fact, with their sensuous nature, their manifold striving, their adverse destiny, their immense calamities, the Celts are the prime authors of this vein of piercing regret and passion.[8]

While one strain of British nationalism was trumpeting "Rule Britannia" and imperial expansion, another was looking into the pre-Christian and non-classical past to find different sources of energy and validation. It was not the last time the Celts would be invoked as a paradigm to justify an extra-national perspective. In 1991, just around the time the fall of the Soviet Union was allowing eastern European states to join the European Union, a grandiose museum show in Venice called *I Celti* hailed the Celts as embodying the "First Europe." The show was light on actual artifacts, which was more than made up for by the part-political, part-poetic effort to assert the continuing impact of Celtic heritage in the European present.

From the beginnings of the revival, the Celtic sense of "natural magic" was also an obvious lure for poets and artists of all stripes. But, whatever the openness to the Celtic influence, or the hostility to it, in the writers and politicians of the nineteenth century, the literature of horror owes a special debt to the Irish. In fact, it is remarkable how many horror authors have a share in what I might call the eerie/Eire tradition. Edmund Burke, the eighteenth-century theorist of the sublime and the beautiful, was born in Dublin. Although he was raised in his father's religion as an Anglican, it is difficult not to see the affinities in his writings, both aesthetic and political, with a world where the awesomeness of nature and the traditions of the past color the emotions of the present. Charles Maturin, whose father was dean of Saint Patrick's in Dublin after Jonathan Swift, wrote the popular Faustian novel *Melmoth the Wanderer* (1820). Sheridan Le Fanu, perhaps the greatest ghost story writer in English of the nineteenth century, was born in Dublin, flourished in the same era as Poe, and wrote among many other short stories and novels "Carmilla" (1872), perhaps the first lesbian vampire tale, as well as the Dr. Hesselius stories, featuring a detective of the occult. Oscar Wilde was also born in Dublin, his father an ophthalmologist who wrote books about Irish antiquities and folklore and was a lifelong Irish nationalist. Maturin was Wilde's great-uncle by marriage, and when Wilde left England for Europe after being released from jail, he called himself Sebastian Melmoth. Bram Stoker, the author of *Dracula,* worked as a theater critic for the Dublin *Evening Mail,* when it was co-owned by Le Fanu. A friend of Wilde since university days, he married an early girlfriend of Wilde's.

Wilde and Le Fanu, like so many of the other Irish writers, were Anglo-Irish, more Anglican than Catholic in upbringing. But all of them flourished at a time in the late nineteenth and early twentieth centuries when an explicit invocation of the role of the Irish past in both politics and the arts was taking place. Finally in this array I should mention a family of writers not usually associated with Ireland, but definitely part of the gothic tradition. These were the Brontë sisters. They were the daughters of Patrick Brunty, an Irish farm laborer whose abilities caught the attention of a local clergyman who paid to send him to Cambridge, where he changed the spelling of his name.[9]

Like the Catholicism of many South American countries, in Ireland a hearty portion of native beliefs mingle with whatever theology and imagery have been imported from Rome. The farther from the Vatican, the more likely it is that some intriguing syncretic accommodation is reached between the church and the old religion of the past, particularly, in Ireland, the Celtic past with its earth and sky and sea paganism.

In the midst then of the open future proclaimed by the forward-looking revolutionaries and scientists and early industrialists of the late eighteenth century, and in contrast with those who looked to the past for its untainted wells of purer language and feeling, the gothic novel is filled with anxiety about the past. Turning its face against a world of progress and change and daylight, gothic horror emphasizes how alienated its characters have become from both the past and nature. Often hostile or indifferent to the knowledge that has been gained from science and industry, the gothic novel embodies a feeling that real knowledge has been lost. The gothic presumption is the difficulty or inability amid overpoweringly dark forces of knowing anything with certainty. Often there is no privileged point of view, no omniscient narrator, no one to see the story whole, and so the reader is kept in the dark as well. No wonder then why the gothic mode becomes so popular in the United States, the newly hatched country, born in the eighteenth century without a past, innocent and untrammeled and with an unlimited future, but thereby everlastingly debarred from a deep history of its own. Whereas it could easily be argued that the gothic novel is a subordinate form in England compared with the more realistic worlds of Dickens, Thackeray, and Eliot, in the United States it is a much more important genre. So many American authors carry the gothic strain— Charles Brockden Brown, Nathaniel Hawthorne, Herman Melville, Mark Twain. In their works, the entrepreneurial, willfully autonomous self so characteristic of nineteenth-century America has to face the wound of a past he has tried so decisively to leave behind. It is a theme always ready to be resurrected in times when the blithe American orientation toward the future gets out of control, for example in the horror film *Poltergeist* (1982), in which the unthinking developer of middle-class suburban tract housing has to face the consequences of having built over a Native American burial ground.

In gothic fiction the most all-enveloping and immediate way the past makes its appearance is in the discovery of the story itself, and the most prevalent method of making the supernatural story seem real is the device of the discovered manuscript. The first gothic novel, Walpole's *Otranto,* announces on its title page that it has been "translated by William Marshall, Gent. from the original Italian of Onuphius Muralto, canon of the Church of St. Nicholas at Otranto." The story, we are told, happened sometime between 1095 and 1243, and the book, found in a library in the north of England, had been printed at Naples in 1529. Not until the second edition in April 1765 does the name of the actual author, Horace Walpole, appear. The subtitle is now "A Gothic Story," and in a new preface the author explains how he tried "to blend the two kinds of romance, the ancient and the modern," the improbable work of the imagination with the probable actions of human nature.

Walpole's original effort to place his work in a distant, mysterious past, reverberates down the centuries, imitated in *Frankenstein* by the monster's diary (unlike the movie Frankenstein monster, the novelistic one can read and write) and by Hawthorne in *The Scarlet Letter,* in which he introduces his story by claiming that the evidence for it was found in the musty archives of the Salem customs house where he worked, "in a small package, carefully done up in a piece of ancient yellow parchment," the notes of an antiquary himself eighty years dead that tells the tale of Hester Prynne and the Reverend Arthur Dimmesdale. Always the past enshrouds the present with its dark crimes and tumultuous passions, often having to do with a shadowy family inheritance. Each manuscript leads back in the past to another source, and the original tale can be grasped only through a succession of veils. Like the wary traveler in front of a dark foreboding mansion, the reader cannot cross into the world of darkness and terror directly, but only by the tenuous bridge of old, retold stories. So too Buffy the Vampire Slayer and her friends always have to consult the ancient texts in the school library before sallying forth to defeat the vampires and demons from the Hellmouth that lies beneath Sunnydale High School. Behind the kaleidoscope of earthly change and appearances lies the unchanging, eternal truths of horror.

This pretense that the story has been transmitted from long ago or has come to us filtered through a series of authentic storytellers who are more or less neutral observers is imitated in many stories of horror. But it is also characteristic of a kind of literature that tries to turn its face against placid everyday life to tell tales of heightened passion and feeling. Toward the end of the eighteenth century, many writers tried to create a more authentic literature of feeling through a kind of literary fraud that sought to get away from the "normal" in literature by assuming the cloak of past authority. Thomas Chatterton, before he committed suicide at the age of seventeen, published a book of poems that he claimed was written by a fifteenth-century poet named Thomas Rowley, which Chatterton said he found in an old trunk. Although Robert Burns was one of seven sons of a Scottish farmer, he was well educated in literature, foreign languages, and mathematics, yet he wrote many of his poems in the dialect language of peasants.

What unites these different writers is the urge to find a language for emotional authenticity, to get away from the inherited norms of writing and assume the cloak of another kind of authority, whether that comes from the

past or from otherwise socially excluded groups in the present who have preserved that past memory. Pretending that a story is real because it has been
told by someone other than an author is another variation of the same basic
strategy. *Frankenstein,* as we have seen, is a virtual Chinese box of stories
within stories. We enter through the supposed diary of a young man named
William Walton, who happens to meet on shipboard another man, rescued
from the ice, Victor Frankenstein, who starts to tell his own story, within
which we find the story told by the monster he has created. Another benefit
from the pretense of the discovered manuscript is that it makes the story seem
more authentic. Similar to the multiple perspectives in *Dr. Jekyll and Mr.
Hyde,* it resembles a documentary beginning, an assertion of actual dates and
times, the better to make us believe that the events are real. In this way,
Dracula, almost a century and a half after *The Castle of Otranto,* tells its story
through diaries, newspaper clippings, and even primitive wire recordings and
typewritten transcripts—a technique imitated in the next century, for example, by Stephen King in his first published novel, *Carrie* (1976).

In some works a monster like Dracula comes from the past and, in order
to be defeated, has to awaken the heroic potential of the present. In others,
like *Wuthering Heights,* the normal audience of the present is nostalgically
treated to the stories of the grandeur of the past, the ill-fated love of Cathy
and Heathcliff, before which they can only stand amazed. For most novels of
terror, like most films (at least the good ones), do not and cannot plunge us
immediately into their dark worlds, but must lead us in through the passageways of normality, attended by people like ourselves, before the monster, or
the hero, is glimpsed. William Walton listening to Victor Frankenstein's tale,
Jonathan Harker on his way to Dracula's castle, the visitor from the south of
England Mr. Lockwood hearing the history of Wuthering Heights from the
housekeeper Nelly Dean—all are bridges from our daylight world into a grim
or romantic, but always passionate, world of past strangeness.

THE CHURCH OF DRACULA

It is the fault of our science that it wants to explain all; and if it explains
not, then it says there is nothing to explain.

—Bram Stoker, *Dracula*

The quintessential monster from the past appears most fully formed in
Bram Stoker's *Dracula.* The folk myth of the vampire, as collected and

codified in Stoker's work, answers the question of the lost past by harkening back not just to a medieval past but to a pre-Christian world. The beginning of this chapter has echoed some of the themes and concerns of Chapter 2. Rightly so, for with the vampire, we have come full circle to the intimate relation between horror and religion not created but certainly amplified for the early modern era by the Protestant Reformation. The Reformation break with the past, in which prayers for the dead were at first prohibited, implied that society was no longer a community of the living and the dead. How to cross the boundary between death and life became a crucial issue. One possibility was the ghost; another way to remedy that deficiency would become the vampire undead.

It is intriguing how the vampire story presents itself so explicitly as an alternate religion, responding in a variety of ways to changing ideas of the nature of God, Christ, and Satan within orthodox Christianity. In vampirism, as arrayed in *Dracula* and its descendants, there are as many rites, rituals, and sacred objects as in Christianity itself, making vampirism not just an older religion but also a religion with its own hierarchy and its own promise of defeating death—through vampire immortality. In vampirism, instead of sin being in Augustine's terms a turning away from God, it is an active principle.

Hawthorne's customs-house clerk in *The Scarlet Letter*, before he finds the manuscript that fires his imagination, bemoans the fact that he lives in the United States, a country without a mysterious past and therefore one without passion and romance. But *Dracula* with its up-to-date methods of communication implies that even in the enlightened and civilized present, primitive horror still exists. The present is the place of dullness and conformity, the past the place of energy and excitement. Like *Dr. Jekyll and Mr. Hyde*, *Dracula* continues the movement of the tale of horror from long-gone or faraway exotic places to the contemporary, familiar world. Today we may look back upon their tuxedos and top hats, their gaslit streets and sumptuous drawing rooms, as typically Victorian. But for their early readers this was the present, their normal lives. This transition from the glamorous but distant setting to just around the corner parallels the change from upper-class castles to more middle-class and recognizable locations, in a way strikingly similar to how traditional Japanese ghost stories metamorphosed into nineteenth-century Kabuki ghost plays—implying the presence of a new middle-class audience for such stories in both cultures.

Yet at the same time that it has become more contemporary, the world summoned up in *Dracula* is also the product of a deep and almost forgotten past that among other things represents a pre-Christian paganism, linked with the Celtic, that is rooted in earth and nature, where power is associated with animal familiars as well as with animal shapes like the bat and the wolf that the vampire can turn into—"the children of the night."[10] The novel *Dracula* appears at a time when comparative religious studies and the anthropological view of primitive cultures, as in works like J. G. Fraser's *The Golden Bough* (1890), have undermined the claims of unique spiritual truth made by the organized religions by showing their common roots as well as, in Rudolf Otto's sense, implying that all religious experience begins in the numinous. It was also a period that sowed the seeds for artistic modernism, which drew upon what was conceived of as the primitive and the natural to replenish worn-out forms, whether it was T. S. Eliot's use of myths in *The Waste Land,* Picasso's of African art, or Stravinsky's of folktales and ancient ritual in *The Firebird* and *The Rite of Spring.*

In accord with the same preoccupation with the energies of the pre-Christian world, Dracula arrives in England aboard a ship called the *Demeter,* named for the Roman goddess of earthly fertility. So too, in this connection to nature and the earth, Dracula might be associated with the late-nineteenth- and early-twentieth-century literary preoccupation with the figure of Pan, the archetypal nature god. Pan, like his more monstrous kin, represents a powerful instinctive world whose claims on human attention and understanding have been either ignored or glossed over in the rise of conventional religion. Central to Pan's power is his connection to nature and to human sexuality. An important forerunner in this tradition is Arthur Machen's famous tale "The Great God Pan" (final form, 1894), in which Pan has mated with a human woman to create a half human, half monster—a plot turn that looks forward to such later stories as *Rosemary's Baby* (1968), as well as the impregnation of Ripley by the Alien in *Alien 3* (1992). In a somewhat more benevolent mode are E. M. Forster's "The Story of a Panic" (1903) and J. M. Barrie's *Peter Pan* (1904), subtitled *The Boy Who Wouldn't Grow Up.* Both associate the figure of Pan with a youthful vision of the world rejected by blind adults—akin to the Romantic view of the child's vibrant sense of the wonders of nature that are lost when adulthood looms.[11]

Such stories, along with figures like Dracula and the god Pan, dramatically revive the tension between the newer and the older religions and raise the question of how effectively Christianity has repressed or transformed the religion of earth. Many of the scholarly arguments about the reality of witchcraft, for example, especially over whether it has any verifiable roots in pre-Christian religion, are themselves products of the gothic revival of the late eighteenth and early nineteenth centuries. Before the modern vampire made his maiden appearance in John Polidori's tale *The Vampyre* in 1821, there existed a semi-coherent history of aristocratic sadists who believed that the blood of innocents would keep them young. The most memorable upper-class murderers were two late-medieval human monsters: Gilles de Raies (1404–1440), the military companion at arms of Joan of Arc in his twenties and one of the richest nobles in France, who was tried and convicted of heresy for kidnapping, sodomizing, and murdering more than two hundred lower-class boys and girls; and Elizabeth Bathory (1560–1614), niece of the king of Poland and countess of Transylvania, supposedly a sadist who whipped her servants unmercifully until she discovered by accident that blood was making her feel younger, then bathed in the blood of servants until she made the mistake of deciding that she needed more upper-class female blood and started killing young women of good families. After that she was arrested and walled up in her castle until she died. Although Gilles de Raies has a claim to be the inspiration for the folktale character Bluebeard, he didn't in fact murder his wives. In any case, both de Raies and Bathory are now primarily known only to historians, connoisseurs of straight-to-DVD horror films, and fans of the Hammer Studio movies from the 1970s like *Countess Dracula* (1972) and *Old Dracula* (1974), in which David Niven as Dracula gets blood from Playboy bunnies to resurrect his dead wife.

No details of the histories of either Gilles de Raies or Elizabeth Bathory include references to fangs or bite marks on the necks of their victims, perhaps because at the time drinking and bathing in blood were also part of the accusations against witches, along with drinking semen and breast milk—a general hankering to drain precious bodily fluids. The sanguisuga, for example, and the vrykolakas were creatures of the night whose undead bloodsucking activities were reflected in many other cultures, but with hardly the centrality among monsters later assumed by the vampire. Like ogres and other such monsters, they often focused on children as appropriate victims, in a familiar effort to explain childhood death as the result of diabolic forces. Joshua Trachtenberg, in *Jewish Magic and Superstition: A Study in Folk Religion*, also mentions the frequently found medieval view that Jews took blood for longevity, an ancient anti-Semitic calumny that could obviously be easily assimilated to the panic over vampires. The fear in numerous places was obviously real. Recently, in a graveyard near the Bulgarian town of Sozopol, skeletons were found dating from the fourteenth century, with metal objects shoved into their bodies to prevent them from rising again. Such twice-told tales of vampires with aristocratic bloodlines merge with stories of the undead who rise from their graves to ravage the rural countryside, creating the modern conception of the vampire.

Many such stories were brought together in the eighteenth century by the prolific Benedictine monk Augustin Carmet in his *Traité sur les apparitions des espirits, et sur les vampires, ou Les revenants de Hongrie, de Moravie* (1751, Treatise on the Apparition of Spirits, and on Vampires, or The Ghosts of Hungary, of Moravia). Carmet, also the author of a six-volume commentary on the Bible, collected the stories and highlighted their strangeness but was a bit vague on whether he believed them or not. Even before his book appeared in France there was enough knowledge of the vampire's general characteristics that the OED could claim the word first appeared in English (as *vampyre*) in 1734, and it was already being used metaphorically to refer to anyone who preys upon another ten years before Carmet wrote. With explicit acknowledgment to Carmet, Voltaire in his *Philosophic Dictionary* (1764) specifies the vampire as predator with analogies that, in the nineteenth century, were repeated by Friedrich Engels and later by Karl Marx:

> We never heard a word of vampires in London, nor even at Paris. I confess that in both these cities there were stock-jobbers, brokers, and men of business, who sucked the blood of the people in broad daylight; but they were not dead, though corrupted. These true suckers lived not in cemeteries, but in very agreeable palaces.

By the usual historical process through which fears coalesce a variety of facts, fictions, and half-truths, these superstitions and folktales became constellated around stories about the cruelty of Vlad III, three-time ruler of Wallachia, which began circulating by the end of the fifteenth century. More than four hundred years later, Vlad, whose patronymic was Dracula, was called upon by Bram Stoker to take his place in the modern mind as the king of the vampires.

Despite the fact that Vlad historically defended Christianity against Islam, in the vampire tradition, as codified and passed down by Stoker, no other archetypal monster so clearly represents as direct a threat to Christianity as the vampire. More than the Frankenstein-like creator competing with God, Dracula is the "ancient adversary," the opponent of God, with his own twisted version of Christian rituals. The need to drink blood—"The blood is the life"—mocks the Eucharist, just as the revulsion from the cross and holy water implies the continuing combat with Christianity, in which the vampire promises its chosen acolytes a triumph over death in the immortality of the undead rather than the Christian heaven, an immortality within the world and time, rather than outside in some timeless place. The vampire story thus illustrates the way religion in general and Christianity in particular underlie and shape the nature of horror. Frankenstein's Creature is anguished to discover his monstrousness; Dr. Jekyll fears and loathes Mr. Hyde, although he can't resist becoming him; the Wolfman, at least in the Hollywood retelling, similarly makes an involuntary transformation after fruitless resistance. In contrast, the natural monster just is who he is. Dracula also is self-accepting and self-centered, though much more articulately so. He is after all a count, an aristocrat high in social status, totally comfortable with his monstrous desires. Most monsters are singular and alone, but Dracula has acolytes and in effect his own alternate church, complete with ritual occasions and objects. In no horror genre other than the vampire are there so many motifs, ritual objects, taboos, plot turns, and characters: wooden stakes, crucifixes, a coffin filled with native earth, fangs and pointed teeth, capes, tuxedos; the list goes on: fear of garlic and the destructiveness of sunlight, no reflections in mirrors, wounds that heal immediately, no interest in food, great strength, bites on the neck, coldness of flesh.

SEX AND THE SINGLE MONSTER

The seductive power of the vampire reflects the appeal of Satan or, more immediately in literary history, the mesmerizing Byronic hero. It is no accident that Polidori's story bases the vampire character Lord Ruthven on Byron. Byron's public image, like that of Satan and a gothic hero/villain like Don Giovanni, partook of the fallen angel, alienated from God and the world, doomed to wander endlessly over the earth, racked with sin and guilt, but unbowed and unrepentant. Like Dracula, his mesmerizing, commanding eyes were one of his prime characteristics, drawing women and men to him in equal quantities and with equal subordination, encapsulating his hypnotic power over others.

Sexual attraction was one of the most potent and mysterious of invisible forces in a world before psychology and biochemistry. No wonder perhaps that it was so closely linked to the diabolical. Satan in Protestant countries is often a figure of illicit sexuality, as the obscene rituals ascribed to witches in the seventeenth century testify. In Catholic and Islamic countries, by contrast, he is much more a general oppositional religious and political figure rather than a personal tempter. The vampire thus embodies the non-normative sexuality that the monster represents generally. But, intriguingly enough, Dracula as described by Bram Stoker has no visibly seductive characteristics. He is "a tall old man, clean shaven save for a long white moustache, and clad in black from head to foot, without a single speck of color about him anywhere." Like the witch, who was considered to have an innate ability to fascinate without having necessarily the material means, the literary Dracula is seductive without any physical characteristics we might conventionally associate with seduction. When Dracula moves from the literary world to the mediums of theater and film, however, with the honorable exception of the gruesome Count Orlok played by Max Schreck in F. W. Murnau's *Nosferatu*, that pure allure has to find a visual equivalent and so Dracula's look becomes more suave and even handsome, to emphasize his connection to more conventionally seductive male figures.

In addition to his charismatic qualities and virtually instant control over most women, the vampire is also usually an aristocrat and the most articulate of monsters, able to talk clearly and coherently, unlike so many of the others, who either have no language or are lower class and mutter unintelligibly. From Lord Ruthven and Dracula down to the Addams family, wealth and aristocracy are part of the vampire's DNA, just as his dangling of immortality as a lure for the chosen of his victims promises the opportunity to become one of the elite. Since the expunging of statutes against witchcraft in the eighteenth century, crime began to belong legally in the realm of the police and fictionally in the realm of the detective. But evil was not a crime in the same sense. Whereas witches had been tried for their contacts with diabolical forces, what would it mean to try a vampire? So the special quality of evil represented by the vampire stands outside the system of human justice, just as aristocrats in earlier ages had often been exempt from laws that others had to follow.

If horror on one side is allied to religion in its preoccupation with the uncertain line between the living and the dead, on the other it bears strong affinities with pornography in its characterization of women as both sexual victims and sexual predators. I have been writing of "he" and "him" to characterize the vampire, but, although the common twentieth-century image of the vampire is male—thanks to Dracula and its descendants—women can certainly be vampires as well. As it appears in much of horror as well as in the tradition of the detective, the power of the feminine is a central part of the vampire story. In fact, although most nineteenth-century literary vampires tend to be male, many of the traditional vampire characteristics are already present in one significant early literary version of the female vampire, Goethe's ballad "The Bride of Corinth" (1797), in which a pale, cold to the touch, blood-drinking undead young woman denounces the Christianity that has shut her into a nunnery to die and tantalizes her living former lover.[12] This kind of vampire femme fatale is mirrored also in such poems as John Keats's "La Belle Dame Sans Merci" (1819), the heartless woman who lures men to their destruction, and "Lamia" (1820), the man-eating female monster from Greek mythology with the head and breast of a woman and the body of a serpent. Another significant early version of the power of the female vampire is Sheridan Le Fanu's "Carmilla" (1872), with its main character what may be an evocation of the wild women of Irish legend, the bloodlust of Elizabeth Bathory, and the overt sexuality of the perhaps Celtic sheela na gig sculptures found so frequently in Ireland.

Such predatory females heavily influenced nineteenth-century painters, who added other mythological women like Lilith, the supposed first wife of Adam, also portrayed as half woman, half snake; Salome, usually brandishing the head of John the Baptist; the Sphinx, with the head of a woman, body of a lion, and the wings of a bird; and a host of other lesser known feminine blood-drinkers and devourers. In fact, if one were to consider primarily the depictions of the vampire in nineteenth-century art, it would be easy to conclude that vampires were predominantly women. Descending from characters like the "dark lady" of Shakespeare's sonnets, or Matilda in *The Monk*, with her sexual avidity and diabolical connections, the "dark woman" of nineteenth-century fiction easily metamorphosed into the soul-destroying vampire, preying especially on male weakness and suppressed desire. As Jonathan Harker says of his sight of the three wives of Dracula, "I felt in my heart a wicked, burning desire that they would kiss me with those red lips." These were the women that the Marquis de Sade described as *toujours plus*, always more, sapping male strength (and semen) endlessly.[13]

In the later eighteenth century mesmerism came into vogue as a therapy that supposedly corrected and rechanneled the errors of the invisible flow of feeling. As used by male practitioners, however, it was often accused by its opponents of being sexually predatory as well. Yet that kind of mesmerizing charisma was also not exclusively male. In numerous mesmeric stage presentations, the prime figure was a woman, who was thought because of her gender to have better entrée than a man to the invisible world. The power of such women, even in the face of efforts to define true femininity as passive and morally upright, the so-called "angel in the house," was underscored by their pervasive role in the contacts with the spirit world that also fascinated the nineteenth century. Women's marginalization in a male-dominated society thus turned into a source of power and energy. The language of electricity and mesmerism became part of the description of charisma generally, especially in women. As Margaret Fuller writes in *Woman in the Nineteenth Century* (1854), "The electrical, the magnetic element in Woman has not been fairly brought out at any period." It was a species of attraction that was housed in the body but was distinct from it, like the appeal of the unsightly Dracula. As Fuller says, in speaking of Miranda, a character based on herself, "She was fortunate in a total absence of those charms which might have drawn to her bewildering flatteries, and in a strong electric nature, which repelled those who did not belong to her, and attracted those who did." Appropriately enough for this mesmeric connection, in *Dracula* Professor Van Helsing explains that the oddness of Transylvanian geology accounts for the presence of its vampires:

> There are deep caverns and fissures that reach none know whither. There have been volcanoes, some of whose openings still send out waters of strange properties, and gases that kill or make to vivify. Doubtless, there is something magnetic or electric in some of these combinations of occult forces which work for physical life in strange ways.

In the face of the conventional nineteenth-century polarity of the passive woman and the active man, the vampire, whether male or female, asserted an unbounded sense of both sexuality and selfhood. Vampires, like the devil, flourished in boundary places, at crossroads, on the verge between life and death, normal and abnormal, heterosexual and homosexual, male and female. To combat them properly required a similar ability to bridge what otherwise seemed to be incompatible differences. *Dracula* the novel stages some of these issues in its own extreme way. Mina Harker in the movie versions of Stoker's tale is usually eclipsed by Dracula himself. But in the novel she is a crucially important character, his great antagonist, as much if not more than Van Helsing. And where does her power come from? Although Dracula forces her to drink blood from his breast, in "that terrible and horrid position," she has the fortitude to lead her companions to Dracula's lair in Transylvania and use her telepathic connection with him ultimately to help them destroy him. And it is exactly her own doubleness, her ability as a "New Woman" to bridge conventional gender polarities, that allows her to do this. As Van Helsing says of Mina admiringly, "She has man's brains—a brain that a man should have were he much gifted—and a woman's heart." In the novel Van Helsing and Mina become complementary figures. He is the man who has emotions and can laugh and cry like a woman; she is the woman who has "the brain of a man." She also self-consciously either subordinates herself to the "strong, brave" men as a kind of child, or else acts like the nonsexual, comforting earth mother. Both Van Helsing's and Mina's kind of psychological androgyny seems to be what Stoker believes is the only response possible to male abjection before the power of female sexuality.

Unlike "normal" men, the male vampire is fatally attractive to both women and men, while the female vampire, with the exception of Carmilla and her descendants, tends to prey primarily on male weakness. Images of women, ennobling and derogatory, abound in nineteenth-century visual art. But the decade that sees the appearance of *Dracula* has some choice examples with a vampire twist. Edvard Munch's painting *The Vampire* (1895), for example, shows a woman with flowing red hair bending voraciously over the neck of a passive man. Philip Burne-Jones's painting *The Vampire* (1897) features a woman in nightclothes straddling a supine and seemingly unconscious man on a bed. On seeing it, Rudyard Kipling was supposedly inspired to write his poem "A Fool There Was," which begins "A fool there was and he made his prayer / (Even as you and I!) / To a rag and a bone and a hank of hair / (We called her the woman who did not care), / But the fool he called her his lady fair / (Even as you and I!)." Instead of the vampirism of Munch's painting or the explicitly sexual depletion depicted in Burne-Jones's, Kipling's fool is stripped of all his money and possessions by "the woman who did not care." Kipling's poem in turn lent its title to the 1915 film in which Theda Bara plays a woman who seduces a devoted husband and father away from the straight and narrow. Bara was perhaps the first sex symbol movie star in America, and not incidentally helped popularize the term *vamp* for a sexually predatory woman. Publicity photos showed her half-naked and intertwined with a skeleton representing her depleted male lover, while movie magazines gave out the titillating story that her name was an anagram of ARAB DEATH. In reality she was Theodosia Goodman, born in Cincinnati. But the connection of such a female figure to orientalist exoticism and sensuality elaborated the vampire tradition in a direction that would lead to later figures like the dragon lady and the femme fatale.[14]

One of the most intriguing and problematic aspects of the vampire tradition is the difference between killing a victim by draining all of its blood or, instead, making the victim an acolyte and associate by infecting it with the vampire spirit. Even within the cohort of old and new vampires there is also a hierarchy, in *Dracula* the difference between the abject follower Renfield, the voracious Lucy Westenra, and the more powerful Mina Harker. How is this decision made? One decisive factor seems to be analogous to the relation between lust and love, the deadly bite akin to a one-night stand and the deeper connection to the potential beginning of a future relationship. As one of the group of nomadic vampires in Kathryn Bigelow's late-blooming addition to the tradition *Near Dark* points out when the group wants to kill the young Caleb for exposing them, "He's already turned." That is, he is already one of us. Part of the dramatic tension in *Breaking Dawn* (2008), the final novel in the *Twilight* series, is how both sex and pregnancy will affect Bella, the human married to Edward the vampire—a crisis resolved only when Edward turns her into a vampire as well.

As in Goethe's "Bride of Corinth," there is thus often a potential connection between love and death in the vampire story, a motif whose significance in vampire lore may also be implicit in *Dracula*. As one of Dracula's wives says to him as he begins to feed on Jonathan Harker, "You yourself never loved; you never love!" To which Dracula responds that he has loved in the past. For the most part, the male or the female vampire is beyond the lure of love and remains, as in Kipling's poem, self-sufficient, although Tod Browning's *Dracula* film suggests even further that Dracula has a soft spot for Mina, bringing her down into the tombs to lie in a coffin next to him, a connection she exploits in her plans to defeat him. In the course of the twentieth century, these brief references to a love in the past and an affinity in the present become elaborated into the idea of the lost love for which the monster searches. Two other types of fantasy influence it. One is the Undine story, a modern descendant of the classic stories of human beings who mate with gods, which begins as the tale of a water nymph who loves a human and has to face the dilemma of staying nonhuman and immortal, or becoming human for love and having to face death. The other is the appearance of a twentieth-century monster, the Mummy, whose primary quest is to find in the present the woman whom he loved in the past. First appearing in the 1932 film inspired by the 1922 opening of King Tut's tomb, the Mummy's problem is his inability, like that of the Frankenstein monster, to find the mate he yearns for. The contrast is between monster immortality and human mortality, between an eternal life alone and a deep but temporally limited love. When the Mummy is revived, he seeks to bond with the reincarnation of his lost love, or else he must wander the earth forever, unrequited and alone. Like the Greek and Roman gods, such a monster, while seemingly beyond human impermanence, still can be subject to human emotions.[15]

Although one poster for the 1931 *Dracula* included the line "the story of the strangest passion the world has ever known," that was hardly a major theme in the film. But when these influences are later mingled more concertedly with the vampire story, as in Francis Coppola's *Bram Stoker's Dracula* (1992), love restores a humanity that the vampire otherwise lacks, and simultaneously makes him a more pathetic, and sympathetic, figure. The love that transcends death becomes the true afterlife, rather than any lonely ersatz immortality or even the religious hope of heaven. The passion that lasts beyond the grave connects as well with the way the vampire story can also be read as an elegy for the lost grandeur of the past, the feelings and beliefs that have been repressed by the modern world but still simmer undiminished beneath the surface. At a time in the late nineteenth century when European and American society seems to be more in motion than ever before, moving forward technologically, politically, and economically, Dracula represents the inexorable pull backward into a terrifying past, ready and eager to take its revenge.

❧

Akin to other elements in the genre story, sexuality and attitudes toward the body in horror mutate, responding to new contexts and new ideas. Like a funhouse mirror, the form reflects cultural changes in attitudes toward gender in distorted, heightened ways. One early source of the sexual fear of the natural or created monster was the possibility of both giant sexual parts and incessant mechanical repetition. Behind such ideas are eighteenth-century ideas of the body as machine. John Cleland in *Fanny Hill* (1748) uses *machine* to refer to the human body in the throes of sexual pleasure as well as a synonym for penis. By the end of the century, instead of invoking the uniquely created machines that inspire Victor Frankenstein, the mechanical has become identified with the repetitive as a legacy of the Industrial Revolution. Yet the same uneasy relation between the mechanical and the organic, as well as the question of the created monster's capacity for feeling and sexuality, will be revived in the twentieth century with the advent of robots, androids, and cyborgs—part human and part mechanical creatures that call into question the integrity of the human body.

Each major variety of the monster seems to have its own relationship to sexuality. Zombies, as a subordinate form that emphasizes the group, have the least potential. The vampire story, with its large quotient of sexuality and its hero's charismatic appeal to both men and women, is principally heterosexual in implication, although from Sheridan Le Fanu's "Carmilla" onward, it has had a strong lesbian appeal as well. *Frankenstein,* with its emphasis on the ability of a man to create new life without the need for a woman, has allowed homosexual implications, as explored in Andy Warhol's *Flesh for Frankenstein* (1973) as well as Christopher Isherwood and Don Bachardy's script for *Frankenstein: The True Story* (1973).

The vampire may be the most prominent standard bearer of the sexual theme in horror, but its tributaries flow through all four of the basic monster types, involving not just or even primarily genital sex but everything to do with gender, male-female difference, the sense of bodily integrity, sexual norms and their contraries. As I shall discuss in the final chapter, such themes gather more power and importance with the advent of the movies and visual media generally, because images that were otherwise conveyed primarily by words on a page are now come to life before our eyes. Not that associating the horrific with the sexual had to wait for Freud and the movies to appear. When the English caricaturist Isaac Cruikshank chose to parody the erotic effects of Lewis's *The Monk* in an 1801 engraving titled *Luxury,* he drew a woman backed up to a blazing fireplace. In one hand she holds the novel while the other is under her dress, clearly masturbating.

Both the fear of sexuality as well as its undeniable attractiveness is often a major theme of the visual categories of the horror story, and its centrality is first emphasized by early stage versions of works like *Dr. Jekyll and Mr. Hyde,* which invariably add female characters to what is otherwise an almost entirely male plot—a change elaborated even more by the movie versions. Although lust has canonically been characterized as the least culpable of the Seven Deadly Sins, the control and repression of sexuality has been a prime concern of Christianity throughout its history, especially in its dualistic mode. If the physical world is naturally evil, then the body is evil as well, or is at least the place where evil most easily enters. *Inter faeces et urinas nascimur* ("we are born between shit and piss") says the medieval theologian Bernard of Clairvaux, attributing the phrase to Augustine. From such a viewpoint, the body itself becomes a kind of monster that must be tamed.[16]

Augustine in his *Confessions* frequently wrestles with his own lusts in an effort to become a good Christian. In films, although the explicit context is often secular, this focus on both the body and the sexual again recalls horror's religious roots. Unlike Augustine's struggles with his own desires, modern versions of the struggle also emphasize the power of the feminine, either as virgin or wanton. One indelible image from the early history of movie horror is thus the monster carrying off a woman, often dressed in white flowing robes, perhaps asleep, perhaps kicking and screaming, with others in hot pursuit, armed and frequently carrying torches. The monster's purposes are never quite made clear—is it to desire, to ravish, or even to worship? Cesare in *Caligari,* the Creature in *Frankenstein,* the Gill-man in *Creature from the Black Lagoon,* King Kong—the list goes on. One interpretation of the fear of the monster may be the fear of the Other who aims to attack "our women," and the images of pursuit do often recall a lynching. But the monster's motivation, as in the Frankenstein story, is also often akin to the human desire to have a mate and no longer be a solitary being.

In terms of literary history one could trace the motif of the monster's attraction to the woman back to the novels of Ann Radcliffe, with their youthful and presumably virginal heroines, endangered and oppressed by male tyranny. The vulnerable woman in horror therefore draws upon past images of innocence, but the monster may have a share of that innocence as well, and feel more affinity with the oppressed feminine than with the mobs of men who pursue him. Living in a presexual moment or on the verge of adult sexuality, characters like Regan in *The Exorcist* or Carrie in Stephen King's first novel are particularly welcoming to supernatural forces, for good and for evil: Regan as a battleground between demon and exorcist; Carrie discovering her own supernatural powers as she is torn by the petty evil of her teenage tormentors and the more deadly evil of her mother's extreme version of Christianity.

With the decisive shifting of the audience demographic of horror films from adults to young adults in the 1970s, Carrie's Ewen High School is an appealing setting within which to dramatize issues of dawning sexuality and its repercussions. In other films of the period, teenagers having sex is frequently a way to ensure that they will become the monster's prey. Jason Vorhees of the *Friday the 13th* films and Michael Myers of the *Halloween* films are only two of the inexorably stalking monsters who seem most upset by this. Frozen at early stages of their development, part of the hostility toward sexuality of these teenage monsters seems to lie precisely in their refusal to grow up. Like murderous Peter Pans, they aim to rid the world of the sexual feelings and actions they cannot share. Slashers like them are again seemingly secular and individually motivated, but their disgust with sexuality still connects them to a religious tradition of horror. Historically, the monster frequently invades the bedroom first of all. The house in horror is often an image of the body, a metaphor for the different aspects of the self, the self with other people and the self alone. The body is generally under attack in horror, and the bedroom—the place of sex, sleeping, and dreaming—is the place of greatest vulnerability.

I began this study by quoting the eighteenth-century writer Edward Young, who said, "We love to be at once, miserable, and unhurt." It is a sentiment frequently echoed down to the present as a way of understanding not only the appeal of horror films, but also all sorts of vicarious experiences. To the extent that the body is a central element in personal identity, the aesthetic experience of the movies is a time away from the body's immediacy and into the realm of imagination and feeling—which may explain the urge to consume popcorn and candy so avidly during a film. Accordingly, while literary horror has its share of violence against the body, twentieth-century cinematic horror has made it a much more central part of its stories.

The visualization of the monster allowed by the movies plays a crucial role in the psychological connection between the film and its audience. When we watch, we are to a certain extent disembodied, more in touch with the unconscious world of dreams than with our immediate physical selves. Similarly, the modern world of fame, so expanded by the movies, specifically encourages an emotional and even an erotic connection to these present/absent figures on the screen, the ghostly famous ones you have never met. "I see dead people" is thus a quintessential movie experience that becomes more and more compelling as the movies age, when the performers we see so full of life on screen are themselves long gone. Horror exploits this central aspect of the moviegoing experience by its many attacks on the bodies on screen through sexuality and violence, while at the same time offering the consolation of resurrection for the audience after the film is over.[17]

CHAPTER 8

Horror in the Age of Visual Reproduction

... the eye sees not itself / But by reflection, by some other things.
—Shakespeare, *Julius Caesar*

In addition to images of vampire-like women in the paintings of Munch and others, the late 1880s and the 1890s mark an auspicious reinvigoration of the literature of horror and the supernatural as well as the literature of detection and rational logic. Doyle's Sherlock Holmes (*A Study in Scarlet,* 1887), Stevenson's *Jekyll and Hyde* (1888), Wilde's *The Picture of Dorian Gray* (1891), and Stoker's *Dracula* (1896) all introduce many characters that to a greater or lesser extent have managed to slip out of their original literary confines to become generalized figures who might appear anywhere in popular culture. In addition, it hasn't entirely escaped attention that the same period marks the early appearance of some of the major works of Sigmund Freud, *Studies on Hysteria,* co-authored with Josef Breuer (1895), and *The Interpretation of Dreams* (1900). As the intertwined genesis of the Industrial Revolution and the gothic in the eighteenth century implies, horror turns its face against the optimistic future and rejects any idea of progress understood solely in terms of social, scientific, or technological advance. Instead it brings us back to the repressed facts—preeminently death, but also the world of the spirit—which can never be improved upon in the way you can make a more efficient factory or a better computer. One way then to consider this widespread eruption of horror motifs and story lines in the art and literature of the late nineteenth century is as part of a general attack on the Victorian cult of progress that also included a host of other fin de siécle phenomena like the rise of Catholic mysticism, the Aesthetic movement, and even the sinuous natural forms of art nouveau, which recall those of the arabesque.[1]

Yet still another major event of the 1890s was the appearance of the embryonic motion picture industry, in the projectable films of the Lumière brothers, Auguste and Louis, and those of Georges Méliès. Just as early printing had been instrumental in fostering the circulation of Reformation ideas about the accessibility of the Bible in vernacular languages rather than Latin, graphic art aided immeasurably in the dissemination of images of the monstrous. The Papal Ass and the Monk Calf, those early figures of Lutheran and Calvinist polemic, served both functions admirably, as analogues to the general preoccupation with monstrous births and as allegorized attacks on the Catholic hierarchy. It was a style of propaganda that expanded in the twentieth century with the rise of new modes of visual technology, enhancing the persuasive power of images and creating a whole repertoire of new and refurbished monster depictions.

The movies thus constituted a leap forward in the evolution of attitudes toward both the natural and the supernatural, the rational and the irrational, the visible and the invisible worlds. The gothic emphasis on the inability to describe the truly horrific—the awesome ineffability of the demonic—a tradition still honored in the twentieth century by writers like M. R. James and H. P. Lovecraft—was augmented by another of the new technologies, radio, which invited the hearer into an otherwise invisible world filled by one's own imaginings. But the essence of a movie was to be seen. In masterpieces of silent film horror such as *The Golem, The Cabinet of Dr. Caligari,* and *The Student of Prague,* the style of German expressionism, previously developed in painting and theater, conveyed with its unrealistically painted sets, its abrupt angles and shadows, the twisted lettering of its intertitles, and its general air of tortured artifice an uncertain world of extreme states of emotion, peopled by characters, like those in the stories of Poe, often on the verge of or plunged deeply into madness. Such artifice aimed in part to critique the moral emptiness and superficial reality of the fourth-wall stage of nineteenth-century drama, with its pretense to mirror reality. To define the world only by its visible and material circumstances was insufficient. Expressionism illustrated instead the reality of the mind and the feelings, in all their confusions and distortions.

In 1919, during the heyday of German expressionist filmmaking, Sigmund Freud published an essay called "The Uncanny" (Das Unheimliche). In it he focuses on this word, which pervades the fantastic tales of the German

Romanticist E. T. A. Hoffman like "The Sandman," and uses it as springboard to an essay-long discussion of its paradoxical meanings. After a survey of comparable words in other languages, Freud distinguishes between two senses of the word in German: familiar and comfortable; concealed and hidden. It is familiar because it is everywhere, but it is hidden because, like the knowledge that one must die, it has been repressed. The vague but persistent sense of dread that is the feeling of the uncanny often occurs "when the boundary between fantasy and reality is blurred" (150). It is a definition that well describes the clash between the normal and the abnormal exploited by expressionist horror. It is suitable as well to more modern depictions, when it is not the strangeness of the monster that terrifies but the ordinary context in which it appears, like the bland public spaces of Stanley Kubrick's film of *The Shining,* the luxurious hotel lobby or the men's room that belong to no one and therefore seem to represent safety, but in fact are filled with demons.

∽◦⊙◦∾

Before considering in more detail what elements in the physical nature of movies and movie-making (and television and any other narrative visual medium) contributes to the longevity of horror, I must come back again to my early analogy between horror and religion in the area of ritual. What is honorifically called ritual in religion bears a close resemblance to what is less respectably referred to as genre in the arts. Religious ritual and aesthetic genre share two aspects of myth, the unchanging truth and the constantly changing context, God's (or the artist's) purpose on the one hand and my specific problem on the other. The ritual is meant to encompass all human situations, but it must also feel immediately relevant to whatever specific anguish the worshiper is experiencing. The genre story may have an unalloyed essence (Frankenstein is a monster created by a man who cannot control it) as well as a meaning that transforms with every new context (as technology develops, robots can potentially become the masters of human beings). One question then is whether the significance of the story is in its basic meaning, or does its meaning depend on its ability to continue to transform?

Like ritual, genre creates a community of viewers with similar and overlapping experiences. But unlike prayer or other religious rituals, genres cannot merely be repeated endlessly and expect the same responses from their audiences. A variety of originality has to be present for the genre work to be more lasting than others that may closely resemble it. Working within a preexisting form, the creator wants to do more with it, to compete with previous examples. Whereas absolute originality at least claims to do something that never existed before, genre originality perfects, changes, and interprets a tradition. Genre creativity in this sense is a species of rereading. It may accomplish this by stepping outside, revising the context in which the story appears—or by delving inside, teasing out potentials in the stories that others had not seen or ignored. The most long-lived genres embody cultural myths, stories we tell each other to make sense of the world we find ourselves in, not factually so much as emotionally. Genres express our fears and desire—as shaped by a series of stories, characters, and motifs—and keeps playing variations on them until people grow tired, which for some may take a very long time. The repetition of genre formats satisfies their audiences until changes in society and culture and human consciousness make them neither amusing nor engaging. Horror, it must be said, has had a longer run than many genres, and its hardy evolution over the nineteenth, twentieth, and into the twenty-first century implies the continuing vitality of its characters, plots, and terrors to the dream life of its audience. So long as we have our hopes and fears, we will have ways of staging, expressing, exacerbating and, for the moment at least, purging them.

How then did the movies make such an enormous and continuing contribution to the presence of the monstrous in the human imagination? At various moments in previous chapters, I have commented on the impact of the new arts of visibility in the nineteenth and twentieth centuries, especially photography and motion pictures, on the imagination of horror and the definition of the monstrous. In the simplest and most obvious terms, movies add visual power and impact to characters and situations that have their roots in literature and verbal description, intensifying and expanding horror traditions. In so many ways, film can be more explicitly gothic than the prose fiction that took its own cues from picturesque painting: storms pound the roofs of dark houses, lightning flashes, curtains blow in the wind—raging nature appears directly. As a visual medium, film can also exploit more than literature the lure of the partially seen, the vague forms at the edge of vision that draw the viewer onward down the dark corridor to the door that shouldn't be opened. The visual tradition that influences the look of the 1931 *Frankenstein,* for example, is as strong as or even stronger than its literary ancestor. Its contrasts of light and dark and its extreme camera angles invoke *The Cabinet of Dr. Caligari;* its laboratory draws upon the one in which Rotwang creates the robot Maria in *Metropolis;* and its image of the inarticulate, awkward, and shambling Creature owes more to *The Golem* than to Mary Shelley's handsome (although dead), eloquent, and physically adroit monster. In literature vague description can invoke dread images fostered by the reader's own fears, but movies must show, and in showing create a tradition of their own. Mr. Hyde is loathed at first sight by Enfield, but he is very difficult to describe: "He must be deformed somewhere; he gives a strong feeling of deformity, although I couldn't specify the point." In any Jekyll and Hyde film, of course, that "point" must be given a local habitation and a name, depending on the director's vision for the story. Rouben Mamoulian for the 1931 version considered Hyde to be an aborigine, while Spencer Tracy for Victor Fleming's 1941 version used very little special makeup to emphasize Hyde's psychological origins.

But the influence of the movies goes beyond visual details and the elaboration of individual stories. One way of accounting for the power of its stimulus might derive from the twin genesis of film in the contrast between the realistic settings of the Lumière brothers and the imaginative theatrical constructions of Méliès, an uneasy symbiosis that has long been considered a metaphor for the double nature of movies themselves. Almost immediately the two forms were amalgamated. In *Sherlock Holmes Baffled* (1903), one of the earliest Holmes films, an appearing and then disappearing burglar leaves the great detective totally confused, as the seemingly normal setting is infused with heavy doses of movie magic. The movies thereby reinvigorated horror stories and traditions by a variety of photographic and cinematic techniques—double exposure, superimposition, stop motion—that allowed a potentially nightmarish manipulation of time and space. Accordingly, there was a significant though scant number of early film versions of classic horror tales. But it was most significantly with the establishment of the studio system of production in the 1920s and the coming of sound in the 1930s that the more infrequent productions of literature and the other arts were decisively superseded by an art form now turned into a business that emphasized repetition as much as originality, speeding up the aesthetic transformation of inchoate fears into recurrent myths and stereotypes.

Horror, like all genres, literary and artistic, has two basic elements. One is its traditional way of telling a story, with repeated characters, plot turns, and motifs. That aspect is to a certain extent invariable and even perhaps eternal, based for some critics on the innate structures of the human mind and for others on the primitive responses of early humans, or some combination thereof. The second dominant element is the way these patterned and ritualized stories interact with the ongoing movement of history, with specific historic events and individuals. There is certainly plenty of evil in the world, and the twentieth and twenty-first centuries have served up heaping portions on the grand scale. Whether the Holocaust or the Gulag or the activities of the latest serial killer constitute evil in the theological sense that worried churchmen and ordinary people after the Lisbon earthquake is a matter of either taste, philosophical inclination, or religious upbringing. What does seem worth entertaining as an idea is the link the Marquis de Sade made between the events of public history and the inner life tapped into and shaped by art, when he praised *The Monk:* "In an age of violence and revolution, the writer can move his audience only by invoking monstrosities comparable to the harsh realities of the world in which his readers live."

Of course, the connection between their internal aesthetic forms and the external world of history and events is true of genres other than horror. But horror in particular draws upon analogies with filmmaking that enhance its power. Consider, for example, the creation of the Frankenstein monster. Although the original novel was written at a time when people were fascinated by electricity and galvanism as creative and therapeutic forces, the scene hardly takes up half a page. Yet it is a spectacular set piece in the film, taking place in a sumptuous laboratory outfitted with a host of intricate "scientific" devices. In *The Bride of Frankenstein* a few years later, it has become even more elaborate, and in both scenes the crucial element is the lightning that will animate the creatures. In the early 1930s mesmerism may no longer be the latest news in the way it was when Mary Shelley wrote. But the technology of filmmaking dictates a more elaborate presentation. Like film itself, these monsters are created by light. So too, akin to the stories of which they are a part, the creatures are created from preexisting and dismembered parts of the dead, to be brought back to life and vitality, as each new version of the story seeks to be, cannibalizing the past to create a new work in the present.

Film also modifies the image of the vampire. As I have pointed out, Bram Stoker himself brought together a host of different elements in the vampire tales and superstitions to create *Dracula,* emphasizing some, downplaying or ignoring others. *Nosferatu* (1922), the unauthorized film adaptation directed by F. W. Murnau, stuck closely to the characterization of Dracula in the novel as a horrid-looking older man with a long white mustache and hairs in his palm. He was played by an actor named Max Schreck, whose apparently real name means fear, terror, or dread in German. But just as the American actor-playwright William Gillette added visual nuances to the image of Sherlock Holmes in his 1899 play, including the deerstalker hat and meerschaum pipe, and just as Victor Frankenstein was invariably supplied with a grotesque lab assistant otherwise absent from the novel, so later versions of *Dracula* eliminated the ugliness of the Dracula of the novel and added new touches—the often strikingly handsome features and seductive visual appeal of the Count (a revival of the Byronic hero), the constant dress in evening clothes, and the de rigueur stake in the heart. At the same time film encouraged other details to become more prominent, like Dracula's lack of reflection in mirrors and the stress on his hypnotic eyes. As befits a nonvisual story, there is also little mention in the novel of Dracula's inability to appear during the day. Van Helsing does say that he loses his power at daylight, but mentions nothing about disintegration, which awaits Murnau's *Nosferatu* to be made an essential part of the vampire characteristics.[2]

Vampires, like new versions of the same genre story, wake from the dead when they are nourished with new blood. The creation and longevity of monsters can therefore be seen as analogies to the filmmaking process, close enough to warrant an almost symbiotic relationship between horror stories and the special nature of cinematic form. The people we see on the screen are present to us even though they are physically absent, much as our own images in mirrors are present without any specific visual embodiment. Dracula's lack of a reflection therefore corresponds with a special intensity to the way we experience movie actors and especially stars as being both here and not here, evasive mirrors of ourselves or the way we would like to be.

The created monster film also draws richly on the technological apparatus of filmmaking, mimicking the process of film creation itself. The monster that escapes its human creator thus offers a matching image to this new art form, so entangled with mechanical processes that it threatens to escape the control of its artistic creator. Intriguingly, some of these early films also restage the Shelleyan symbiosis of creator and creation by their casting. Elsa Lanchester, for example, plays both Mary Shelley in *The Bride of Frankenstein* as well as the Bride herself, and is the speaker who tells us the story of the creation of her own doppelgänger. The unavoidable way in which we call the creature Frankenstein after his creator is analogous to how actors and characters merge in our minds. Human sexual creation, artistic creation, divine creation, and monstrous creation are thus aligned in both analogy and competition with each other.

In this way, it is perhaps no coincidence that the classic early formulation of the primary human and quasi-human monsters occurred at the beginning of the sound era—*Frankenstein, Dracula, Dr. Jekyll and Mr. Hyde*—when the ability of performers to speak set them free from the silent world, where they were essentially another form of object in a realm in which the director was the prime artist. As the movies gained a voice, a rebalancing occurred between the director's overall vision of the film and the actor's escapability from the director's control. While the inarticulateness of the Frankenstein monster reflects the ability of the director to manipulate the performer, the transformation at the heart of *Jekyll and Hyde* bears more than a passing resemblance to the ability of the actor to metamorphose into multiple roles, and thereby evade the director's domination. The Jekyll and Hyde film, with its leading actors performing two roles, at the same time also can allude to the audience's growing awareness of the contrast between the onstage and offstage presence of stars fostered by fan magazines and the media. The star system thus transfers its charisma to these fictional characters, most clearly when they are impersonated by numerous actors, as each tries to put his definitive stamp on Dracula or Sherlock Holmes.

Correspondingly, the ways in which the vampire film plays with transformation—as characters change into bats, wolves, and other nonhuman forms—invokes the illusionistic ability of films. It is one thing to say or write that the vampire transformed; it is another to witness it. And the audience that can both appreciate and be frightened by the transformation is not only one whose understanding of the vampire story has become more sophisticated with repetition but also one more knowledgeable about the resources of the movies to be able to tell that story.

In the thirst for stories of fear and trembling, movies and later television began rummaging through myths and superstitions to find suitably monstrous creatures, sometimes in their natural habitat, whether on an isolated island or in the distant past, but later much closer to home. That movement from the faraway and exotic to the familiar and nearby is a constant in the evolution of cinematic as well as literary horror. The past cannot remain in the past where it was safely entombed and forgotten. Angry and insulted, it must summon up its power to plague the present. Perhaps this resentment explains the motivation of the demon Pazuzu in *The Exorcist,* who lures Father Merrin into a combat over the body of a twelve-year-old girl in Washington, D.C. He first appears in the shape of an archaeological object, an amulet dug up somewhere in northern Iraq, subject to scholarly analysis. How demeaning to a great evil from the past! Merrin would pay. The quickening and elaboration of genre history accomplished by the movies was thus unparalleled in the art forms of the past. Just as Elizabethan and Jacobean theater brought onto the stage ghosts that the English Reformation and the attack on the concept of Purgatory had supposedly banished from religion, so the movies, with their ability to show people and things that are not there, gave new energy to the life of the invisible world, both dead and undead.

SYMPATHY FOR THE DEVIL

As I've tried to show, the extent that a genre story retains its power in the generations after it first appears depends on how its meaning changes and metamorphoses in response to new contexts. The basic story and characters may be the same, but depending on the period in which it appears, different elements are emphasized and brought out. One example is how *Frankenstein* can absorb cloning and organ transplants; another would be the connection between *Dracula* and AIDS. Sometimes a genre continues what is essentially the same story. Frankenstein and Dracula were always able to be reborn, and therefore there are sequels. Other times, a genre repeats a story but with changes and modifications that make it a departure from the original. But there is still a family resemblance, in the way that all brain stories or replicant stories resemble *Frankenstein,* and all stories of doubling and transformation resemble Jekyll and Hyde.

What about the changing social context? Early in *Dracula,* after Jonathan Harker has complimented him on his English, Dracula describes himself in a famous biblical phrase that is picked up later by Robert A. Heinlein for his novel about an extraterrestrial on earth. Dracula says that however good his English may seem, in London he would always be seen as "a stranger in a strange land." At home he is a noble, but there he would marked out as different. "Stranger in a strange land," as used by Dracula, is a phrase that cuts in at least two directions: he may be strange but the land itself is strange as well—and who among us hasn't felt that sense of being different, of not fitting in, most obviously when traveling. For a moment at least we are invited to identify with Dracula, and perhaps also contemplate the potential links between him and the eastern European Jews, who were also resettling in the East End of London in the years that Dracula made his new home in Carfax Abbey. The 1931 *Dracula* may allude to this possibility by having Dracula wear a medallion closely resembling a six-pointed Jewish star when he greets his English guest at the beginning of the film.[3]

As the resident of a foreign country as well, Dracula is a challenge to English nationalism. The connection between nationalism and a paranoia about the foreign and alien always lies beneath the surface of horror and arises with special strength during wartime or the threat of war. It's a theme that has been entirely dropped from the movie of *Dracula,* but it is still noteworthy that his manly antagonists in the novel include an American, Quincey Morris, "a moral Viking," who dies at the end but not before plunging his Bowie knife into Dracula's heart. Foreign blood may contaminate, but the sacrificial new blood from America can energize England. The basic idea has its descendants in the superheroes of the present, who bridge the national paradox of simultaneously being "number one" and yet fearful we will be toppled by the mysterious power of the zombie apocalypse.[4]

With this precedent in mind, perhaps, the vampire, more than any other form of the monster, can become a stand-in for other marginalized groups in a society. He is the opposite of the Frankenstein monster, who so longs to be considered normal and to be accepted despite his obvious strangeness. In the novel, the Creature spends hours watching the interactions of the De Lacey family, hoping to learn conventional social behavior, longing to be accepted by them and others. In the early films, this desire becomes even more acute. In the four-year transition from *Frankenstein* (1931) to *The Bride of Franken-stein* (1935), significant changes have occurred that are made explicit by the frame story, in which Byron, Shelley, and Mary Shelley discuss what was most appealing about the original story, complete with clips of the earlier film. In a sense, this is the dawn of a genre self-consciousness in which there is a greater use of the resources of the film medium, with the films themselves explicitly or implicitly meditating on their predecessors and highlighting their deviations from them.

In the first film, following a play version by John Balderston, the effort of Frankenstein (called Henry rather than Victor) to create the monster is specifically contrasted with his pending marriage to Elizabeth. When the burgomaster and others are asking when the wedding will happen, Henry's father, the Baron, a domestic tyrant who continually babies Henry, thinks that there's another woman involved in the delay. Although a superannuated duffer (with an odd lump on his neck), the Baron is still sexually competitive with his son. At the end of the film, after the half-dead Henry is recuperating from his fall from the windmill, the Baron stops the twittering group of housemaids bringing a bottle of wine to the convalescent and drinks it himself, toasting without discernible irony "a son for the house of Frankenstein." Henry for his part wants to lock up *both* the monster and Elizabeth. When he is distracted, the monster enters the bedroom where Elizabeth has been dressing in her wedding gown and carries her off, hardly for sexual purposes, since it seems that, as it happened with little Maria at the lake, he is more entranced by her bouquet of flowers than by her body.

In the second film, by contrast, this quasi-oedipal situation, as well as the Henry-Monster-Elizabeth triangle, is ignored entirely in favor of a greater focus on and humanization of the monster, especially in his desire for a mate. *The Bride of Frankenstein* thus invents the ways to do a proper sequel, sometimes seriously and sometimes playfully reinterpreting the original by showing events from a somewhat different point of view, in the process parodying Christian resurrection by the rebirth of the monster from the water under the flaming windmill. While Dracula is, like Mr. Hyde, a non-Christian and even an anti-Christian figure, the monster of the *Bride* becomes associated more and more with the suffering Christ. To underline this image of victimization, after the Creature is captured by the townspeople, he is trussed up in virtually crucifixion fashion, while the torch-bearing anger of their collective action invokes something of the national and international mob violence of the early twentieth century.

While the Creature is the object of the hate-filled gaze of others who are repelled by his appearance, Dracula's penetrating eyes, as translated into film, associate him with the gaze of the camera and its control of the image. But exactly that abjectness makes the Creature into a victim with whom we are asked to sympathize. His pitiable primitiveness and innocence contrasts sharply with Dracula's unrepentant evil, and makes him the kin of all involuntary monsters—the zombies of George Romero's films (so unlike their implacable brain-eating descendants) as well as creatures like the Wolfman, a shape shifter like Dracula, but one who hates what he turns into. Unlike Dracula who glories in his difference, the Creature, resembling King Kong and other natural monsters, is an outcast through no fault of his own. Throughout the film are numerous medium and close-up shots of his beseeching hands, asking for understanding rather than threatening violence. Even Karloff's makeup seems to have softened as well from the first *Frankenstein,* and, instead of the transplant of a brain, the story stresses the transplant of a heart. All of these more plaintive elements help restore something of the sympathy for the monster's plight in Shelley's novel: "Who was I? What was I? When did I come? What was my destination?"[5]

Most visually self-conscious of all, of course, is the scene with the blind hermit in the *Bride,* which takes off from an incident in the novel that finally alienates the Creature from his beloved De Lacey family. I have written elsewhere of the aesthetic shiver that occurs when there is a participant in an art form that cannot appreciate the art form—like a purposefully clumsy dancer in ballet or a deaf percussionist like Evelyn Glennie, who feels sounds and rhythms through her body. If the confusion of one sense for another is termed synesthesia, this effect might by analogy be called dysesthesia, a clash between senses. A blind person in a movie may be the most striking example, as in the *Bride,* where the hermit cannot see the visual monstrousness that disgusts other viewers, and so can appreciate the Creature for his childlike inner nature. In the novel the Creature and the blind father of the De Laceys converse in full sentences and elaborate politeness, while in the film the virtually inarticulate monster is taught a few rudimentary words by the hermit while he is soothed by the hermit's violin playing. Without a family himself, the hermit feels keenly his kinship with the Creature, as a fellow outsider to the "normal" human community.[6]

Far from being exclusively negative, then, as attitudes toward human difference evolve, the story of the monster could encompass the way either prejudice or sympathy views the outsider, any outsider. Already during the era of its first publication, analogies were made between the Frankenstein monster and the lower classes and slaves. Stephen Crane's 1898 story "Monster" describes how an African-American man is called "monster" by the residents of his small town after he is disfigured when rescuing the son of his employer from a fire. When the employer's family takes him in, they are rejected by the town as well. By contrast, the monstrous for H. P. Lovecraft in his Cthulhu horror stories of the 1920s is akin to all the alien groups he feared personally: women, Jews, immigrants, foreigners of all sorts, the list is long. Guillermo del Toro, the inspired director of such horror films as *Pan's Labyrinth* (2006), has remarked that the gothic teaches us to "understand otherness." But the image of the monstrous can work in many often contradictory ways: the other to fear, the other to be fascinated by, the other to sympathize with, and the other to identify with.[7]

As monsters enter the modern period and are made flesh by movie actors, it becomes more transparently obvious that they can serve as stand-ins for any group considered abnormal by society. While this sense of alluring but repugnant difference is a potential interpretation or nuance in the presentation of any monster, it is most appropriate for the vampire. *Blacula* (1972) starred the African-American Shakespearian actor William Marshall as Mamulwalde, an African prince turned into a reluctant vampire by Dracula. He later is released from his coffin in the twentieth century and, in a plot turn that reflects the

Undine mode of the vampire story, goes to search for his lost love. But after he has turned her into a vampire and she is killed, in despair he commits suicide by going out into the daylight. The pathos of the story looks forward to later versions of the good or at least morally ambiguous vampire, like Angel in the *Buffy the Vampire Slayer* TV series (1997–2003) and the black human-vampire hybrid *Blade* (1998) who hunts his evil brethren.[8]

The fear of outsiders is therefore given shape by the imagery of the monstrous. Whereas the early history of modern monsters emphasized their general deviation from the norm, later interpretations identified them with whatever group was considered a threat to established society, with the assumption that they were organized, much like the witches of seventeenth-century mythology. I argue no direct causality between, say, the influx of Jews into late-nineteenth-century London and Dracula, the monster from eastern Europe. But the imagery of the monstrous is remarkably portable in an atmosphere of paranoia that encourages the fearful to apply whatever dreadful images are most ready at hand to shape and justify their fears. As the world became more complicated, and as populations needed to be persuaded or manipulated into believing it was worthwhile to fight certain enemies, the language of monstrosity becomes a significant factor in how reality is understood. Reason may balk and ask complicated questions, but fear can forge into iron prejudice the movie-derived "knowledge" about zombies with the image of crowds of Central and South American immigrants, or Islamic fundamentalist suicide bombers—faceless hordes bent on destroying our way of life. The fear that a worldwide conspiracy against Christianity existed was articulated in such documents as the anti-Semitic hoax *The Protocols of the Elders of Zion* (1903), coming from the same uncertain prewar period as *Dracula*. Put together with the characterization of the capitalist as vampire in Marx's *Capital* and the popular anti-Semitic identification of Jews with money, for simple minds it easily coalesces with the vampire church Dracula seeks to create. Words and images may hurt, but they don't kill. Yet they can influence how we think about those we love and those we hate.[9]

❧⊙❧

In the more secular light of the modern period, religiously inflected tales of horror in which souls are sold to Satan in a gloomy gothic atmosphere of sublime awe are far less prevalent than everyday monsters who stalk their victims in familiar sunlit settings. The horror of the 1970s and later is marked by this merging of the monstrous and the frequently commonplace details of daily life. The visual trappings of the gothic have almost vanished; blowing curtains and dark hallways rarely make much of an appearance. But even the most secular of horror creators, like Stephen King, still retain something analogous to religious ideas about the relation of life to death, as well as a close relation to religious forms of worship, the rituals of repetitions, the prayers for intercession, still enticing for believers and nonbelievers alike.

Dracula's move from his eastern European castle to London was a prime early example of the tendency of the monstrous to cease being exotic in place or set back in time and come closer and closer to home. The leafy suburban streets of *Halloween* or *Nightmare on Elm Street,* the shopping mall of *Dawn of the Dead,* the Georgetown of *The Exorcist,* or the luxury hotel of *The Shining* typify the invasion of "normal" space by abnormal forces. The monsters are not safely tucked away overseas or in the past; perhaps less comically than *The Munsters* or *The Addams Family,* they live next door. Like the appalling Mr. Hyde who emerges from the respectable Dr. Jekyll, this presence of horror in a normal setting creates a bridge to the audience, transforming the familiar into the unfamiliar and the cozy into the terrifying. Part of this cocoon of normality is the frequent presence of references to other areas of popular culture in a cushioned and domesticated form of horror, as the children being babysat by Laurie, the Jamie Lee Curtis character in *Halloween,* ask to watch a horror movie or how Danny, the young boy in *The Shining,* has a toy Volkswagen with a play monster coming out of the roof.[10]

How much self-awareness can a genre take? Neither *Kiss Me Deadly* nor *Chinatown* with their attacks on the detective's blithe ignorance managed to destroy the figure, although they certainly had a role in forcing many later fictional detectives into a closer relation with established institutions like the police. Horror, however, seems to be able to absorb a self-consciousness of its own assumptions much more seamlessly. In the early phases of horror films and literature, those assumptions were still being developed, so it was logical that both audience and characters were ignorant of them. At the beginning of the film of *Dracula,* Edward Van Sloan, who plays Van Helsing, appears before a stage curtain and warns the audience of the frightful nature of what will unfold. In the middle phase, the characters are ignorant (of, say, being in a haunted house), while the audience is knowing (don't open that door!). By the third phase, as both horror movies and horror fiction of the late twentieth century emphasize time and again, an era in the history of horror had been reached when neither characters nor audience could profess to be ignorant of its traditions and characteristic plot turn and motifs.

After the great age of movie horror that begins with *Frankenstein, Dracula, The Invisible Man, The Wolfman,* and *The Mummy* in the 1930s, there was little significant innovation. The World War II period saw some horror films, most notably the stylish innuendos of Val Lewton. But the number of films was small, and many were set in the Victorian past, as if the horrors of war were so apparent in the daily newspapers that cinematic horror shouldn't even try to match them. By the late 1940s and 1950s, horror was to a great extent relegated to the second half of double features and produced by independents or by the less prestigious studios. Many of these films were memorable and became cult classics, but they were often made on shoestring budgets. With the late 1960s and the 1970s, however, came a whole group of directors with a special affinity for horror, who rarely if ever focus their talents on another kind of movie: George Romero, John Carpenter, Wes Craven, Tobe Hooper, David Cronenberg, Joe Dante, Sam Raimi, and others. Many got their start in independent studios like Roger Corman's American International Pictures, while someone like Romero, whose first film was *Night of the Living Dead* (1968), originated even farther away from Hollywood. Shot, like many of his later films, in the Pittsburgh area, *Night of the Living Dead* cost $114,000 and grossed $12 million in the United States and $18 million abroad. Romero's pioneering revision of the image of the zombie, the film engaged social issues of racism and satirized consumerism. It was also heavily criticized, somewhat for blood and gore, but even more extensively because its hero, played by Duane Jones, was African-American. Horror was being forced to live up to its socially subversive potential.

The major Hollywood studios, although floundering financially at this time, still thought of horror as B-pictures. But with the growing mainstream respectability of horror as a genre, bigger available budgets, and enhanced special effects, directors like Ridley Scott and Stanley Kubrick, otherwise not identified with horror, plunged in as well. All were to different degrees adroit at exploiting this new era of self-consciousness in the history of the genre. *Scream* (1996) and its successors, for example, play with the paradox of audience awareness by presenting characters who know all the horror film tropes—the scary phone call that comes from inside the house, the unbeliever who is the first to be killed—yet are nevertheless victimized by them. *Scream,* like such horror franchises as *Halloween, Friday the 13th,* and *Nightmare on Elm Street,* also exemplifies the frequency with which the new horror emphasized protagonists who were similar to the members of the audience. Unlike the middle-class and upper-middle-class characters in *Dracula,* say, these were teenagers and young adults. The monsters in *Halloween* and *Friday the 13th* were of a similar age, but whereas Freddy Krueger in the *Nightmare* series was more akin to Dracula in his verbal wit, Jason Voorhees and Michael Myers were virtually zombie-like in their silent implacability, monsters who have never grown up because of their attachments to their mothers and therefore take revenge on the teenage sexuality they are incapable of enjoying.[11]

Teenage sexual uncertainty also had some bearing on a new horror trope, made spectacularly visible by constantly improving special effects: the slippery boundaries between the body and the mind as well as the problematic relation of the body to personal identity. The continuities between the dream world of the movies and the fantasies and fears of the mind fostered the potential for a character's alienation from a body that was out of control.[12] When Freddy Krueger bursts from the chest of Jesse in *Nightmare on Elm Street 2* or the alien infant from the chest of Kane, the executive officer of the spaceship *Nostromo,* in *Alien, Frankenstein*-like themes of men giving birth to monsters have been updated for a new era. The difference between the monster out there and the monster that is me becomes a more pressing issue, as the presence of robots, androids, and replicants raises further questions about the elements of human identity. The change from the original version of *The Thing* (1951) and the 1982 remake illustrates the metamorphosis. In the 1951 version the monster looks like a big, somewhat weird guy in a space cadet–type uniform, identifiable in the midst of the Cold War with the Communist menace. The 1982 version goes back to the original short story by John W. Campbell, Jr., and makes the monster a shape-shifter, with the full advantage of special effects. Instead of the military and scientific people in the polar station in 1951 trying to band together against the invader, the 1982 crew realizes that the monster could be any one of them. Suspicion and paranoia turn them against one another, until finally only two are left to freeze to death, each wondering if the other is the monster.

An eccentric but fascinating example of the bodily monster is Michael Jackson's 1983 song and music video "Thriller," which in essence presents the star as a kind of monster, perhaps the *monstre sacré,* or sacred monster, defined by Jean Cocteau as a public figure, a celebrity whose strange behavior and eccentricities are tolerated and even celebrated by his or her fans. The thirteen-minute film begins with Jackson and his girlfriend on a date. He runs out of gas in a dark wood. As they walk along, the moon appears and Jackson turns into a werewolf, who chases the girl through the forest. Then it turns out that it is all a movie being watched by Jackson and his girlfriend, who doesn't enjoy being scared. They leave the theater and he begins to sing the title song as they walk past a cemetery from which the undead emerge and Jackson joins them in dancing. Throughout, the film plays with familiar horror images, including the horror actor standby Vincent Price as the narrator, as well as self-conscious movie-within-a-movie motifs. At the end all the werewolves and zombies, including Michael Jackson's affinity with them, turn out to be a nightmare the girlfriend is having. Life seems to have returned to normal. But at the last moment, Jackson turns to the camera and flashes his yellow eyes. In different degrees "Thriller" is a teenage date movie ("I'll save you from the terror on the screen"), a showcase for Jackson's dancing and singing, and a virtual anthology of older horror traditions. But it has an unsettling prophetic side as we look back on it, virtually foretelling the image of Michael Jackson's own metamorphic body in the public eye—sacred monster indeed. For all the self-conscious play with genre motifs and the distance that implies, horror seems to have captured him as well.[13]

When such late films pay homage to a long tradition, the message to the victimized characters and the audience alike is: you think your knowledge of horror as a fictional genre distances you from what is happening, but we're still going to scare you/kill you anyhow. This clash between the knowledge of horror conventions and the inability to escape them had taken a more potentially benevolent turn in Peter Bogdanovich's innovative film *Targets* (1968), made for Corman's American International. *Targets* optimistically presents a story in which old horror, as represented by Boris Karloff's character of the actor Byron Orlok, defeats new horror, in the person of a young, clean-cut suburban husband and Vietnam War veteran, who has murdered his family and gone on a shooting rampage in the San Fernando Valley. Holed up behind the screen of the drive-in, he randomly shoots viewers in their cars. In the movie on the screen, the younger Karloff plays one of his many horror roles, while the real Orlok advances on the young man, confused by the double Karloff of film and reality, and slaps him into submission. "Is this what we were afraid of?" says Orlok contemptuously. Amid the new horror of mass murderers and the "normal" insane, old-style horror is oddly comforting.

Indelibly marking the horror films of the 1970s and after is thus a stress on the horrors of the normal, the normal neighborhood, the normal house, the normal body, and the ease with which they all can be invaded by demonic forces. The mind is the first defense to fall, and it falls most easily in dreams, where the boundaries of the physical body can be breached again and again. As with the changing nature of the detective story, another kind of knowledge that can't be ignored by modern horror is the knowledge of psychology, along with the ideas of Sigmund Freud and Carl Jung about the unconscious, and the new resources for rational and natural explanation they supply. One detail lost in the transition from Stephen King's novel to Stanley Kubrick's film of *The Shining* is how desperately Jack Torrance tries to tell himself that what he's experiencing are hallucinations, and summons up Freud to try to explain Danny's trances and fear of the hotel to Wendy.

The Shining, with its "Dad goes crazy" story, brings up another significant aspect of normality exploited by so many of the horror stories of the 1970s and after that yet stretches back to the beginnings of the gothic: the horror of family relations. It's a useful bridge between the psychologically inflected neo-noir detective and what happens to horror in the 1970s, especially in terms of the crucial gap between what can be explained and what can't. Jake Gittes can figure out Noah Cross's plan for buying up land in the valley cheaply and then arranging a water supply and annexation into the city of Los Angeles that will make it worth immensely more than he paid for it. But how will he or we ever understand the reasons behind Cross's incest with his daughter and his plans for their child? The only reason Cross gives himself is hardly a reason: "Mr. Gits, Very few people have to face the fact that, given the right circumstances, they are capable of anything."

The contrast between Stephen King's novel *The Shining* and Stanley Kubrick's film can highlight some of the central motifs in this focus on the family.[14] Just as so many genre films of the 1970s and 1980s are metagenres, explicitly aware of their own assumptions, King is a student of the history of horror. The past constantly infuses the present in *The Shining*. But the book and the movie treat that theme in very different ways. In the novel, with its epigraph from Poe's "Masque of the Red Death," the endless party that occurs in August 1945 at the Overlook Hotel resonates with the story of the people trying to stave off death and survive the plague in Poe's story. Time seems to be frozen in both places, like the clocks in a gothic haunted mansion. But Kubrick has his own pipeline to the gothic. As Jack Torrance drives to the hotel and then later as he drives back with Wendy and Danny, we are visually back in the realm of the sublime and the picturesque—the tiny car driving along the solitary road amid the majestic mountains. In the novel Wendy says it makes her nauseous, it's so awesome. On the soundtrack is not only music by some contemporary composers such as György Ligeti and Krzysztof Penderecki but also allusions to Hector Berlioz's *Symphonie Fantastique*, an often nightmarish piece from early-nineteenth-century romanticism. The portentous music and the odd noises on the soundtrack contribute to the feeling of apprehension and uneasiness. Driving to the Overlook Hotel amid the grandeur of nature, the Torrances come closer as well to the invisible world of transcendence and darkness. At the end of *Chinatown* the camera, previously tied to Gittes's detective perspective, for the first time rises up and gives us a wider view as he disappears into the distance. By contrast, in *The Shining* we are introduced to an omniscient perspective from the start, as the camera swoops over the lake and mountains, soaring above the car and the hotel.[15]

In *The Shining* and in many other of his stories and novels, King explores the ambiguous connection between the tangled life within people and the horrors outside, what reason can understand and where it throws up its hands. The two primary traditions of horror are the scientific and rational versus the religious and supernatural. Both *Frankenstein* and *Jekyll and Hyde* are "possible"; *Dracula* is not. While such works continue to exist, the new horror of the 1970s and after emphasizes a third possibility, in which religion is not a factor. Here the supernatural and the subjective are both present, but the line between what is in a character's head and what is in the world is difficult to resolve. This ambiguity is already an issue in adapting Stephen King's work to the movies, in which it is so difficult to convey thoughts and memories and everything we call backstory without seeming too obvious. In the novel we are in their minds; in the film, we see them—and this is most true of Jack—from the outside, which makes him more opaque and finally a demonic caricature rather than someone who in part has "normal" problems like rage and alcoholism. So Jack's relationship with his alcoholic father disappears in the film, along with the story of the wasp's nest he tries to destroy that brings that conflict back. Similarly, the time he broke Danny's arm in a drunken fit is alluded to so briefly it can be easily missed, and so many other nuances that appear in italics and parentheses in the book (to designate thought and memory) have to be dispensed with. Without the novel's access to the minds of its characters, we have little appreciation of his love for Danny and how it divides him. Is Jack a blocked writer who wants literary success above all, an alcoholic, an abusive husband and father, a loving father, a crazy person, the victim of a diabolical place? Objective explanation, subjective explanation, supernatural explanation—the line between what is monstrous but humanly possible and what is actually eerie and bizarre is crossed again and again, and none is finally decisive.[16]

To compensate for its lack of access to the inner lives of the characters, the camera moves incessantly, following them through the labyrinth of the hotel, backing up in front of them, seeing them from a distance, creating the fore-boding space of the hotel and our apprehensions about it. This sense of space is something that films can preeminently construct, and in the history of hor-ror it derives particularly not only from the enclosed paranoid spaces of Poe's short stories, like "The Masque of the Red Death," but also from the tradition of the haunted house film. In fact, with Poe in mind, one could see *The Shin-ing* as a reimagining of two basic elements in "The Fall of the House of Usher," with "house" referring to both the enclosing physical building and the family genealogy. By the 1970s and 1980s, in line with the general normalizing of horror, the malevolent house is not the grand estate or the country mansion of the rich, but a seemingly normal house in suburbia or a luxurious hotel.[17]

The sense of a maze-like hotel, recalling the catacombs of death under the cathedral in *The Monk* and other gothic tales of mysterious hallways and creaking doors, coincides with other elements of the gothic in *The Shining*. The picturesque aspects of the landscape, the oppressiveness of the snow-storms, evoke the gothic sense of a vengeful natural world, as do both King's topiary animals in the novel and the outdoor maze of Kubrick's film—both human distortions of nature. In another nod to cinematic horror traditions, Jack is frequently seen reflected in a mirror to signal his growing doubleness. Virtually every scene in which Jack sees a ghost includes a mirror, except the scene where he is locked in the kitchen storage room, where he only hears a ghost. Yet in other ways the film of *The Shining* has brought the darknesses of the gothic into the brightly lit horrors of the present. Like the suburban street of *Halloween* or the shopping mall of *Dawn of the Dead,* the Overlook Hotel of *The Shining* emphasizes that the blandest, most impersonal public spaces can nevertheless give birth to horror. This too, I would say, registers the im-pact of an age of assassination and mass murder becoming more a part of the American scene since the 1960s, and the feeling that no place is finally safe.

The sense of foreboding created by the camera and the soundtrack in the film is due primarily in the novel to Danny's possession of "the shining," which lets him know the inner thoughts of other people, in a way similar to that of the author. Even then, however, there are things he doesn't understand because of his age, adult matters like sex and corruption.

Poised against the forces of demonic malevolence is the shining itself, the affinity shared by Danny and Dick Hallorann, the African-American chief cook at the hotel. Both book and film thus reflect a growing interest in the paranormal in horror films of the period—telekinesis, telepathy—that have helped engender several different races of superheroes, like the X-Men, the

Fantastic Four, and the Guardians of the Galaxy. Originating in Marvel Comics in the early 1960s and now an elaborate film franchise, these heroes of the paranormal appeal with obvious intensity to their teenage and preteenage audience as compensation for their own uncertainty about who they are. The shift in emphasis from the nineteenth to the twentieth century in this process of identification with fictional characters may be roughly defined as the shift from learning that your alternate identity is more demonic than you realized to learning that it is actually grander and more heroic. Discovering that instead of being an outsider, you have a special gift, a connection to others like yourself outside the family, is a heady fantasy. In King's novel, it also stands for a humanistic sense of affinity, a heightened version of what in normal people would be empathy, an enhanced power and capacity of the self.[18]

But a crucial difference between the novel and the film of *The Shining* is how that enhanced capacity is used. To a great extent the basic psychological conflict in the novel is oedipal. Jack becomes gradually absorbed into the hotel's male world of past status and privilege and prejudice through his overwhelming desire to write his novel and become famous. Like the people in "The Masque of the Red Death," he believes that recognition and riches will keep away death. But in the novel, unlike the film, it is very clear that the hotel may be more interested in Danny with his shining than in Jack, and Jack's competitiveness helps turn him into the primitive paternal monster, who in Danny's dream tries to prevent Danny from contacting Hallorann through the shining "because I am your FATHER!" Jack aims for greatness in the future, but in the film the hotel ultimately swallows him into its past with the brilliant final image of his presence at the Fourth of July ball in 1921.

The novel ends differently, making a useful contrast between King's use of horror motifs to project a basic sense of optimism about the human condition and Kubrick's greater pessimism. In the film (spoiler alert) Danny draws upon the shining to send Hallorann on a long, laborious trip from sunny Florida to the snowbound Overlook. Hallorann walks into the hotel, intent on helping Danny, and is quickly killed by the ax-wielding Jack. Despite the name of the film, despite the bond between Danny and Hallorann, as far as Kubrick is concerned the shining finally doesn't work, and the only point of Hallorann's visit is to bring a working Sno-Cat. Danny then maroons Jack in the snow-covered maze by a trick rather than by any extrasensory ability, and Wendy, like a Final Girl in numerous other horror films of the period, drives them to safety in the Sno-Cat while Jack freezes to death. For Kubrick, Danny and Hallorann's special ability is useless, and their psychic bond wasted. But in the novel, by contrast, people do connect, things do work out, and the shining is effective. Even when the Jack of the novel is trying to kill him with a roque mallet, Danny's shining manages to find the core of loving father beneath Jack's mania and for the moment stop him. While King's novel ends with the unattended hotel boiler blowing up, Kubrick's film ends with the frozen corpse of Jack in the maze. Both the novel and the film are great meditations on the traditions of horror, but while one winds up hot, the other stays cold.[19]

THE VAMPIRE VARIATIONS

A story that is already known in its general outlines and some of its aspects can be artistically useful as a pattern that can be played against. Genre is in this way comparable to a repertory company in which one of the pleasures of seeing a new production is to appreciate a known actor in a different role. Movies have made this pleasure part of their basic repertoire of effects, as we watch both stars and character actors metamorphose from film to film—the main difference between them being that the stars usually have a more restricted palette from which to draw the colors of the new role.

Yet for the story (or the actor) to be recognizable in its new incarnation there have to be some elements that harken back to the past amid the new. The vampire story, because it boasts so many elements, is rich in the number of its transformations, especially from the 1970s onward, when there arises a whole new audience for horror, nurtured on the monster shows of late-night television in the 1950s and 1960s, when the classics and many others, worthy and unworthy, were repeated again and again, as well as youthful readers of EC Comics, which in the 1950s featured such titles as *The Vault of Horror* and *Tales from the Crypt*.

Yet the basic question remained: To be recognizably a vampire story post-*Dracula* the tale, whether written or visualized, has to stay within conventions. But which ones? For some forty years, the basic look of Dracula remained stable. But the scouring of 1930s film archives by 1950s television created a self-consciousness about the history of the horror form, first appearing in the realm of fandom with the magazine *Famous Monsters of Filmland* (1958), edited by the horror buff and collector Forrest J. Ackerman, and later with *Fangoria* (1979), and the horror-scifi-noir-European art cinema hybrid *Video Watchdog* (1990). With this revaluation of the monster legacy, when all were in one way or another revised and reinterpreted, Dracula changed as well. Throughout the 1960s vampire stories had been made repeatedly, in the films produced by Hammer Studios in England, as well as those directed by Mario Bava in Italy, Jess Franco in Spain, and Jean Rollin in France.[20] Like the visual changes in the look of the vampire, these films concentrated on the vampire surface with greater stylization, more lavish period costumes, and more explicit scenes of violence and sex, even crossing into the pornographic. But emerging gradually from these generally B-movies were themes and pre-occupations that would later appear in mainstream productions. One element in the new view of the vampire story was a revival of interest in its actual historical foundations, going back into the real and legendary material that Stoker had brought together in his novel.

In 1972 Radu Florescu and Raymond T. McNally published *In Search of Dracula,* the first of many books associating the fictional vampire with the fifteenth-century Transylvanian despot Vlad III, or Vlad the Impaler, while generally glossing over the fact that Vlad was a defender of Christianity against the Islamic Ottomans, whereas Dracula is at the very least an enemy of Christianity. Florescu continued this impulse to anchor fictional monsters in history with books on what he argued were the real-life origins of the Frankenstein monster as well as Dr. Jekyll and Mr. Hyde. Despite the fact that Horace Walpole never went to Otranto or Bram Stoker to Transylvania, this urge to argue that there was a verifiable reality behind the demonic presence interestingly replicates the tension between natural and supernatural explanation that animates so much horror to begin with. If there is a real Dracula, in some sense the fear of the unknown can be allayed, and the emotional grip of the story loosened while still being enjoyed. In the same era, the imagery of the monster made its debut in even more disparate areas of popular culture. In 1971 General Mills came out with Count Chocula and Franken Berry cereals, and in 1972 Count von Count first appeared on *Sesame Street,* introducing young children to the imagery of monsters entirely shorn of the stories that gave them birth.

The urge to sequel in horror, as contrasted with the detective who continues on to the next case, embodies the relentless survival of the monstrous in the world and summons up the Christian roots of horror in the imagery of resurrection. Universal in the 1930s had already experimented with genre mutation by combining monsters in such films as *Frankenstein Meets the Wolfman,* a trend that reached logical absurdity in films like *Billy the Kid vs. Dracula* (1966), and pushed forward with the likes of *Freddy vs. Jason* (2003).[21] The 1970s and 1980s then saw a more intense elaboration of monsters than had existed under the studio system. Whereas the monsters of literature tended to inhabit the novel of their creation and nothing more, movie monsters were destroyed only to be resurrected in sequels. Between 1978 and 2009, there were twelve *Friday the 13th* films, eight *Halloweens,* and seven *Nightmares on Elm Street,* to name only the most prominent, without counting any TV or straight-to-video versions—so many that they are now referred to as "franchises," like fast-food chains.[22]

More interesting, in terms of the evolution of the vampire myth, were the self-conscious rereadings accomplished by both literature and film during the 1970s, in which the tradition is analyzed for what it can say to an audience already familiar with its assumptions and its explicit or hidden assumptions about the world. An ambitious film in this direction was George Romero's *Martin* (1978), which asked the basic question: If there are so many details in the vampire story, which are essential and which can be done away with? Martin, a seemingly normal kid, has vampire visions that seem to come from old movies, and is convinced that he is a vampire, in some way, although he insists there's "no magic" about it. Martin does drink the blood of his victims, but because he has bad teeth he has to use a razor blade to cut them. His eastern European grand-uncle, whom he lives with, also believes Martin is a vampire and treats him that way, uselessly brandishing garlic and crosses that don't affect Martin at all, but finally killing him with a stake through the heart. Was he really a vampire or just persuaded he was because of his background, his movie-going, and his blood-drinking desires? The line between the supernatural and the psychological gets crossed again and again.

Among numerous other variations of the vampire story in the 1970s were a version of Dracula produced by Andy Warhol as well as a kung fu Dracula from Hammer Studios. With the general trend in the 1970s of bringing horror closer to home, Stephen King's *Salem's Lot* (1975) situates a vampire novel in contemporary New England, while Anne Rice's *Interview with the Vampire* (1976) became the first of many minglings of vampire tradition with the southern gothic atmosphere of Carson McCullers and Flannery O'Connor. In 1979 came three films that in their differences showed the concerted cultural effort to retool the Dracula story and bring it up to date. *Love at First Bite* (with George Hamilton as the Count) played it for laughs, *Dracula* (Frank Langella) asserted a greater fidelity to the original novel, while in *Nosferatu* the German director Werner Herzog mined Murnau's original.

From the 1970s to the next vampire revival in the 1990s and beyond, these various modes of resurrection continued: Going back to the original novel,

Coppola's *Bram Stoker's Dracula* (1992), despite its title assertion of original authenticity, in fact elaborated the lost love motif of *The Mummy* as well as introduced a scene not in the novel in which the Count goes to an early nickelodeon. Underlining Dracula's search for his lost love Elisabetha (another detail not in the novel) was Coppola's use of Annie Lennox's "Love Song for a Vampire" behind the final credits: "Let me be the only one / To keep you from the cold." As appealing as the theme of lost or unrequited love might be in general, it is immensely enticing for an audience in its teens and early twenties, that major target demographic for horror films. I've mentioned how from *Halloween* onward teenagers have become leading perpetrators as well as victims. In the same year of Coppola's *Dracula* appeared the film of *Buffy the Vampire Slayer,* followed five years later by the long-running TV series, in which the title character, starting in her southern California high school (unknowingly built over the Hellmouth), fights vampires and other assorted demons with the help of a handful of friends, as well as the school librarian, who is the Watcher assigned to develop her abilities. The creator of Buffy, Joss Whedon, somehow manages to mingle a knowingness about horror traditions with often genuinely frightening stories as well as fraught emotional situations familiar to anyone who has passed through the teenage years—all with a frequent comic touch that reveals a self-consciousness about the form without ever lapsing into parody.

Another telling aspect of *Buffy's* ongoing plot is her constant but vexed attraction to the "good" vampire Angel, a theme that of late has had its most elaborate presentation in both the *Twilight* and the *True Blood* series of novels and films, which also maintain the tradition of geographic specificity, the Pacific Northwest in *Twilight* and southern gothic Louisiana in *True Blood.* Only rarely in such versions is the gender dynamic the other way around, with a "normal" boy being attracted to the vampire girl. Like good girls in the 1950s fascinated by bad-boy bikers, these heroines are both attracted by the outsider and in various ways want to domesticate him.

Romero's *Martin* had the effect of questioning the elements in the vampire story and asking how many could be omitted while keeping it still recognizably about vampires. One film from the 1980s took the elements of the vampire story and reinterpreted them in a fully original way—*Near Dark* (1987), directed by Kathryn Bigelow and written by Bigelow and Eric Red. *Near Dark,* like so many of the "new" monster movies, is set in the present and has few of the visual hallmarks of the classic horror stories—no odd angles, raked shadows, or other gothic and expressionist signals that this is a horror movie. In fact, for the innocent viewer it might take several minutes before she or he realizes that this is in fact a vampire movie. Roadhouses, motels, bus terminals, plowed fields beside roads lined with electric poles—all seems familiar and down home. Yet at the same time all the signals are there, garbed in the form of normality, if you chose to notice, or will notice in retrospect: a mosquito penetrating the arm of a young man in a cowboy hat whiling away a dull night in a western town until he and his friends spot an attractive young girl; the Lugosi-like innuendo of the boring banter between Caleb, the young protagonist, and May, the girl, eating an ice cream cone: "Can I have a bite?" "Bite?" "I'm dying for a cone?" "Dying?" Language becomes charged, suggesting deeper meanings beneath its surface, just as Caleb's sense of reality will suddenly split apart to discover what lies beneath. Instead of Dracula's enclosed world of the castle and the city, *Near Dark* is set in open spaces. No one has fangs or shapeshifts, and there is no home earth except for the American land itself. In their contemporary secular world, no one brandishes a cross or crucifix. Nor is there any Van Helsing–like authority to tutor us in vampire lore. We know it already, and any other forms of authority in the film, whether police or fathers, are either no help or helpless.

As the film develops, it turns out that May is part of a vampire family that travels around the Southwest and the Midwest, moving by night, hiding by day, staying alive by finding victims. Most crucially this family of vampires, joined by their need for blood but put together by happenstance, looks more like a bunch of hoboes dressed in a conglomeration of clothes picked up from a thrift shop or a dumpster. No capes and tuxedos for them, no drawing rooms and cordial upper-middle-class chitchat. Not only have the vampires fallen from their elite status, the whole genre seems to have fallen, its dignity and class status lost. Jesse, the quondam father of the "family," sports fingernails that specifically recall Max Schreck's talons in *Nosferatu*. As he tells Caleb, he fought for the South in the Civil War: "We lost." Like Walton in *Frankenstein* or Jonathan Harker in *Dracula*, Caleb is the normal person moving into the sphere of the abnormal and in the process showing that normality may just be a thin skin over the demonic, as he tumbles from the wide-open spaces into the enclosed world of the vampire family and their succession of hijacked campers, station wagons, and RVs.

Yet even in the abnormal there are reflections of normality, most obviously Caleb's growing feeling for May, like a beloved who comes from a weird family that you still must deal with if you expect to keep her. When Caleb's real family and the vampire family meet, he tries to protect his real family at the same time that he tells his father "I'm with them now." The desire to be accepted is strong, even by a monstrous family out of legend. Later, Caleb becomes human again through the blood transfusions given to him by his father, a veterinarian. This an important new emphasis in the vampire story, although with precedent in *Dracula,* where it is attempted unsuccessfully with Lucy Westenra and successfully with Mina Harker.[23] This possibility helps resolve the basic vampire conundrum: Why do certain people who are bitten die, while others survive to become acolytes? Allowing the reversal of the vampire's bite emphasizes the potential ease of passing between the living and the dead, or at least the living and the undead, as well as giving strength to the theme of giving up immortality and becoming human for love. But finally, when all the vampires are destroyed except for May, and she is restored to Caleb and humanity by another blood transfusion, the feeling is not of triumph but of elegy and mourning. Human love may have triumphed over vampire immortality, but magic is gone from the world. Even in their fallen nature, Jesse and the family were a connection to a grander but vanished history, emissaries from a lost past to the bland ordinariness of the present. As in so much of horror, once the monster has been defeated, the world has lost its vitality and the survivors face a drab future.[24]

MAPPING THE SUPERNATURAL

Protestantism begins in great part as an attack against the way Catholicism had absorbed images from the spiritual domain, both positive and negative, angels and demons, into theological doctrine. Its solution, mirroring a similar emphasis in Islam, was to purge the new religion not only of representation but also of any efforts to ease the dead into the invisible world. But by now, some four and a half centuries after the Reformation, the arts of visual media have so prevailed, in the West at least, that the representation of both divine and diabolical forces, monsters of all sorts, has become a normal language of praise and contempt. Such images originating from the secular sphere do not replace religion, but they crucially interact with it, raising and then for the moment placating fears. To the extent that the gothic first connects horror and religion, then gradually disentangles the two, it is particularly preoccupied with the illegitimate uses of authority, and how individuals are manipulated by conventions imposed on them from above, whether by human fathers, political fathers, or the divine father. The coming of the detective reestablishes that sense of authority, based on his purely secular resources of reason, analysis, and personal intuition. But the gothic view of the individual's frailty before demonic forces remains powerful. In most modern horror, God the benevolent father is absent. He is what theologians call the *deus absconditus,* the disappeared god, the creator who, like Victor Frankenstein, doesn't care anymore about his creation. And in so many films human fathers (and frequently mothers) either fail or become malevolent.

Some readers might be pleased to see contemporary films and writers being mentioned in a book that tries to take a long view of horror, while others could reasonably feel a precipitous decline in grandeur from the works of the past as well as from the spiritual concerns that gave horror such a cultural centrality in earlier ages of religion. The B-movie horror pictures of the 1950s, with their flimsy sets, ridiculous plots, and histrionic acting, in certain ways produced shivers made more palpable by the contrast with their inadequate materials, while the more material and plausible horrors created by the computer-generated graphics of the present may create an immediate shock but then are easily dismissible, because they are horror rather than terror, unable to plumb the audience's deepest fears. But no matter how trivial the nuances that separate many contemporary horror works from their illustrious predecessors, the continuing allure of the basic forms of monstrousness still shapes much of our views of the world outside, the world that is out to get us. This demonization of whoever is the current enemy calls upon images that have been developed since the end of the eighteenth century, the beginning of the modern age.

I've discussed the ways in which monsters can easily be made to represent, both positively and negatively, the out groups in society, or whatever group or individuals are presently creating fear and anxiety. After delving for many pages into monsters, ghosts, and prodigies of all sorts that still haunt our imaginations and shape our attitudes and responses to the real threats of the world, it is time to see whether any connections between them can be made. Are there qualities that unite all monsters, continuities in the monster array, a family resemblance? To clarify some relationships, and perhaps in passing to discover some hidden pathways between monsters, I began this book by saying that it seems possible to reduce the number of essential monsters to four: the natural monster, the created monster, the monster from within, and the monster from the past. Here, therefore, I will step away from the contrast I have been pursuing between the world of detective causality and the world of unverifiable supernatural phenomena, and try to establish a taxonomy of the monstrous that explains the connections between the monsters of the last two or three hundred years.

To decide whether monsters arise from the inherent fears of an eternal human nature or are the products of a specific historical period is unnecessary. They take their shape from the interplay between the fears of an invisible world and the special fears of an era: the natural monster from fears of a physical world out of control; the created monster from fears of human aspiration and scientific advancement; the monster from within from fears of the resurgence of a dark inner self repressed in the name of civilization; the monster from the past from fears that the present has lost the power and intensity of the world of more ancient times. These four basic types are not entirely separate from one another but often tangentially connect with or overlap in the manner of Venn diagrams, giving birth to new forms of the monstrous: the Wolfman can thus be seen as a hybrid of the monster from within and the monster from nature, while the zombie combines the implacability of the created monster with the monster from the past's desire to create a new order for the world. Depending on your taste for variety, the four categories may not be able to account for all possibilities, but in the branching tree of artistic horror, they and their variations and combinations leave little to be unassimilated. Thus, even when a seemingly new monster appears, like the demonic janitor Freddy Krueger of *The Nightmare on Elm Street* series, he is unmistakably based on the pitiless, ubiquitous Frankenstein Creature amalgamated with the verbal dexterity and shape-shifting of Dracula, and, because he inhabits the dreams of his victims, more than a touch of the Mr. Hyde of the interior self.[25]

One pervasive form of the earliest monsters, as we have seen, has its roots in religion, and partakes in one way or another of the qualities associated with Satan. In the Romantic secularization of that satanic role, the monster has some of the qualities of the lonely individual, whose sin separates him from normal society, at once a source of strength and misery. The monsters of nature, which in the past amazed local people, were also assimilated to religious purposes by being considered messages from God looking for an interpreter, another way for the priesthood to assert its authority and its exclusive understanding of the invisible world. They too received a turn from the Romantic perspective, with nature now being conceived as the benevolent alternative to the organized social world, and a place of renewal and reinvigoration. From that complex came forth the Frankenstein monster, simultaneously a gruesome threat and an innocent child of nature who only wants to be accepted by a human creator, who believed science and reason were enough to ensure his continuing power. That human creator of course goes forward into his

many mad scientist descendants, while the monster as destructive but innocent child goes forward into mutants (like the children sired by aliens in *The
Village of the Damned*) or into the many versions of teenage monsters that
populate the 1950s (*I Was a Teenage Frankenstein, I Was a Teenage Werewolf,*
etc., etc.). Not incidentally, the natural world revolts and becomes monstrous
when human science goes into what is considered forbidden territory, as it
does with the creation of the atomic bomb, which releases so many monsters
onto the screen in the 1950s.

Meanwhile, the growing awareness of the structure of society and the
growing analysis of power relations within society gives birth to the monster
from the upper classes, the blood-sucking vampire that preys on those beneath him. But at the same time on the personal level, the sympathy for such
a monster appears in the theme of love, for, like the earlier satanic figure, the
vampire is also lonely and in need of a mate. The growing knowledge of psychology, as well as Darwinian ideas of our closeness to our animal forebears,
then bring into focus the monster from within, the submerged, bestial self,
with his kinship to the Creature first created and then difficult if not impossible to bring back under control.

In the contemporary world, the vampire has so far had the dominant spot,
with the werewolves as subordinate, as in *Twilight,* where the upper-class and
sophisticated vampire gets the girl, much to the upset of the native-born
werewolf. But the vampire must share the monstrous crown with another
form of the monster that is particularly native to the twentieth and twenty-
first centuries—the zombie. Unlike the traditional individualist monsters,
zombies are a group with a mass mind and so more susceptible to being identified with contemporary fears of advancing hordes. They lack both an obvious leader as well as the individual charisma that marks the vampire. So too,
it's hard to know who might be a vampire, while zombies are pretty obvious,
with their decaying skin and their relentless desire to feed on brains. In other
words, the vampire is connected to fears of a hidden, sexually arousable, self,
while zombies have an obvious connection to social fears about being overrun
by faceless multitudes. An early, proto-zombie version of this fear appeared
for the first time around 1910 in Robert Ripley's *Believe It or Not!* newspaper
panel. Called "The Marching Chinese," the cartoon showed an endless group
of four abreast Chinese, anonymous under their coolie hats, tramping across
the globe. Accompanying it was the statement (mathematically mistaken)
that the march would continue forever because more babies would be born to
replace those that die along the way. To add a note of authenticity—and to

nod at the potential threat to national sovereignty—in the small print at the bottom, it says "based on U.S. Army marching regulations."[26]

As a group, zombies can represent general fears of being invaded and, in a characteristic of zombies that is emphasized over the years although hardly present in the original Caribbean-set stories, the fear of being consumed, cannibalized. This theme of consumption in all its aspects is present early on in George Romero's second zombie movie, *Dawn of the Dead* (1978), in which a whole set of scenes takes place in a suburban mall, a new phenomenon at the time, invaded by zombies. The "explanation" given is that the same virus that allowed them to rise from the dead also reduced their IQs to 25 and made them long for activities where they felt the most happiness—shopping. Whereas the comic vampire film (for example, *Love at First Bite* or *The Fearless Vampire Killers*) is a relatively minor aspect of vampire tradition, Romero's revision made his zombies both threatening and comical at the same time, in part mocking a high seriousness that vampire stories and films usually try to maintain.[27]

✺

What new can happen? We are now sixty years or so into a horror phase that started in the late 1960s and early 1970s. The detective effort to regain control over an uncertain world of crime and evil still works with some success through a combination of technology and intuition in literary fiction and long-form television, especially in the police procedural shows, as well as such hospital shows as *House* and *Bones*. But it seems nearly dead as a form for traditional cinematic narrative. In addition, as I have mentioned, those shows focus on working with others in an environment where crime is a constant, rather than the more solitary situation of the classic detective. Accordingly they are often less about crime solving than about relations between members of the team, or between the cops and the criminals.

But the horror mode continues to flourish in novels, film, and television— and in many different forms, from the genre playfulness of Joss Whedon in *Buffy the Vampire Slayer* and *The Cabin in the Woods* to the extreme slasher nightmare plots of the *Saw* and *Hostel* films. Asian horror, influenced by native traditions as well as Western forms, has flourished and in turn influenced new horror in the West. From the 1990s into the first decade of the twenty-first century various TV series and films try to bring the two forms together. Of special interest were the 202 episodes of Chris Carter's *The X-Files* (1993–2002), because that show tries to resolve the clash between the closed explanation of the detective story and the open-endedness of the supernatural story by having its two main characters represent different perspectives on what a problem is: the analytic rationalist doctor Dana Scully and the FBI agent believer in the supernatural and the extraterrestrial Fox Mulder. The tag line for the series proclaims "The Truth Is Out There," but it never quite says where.

Since the era of the gothic, horror has shown itself to be a flexible genre, able to absorb and work its magic on newer and newer aspects of the modern world. In the increasingly secular society that came into being with the revolutions both political and scientific of the eighteenth century, it has managed to become the prime artistic place where the spiritual and psychological fears about the modern world can be articulated and, as those fears have changed, it has also mutated both in terms of the internal history of the versions of the form and the external history of public events. A crucial part of our collective social imagination of the horrific is thus the offspring of the justifiable Enlightenment hostility to any explanation that invoked the invisible world. Whereas the atomic bomb and the prospect of universal destruction undermined the authority of the detective and his promise to make sense of the world of visible things, uncertainty is an essential part of horror. A film like *The Matrix* (1999) highlights the contrast. In *The Matrix* all life is false consciousness. Nothing is real but everything is experienced as real. Visually we are back in something resembling neo-noir, the gritty life of the city, with characters named Trinity and Morpheus, the god of dreams. The mode here is to a certain extent horror mixed with science fiction, but it is decisively anti-detective, because the detective story depends on the real. The detective's and our own faith in the reasonableness of reality and the rationality of putting facts together and getting an answer—turns out to be an illusion. Instead, everything is stylized and premeditated—much as in the movies.

Like popular culture generally, horror is an unending conversation about irresolvable fears. Now, as every childhood tale and horror story from our own culture and a variety of others is being ransacked to be told again and again—in movies, television, and video games—that process has been speeded up tremendously. The history of horror and the monstrous, both in itself and as it contrasts with the much shorter history of detection and analysis, thus stages again and again the basic modern conflict between the belief in the visible, quantifiable world and the belief in the invisible, unquantifiable world. And, as the continuing vitality of horror as an artistic form illustrates, our emotional tendencies, whether culturally inherited or developed through experience, are available to us more immediately and readily than are the tools of analysis and reason. Those tools, along with their method of interrogating, calculating, organizing, and deducing can themselves preempt and distort a more direct response to emotion-laden situations and events. Yet without the respect for facts, without the detective, an anti-intellectual view of science threatens to prevail, whose residue is only naked fear. Obviously we need them both, the detachment of objectivity and the involvement of emotion. But just as the scientific and rational bent is too often ignored by those who want primarily to believe, the emotional response has either been shoved to the side or disregarded, considered the response of the ignorant and biased, rather than brought into the air and potentially understood.

Through exploring the history of horror, I have tried to emphasize the vital and necessary interconnection between the world of reason and the world of the imagination, the realm of fact and the realm of feeling. We all live with the invisible world, if only the memory of departed friends and family. The religious may live with devils and angels, the intellectual with ideas, the historian with people from the past, the scientist with particles and reactions beyond the reach of human, microscopic, or telescopic sight—all invisible, some believed in because of facts, some because of faith, some because of feeling, but all unseen.

Notes

1. Antonio Damasio, *Self Comes to Mind: Constructing the Conscious Brain* (New York: Pantheon, 2010); Michiko Iwasaka and Barre Toelken, *Ghosts and the Japanese: Cultural Experience in Japanese Death Legends* (Logan: Utah State University Press, 1994). See also Laure Murat, *The Man Who Thought He Was Napoleon: Towards a Political History of Madness*, tr. Deke Dusinberre (Chicago: University of Chicago Press, 2014). In late-nineteenth-century France, women with mental illness frequently thought they were Joan of Arc. For an intriguing study of how cultural assumptions influence the expression of mental illness, see T. M. Luhrmann, R. Padmavati, H. Tharoor, and A. Osei, "Differences in Voice-Hearing Associated with Psychosis in Accra, Chennai and San Mateo," *British Journal of Psychiatry* 206 (January 2015): 41–44.
2. The word is a Middle English version of *baboon,* referring to a foolish, stupid person as well as to the monkey.
3. See Joshua Trachtenberg, *Jewish Magic and Superstition: A Study in Folk Religion* (New York: Behrman's Jewish Book House, 1939), for the roots of such syncretic beliefs in early Judeo-Christian thought.
4. See, for example, Michael Camille, *Image on the Edge: The Margins of Medieval Art* (London: Reaktion, 1992); Debra Higgs Strickland, *Saracens, Demons, and Jews: Making Monsters in Medieval Art* (Princeton: Princeton University Press, 2003).
5. The classic statements in English of the compatibility of supernatural and natural causes are Thomas Burnet, *The Sacred Theory of the Earth* (1691), Joseph Butler, *Analogy of Religion, Revealed and Natural* (1736), and William Paley, *Natural Theology, or Evidences and Attributes of the Deity* (1802), which popularizes the idea of the

Watchmaker God, leading directly to the current view of intelligent design. For more details on the earthquake, see Nicholas Shrady, *The Last Day: Wrath, Ruin, and Reason in the Great Lisbon Earthquake of 1755* (New York: Viking, 2008).

6. Mark Larrimore in *The Book of Job: A Biography* (Princeton: Princeton University Press, 2013) remarks that "the book of Job shows that the problem of evil must remain an open wound," even though theodicy per se is no longer a problem in the West, since suffering and evil in the world can be acknowledged without asking whether they are part of God's plan. In 1759, the same year as the publication of *Candide,* Samuel Johnson in England published *Rasselas,* the story of a young prince who grows up in Happy Valley, then leaves to find happiness in the world, only to discover it does not exist.

7. *The Causes and Cure of Earthquakes* (1750). John Wesley would later write *Serious Thoughts occasioned by the late Earthquake at Lisbon* (1755).

8. Goethe, *Dichtung und Wahrheit* (Truth and Poetry), https://archive.org/stream/auto-goethe00goetuoft/autogoethe00goetuoft_djvu.txt, 19.

9. The 9/11 terrorist attacks have similarly been cited as background for the increasing numbers of self-identified atheists in the United States.

10. The word *demiurge* comes from the Greek for artisan or skilled worker. In some versions of Gnosticism the Demiurge is identified with pagan high gods like Zeus or Jupiter. The gnostic view continues to have currency among believers. A nationwide study from Baylor University in 2006 described the four major ways Americans viewed God: authoritarian (31.4%), benevolent (23.0%), critical (16.0%), or distant (24.4%). *Los Angeles Times,* September 16, 2006, B2.

11. Thanks to Jack Miles for pointing me to a crucial passage in Isaiah 45:7: "I form light and create darkness, I make weal and create woe, I Yahweh do all these things." As a residue of this earlier dualism from which monotheism was fashioned, some biblical scholars also point to how one of the Hebrew words for God, *elohim,* is, oddly, a plural. From the later perspective of Christianity's triumph, such a dualistic point of view helps resolve the seeming clash between the wrathful God of the Old Testament and the loving Father and God of mercy of the New Testament. For a useful discussion of these issues, see C. G. Jung, *Answer to Job,* tr. R. F. C. Hull (London: Routledge & Kegan Paul, 1954).

12. C. G. Jung, *Aion: Researches into the Phenomenology of the Self* (Princeton: Princeton University Press, 1951), 61. Satan in Arabic means "adversary," and so the frequently repeated phrase "the Great Satan" used by Islamic fundamentalists to denote the West in general and the United States in particular similarly follows the evolution of the nature of Satan in Christianity. The prime devil in Islam is called *Iblīs.* He is a *jinni* who refused God's command to bow to Adam, individuality itself being the source of sin.

13. Marquis de Sade, "Reflections on the Novel" (1800), in *The 120 Days of Sodom and Other Writings,* tr. Richard Seaver and Austryn Wainhouse (New York: Grove, 1994), 109. The word *escapism* did not appear in English until the 1930s, when it was first used to refer to the vogue for erotic poetry and drinking songs during the otherwise savage wars of antiquity.

14. A fuller discussion of horror and psychology appears in Chapter 5.

15. Jürgen Habermas in *The Structural Transformation of the Public Sphere* (Cambridge: MIT Press, 1991) situates the beginning of the public sphere in the eighteenth century, although there are obvious precursors in the coffeehouse gathering places and the newsbooks of the seventeenth century.

16. Barry Glassner, *The Culture of Fear* (New York: Basic, 1999). See also Joanna Bourke, *Fear: A Cultural History* (London: Virago, 2005), and "Fear and Anxiety: Writing About Emotion in Modern History," *History Workshop Journal* 55 (2003): 111–33. Bourke's analysis focuses on the response to actual fears like cancer, nuclear war, AIDS, immigration, and so on, from a history of science, psychology, and technology perspective. She also includes a wealth of material gleaned from letters and diaries that help characterize the relation between fear as individual response and fear as a socially conditioned assumption. Noël Carroll in *The Philosophy of Horror: Paradoxes of the Heart* (New York: Routledge, 1990) discusses from both a philosophical and historical perspective the aesthetic means by which works of horror seek to inspire fear in their audiences.

17. Stephen King, *Danse Macabre* (New York: Everest House, 1981), 156.

CHAPTER 2. BETWEEN HOPE AND FEAR

1. John of Damascus, *An Exact Exposition of the Orthodox Faith* (book III of "Fountain of Wisdom"), book II, chapter XV. He considers shame, or fear of being blamed, to be the most extreme form of fear. I have used here the usual English translations. In Latin, however, the terms have somewhat different nuances, especially consternation (*admiratio*, or wonder) and panic (*stupor*, or amazement). For the text, see http://www.stmaryofegypt.org/library/st_john_damascene/ exact_exposition.htm. John Trusler, *The Distinction Between Words Esteemed Synonymous in the English language, . . . By the Rev. Dr. John Trusler. In two volumes* (London, 1794–95).

2. Ann Radcliffe, "On the Supernatural in Poetry," *New Monthly Magazine and Literary Journal* 19 (1826): 149. Radcliffe died in 1823. The essay was published posthumously. Robespierre, speech to the National Convention, February 5, 1794, "La terreur n'est autre chose que la justice prompte, sévère, inflexible."

3. Although gothic style was often stigmatized, gothic precedents played an important role in seventeenth-century politics, when the Anglo-Saxon witenagemot (council of wise men) was invoked against the monarchical "Norman yoke" brought into England by William the Conqueror. See Samuel Kliger, *The Goths in England* (Cambridge: Harvard University Press, 1952); J. G. A. Pocock, *The Ancient Constitution and the Feudal Law* (Cambridge: Cambridge University Press, 1957).

4. Walpole's Strawberry Hill still exists on the grounds of St. Mary's University College in London. Fonthill Abbey is now almost entirely demolished, but some version of its grandeur may still be found in scenes from the 1931 film of *Dracula,* when Renfield visits Dracula's castle.

5. The King James Version translation of the phrase from Exodus is also disputed. In the American Standard Version it is rendered as "sorceress." In the Septuagint, the

Greek Old Testament, the word translated as "witch" is equivalent to the word meaning herbalist, especially one who dispenses poisons as well as beneficent nostrums.
Other interpretations argue that the passage, instead of saying that witches should be
killed, really means a sorceress should not be allowed to raise the dead, which would
accord with the implications of the Witch of Endor passage. See, for example, Victor
P. Hamilton, *Exodus: An Exegetical Commentary* (Grand Rapids, Mich.: Baker
Academic, 2011). It has also been suggested that the use of "witch" as the translation
in the King James Version is a contemporary nod to James's well-known antipathy
to witches.

6. Augustine, *The City of God,* Book XXI. See also Augustine, *Confessions,* Book IX.

7. Ghosts often play a role in revenge plots, and it is tempting to see a connection between their desire for payback and revenge stories generally, especially in terms of the
revenger's obsessiveness.

8. In Japan, ghosts are differentiated from supernatural figures. They are generally
vengeful and have no feet.

9. Spiritualism is discussed further in Chapter 5. The ghostly past might be invoked in
other ways to soothe the feelings of the present. Arthur Machen, an important writer
of ghost stories, as a journalist in World War I invented the tale of a troop of medieval
English warriors appearing on the battlefield to avenge a British defeat; Alan E.
Bernstein, "The Ghostly Troop and the Battle Over Death," in Mu-chou Poo, ed.,
Rethinking Ghosts in World Religions (Leiden: Brill, 2009), 115–62.

10. Hel is also a common woman's name in German. When Fritz Lang's epic futuristic
film *Metropolis* (1926) was shown in the United States, every reference to and scene
involving an important character named Hel was cut out of the film to spare the
tender sensibilities of the audience.

11. Thomas Hobbes, *Leviathan,* ed. C. B. Macpherson (Harmondsworth: Penguin,
1968), I, ii, 92. Hobbes here follows Jean Bodin in *De La Demonomanie des Sorciers*
(1580), which argued that witches should be persecuted and prosecuted. Like James I
in his *Daemonologie,* Hobbes and Bodin connect the need for a single principle of
authority in the state to the need to expunge any real or fancied opponents.

12. *Vox in Rama,* a papal bull said to have been issued in the 1230s by Pope Gregory IX,
is cited by some historians as the first official instance of the idea that it is the devil
who prevents people from embracing Catholicism as the true religion, as well as
the origin of the belief that black cats were the minions of Satan. The institutor of
the papal inquisition to police heresy, Gregory also canonized Francis of Assisi, the
well-known animal lover (although not cats?) and promulgated "the perpetual servitude of the Jews," which effectively prevented them from having any direct political
power.

13. Keith Thomas, *Religion and the Decline of Magic* (London: Weidenfeld and Nicolson,
1971), 761. In 1484, Innocent VIII, at the instigation of the Dominican inquisitor
Heinrich Kramer, issued the papal bull *Summis Desiderantes,* which declared witchcraft to be heresy. In 1487 Kramer and Jakob Sprenger published *Malleus Maleficarum*
(The Hammer of Witches), which became the basic text for prosecuting and execut-
ing witches throughout Europe, despite later condemnation by the church.

14. Although legal precedent for dealing with witches came originally from Roman times, "only in the Christian west" was witchcraft assimilated to heresy and "rendered felonious." See Daniel N. Robinson, *Wild Beasts and Idle Humours: The Insanity Defense from Antiquity to the Present* (Cambridge: Harvard University Press, 1996), 4. The widespread paranoia about the secrecy of the gatherings of witches had direct analogy in England to the Elizabethan and Jacobean laws against recusant Catholicism with its "priest holes" and Guy Fawkes–like conspiracies. The terms *witches sabbath* (or sabbat) and *coven* appear in English for the first time in the mid–seventeenth century.

15. On King James, see James Sharpe, *Instruments of Darkness: Witchcraft in England, 1550–1750* (London: Hamish Hamilton, 1996), 50. Neither the writing nor the first performance of *Macbeth* can be dated with total accuracy. Most scholars choose 1606 as a probable time of writing and 1608 for the inaugural performance. According to some critics, James after 1599 became more skeptical about the power of witches, perhaps because the idea of an alternate diabolical church was not as important in England after the Reformation created Anglicanism. Demons in England, with some exceptions, tended to be identified as part of a Catholic conspiracy rather than a sabbath of witches. The Witchcraft Act of 1604 was not repealed until 1736, when Parliament made accusations of witchcraft and sorcery illegal.

16. Reginald Scot, *Discoverie of Witchcraft,* chapter 3, p. 5; https://archive.org/details/discoverieofwitc00scot. Although Scot did believe in the supernatural, he considered witches to be primarily suffering from mental illness and blamed the Catholic Church for fostering the belief in their powers. In his combination of a belief in demons and Satan's kingdom along with a psychological interpretation of witchcraft claims, Scot's argument reflects that of the Rhineland doctor Johann Weyer in *De Praestigiis Daemonum* (On the Illusions of Demons), 1563. For more on early skepticism about witchcraft, see among many others Sharpe, *Instruments of Darkness;* Moshe Sluhovsky, *Believe Not Every Spirit: Possession, Mysticism, and Discernment in Early Modern Catholicism* (Chicago: University of Chicago Press, 2007); Lyndal Roper, *The Witch in the Western Imagination* (Charlottesville: University of Virginia Press, 2012).

17. Compare George Eliot's novel *Adam Bede* (1859), in which a female Methodist preacher named Dinah appears prominently, although Eliot makes little of the connection to Wesley's strong belief in ghosts. It's undeniable that a large portion of witch hunting has more than a tinge of misogyny. According to the *Malleus Maleficarum,* men were less susceptible to the power of the devil than were women because Christ was a man. In a wider theological context, this kind of attitude also constitutes an attack against the importance of Mariolatry in the Catholic Church in favor of a more masculine definition of holiness.

18. Historians of witchcraft have pointed out how often those accused had been midwives or assistants at lying-ins, and therefore susceptible to be accused if anything out of the ordinary occurred.

19. In 1938 as well, the *New York Times* uses "witch hunt" in an article about government investigation of business monopolies. The next year John L. Lewis, the head of the Congress of Industrial Organizations, or CIO, bars Communists from any role in the

union, but he promised there would be no "witch hunt." The references continue until they reach a high-water mark in the Cold War 1950s.

20. Already in eighteenth-century England, there is a shift to a doctrine of works as an important element of Protestantism. By the twenty-first century, the United States, predominantly a Protestant country, led the world in charitable giving, whereas Catholic Italy has an anemic charitable tradition. See Francesco Antinucci, *Cosa pensano gli Americani* (Roma: Laterza, 2012).

21. Stuart Clark, *Thinking with Demons: The Idea of Witchcraft in Early Modern Europe* (Oxford: Clarendon Press, 1997), 459. See also Thomas, *Religion and the Decline of Magic,* 308, where he speaks of the "ecclesiastical anxiety to repress popular magic." In parts of Germany where there was an uneasy truce between Protestants and Catholics, there was a Protestant zeal for stamping out popular beliefs and activities considered pagan, while Catholics were frequently more open and syncretic. In such situations, governmental authority was often more eager than the religious to eradicate heresy, while the Catholic Church sought to weed out those who "mistake demonic possession for divine inspiration"; Sluhovsky, *Believe Not Every Spirit,* 62.

22. "[O]nce Catholicism had become isolated as one church among several, its exorcisms began to be an identifier of distinctly Catholic forms," according to Sarah Ferber, *Demonic Possession and Exorcism in Early Modern France* (New York: Routledge, 2004); "the position of exorcism within Catholicism can also be understood in the context of a shared desire to keep religion above popular control and in the hands of the learned" (38, 54).

23. In the polemics of the seventeenth-century English civil wars, a similar move postulated that English political traditions owed more to establishment of the Anglo-Saxon parliament than imposed Norman monarchical traditions, and gothic thereby became associated with the parliamentary and anti-royalist point of view.

24. See Jean-Claude Schmitt, *Ghosts in the Middle Ages: The Living and the Dead in Medieval Society,* tr. Teresa Lavender Fagan (Chicago: University of Chicago Press, 1998), 14. For more on the background of the idea of purgatory before it was formalized theologically, see Isabel Moreira, *Heaven's Purge: Purgatory in Late Antiquity* (New York: Oxford University Press, 2010).

25. Augustine, *The City of God,* Book XXI. In section 13 he says that some sins have temporary, purgatorial punishment, while in section 24 he denies that prayers to saints have any efficacy in ameliorating punishment after death. Peter Brown, "The Decline of the Empire of God: Amnesty, Penance, and the Afterlife from Late Antiquity to the Middle Ages," in *Last Things: Death and the Apocalypse in the Middle Ages,* ed. Caroline Walker Bynum and Paul Freedman (Philadelphia: University of Pennsylvania Press, 2012), 41–59. See also Peter Brown, *The Ransom of the Soul: Afterlife and Wealth in Early Western Christianity* (Cambridge: Harvard University Press, 2015). By contrast, in the Islamic interworld (*barzakh*) the soul waits for Judgment Day and no intercession is possible.

26. The full title of Bunyan's seventeenth-century religious tract is *The Pilgrim's Progress from This World to That Which Is to Come; Delivered under the Similitude of a Dream.*

27. The official church recognition of Purgatory came at the Council of Lyon in 1274, as part of an effort to bring the Greek church back into the fold. It was reaffirmed at the Council of Florence in 1439, which had a similar purpose.

28. From about the twelfth century onward, a site referred to as St. Patrick's Purgatory, on Station Island in Lough Derg in the west of Ireland, has been a pilgrimage site. According to legend, St. Patrick was shown by God a cave there so that he could give substantial proof of Purgatory to those he was trying to convert. There were analogous arguments over the geographic site of Hell as well. Was it under the earth, like the land of the dead in classical literature, or, as some eighteenth-century theologians argued—without the benefit of seeing the *Alien* films—might it be in outer space?

29. All intercessory activities were abolished by laws in 1545 and 1547, during Edward VI's reign. The material (and oversimplified) reason for the original confiscations of the English Reformation has often been cited as the Crown's need for money for war. See Ralph Houlbrooke, *Death, Religion, and the Family in England, 1480–1750* (Oxford: Clarendon, 1998).

30. On the theological underpinnings of sixteenth- and seventeenth-century *ars moriendi,* see Kevin Laam, " 'For God's Inheritance Onelye': Consolation and Recusant Identity in Robert Persons's *Christian Directorie,*" in *The Reformation Unsettled: British Literature and the Question of Religious Identity,* ed. Jan Frans van Dijkhuizen and Richard Todd (Turnhout, Belgium: Brepols, 2008), 205–24.

31. Stephen Greenblatt, *Hamlet in Purgatory* (Princeton: Princeton University Press, 2001), 239. See also Eleanor Prosser, *Hamlet and Revenge* (Palo Alto: Stanford University Press, 1977), on ghost-counting on the stage. She says fifty-one ghosts appear between 1560 and 1610. Greenblatt also notes how much more interested Shakespeare was in ghosts as characters than other major playwrights like Christopher Marlowe and Ben Jonson (154). Other critics argue that ghosts, like other references to Catholic rituals and ideas, when transformed into fiction, become more metaphoric than doctrinal. See, for example, Gillian Woods, *Shakespeare's Unreformed Fictions* (New York: Oxford University Press, 2013).

32. Thomas, *Religion and the Decline of Magic,* 703.

33. See George Starr, "Why Defoe Probably Did Not Write *The Apparition of Mrs. Veal,*" *Eighteenth-Century Fiction* 15 (2003): 421–51.

34. The Cambridge Platonist effort to merge science with theology was in many ways a more extreme version of the work of Robert Boyle and Isaac Newton, who maintained an interest both in experimental science and in religious thought. For further discussion, see Chapter 4.

35. "Burnt-over" referred to the idea that there had been so many religious revivals in the area that no inhabitants were left to convert. The First Great Awakening was almost a century earlier and similarly emphasized personal salvation. For more on the spiritual and anti-rational in the age of Enlightenment, see Joscelyn Godwin, *The Theosophical Enlightenment* (Albany: State University of New York Press, 1994), and Paul Kléber Monod, *Solomon's Secret Arts: The Occult in the Age of Enlightenment* (New Haven: Yale University Press, 2013).

36. The first table-rapping séances were conducted by the Fox sisters in 1848; Morse had developed the telegraph and the code some ten years before. In Roberto Rossellini's film *La Macchina ammazzacattivi* (The Machine That Kills Bad People, 1952), a small-town photographer is given (by a demon, it turns out) a camera that can kill

bad people. The photographer soon realizes that telling the good from the evil is a difficult task.

37. Blavatsky thought the medium séances contacted powerful spirits with special knowledge, not just the deceased in general.

38. Francisco de Goya Lucientes, *Saturn,* Museo del Prado, https://www.museodelprado.es/en/the-collection/online-gallery/on-line-gallery/obra/saturn-devouring-one-of-his-sons/.

39. *Northanger Abbey* was begun in 1798 and sold to a publisher in 1803, but published only posthumously in 1818. I wonder if the long delay between its writing and publication might have been due to a publisher who earlier saw more profit in the market for unalloyed terror. By 1818 a parody was more welcome.

40. See Clark, *Thinking with Demons,* 592, on the eighteenth-century end of sacerdotal monarchy.

41. The possessed were usually referred to as "demoniacs."

42. Although the common view of exorcism considers it preeminently an aspect of Catholicism, some Protestant groups have doctrinal views of it as well. In 1975, for example, the Anglican House of Bishops published guidelines for "the ministry of deliverance" (i.e., exorcism). "In every Anglican diocese in the country the bishop has an adviser (or advisers) overseeing this work." Reverend Prebend Paul Towner, letter to the *London Review of Books,* May 23, 2013.

43. The frequent lack of either a dominant single God above or a single devil below in Asian religion similarly tends to characterize evil as mischief or chaos rather than a separate principle.

44. Elaine Pagels in *The Origin of Satan* (New York: Random House, 1995) argues that the Old Testament role of Satan implies his significance as a divisive force within Judaism, rather than an enemy from without.

45. The conversations were held at Ambrose's Tavern, hence the name. Hogg was born near Ettrick in the Scottish borders region.

46. The general sentiment goes back to Aesop, but Franklin's formulation comes from the English political theorist Algernon Sidney, who was executed for supposed participation in a plot to assassinate Charles II and his brother James.

47. In addition to Hogg's "double-goer" in *Blackwood's Magazine,* Sir Walter Scott used "double-ganger" in *Letters on Demonology* (1830).

48. Similarly, Washington Irving in "The Legend of Sleepy Hollow" (from *The Sketch Book of Geoffrey Crayon,* 1819–20) never quite says that the Headless Horseman was Brom Bones intent on scaring Ichabod Crane away from Katrina Van Tassel, but it's fairly clear that Crane's terror is in the eye of the beholder rather than in the spirit world. The past that preoccupies Hawthorne in his most famous novel, *The Scarlet Letter,* is the era of the Salem witch trials.

CHAPTER 3. TERROR, HORROR, AND THE CULT OF NATURE

1. Augustine in *The City of God* is cited as the usual source for the first etymology, the medieval theologian Isidore of Seville for the second. By the Middle Ages *monstrum* also referred to a sign or a portent.

2. The pioneering surgeon Ambroise Paré in *Des Monstres et Prodigies* (Of Monsters and Prodigies, 1573) divided monsters into three categories: less than nature, more than nature, and conglomerate. Arguments over the conglomerate human-divine nature of Jesus characterize theological discussions in the early centuries of Christianity. See, for example, Elaine Pagels, *The Gnostic Gospels* (New York: Random House, 1989).

3. See Fred C. Robinson, *Beowulf and the Appositive Style* (Knoxville: University of Tennessee Press, 1985), 71; Andy Orchard, *Pride and Prodigies: Studies in the Monsters of the Beowulf-Manuscript* (Cambridge, England: D. S. Brewer, 1995).

4. Cicero's *On Divination* catalogues many of these beliefs, usually for the purpose of debunking them.

5. Carlin A. Barton, *The Sorrows of the Ancient Romans: The Gladiator and the Monster* (Princeton: Princeton University Press, 1993), calls them "guardian monsters" (170). The connection of such natural monsters to the earth is reflected in the numerous instances of a series of high hills being referred to as a sleeping giant.

6. Nate Schweber, "In New Jersey, a Knot in a Tree Trunk Draws the Faithful and the Skeptical," *New York Times,* July 23, 2012, A17.

7. The tribe without heads but with faces in their chests were a mythologized version of the Ethiopian Blemmyes. John Spencer, who coined the word *teratoscopy* in his *Discourse Concerning Prodigies* (1665), was in fact arguing against the excessively free interpretations of prodigies and monsters as a threat to government and religion. For an image of Dürer's engraving see, for example, http://www.wga.hu/support/viewer_m/z.html.

8. Ottavia Niccoli has pointed out that in Italy after 1500 the appearance of monstrous births was considered to refer more to personal sin than to political or religious issues, perhaps because of a pact between Charles V and the papacy. The interpretation continues in Germany with the Reformation, however, and in certain areas there were still antipapal monsters; "after 1530 the elites rejected any sort of involvement with the world of folklore." Ottavia Niccoli, *Prophecy and People in Renaissance Italy* [1987], tr. Lydia G. Cochrane (Princeton: Princeton University Press, 1990), 190, 193.

9. Betty A. Schellenberg, "Coterie Culture, the Print Trade, and the Emergence of the Lakes Tour, 1724–1787," *Eighteenth-Century Studies* 44 (Winter 2011): 205. See also Betty A. Schellenberg, "Imagining the Nation in Defoe's *A Tour thro' the Whole Island of Great Britain,"* *English Literary History* 62 (Summer 1995): 295–311.

10. The previous two paragraphs are partially drawn from my essay "The Genre of Nature" in *Refiguring American Film Genres,* ed. Nick Browne (Berkeley: University of California Press, 1998).

11. See, for example, Jacques Le Goff, *The Birth of Purgatory* [1981], tr. Arthur Goldhammer (Chicago: University of Chicago Press, 1984); Carlo Ginzburg, *The Cheese and the Worms: The Cosmos of a Sixteenth-Century Miller* [1976], tr. John and Anne C. Tedeschi (Baltimore: Johns Hopkins University Press, 1980).

12. The *Philosophical Transactions* of the Royal Society detail numerous examples of strange human and animal births. Edmund Halley, the astronomer, for example, published "An Account of Animal Resembling a Whelp Voided *Per Anum,* by a Male Greyhound, and of a Roman Altar," *Philosophical Transactions* 19 (1695–97): 316–18.

In 1726 a woman from Surrey named Mary Toft claimed to have given birth to rabbits after sighting one during her pregnancy. Exposed as a hoax, it still fooled many doctors.

13. Daniel Defoe's *A Journal of the Plague Year* (1722), which deals with the plague of 1665 in the voice of a contemporary witness, spends much of its time trying to answer the question why London in particular was struck with disaster. At the end, the narrator can conclude only that there is no final reason for either the coming of the plague or his own survival.

14. According to William E. Burns, after the London earthquake of 1750, Hume's publisher refused to do a second edition of the *Enquiry* because of the inclusion of the essay on miracles. *An Age of Wonders: Prodigies, Politics and Providence in England, 1657–1727* (Manchester: Manchester University Press, 2002), 138.

15. See Richard Altick, *Shows of London* (Cambridge: Harvard University Press, 1978), 36.

16. Barnum called his exhibition of strange people (and objects) the American Museum (1841). In 1889 his performers held a meeting in which they told Barnum they wanted to be called prodigies, not freaks. Since the 1960s the study of fabulous creatures has been termed cryptozoology, while the creatures themselves are termed cryptids.

17. The older meanings of *grammar, gramarye,* and *glamour* are revived in the eighteenth century, along with a cognate word *grimoire,* a magician's manual for evoking demons. The witchcraft usage of *spell* dates to the seventeenth century. *Hex* and *hag,* associated words, date to the sixteenth century.

18. For more on the natural/hypernatural/supernatural distinction, see Lorraine Daston and Katharine Park, *Wonders and the Order of Nature, 1150–1750* (New York: Zone Books, 1998), 212. The authors tend to use the word *preternatural* for the middle term. Although that is more usually a synonym for supernatural, the distinctions are similar. Tzvetan Todorov's literary critical distinction between the fantastic uncanny (an illusion: preternatural or hypernatural) and the fantastic marvelous (the supernatural) is another descendant of such arguments. See *The Fantastic: A Structural Approach to a Literary Genre* [1970], tr. Richard Howard (Ithaca: Cornell University Press, 1973).

19. To enhance their sublime power, Edmund Burke also thought that paintings should be seen alone, rather than as part of a social occasion. For a different view of the relation between the general and the detail in art, see William Blake's marginal comments to his copy of Sir Joshua Reynolds's *Discourses on Art:* "Minute Discrimination is not Accidental. All Sublimity is founded on Minute Discrimination" and "Without Minute Neatness of Execution the Sublime cannot Exist! Grandeur of Ideas is founded on Precision of Ideas."

20. See also Uvedale Price, *Essay on the Picturesque, As Compared with the Sublime and The Beautiful* (1794). For visual parodies of the cult of the picturesque see Thomas Rowlandson's "The Tour of Dr Syntax in Search of the Picturesque" (1809).

21. I am referring to the 1930s films of *Dracula* and *Frankenstein* here. In the novel of *Dracula* it is Jonathan Harker who is being met, while in *Frankenstein* it is Victor who is the somewhat mad scientist. These and other changes from book to film are discussed in Chapter 4.

22. As the background to her literary output, Radcliffe was politically a Whig, religiously a Dissenter (a non–Church of England Protestant), and a supporter of the French Revolution.

23. Edison had invented the phonograph in 1877.

24. With its mingling of a local demon, the Jersey Devil, and modern technology, *Blair Witch* is an intriguing update of Ambrose Bierce's 1893 short story "The Damned Thing," in which a man is murdered by a creature that is invisible to the human eye because it is an actinic (ultraviolet) color. Another contemporary version of the invisible monster appears (?) in Guy de Maupassant's story "The Horla" (1887), this time as a kind of Brazilian vampire. This variation is elaborated in the film *Predator* (1987), in which the invisible monster is an alien from another world, sporting Rastafarian dreadlocks, hunting earthlings for sport.

25. There are of course literary precedents for all of these narrative tricks: the interpolated tales of *Don Quixote,* the double plots, masques, and songs of Shakespeare, etc. The difference in the gothic is to deploy them in the service of arousing feelings of fear and uncertainty.

26. Horace Walpole did take the Grand Tour, but the actual castle in Otranto, Italy, bears no resemblance to the one in the novel.

27. *Fingal* was in fact written by Macpherson. It is one of a large number of literary frauds of the period, in which contemporary writers take on the masks of fictionalized writers from the past.

28. Sebastian Hensel [his sister Fanny's son], *The Mendelssohn Family (1729–1847) from Letters and Journals,* tr. Carl Klingemann (New York: Harper, 1881).

29. Leslie Fiedler, *Love and Death in the American Novel* (New York: Stein and Day, 1966), 47.

30. Examples of the Green Man carvings across Europe are those in the roof bosses of England's Norwich Cathedral, as well as the Seven Green Men, a series of seven green men carved in the thirteenth century on to the facade of St. Nicholas Church in Nicosia, Cyprus.

31. The Green Knight of the fourteenth-century poem *Sir Gawain and the Green Knight* serves as both monster antagonist and mentor to Sir Gawain. He seems to belong to a pre-Christian world that may be antagonistic to, but is in the end harmonious with, the Christian one. Both heroes (Rambo) and monsters (Dracula) often imagistically arise from the earth. The long-lived television series *Buffy the Vampire Slayer* draws on the knowledge gained from magical books to combat the creatures that pour out of the Hellmouth beneath the local high school. At the same time the religious commitment of *Buffy* is vague, with, for example, the cross around Buffy's neck appearing and disappearing until it is finally almost entirely dropped in the later seasons.

32. H. L. Mencken in 1936 uses the word to mean "dull-witted."

33. Although "vodou" is now the preferred spelling, I use "voodoo" for its historical relevance.

34. Another comic zombie film of the period was *Zombies on Broadway* (1945), with Bela Lugosi again as a zombie-creating mad scientist.

35. Arguments begun in the distant past continue over whether "monsters" rightly refers also to giant creatures, like Monstro the whale in *Pinocchio* (1940) and the heroine of *Attack of the Fifty-Foot Woman* (1958), or should be reserved only for clearly freakish beings. But the "fact" remains that monsters in the strict sense are usually quite large.

36. Browning himself had run away to the circus at sixteen. The controversy over *Freaks* virtually ended his filmmaking career.

CHAPTER 4. FRANKENSTEIN, *ROBOTS, AND ANDROIDS*

1. In *Mary Shelley: Her Life, Her Fictions, Her Monsters* (New York: Methuen, 1988), Anne Mellor points out that, in a deleted scene in the novel, Victor visits Bacon's rooms at Oxford (69). Another forerunner of the modern created monster is Talus in Edmund Spenser's *The Faerie Queene,* Sir Artegal's metal servant, who punishes villains with his iron flail.

2. Although Victor's collecting of body parts takes place in Switzerland, it reflects the medical situation in England. Since only executed criminals were legally considered appropriate for dissection, the advancing science of anatomy collided with the decreasing number of capital crimes. As a result, surgeons would often buy disinterred corpses supplied by "resurrectionists." Less scrupulous suppliers, like the famous Burke and Hare, would hurry their victims into the grave by murder. All these activities, criminal and otherwise, were halted by the Anatomy Act of 1832, which gave doctors and medical students legal access to both unclaimed and donated corpses.

3. *Golem* in Hebrew essentially means unformed matter. It is used once in the Bible, Psalm 139, in which the Psalmist talks about being made by God from "unperfect substance" (King James Version).

4. At the end of *Iron Man 3* the superhero industrialist Tony Stark throws the metal boss away, saying, "We make our own demons."

5. On the eruptions and weather patterns, see Alexandra Witze and Jeff Kanipe, *Island on Fire: The Extraordinary Story of Laki, the Forgotten Volcano that Turned Eighteenth-Century Europe Dark* (London: Profile Books, 2014); on 1816 in particular, see William K. Klingaman and Nicholas P. Klingaman, *The Year Without Summer: 1816 and the Volcano that Darkened the World and Changed History* (New York: St. Martin's, 2013).

6. In Ovid's version of the myth, Prometheus also creates human beings out of mud and rainwater.

7. Mellor, *Mary Shelley,* 45–46.

8. Blake, *The Marriage of Heaven and Hell* (1790); Shelley, *A Defense of Poetry* (1821), published posthumously in 1840.

9. Shelley seems to have in mind here Henry Fuseli's painting of Shakespeare's *Hamlet,* Act I, Scene IV, from 1796.

10. Like Heathcliff, Emily Brontë's father Patrick himself came from far down in the social scale.

11. Descartes wrote: ". . . it seems reasonable since art copies nature, and men can make various automata which move without thought, that nature should produce its own

automata much more splendid than the artificial ones. These natural automata are the animals." Letter to Henry More, February 5, 1649, in *Environmental Ethics: Divergence and Convergence,* ed. S. J. Armstrong and R. G. Botzler (New York: McGraw-Hill, 1993), 284–85.

12. Robert Boyle, "These living Automata, Human bodies," *A Free Enquiry into the Vulgarly Receivd Notion of Nature: Made in an Essay, Addressd to a Friend* (1686). See also Robert Boyle, *Treatises on the High Veneration Man's Intellect Owes to God: On Things Above Reason: and on the Style of the Holy Scriptures* (1684). In his will Boyle endowed a series of lectures to consider the relationship between Christianity and natural philosophy as well as to argue the truth of Christianity against atheists, Muslims, Jews, and other infidels, while glossing over or ignoring any internal Christian arguments.

13. Patricia Fara, *An Entertainment for Angels: Electricity in the Enlightenment* (New York: Columbia University Press, 2002) 2.

14. Quoted in Fara, *Entertainment for Angels,* 1.

15. The names of the early experimenters are still with us in words like *volt* (Alessandro Volta), *galvanism* (Luigi Galvani), *watt* (James Watt), and others.

16. Fara, *Entertainment for Angels,* 80.

17. The libretto for *Così Fan Tutte* (1790) includes a tip of the hat to Mesmer, when the maid Despina, disguised as a doctor, passes a mesmeric stone (*pietra mesmerica*) over the supposedly poisoned bodies of the disguised lovers to revive them. Since the poisoning is also fake, Mozart's, or da Ponte's, attitude toward mesmerism is appropriately ambiguous.

18. In a 1679 letter to Robert Boyle, Newton proposed the existence of an invisible "aethereal substance, capable of contraction & dilatation, strongly elastick, and, in a word, much like air in all respects, but far more subtle," in which light, gravity, and magnetism move. See http://www.newtonproject.sussex.ac.uk/view/texts/normalized/NATP00275. Jonathan Swift later parodies the idea in *A Tale of a Tub* (1704), but the belief that there was an invisible connection between things retained its allure, and marked the gradual shift from a demonological to a scientific (and often pseudo-scientific) language.

19. Mesmerism was introduced in England by Richard Chenevix (1829) and popularized by the physician John Elliotson. Galvanic and electrical treatment for medical and psychological problems continued to have a long history. Alice James, the sister of Henry and William, was treated painfully with galvanic methods. Recently, electroshock therapy has had a resurgence in therapeutic use as researchers and physicians have been able to fine tune and validate its real rather than its imaginary effects.

20. Comparable to hysteria in women was the complaint called invalidism in men (later neurasthenia), or what had earlier been known as valetudinarianism. The Freudian concept of transference bears some intriguing resemblances to the mesmeric bond between mesmerizer and patient.

21. Joanna Bourke, in *Fear,* 25–50, discusses the persistence of fears of premature burial.

22. See, for example, Amy Lehman, *Victorian Women and the Theatre of Trance* (Jefferson, N.C.: McFarland, 2009).

23. Ibid., 98–99. Such activities were not limited to well-known mesmeric performers but indulged as well by amateurs like Jack London's mother, Flora Wellman, who spoke in séances in what were described as the guttural accents of Plume, an Indian chief. See Earle Labor, *Jack London: An American Life* (New York: Farrar, Straus, and Giroux, 2013), 17, 28. The personalities of these spirit guides were often at odds with the everyday personalities of the trance performers, usually freer and less dictated by societal norms. An enchanting film version of this occurs in *The Pirate* (1948), set in the eighteenth-century Caribbean, when Gene Kelly as a traveling performer hypnotizes the staid Judy Garland and she breaks into a raucous song and dance.

24. In more contemporary studies, the psychiatrist Rick Strassman has conducted experiments that attempt to show that the pineal gland produces the psychedelic compound DMT and thus may be responsible for triggering what are referred to as near-death experiences. Research by the neuroscientist Michael Persinger has also sought a connection between electromagnetic fields and ghostly hallucinations caused by the lowering of melatonin levels, controlled by the pineal gland. Perhaps Descartes was on to something after all. For an account of these and other efforts to find connections between the natural and the supernatural worlds, see Mary Roach, *Spook: Science Tackles the Afterlife* (New York: Norton, 2005).

25. Comte de Volney, *The Ruins of Empire,* chapter 6, "The Primitive State of Man"; http://www.gutenberg.org/files/1397/1397-h/1397-h.htm.

26. Acting and the monstrous are discussed further in Chapter 6. The plot of Shaw's *Pygmalion* (1912), on which the musical *My Fair Lady* is based, resembles *Trilby* without the mesmerism. Beerbohm Tree also starred as Henry Higgins in the original production.

27. The racial elements of these transformations and amalgamations are discussed further in Chapter 8.

28. The script for *Metropolis* was based on a novel by Lang's wife Thea von Harbou and co-written by her. Although Lang left Germany after Hitler's election as chancellor, von Harbou continued to work in the Nazi film industry.

29. The variations on this theme are countless, but some significant examples would be the look of the monster in *Alien* (1979), a mechanical being that comes out of an egg in a spaceship modeled on the human body. In its sequel, *Aliens* (1986), Ripley, the heroine, must don a mechanically enhanced exosuit to defeat the alien creature. *I, Robot* (2004) is yet another film in which the hunter turns out to be one of the hunted.

CHAPTER 5. THE DETECTIVE'S REASON

1. Some critics have argued that the reasonable explanations at the end of Ann Radcliffe's gothic novels come about because Radcliffe's Protestant faith and liberal politics militated against any final capitulation to the supernatural. See, for example, Victor Sage, *Horror Fiction in the Protestant Tradition* (New York: St. Martin's, 1988).

2. Balzac models his villain Vautrin in *Le Père Goriot* (1835) on Vidocq as well, illustrating once again how the detective and the master criminal enter cultural imagination at the same time.

3. One of Conan Doyle's first Sherlock Holmes stories, "A Scandal in Bohemia," is to a great extent a retelling of "The Purloined Letter."

4. Poe uses "clue" once each in "The Purloined Letter" and "The Mystery of Marie Rogêt," although both times in the sense of a general key to a solution rather than a detail.

5. The fascination with the spectacle of the city unites such otherwise disparate works as De Quincey's *Opium-Eater*, where London is portrayed as filled with "sublime pleasures and terrifying despair," Nikolai Gogol's "Nevsky Prospekt" (1835), and Poe's "Man of the Crowd." Gogol's story begins like "The Man of the Crowd" with an observation of the different times of day and the different kinds of people on the streets, who move without "a sense of some goal, or, better, of something resembling a goal"; it concludes "God, what is our life! An eternal discord between dream and reality!"

6. Baudelaire's essay is specifically about Constantin Guys, a watercolorist and sketch artist, whose works document the everyday reality of Second Empire life.

7. Bucket, like Wilkie Collins's detective Sergeant Cuff in *The Moonstone* (1858), is usually considered to have been based on Jonathan Whicher, one of the original members of the Scotland Yard detective branch established in 1842. The amount of talk about large and small class distinctions is a characteristic of detective fiction on both sides of the Atlantic that becomes even more marked with the beginnings of the American hard-boiled detective. Racism is often part of it.

8. G. K. Chesterton, "A Defense of the Detective Story," *The Defendant* (1901).

9. It is tempting to read Poe's story as a mockery of that attitude, since Johnson was notoriously someone who didn't like to be alone and walked extensively throughout London. Perhaps he is the 65–70-year-old man, with shabby clothes and yet rich ornaments, that Poe depicts. One of the first guidebooks to London lowlife is Ned Ward's *The London Spy* (1703), which Defoe would certainly have known.

10. Emerson, *Selected Letters*, ed. Joel Myerson (New York: Columbia University Press, 1997), 330 (written in 1847).

11. As often happens in later versions of the detective story, the seemingly detached observer not only has an effect on what he sees but also may be drawn in himself—a plot turn exploited comically in Buster Keaton's *Sherlock, Jr.* (1924), in which a young projectionist studying to be a detective is yanked bodily into the films he is showing.

12. Holmes and Moriarty both seem to fall to their deaths at the Reichenbach Falls. The OED informs us that the word *cliff-hanger* for an episode or story that leaves us unsure of the resolution appears first in 1937, but surely there is some reminiscence of Holmes and Moriarty in the idea, however submerged.

13. Older readers might remember the paperback editions of Agatha Christie, Dorothy Sayers, and others that helpfully often included a map of the town where the crimes occurred so that the reader might trace the distance between the parsonage, the pub, and the millpond where the body was found.

14. R. Austin Freeman's Dr. John Thorndyke is another example of the "thinking machine" style of detective. Agatha Christie's Hercule Poirot and Miss Marple are both efforts to bring together the puzzle-solving detective with the eccentric personality.

15. In the mode of the times, Chan, Moto, and Wong were played by white actors, while the women were not detectives by profession, Hildegard Withers being a school-teacher and Torchy Blane a journalist.

16. Raymond Chandler, "Twelve Notes on the Mystery Story," in *Later Novels and Other Writings* (New York: Library of America, 1995), 1008. This essay is based on notes unpublished in Chandler's lifetime.

17. In *Farewell, My Lovely* (1940), Chandler winkingly refers to the medieval Christian tradition of the knightly quest for the Holy Grail. In it Velma Valento, the nightclub singer Moose Malloy has hired Marlowe to search for, turns out to be the rich, mur-dering femme fatale Mrs. Grayle.

18. Akira Kurosawa's *Yojimbo* (1961), Sergio Leone's *Fistful of Dollars* (1964), and Walter Hill's *Last Man Standing* (1996) all follow the *Red Harvest* pattern.

19. *Film noir* is a French term for American movies that was coined in 1946 by the critic Nino Frank in analogy with the Série Noire novels translated primarily from American writers such as Hammett, Chandler, James M. Cain, and Horace McCoy. It reflected as well the darkly stoic tone of some memorable French films of the late 1930s, often featuring Jean Gabin, not usually playing a detective but an individual struggling against a fatal universe.

20. In hobo slang, *gunsel* means a young man in a homosexual relationship with an older man. Joseph Shaw, the editor of *Black Mask* magazine, would not allow vulgar lan-guage in the detective stories he printed. Hammett included the word to fool Shaw into thinking it just meant a young man with a gun.

21. Edward Dmytryk directed *Murder, My Sweet,* but I have been unable to find a specific credit for the dream sequence. Robert Montgomery tries (and distinctly fails) to find a cinematic equivalent for Chandler's first-person narration in his film of *Lady in the Lake* (1947), in which the camera's and Marlowe's gaze are made one and we see Montgomery the actor primarily when he passes by a mirror.

22. As if to affirm the connection between the detective and the criminal, Humphrey Bogart, before appearing as Sam Spade in *The Maltese Falcon* (1941) and as Philip Marlowe in *The Big Sleep* (1946), had primarily criminal and even villain roles in films.

23. The emblematic name of one detective of the 1930s was "The Lone Wolf." Detective fiction in political contexts other than the United States and England takes correspond-ingly different turns. Persephone Braham, in *Crimes Against the State, Crimes Against Persons: Detective Fiction in Cuba and Mexico* (Minneapolis: University of Minnesota Press, 2004), shows how the basic detective format varies between Cuba, where the state is considered ideal and the criminals are hostile to it, and Mexico, where the state is considered corrupt and the criminals are those in power. See also Barbara Pezzotti, *Politics and Society in Italian Crime Fiction* (Jefferson, N.C.: McFarland, 2014).

24. The theme of masculinity in the hard-boiled detective story is discussed further in Braudy, *From Chivalry to Terrorism* (New York: Knopf, 2003).

25. Also, another cultural hero rose to help supplant the traditional detective—the spy, whose international scope, familiarity with advanced technology, and combat with mega-villains is more in tune with the fantasies of the era.

26. In this way, a wrinkled and weary Robert Mitchum, previously a stalwart of film noir, stars in British versions of *Farewell My Lovely* (1975) and *The Big Sleep* (1978).

CHAPTER 6. JEKYLL AND HYDE

1. To what extent are both the monster and the detective archetypal figures in a primarily Anglo-American tradition? It has been argued that France, with its rationalist tradition, has little taste for the gothic, which has a deeper life in, for example, Italy and Spain. Similarly, the question of the detective's identity and fallibility is not as much an issue in Italian, where the word for detective is *segugio,* from the verb "to follow." Georges Simenon's Inspector Maigret certainly has character, but his point of view is not problematic in the style of the American detective. He more resembles some of his descendants in Scandinavia—like the Swedish Kurt Wallander, the detective in Henning Mankell's novels—who have alcoholism, family conflicts, and other personal problems as part of their characterization, while for the most part maintaining professional clarity in their investigations.

2. Poe's formulation recalls Thomas De Quincey's description of the opium eater as a philosopher possessing "not merely the possession of a superb intellect in its *analytic* functions . . . but also on such a constitution of the *moral* faculties as shall give him an inner eye and power of intuition for the vision and the mysteries of our human nature." *Confessions of an English Opium-Eater* (1821).

3. This mingling of the empirical and the affective in Holmes's character might also be a clue to how his creator Doyle could also believe in spiritualism and, unlike his friend Houdini, be hoaxed by an array of mediums.

4. For the early scientific exploration of this phenomenon, see "A Double Consciousness, or a Duality of Person in the Same Individual . . . " (1817), cited in Ian Hacking, *Rewriting the Soul,* 150. Hacking also refers to the 1791 case of Mary Reynolds, discussed in E. T. Carlson, "History of Multiple Personality in the United States," *Bulletin of History of Medicine* 58 (1974): 72–82.

5. George Grey Barnard, *The Struggle of the Two Natures in Man,* Metropolitan Museum of Art, New York, http://www.metmuseum.org/collection/the-collection-online/search/10105.

6. Nikolai Gogol's short story "The Nose" (1835–36) treats the relation to the double comically. In it, a man awakes to find his nose is missing, and later discovers that the nose has taken on a life of its own, even to the extent of occupying a higher rank in the civil service. After various misadventures the man awakes and discovers his nose is back in its proper place, with no explanation given for its rebellion. In another version, Hans Christian Andersen's "The Shadow" (1847), the double self becomes richer than the master and finally has him executed. An even earlier version is Adelbert von Chamisso's "Peter Schlemihl" (1814), combining the Faust legend with the doppelgänger in a short story about a man who sells his shadow to the devil.

7. Films like those in the *Texas Chainsaw Massacre* series invert the revenge side of the social serial killer tradition by featuring a backcountry family that attacks wayward middle-class travelers and turns their dead bodies into barbecue, while the main killer, Leatherface, is a nonspeaking Frankenstein figure.

8. The script for *Shadow of a Doubt* is by the three-time Pulitzer Prize winner Thornton Wilder, who may have been homosexual, although he never refers to this in any of his writings. Nevertheless, Uncle Charlie (Joseph Cotton) has some kinship with other crypto-gay characters in 1940s films, for example, Waldo Lydecker (Clifton Webb) in *Laura* (1944) and Lord Henry Wotton (George Sanders) in *The Picture of Dorian Gray* (1945).

9. Perhaps too it may explain the fascination in many such films and plays of the period with the behind-the-scenes aspects of theater and film, for example in *All About Eve* (1950) and *The Bad and the Beautiful* (1952).

10. Throwing an even wider net, I would include as a sidebar to these more explicit double films another subgenre of the period, the cop-buddy films, in which partners are of different genders, different races, different countries, even a couple in which one is alive and the other the reanimated dead (*Dead Heat*, 1988), or one an earthling and the other an alien (*Alien Nation*, 1988).

11. *Alice in Wonderland*, 1865; *Through the Looking-Glass and What Alice Found There*, 1871. The director of the 1926 *The Student of Prague* was Henrik Galeen, who also wrote the script for the first film of the *Golem* trilogy. The student in the 1913 version was played by Paul Wegener, who also starred in as well as co-wrote and co-directed *The Golem, How He Came Into the World*. The student in the 1926 version was played by Conrad Veidt, who plays Cesare in *The Cabinet of Dr. Caligari*. The world of German expressionist horror cinema was clearly a very tight circle.

12. One movie version of the story (1960, directed by Roger Corman, script by Richard Matheson) reinterprets the paintings as portraits of the evil ancestors of Roderick and Madeleine, bringing the monster and the portrait together even more decisively.

13. The vampirism of the artist who battens on the lives of his subjects is a frequent theme in the films of Ingmar Bergman, such as *Persona* and *Through a Glass Darkly*.

14. Wilde letter to Ralph Payne, Turnbull Library, National Library of New Zealand. In Arthur Machen's 1894 story "The Great God Pan," the mysterious woman at the center of the tale, the child of a human and Pan, is also first seen in an eerie portrait.

15. In a contemporary version, *The Devil's Advocate* (1997), the satanic figure, the head of a New York law firm, tempts the protagonist with money and status.

16. See Ian Hacking, *Rewriting the Soul: Multiple Personality and the Sciences of Memory* (Princeton: Princeton University Press, 1998). Elliotson became a promoter of mesmerism and resigned his position at the London University hospital when the Hospital Council denounced the practice as fraudulent.

17. Rank's essay first appeared in *Imago*, the Viennese journal of psychoanalysis founded in 1912.

18. W. E. B. Du Bois later uses "double consciousness" to refer to the way the African-American sees himself simultaneously from the inside as a person and from the outside through the eyes of the white majority: "an American, a Negro; two souls, two thoughts, two unreconciled strivings; two warring ideals in one dark body, whose dogged strength alone keeps it from being torn asunder." See "Strivings of the Negro People" (1897) and *The Souls of Black Folk* (1903).

19. *Lectures on Shakespeare and Other Poets and Dramatists,* Lecture XIII, "On Poesy or Art" (London: Everyman, n.d.), 313.

20. In Japanese folklore the nightmare is often personified as a child sitting on one's chest. Angina or transient ischemic attacks could be the actual culprit in both cases, but that's hardly very poetic. Fuseli's painting can be found at https://en.wikipedia. org/wiki/The_Nightmare#/media/File:John_Henry_Fuseli_-_The_Nightmare.jpg.

21. According to Jones's preface, most of his book was written in 1909–10, although it was not published in its present form until 1931. In another of Fuseli's paintings, *The Succubus* (1781), two women lie on a bed, one seemingly asleep, the other awake and distraught, while a dark figure on a horse flies out a nearby window.

CHAPTER 7. DRACULA AND THE HAUNTED PRESENT

1. As I mentioned in Chapter 2, the seventeenth-century political use of supposed gothic precedents to attack the power of the monarchy precedes and in part lays the groundwork for the eighteenth-century embrace of gothic aesthetics. See Kliger, *The Goths in England;* Pocock, *The Ancient Constitution and the Feudal Law;* Nick Groom, *The Gothic: A Very Short Introduction* (London: Oxford University Press, 2012).

2. The effort to connect a humanism rooted in classical ideas with the world of nature is a frequent eighteenth- and nineteenth-century theme, appearing in writers as disparate as Alexander Pope and Henry David Thoreau.

3. Jean Starobinski, *The Invention of Liberty, 1700–1789* (New York: Skira, 1964), 181.

4. The capital of Roman Britain was a former Celtic fortified settlement called Camulodunon, which some scholars have argued is the source for the name Camelot.

5. Molds have also been discovered with slots for metal casting of both crosses and hammers. "Thor the Viking Thunder God," compiled by D. L. Ashliman, http://www.pitt.edu/~dash/thor.html.

6. R. F. Foster, *Modern Ireland, 1600–1972* (London: Allen Lane, 1988), 208.

7. Tiw is a war god comparable to Mars. Woden or Odin is usually considered akin to Mercury as a leader of souls and agent of communication.

8. It would be intriguing to connect this revival of the Celtic with the Catholic resurgence called the Oxford Movement that occurred in the 1830s and 1840s, with John Henry Newman as its prime literary figure. Together they might be considered the second era of the gothic cultural revival in England.

9. Another significant inheritor of these Irish traditions is Lord Dunsany, who came from one of the oldest Irish families and lived in the oldest continuously inhabited house in Ireland, Dunsany Castle. He was a prolific writer who created mainly fantasy worlds, and was therefore a forerunner of J. R. R. Tolkien, C. S. Lewis, and J. K. Rowling. In an odd but tempting detail, the somewhat unusual name of Lucy Westenra in *Dracula* harkens back to a family of Irish landowners of the seventeenth century.

10. Dracula is also associated with Celtic warrior cults like the Berserkers. See Braudy, *From Chivalry to Terrorism.*

11. In this period also appeared some of the earliest scientific investigations of the nature of sexuality, including Richard von Krafft-Ebing's *Psychopathia Sexualis* (1886). For

more on the figure of Pan, see Patricia Merivale, *Pan the Goat-God: His Myth in Modern Times* (Cambridge: Harvard University Press, 1969).

12. Like Byron, Shelley, Mary Shelley, and Polidori trading ghost stories by the shores of Lake Geneva, Goethe writes his in a competition with his friend Friedrich Schiller.

13. For more on depictions of the female vampire, see Bram Dijkstra, *Idols of Perversity: Fantasies of Feminine Evil in Fin-de-Siecle Culture* (New York: Oxford University Press, 1986).

14. The man and woman in Burne-Jones's The *Vampire* are supposedly Burne-Jones himself and the actress Mrs. Patrick Campbell. For an image, see https://en.wikipedia.org/wiki/Philip_Burne-Jones#/media/File:Burne-Jones-le-Vampire.jpg. In 1917 Theodosia Goodman's family changed its name legally to Bara.

15. The Undine story enters literature in 1811 in a novella by Friedrich Fouqué and was quickly popular across Europe, inspiring operas and ballets. A related branch of the Undine story, Hans Christian Andersen's "The Little Mermaid," appears in 1837.

16. Pope Gregory I codified the order of the Seven Deadly Sins in the sixth century as pride, envy, wrath, sloth, avarice, gluttony, lust. This declining order from spiritual to physical sins is followed by Dante in the *Inferno,* and becomes widespread by the fourteenth century.

17. The *Nightmare on Elm Street* series, for example, expands upon this theme by making it clear that what happens to you in dreams can kill or injure you in real life.

CHAPTER 8. HORROR IN THE AGE OF VISUAL REPRODUCTION

1. One of the earliest works of fiction to exploit an aspect of this crowded decade was, appropriately enough, written by the son of a psychoanalyst: Nicholas Meyer's *The Seven-Per-Cent Solution* (1974; film version, 1976), in which Freud and Holmes solve the kidnapping of one of Freud's patients, while Freud also cures Holmes's cocaine addiction.

2. Sidney Paget, the illustrator of the first series of Doyle's tales in the *Strand,* introduces Holmes's deerstalker hat and the Inverness cape, neither of which he wears in the stories. Gillette made the meerschaum iconic, rather than the short black pipe of the stories, supposedly because it made it easier for him to deliver his lines. Vanishing at daybreak may come from the traditions of ghost lore. In contrast with these added details, others are dropped: the idea that a wild rose on his coffin can overpower the vampire, for example, is a motif that falls by the wayside entirely.

3. The character here is Renfield, rather than the Harker of the novel. In the Spanish-language version, filmed in the evening using the same sets, the medallion is absent. Roman Polanski makes a joke of the possibility of the Jewish vampire in *The Fearless Vampire Killers* (1967). When a cross is brandished at one vampire, he says in Yiddish that it won't work. As part of the political context of the period in which *Dracula* appeared, in 1905 the Aliens Act was passed, primarily to restrict Jewish immigration from Russia and eastern European immigration into Great Britain.

4. Dr. Seward says of Morris, "If America can go on breeding men like that, she will be a power in the world indeed." This need for American energy to revitalize England,

especially at a time of an arms race between England and Germany, appears as well in Conan Doyle. In "The Noble Bachelor" (1892), Holmes foresees "our children being someday citizens of the same world-wide country under a flag which shall be a quartering of the Union Jack with the Stars and Stripes."

5. The monster's longing to be normal receives its comic elaboration in the 1960s sitcom families of *The Munsters* and *The Addams Family*, while the extremes of monster family abnormality fuel such films of the 1970s as *The Texas Chainsaw Massacre* and *The Hills Have Eyes*.

6. *Dysesthesia* is otherwise a medical term for an abnormal sense of touch that can cause inappropriate pain. The sympathetic Frankenstein monster in these two great films by the gay director James Whale also expands on the parthenogenic creator-creation dynamic of the original.

7. Elizabeth Young in *Black Frankenstein: The Making of an American Metaphor* (New York: New York University Press, 2008) discusses the positive embrace and revaluation of a monstrous image in the face of a pervasive racism. Analogously, Leilani Mishime explores how the half-human, half-robot cyborg in science fiction films can represent both the prejudices and possibilities of a mixed racial heritage. See "The Mulatto Cyborg: Imagining a Multiracial Future," *Cinema Journal* 44 (Winter 2005): 34–49. Compare the beginning of Ralph Ellison's great novel *Invisible Man*: "I am an invisible man. No, I am not a spook like those who haunted Edgar Allan Poe; nor am I one of your Hollywood ectoplasms."

8. Leonard Wolf in *A Dream of Dracula* (New York: Little, Brown, 1972) traces the theme of the regretful vampire back to the 1936 film *Dracula's Daughter* (290). The urge to renovate the classic story by introducing a new gender, ethnic, or even animal version of the main character is reflected in such later Frankenstein adaptations as *Frankenweenie* (1984) and *Frankenhooker* (1990).

9. The *Protocols* speak of "the King-Despot of the blood of Zion."

10. Sometimes those references to a popular culture outside the film don't date well. Jack Nicholson supposedly ad-libbed the line "Here's Johnny!" in *The Shining* as he axes down the bathroom door on his way to trying to kill his wife and son. By a few decades later, few people under thirty watching the film knew what he was talking about.

11. In appropriate contrast is one of the most suave adult monsters of the new horror—Hannibal Lecter, a psychiatrist.

12. Horror themes of the diseased and/or mutated body are particularly central to the films of the Canadian director David Cronenberg, for example, *Videodrome* (1983), *The Fly* (1986, the remake of a 1958 film), and his adaptation of William Burroughs's novel *Naked Lunch* (1991).

13. The story persists that Jackson in 1987 also tried to buy the bones of Joseph Merrick, the nineteenth-century Elephant Man. Whether or not it is true, it certainly suits the *Thriller* image of the star performer as a kind of natural monster.

14. King intensely disliked Kubrick's film and ultimately helped produce a three-hour TV miniseries version (1997).

15. The obvious flares in the image seem intended to indicate the camera's presence even more definitely.

16. As so often in King's novels, the central character is a writer, and here Jack's alcoholism reflects King's own drinking problem at the time, in perhaps another affinity with the gothic tradition, the identification of writer and monster.

17. The earliest fully formed haunted-house film was *The Cat and the Canary* (1927). Another forerunner was *The Old Dark House* (1932), directed by James Whale and starring Boris Karloff as a sinister butler. Stephen King has said that *The Shining* was influenced by the contemporary haunted-house film *Burnt Offerings* (1976). The year before the film of *The Shining*, *The Amityville Horror* appeared, based on a supposedly real story of a family that moves into a suburban house where murders had been committed.

18. On the origin of widespread interest in the paranormal, see J. B. Rhine's ESP experiments at Duke in the 1950s. Victoria Nelson in *Gothicka: Vampire Heroes, Human Gods, and the New Supernatural* (Cambridge: Harvard University Press, 2012) has argued that the gothic supernatural has transformed into contemporary superhero spirituality.

19. On the "Final Girl," see Carol Clover, *Men, Women, and Chainsaws: Gender in the Modern Horror Film* (Princeton: Princeton University Press, 1993).

20. The attraction of audiences in Catholic countries especially to vampire films is also reflected in the Santo films of Mexico, in which the masked boxer/wrestler fights with vampires, as well as films produced in the Philippines with similar plots.

21. Of late this urge to combination as renewal has produced mashups like Seth Grahame-Smith's *Pride and Prejudice and Zombies* (2009) and *Abraham Lincoln, Vampire Hunter* (novel, 2010; film, 2012).

22. Plus all the Romero *Deads, Chainsaws,* and so on; three *Children of the Corn* and four more made for video; three *Amityvilles* and one TV movie, etc., etc.

23. For both *Dracula* infusions the four men volunteer their blood, without worrying about typing compatibility, which was discovered only some years later in the early twentieth century.

24. The final showdown on a deserted small-town main street also connects *Near Dark* to the western, with its similar nostalgia for a lost warrior world.

25. Stephen King also names four essential monsters in *Danse Macabre*, including Frankenstein, Dracula, and Jekyll/Hyde. But I think he is mistaken to cite the Mummy as number four, who in my view shares too many traits with Dracula and Frankenstein to be called a distinct form.

26. In the West during the Cold War, images of Soviet society, both real and animated, frequently depicted faceless marching thousands, recalling the multitudes of Nazi Germany.

27. The inclusion of comic relief within a general horror context has a long history. As Samuel Coleridge remarked at the beginning of the nineteenth century, "Indeed, paradoxical as it may appear, the terrible by a law of the human mind always touches on the verge of the ludicrous" (*Notes on Hamlet*).

Index